ℜEDEMPTION
of the 𝔇AMNED

VOL. 2: SEA & SPACE PHENOMENA

A Centennial Re-evaluation of

Charles Fort's 'Book of the Damned'

Martin Shough
with
Wim van Utrecht

ANOMALIST BOOKS

Charlottesville, Virginia

An Original Publication of ANOMALIST BOOKS
Redemption of the Damned, Vol.2: Sea and Space Phenomena
Copyright © 2021 by Martin Shough
ISBN: 978-1-949501-18-6

Cover illustration: Jules Verne's fictional moon-shot projectile falls from space to impact the US Navy vessel *Susquehanna*, from the 1870 illustrated edition of *Around the Moon*, courtesy of the Mary Evans Picture Library (maryevans.com). Modified with starry sky and meteor.

Cover design by Seale Studios

For information about the publisher, go to AnomalistBooks.com,
or write to: Anomalist Books, 3445 Seminole Trail #247, Charlottesville, VA 22911

CONTENTS

Acknowledgements v

Foreword by George Eberhart vii

Introduction 1

Part 1: Worlds that Never Were

   1. The Phantom Moon of Venus 5
   2. The Elusive Planet Vulcan 13

Part 2: Stigmata on the Sun & Moon

   3. A "Super-Zeppelin" Eclipses the Sun 33
   4. Followed by a Moonshadow 47
   5. Crows on the Moon 55

Part 3: Transient Lunar & Martian Phenomena

   6. Lights on the Moon 63
   7. The Case of the Missing Eclipse 87
   8. Martian Lights and Clouds 93

Part 4: Fire from the Deep

   9. The Blue fireball 105
   10. *Victoria's* Secret 115
   11. Vast Luminous Wheels 127
   12. Paced by a Fireball off Cape Race 151

Part 5: Plunging Fireballs

13. A Falling Mass of Fire 177
14. Black Meteor: Plummeting Fire & Ice 201

Conclusion 211

Index to Volume 1 213
Index to Volume 2 229

ACKNOWLEDGEMENTS

We are grateful, once again, to Chris Aubeck for helping to inspire this project, and for helping to compile a classified chronological index of cases from *The Book of the Damned*. Thanks also to other members of the Magonia Exchange email group, including Theo Paijmans, Mikhail Gershtein, and Kay Coggin, who have helped locate sources and information for this second volume. Others deserving of special mention include Manuel Borraz Aymerich, Patrick Huyghe, Marc Hallet, and the Mary Evans Picture Library.

Special thanks are due to George M. Eberhart for a generous and erudite Foreword.

Finally, credit is due to Google Maps and Google Earth for images used in several of the Figures, and to Stellarium for charts of the night sky. Other images are individually credited. We have taken pains to seek permissions for their use where appropriate; however, we apologise for any unwitting infringement and would ask any copyright-holder we were unable to find to please contact the publisher with a view to correction in a future edition.

FOREWORD

Charles Fort has not aged well. From a 21st-century perspective, *The Book of the Damned* is a difficult read, riddled with sprawling and oddly constructed paragraphs, abrupt sentence fragments, and an exuberance of dashes. Its often labyrinthine prose leaves many readers yearning for more accessible, if typo-laden, online diversions.

Fort's insistence on interspersing anomalistic data-dumps with abstruse philosophical sidebars on what he calls "intermediatism" (all existence is part of One Universal Thing) tempers the enthusiasm of many readers who only want to be regaled with stories of falling frogs and freakish fireballs.

His penchant for proposing ontologically outlandish hypotheses to counter what is often reasonable skepticism from mainstream scientists, although arguably an early outbreak of postmodernism, casts doubt on his objectivity. Fort's facile dismissal of his own explanations prompts contemporary readers to wonder what his point was.

Those of us who read *The Book of the Damned* before the internet was invented could perhaps more easily take Fort on his own terms. A book was something you read straight through to follow an author's carefully constructed arguments, and all the visionary philosophy, stylistic quagmires, caustic quips, and majestic metaphors were part of the journey—not a distraction.

In order to fact-check Fort, you needed access to a large research library, as I did. Many of my teenage Saturdays were spent spellbound in the stacks of the Ohio State University libraries, tracking down and transcribing articles in *Monthly Weather Review* and *Comptes rendus de l'Académie des Sciences* to see whether Fort was exaggerating or accurate. The task was daunting yet enlightening.

Today the task is no less complicated, but for different reasons. Most of Fort's sources are readily available online through Google Books, the HathiTrust repository, newspapers.com, and other databases. This abundance of source material requires researchers to discover not only what Fort misquoted or inflated, but what he missed entirely.

But Fort's sources have not aged well either.

It's weirdly gratifying to discover that the editors and authors of many 19th-century scientific journal articles got numbers and dates wrong, misquoted or cited their sources poorly, screwed up latitudes and longitudes, took imprecise measurements, and made essential mistakes in geography. In order to assess these old observations, the modern researcher must be armed with up-to-date scientific knowledge, a mastery of archival and digital tools, and the ability to reinterpret the language of the times. In an era when people suffered from ague, dyspepsia, and apoplexy instead of fever, indigestion, and stroke, the terms for scientific measurements, tools, and techniques also require translation.

Martin Shough and Wim van Utrecht use an arsenal of 21st-century tools, both online and in archives, to deconstruct and reconstruct the astronomical, meteorological, and oceanographic anomalies that Fort has puzzled us with since 1919. Yes, Fort cherry-picked his facts to tell a good story, as the authors point out. Nonetheless, they manage to extract the marrow from many of these old bones, and in doing so, take Fort to a new level of relevance.

Reassessing Fort's data is not a job for the faint-hearted. Shough and Van Utrecht are up to the technical and historical challenges, leaving no meteorite unturned in their quest to find reasonable explanations.

Science writer Maynard Shipley wrote an enthusiastic review of Fort's book *Lo!* for the March 1, 1931, issue of the *New York Times,* saying that "Reading Fort is a ride on a comet." Because we now know that comets are merely icy dirtballs, some of that romance has vaporized into a trail of dust and gases. But reading Shough and Van Utrecht is like riding a time-traveling spaceship—when you return from the journey (to paraphrase Shipley), you will find a new and exhilarating appreciation for Fortean anomalies that will color and correct your future reading of science.

George M. Eberhart
Chicago, Illinois
February 2021

George M. Eberhart was senior editor (1996-2020) of *American Libraries*, the magazine of the American Library Association. He served for ten years (1980-1990) as editor of *College & Research Libraries News*, the news magazine of ALA's Association of College & Research Libraries. He has compiled three book-length bibliographies on UFOs and other scientific anomalies. Eberhart holds a bachelor's degree in journalism from Ohio State University and a master's degree in library science from the University of Chicago.

INTRODUCTION

The first volume of this project appeared in 2019 to mark the centenary of Charles Fort's seminal work *The Book of the Damned*. Readers of *Redemption of the Damned, Volume 1*, will find there a brief introduction to Charles Fort and his work. For this second volume we will assume that the reader is at least a little familiar with Fort and with the nature of the material he published.

Suffice it to say that some of the old stories of aerial phenomena collected in *The Book of the Damned* have been retold many times since the advent of Unidentified Flying Objects in 1947. But the treatment has less often been scientifically and historically rigorous. So in *Redemption of the Damned, Volume 1: Aerial Phenomena* we began deconstruction of Fort's magnum opus, for the first time in a hundred years taking all 82 records of strange phenomena observed in the atmosphere between 1777 and 1916, and subjecting them systematically to reanalysis with the tools of 21st century science and digital resources.

The very warm reception given to *Volume 1* by fortean readers, writers and researchers worldwide was gratifying. But Fort collected sightings of more than just things seen in the air. We promised that a companion volume was forthcoming and that between them the two books would radically reappraise the great majority of the most remarkable records collected in *The Book of the Damned*.

True to our word, here in *Volume 2: Sea & Space Phenomena* we turn our attention to two more categories of anomalous observations collected in *The Book of the Damned*: those made by astronomers, of transient unexplained phenomena on other worlds, of phantom moons and planets and other strange bodies in space; and those made by ships' crews of mysterious objects and lights seen in, on, entering, or leaving Earth's oceans.

By and large, the kinds of observations covered in *Volume 1* lent themselves to detailed individual treatments, so that the 82 numbered records could be catalogued chronologically. With the present volume, the type of material and the way Fort presented it necessitated a different format in which, sometimes, organization is by topic, with numbers of records being surveyed and assessed collectively. This is especially so in Part 1 (Worlds that Never Were), Part 3 (in particular Chapter 6 'Lights on the Moon' and Chapter 8 'Martian Lights and Clouds'), and Part 4 (notably Chapter 11 'Vast Luminous Wheels'). Elsewhere the focus is once again on in-depth analyses of individual observations.

Finally, we have included here comprehensive subject indexes for both *Volume 1* and *Volume 2*, which we hope will maximise the usefulness of this project for future researchers.

Putting together this book, and its companion volume, has been a privilege and a labour of love. We hope the reader will enjoy reading it as much as we have enjoyed writing it.

Martin Shough, January 2021

Part 1

Worlds that Never Were

CHAPTER 1 – The Phantom Moon of Venus
CHAPTER 2 – The Elusive Planet Vulcan

CHAPTER 1 – **The Phantom Moon of Venus**

O ne of the oddest mysteries in the history of astronomy is the phantom satellite of Venus, observed many times during the 17th and 18th centuries. Charles Fort reports

> That, in 1645, a body large enough to look like a satellite was seen near Venus. Four times in the first half of the 18th century, a similar observation was reported. The last report occurred in 1767. A large body has been seen -- seven times, according to *Science Gossip*, 1886-178 -- near Venus. At least one astronomer, Houzeau, accepted these observations and named the -- world, planet, super-construction – 'Neith.' His views are mentioned "in passing, but without endorsement," in the *Trans. N. Y. Acad.*, 5-249.[1]

The 1645 observation which started it all was made by Francesco Fontana (1580–1656), a Neapolitan lawyer and astronomer, who in fact saw multiple objects near Venus on different dates over three months. Fontana's own drawing (Fig. 1) depicts one object in front of the illuminated crescent on November 11, *two* lights near the horns on November 15, one near the lower horn on December 25, and one near the centre of the terminator on January 22, 1646. Fontana himself speculated that some, at least, of these appearances may have been "optical illusions".[2]

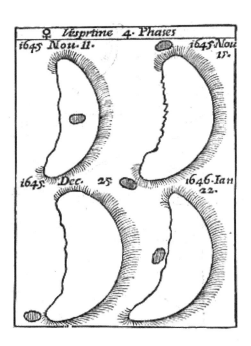

Fig. 1. Francesco Fontana's drawings of the satellite of Venus observed in 1645–1646.[3]

---

1   Fort, *Damned*, p. 186.
2   Paolo Molaro, 'Francesco Fontana and the Birth of the Astronomical Telescope', *Journal of Astronomical History and Heritage,* 20(2), 271–288 (2017);
http://old.narit.or.th/en/files/2017JAHHvol20/2017JAHH...20..271M.pdf
3   https://no.m.wikipedia.org/wiki/Fil:Riccioli-Venus.jpg

Fort says the last observation was in 1767. His source, Martha Martin's *The Ways of the Planets* (1912), actually says 1791 (Fig. 2) and at least one modern commentator agrees the last sighting was in 1791, by Montaigne.[4] However, both dates appear to be wrong.

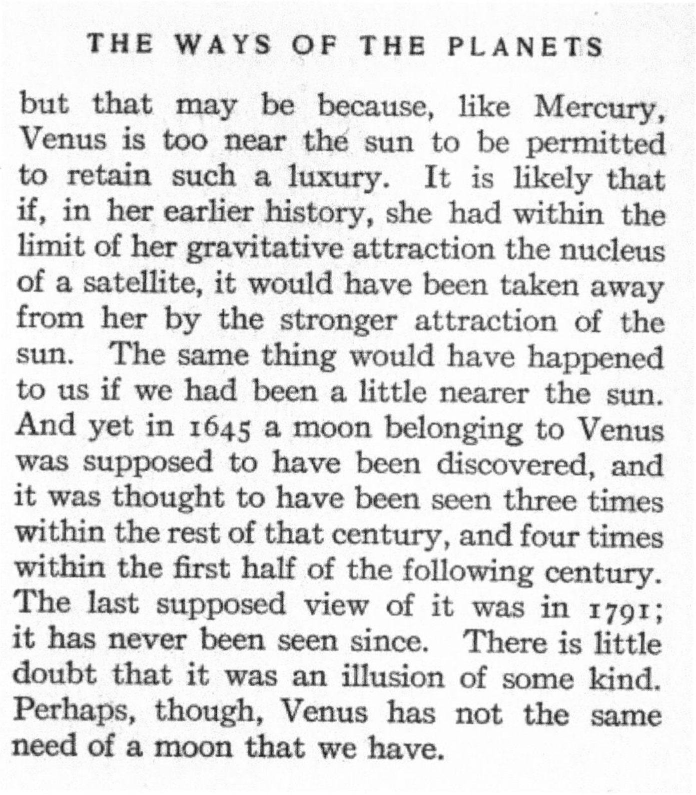

THE WAYS OF THE PLANETS

but that may be because, like Mercury, Venus is too near the sun to be permitted to retain such a luxury. It is likely that if, in her earlier history, she had within the limit of her gravitative attraction the nucleus of a satellite, it would have been taken away from her by the stronger attraction of the sun. The same thing would have happened to us if we had been a little nearer the sun. And yet in 1645 a moon belonging to Venus was supposed to have been discovered, and it was thought to have been seen three times within the rest of that century, and four times within the first half of the following century. The last supposed view of it was in 1791; it has never been seen since. There is little doubt that it was an illusion of some kind. Perhaps, though, Venus has not the same need of a moon that we have.

Fig. 2. Martha Evans Martin, *The Ways of the Planets,* Harper & Brothers, New York, 1912, p. 140.[5]

Jacques Laibats-Montaigne was born in 1716 and died at the age of 72 on December 17, 1788,[6] so we can be confident he made no observation at all in 1791. In fact, in May 17<u>6</u>1 Montaigne's associate Armand Baudouin gave a presentation describing what was then breaking news of Montaigne's observations to the French Academy of Sciences and published two subsequent memoirs on the topic that same year. Montaigne also tried to spot his satellite during the Venus solar transit of June 1761 but apparently never saw it again, although others believed they did. A total of 36 observations were catalogued between 1645 and 1768, more than half of them in 1761.[7] According to certain authorities[8] the only related

---

4   "Mr. X" at www.resologist.net notes: "The last report was made in 1791 by Montaigne, (not 1767)."
5   https://archive.org/details/waysofplanets00martrich. Fort mis-cites the author's name as "Evans".
6   https://www.academie-sciences.fr/en/Liste-des-membresdepuis-la-creation-de-l-Academie-des-sciences/les-membres-du-passe-dont-le-nomcommence-par-m.html
7   Helge Kragh, *The Moon that Wasn't, The Saga of Venus' Spurious Satellite*, Science Networks Historical Studies, Birkhäuser Basel, Vol. 37 (2008), p. 39; biographical sketches, p. 155; http://link.springer.com/chapter/10.1007/978-3-7643-8909-3_3
8   Møller Pedersen, K. & Kragh, H., 'The phantom moon of Venus, 1645–1768,' *Journal of Astronomical History and Heritage*, Vol. 11, No. 3, pp. 227-234 (2008); http://adsabs.harvard.edu/full/2008JAHH...11..227M

observations after 1761 were made by a group of astronomers in Copenhagen, the last being by Horrebow in January 1768, although one source alludes to three later suspected sightings between 1823 and 1892, including one of "a bright spot near the limb of the planet" in February 1884. This last observation was by Charles-Emile Stuyvaert (1851–1908), since 1881 Adjunct Astronomer at the Royal Observatory of Belgium, where he conducted planetary and cometary studies and also took part in the 1882 Royal Observatory Venus transit expedition to Texas.[9]

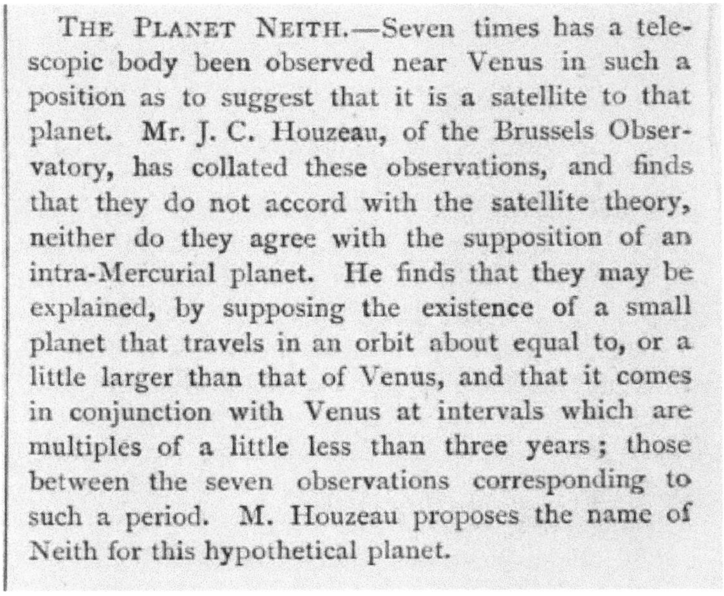

THE PLANET NEITH.—Seven times has a telescopic body been observed near Venus in such a position as to suggest that it is a satellite to that planet. Mr. J. C. Houzeau, of the Brussels Observatory, has collated these observations, and finds that they do not accord with the satellite theory, neither do they agree with the supposition of an intra-Mercurial planet. He finds that they may be explained, by supposing the existence of a small planet that travels in an orbit about equal to, or a little larger than that of Venus, and that it comes in conjunction with Venus at intervals which are multiples of a little less than three years; those between the seven observations corresponding to such a period. M. Houzeau proposes the name of Neith for this hypothetical planet.

Fig. 3. "The planet Neith," Hardwicke's *Science Gossip,* 22 (1886), p. 178.[10]

Fort's sources for Houzeau and his hypothetical planet Neith are shown in Figs. 3 & 5. Jean-Charles Houzeau de Lehaie (1820–1888) was Director of the Belgian Royal Observatory from 1876 to 1883. His idea was prompted by a conviction that observers of the calibre of Cassini could not have been easily deceived, and it was reinforced by an odd numerical coincidence in the dates of the observations, which seemed to occur in multiples of a period which he calculated at 2.96 years.

Houzeau summarised his findings in the Observatory journal *Ciel et Terre* in 1885[11] in an article which also mentions two new observations made nine days apart in February 1884 by Leopold Niesten, a fellow member of the Royal Observatory, and by the above-mentioned Charles-Emile Stuyvaert, whose own sketch – of "an extremely bright point on the disc of Venus, near the illuminated border" – Houzeau also published (Fig. 4). A check using Stellarium finds no stars in close proximity to Venus on either of these sighting dates.

---

9   Stéphane Lecomte, 'Du Satellite de Venus,' *Observations et Traveaux,* Vol. 22-23 (1990), pp. 55-56; http://articles.adsabs.harvard.edu/full/1990O%26T....22...55L

10   http://www.biodiversitylibrary.org/item/18297#page/190/mode/1up

11   'Le Satellite Problématique de Vénus,' *Ciel et Terre,* Vol. 5 (1884–1885), pp. 121-129.

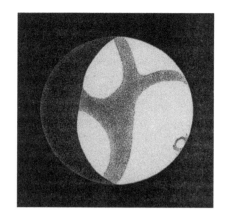

Fig. 4. Jean-Charles Houzeau and Stuyvaert's drawing of a light near the limb of Venus.[12]

Having ruled out a satellite of Venus or an unknown intra-Mercurial planet (*cf.* the phantom planet Vulcan; see Chapter 2), Houzeau came up with the theory of a small planet independently circling the sun close to the orbit of Venus whose orbit had over the ages become coupled with that of Venus due to a gravitational resonance, so that they caught up with one another in a regular period. But to prove his case Houzeau selected only seven of the "best known and best attested" sightings. A critical article in *The Observatory* in May 1886 (Fig. 6) pointed out that Houzeau's list omitted over two thirds of all claimed sightings, including the very first by Fontana in 1645 and the last in 1768,[13] and that including these would destroy the periodicity.

1886.]   NEW YORK ACADEMY OF SCIENCES.   249

We mention in passing, but without indorsement, the speculations of Houzeau, who has attempted to account for some of the older observations of a satellite to Venus, by supposing another smaller sister planet, " Neith," circling around the sun in an orbit a little larger than that of Venus, and from time to time coming into conjunction with it. But the theory is certainly untenable; a planet large enough to show phases, as the hypothetical satellite is said to have done, in the feeble telescopes with which many of the observations were made one hundred years ago or more, would be easily visible to the *naked eye even*. There can be little doubt that all the Venus satellites so far observed are simply *ghosts* due to reflections between the lenses of the telescope, or between the cornea of the eye and the eye lens.

Fig. 5. C. A. Young, 'The year's progress in astronomy,' *Transactions of the New York Academy of Sciences*, 5 (May 17, 1886), p. 249.[14]

---

12 https://www.bestor.be/wiki_nl/images/f/fb/Houzeau.JPG
13 "Roedkiær's observation of 1768 Jan. 4", but this is an error. Peder Roedkiær died in 1767. Roedkiær saw it in 1761 and 1764. Peder Horrebow was the observer on Jan. 4, 1768. See: Kurt Møller Pedersen and Helge Kragh, 'The Phantom Moon of Venus, 1645–1768,' *Journal of Astronomical History and Heritage*, 11(3), pp. 227-234 (2008), 227 (http://www.narit.or.th/en/files/2008JAHHvol11/2008JAHH...11..227M.pdf); Per Pippin Aspaas, *Maximilianus Hell (1720–1792) and the Eighteenth Century Transits of Venus*, 2012; (https://munin.uit.no/bitstream/handle/10037/4178/thesis.pdf?sequence=2).
14 http://www.biodiversitylibrary.org/item/45496#page/265/mode/1up

Later astronomers failed to find any sign of a Venusian moon or of Houzeau's planet Neith. The various positions reported by Montaigne, Cassini *et al.,* could not be made to fit physically sensible satellite orbits, and Houzeau's co-orbital minor planet, whilst acknowledged as an "ingenious" theory, could not have remained near Venus for as long as required to explain the sightings.

Houzeau's theory of co-orbital resonance may not have worked in this case, but it does prefigure in spirit the modern theory of quasi-satellites. A quasi-satellite is a body which, like its quasi-primary, actually orbits around the sun; but the two are coupled together by a gravitational resonance[15] and acquire the same period, although their orbits have different eccentricities. The result is that from the point of view of the quasi-primary, or the planet, its quasi-satellite appears to go around it once a year, even though it is not a truly captured moon. The theory of quasi-satellites is usually said to date from 1913,[16] so it is intriguing that the first real example to be discovered, in 2002, was a quasi-satellite of Venus known as $2002VE_{68}$.

222   *Problematical Satellite of Venus.*   [No. 88.

Jan. 21, corresponds with the increase I noticed Jan. 8. But any such increase or decrease would refer to irregular variation, and not to the rapid and regular variation previously seen, and assumed by me to be due to axial rotation.

MAXWELL HALL.

Jamaica, June 7.

The Problematical Satellite of Venus.

A VERY interesting contribution to the literature of this enigmatical body has recently been made by M. Houzeau (until lately director of the Royal Observatory of Brussels) in an article appearing in 'Ciel et Terre' for 1884, May 15. M. Houzeau is unwilling to believe that the cases in which a satellite was seen near Venus were all illusions, "for all these observations were made either by celebrated astronomers, such as Dominic Cassini, or at least by experienced observers," and it might be added that in the cases of the observations of Short and Roedkiær, the object was seen with more than one telescope, and with several different eyepieces. Short, indeed, actually measured the distance of the "satellite" from Venus with a micrometer, whilst Roedkiær's observations were confirmed on more than one occasion by the other astronomers of the Copenhagen Observatory. M. Houzeau cannot admit the body in question to be a satellite which only becomes visible under accidental circumstances, "first on account of the impossibility of properly representing the observed positions by an orbit described round Venus, and further because the mass of the planet deduced from the least defective attempts would be seven times the real amount."

Some years ago M. Houzeau had suggested that the problematical satellite might possibly be an intra-Mercurial planet. "Let a small planet, revolving within the orbit of Mercury, come on some occasion into so close an apparent approach to Venus as to be visible in the field of the telescope with it, and it would appear beside the larger disk of Venus as a body of smaller size, presenting almost the same phase as the great planet. This is precisely what has been observed."

"There was a method of deciding whether this explanation was admissible. An intra-Mercurial planet could not pass as far from the Sun as Venus does or even Mercury. It could then be seen near the former only at times, when, by its apparent motion, it was not very far from the Sun. If the observations were made sometimes at distances from the Sun in excess of the greatest distance of Mercury, it would be necessary to seek another hypothesis."

In order to test this theory, M. Houzeau therefore drew up the following table of seven of the best known and best attested instances in which the "satellite" of Venus is believed to have been seen :—

1884.]   *Problematical Satellite of Venus.*   223

TABLE I.

No. of the Observation.	Date.	Venus morning or evening star.	Heliocentric longitude of Venus.	Elongation.	Geocentric latitude.	Distance from the Earth. Radius of Earth's orbit = 1.
1.	1645, Nov. 15	E	309°	31°	−2°·0	1·37
2.	1672, Jan. 25	M	162	46	+4·8	0·59
3.	1686, Aug. 28	M	59	38	−0·7	1·17
4.	1740, Oct. 23ᵃ	M	68	46	−0·5	0·60
5.	1761, May 7	E	207	34	+5·4	0·45
6.	1764, March 4	E	59	30	−0·7	1·38
7.	1764, March 28	E	98	35	+1·2	1·24

M. Houzeau points out that this table completely overthrows the suggestion he had made, since in every instance Venus was further from the Sun than an intra-Mercurial planet could possibly be.

The table, however, gives rise to another hypothesis. Expressing the dates in years and decimals of a year, in order better to ascertain the intervals between them, M. Houzeau obtains the following table :—

TABLE II.†

No. of the observation.	Date.	Interval.	Number of periods.	Length of period.
		years.		years.
1.	1645·87			
2.	1672·07	26·20	9	2·91
3.	1686·65	14·58	5	2·92
4.	1740·84	54·19	18	3·01
5.	1761·34	20·50	7	2·93
7.	1764·24	2·90	1	2·90
Total interval .		118·37	40	2·96

It will be observed that the successive intervals are multiples of very nearly the same period, which is almost exactly the length of the interval between the two last dates.

M. Houzeau asks, "Is this agreement, six times repeated, wholly the effect of chance? Undoubtedly it may be only accidental; but

* Old style. The line should read therefore :—
4. 1740, Nov. 3 ‖ M 86 46 +0°·7 0·64.
† The table as given by M. Houzeau is here altered for the true date of Short's observation.

15 https://en.wikipedia.org/wiki/Orbital_resonance

16 Jackson, J. 'Retrograde satellite orbits,' *Monthly Notices of the Royal Astronomical Society*, Vol. 74 (1913), pp. 62-82; http://adsabs.harvard.edu/abs/1913MNRAS..74...62J

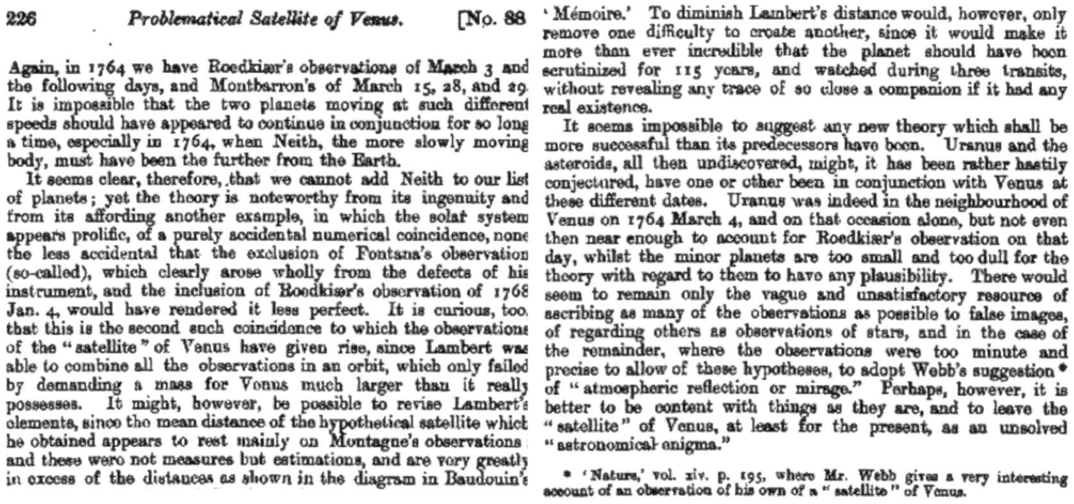

Again, in 1764 we have Roedkiær's observations of March 3 and the following days, and Montbarron's of March 15, 28, and 29. It is impossible that the two planets moving at such different speeds should have appeared to continue in conjunction for so long a time, especially in 1764, when Neith, the more slowly moving body, must have been the further from the Earth.

It seems clear, therefore, that we cannot add Neith to our list of planets; yet the theory is noteworthy from its ingenuity and from its affording another example, in which the solar system appears prolific, of a purely accidental numerical coincidence, none the less accidental that the exclusion of Fontana's observation (so-called), which clearly arose wholly from the defects of his instrument, and the inclusion of Roedkiær's observation of 1768 Jan. 4, would have rendered it less perfect. It is curious, too, that this is the second such coincidence to which the observations of the "satellite" of Venus have given rise, since Lambert was able to combine all the observations in an orbit, which only failed by demanding a mass for Venus much larger than it really possesses. It might, however, be possible to revise Lambert's elements, since the mean distance of the hypothetical satellite which he obtained appears to rest mainly on Montagne's observations and these were not measures but estimations, and are very greatly in excess of the distances as shown in the diagram in Baudouin's

'Mémoire.' To diminish Lambert's distance would, however, only remove one difficulty to create another, since it would make it more than ever incredible that the planet should have been scrutinized for 115 years, and watched during three transits, without revealing any trace of so close a companion if it had any real existence.

It seems impossible to suggest any new theory which shall be more successful than its predecessors have been. Uranus and the asteroids, all then undiscovered, might, it has been rather hastily conjectured, have one or other been in conjunction with Venus at these different dates. Uranus was indeed in the neighbourhood of Venus on 1764 March 4, and on that occasion alone, but not even then near enough to account for Roedkiær's observation on that day, whilst the minor planets are too small and too dull for the theory with regard to them to have any plausibility. There would seem to remain only the vague and unsatisfactory resource of ascribing as many of the observations as possible to false images, of regarding others as observations of stars, and in the case of the remainder, where the observations were too minute and precise to allow of these hypotheses, to adopt Webb's suggestion * of "atmospheric reflection or mirage." Perhaps, however, it is better to be content with things as they are, and to leave the "satellite" of Venus, at least for the present, as an unsolved "astronomical enigma."

* 'Nature,' vol. xiv. p. 195, where Mr. Webb gives a very interesting account of an observation of his own of a "satellite" of Venus.

Fig. 6. Pages from 'The problematical satellite of Venus,' *The Observatory*, 7 (1884), pp. 222-226.[17]

This object is thought to be an asteroid belonging to a family of asteroids whose orbits cross that of the Earth, roaming far from the belt between Mars and Jupiter which was the assumed home of asteroids in the 19th century when Houzeau's theory was mooted.[18] At that time the possibility of asteroids was dismissed because they were too far away, too small, and too dim to explain sightings of bodies showing phases in early telescopes. Today we know that space in the inner solar system is more crowded with objects, and their motions more complex.

Even so, Houzeau's Neith could not be $2002VE_{68}$ or a quasi-satellite like it. $2002VE_{68}$ is thought to be only a few hundred metres across and never gets closer to Venus than about 19 million miles (30 million km, or about 78 times the distance between Earth and our own moon).[19] Whilst the resonances of quasi-satellites are not eternal and bodies may change partners, they only do so slowly over thousands of years, not decades.

Venus also has a trojan asteroid discovered in 2013, that is, one that is in orbit around a Lagrangian point. The Lagrangian points are islands of gravitational stability located near two large co-orbiting bodies, here the Sun-Venus system. There are always five such points. However, Venus's Trojan 2013 ND15 is in L4, many millions of miles from the planet, and, like another temporary co-orbital of Venus, 2001 CK32, it is only around 100 m across. None of these objects can explain the 17th–18th century phantom "moon" of Venus.

After 1768 few people claimed to see the moon of Venus again. Was it a passing delusion or was it real? Could another unknown minor planet, or some more exotic object or objects, have temporarily accompanied Venus for a hundred years or so, only to disappear back into the void? Charles Fort (prefiguring George Lucas' *Deathstar* by 60 years) imagined "Visitors

17 https://archive.org/stream/observatory03gbgoog#page/n241/mode/2up
18 http://adsabs.harvard.edu/abs/2004MNRAS.351L..63M; http://en.wikipedia.org/wiki/2002_VE68
19 In 1766 Johann Titius intuited the pattern that became known as the Titius-Bode Law of orbital radii, noting the "gap" between Mars and Jupiter. The first minor planets or "asteroids" were discovered in 1801–1802, and the concept of a belt, filling the supposed "gap," evolved thereafter. The "law" is regarded today as a coincidence.

to Venus" in a "super-construction," a vessel "large enough to appear like a satellite . . . staying awhile – going away – coming back some other time – anchoring, as it were."

In 1884 the author of the very fair *Observatory* article concluded that most astronomers, having ruled out chance conjunctions of an outer planet or of a minor planet in the asteroid belt, now put the sightings down to stars, telescope defects, or eyepiece reflections, but conceded that this was a "vague and unsatisfactory solution," recommending that it might be better to leave the affair as an unresolved "astronomical enigma."

Three years later, however, in 1887, the astronomical consensus was largely settled by Paul Stroobant in a lecture to the Royal Belgian Academy which is still cited as definitive to this day. The 19-year-old astronomical wunderkind[20] listed all 33 known reports in full and proceeded to explain the "satellites" one by one. Most he explained as small stars near the planet at the time of the observations, and those seen with perceptible discs were nothing but ghost images in the telescope optics, whilst Roedkiær at Copenhagen on March 5, 1761 may have unwittingly observed the planet Uranus twenty years before Herschel discovered it. According to a modern summary Stroobant's criticisms were "so devastating that no one is now talking about Venus' moon."[21]

---

20 https://cds.cern.ch/record/1338962/files/978-3-7643-8909-3_BookBackMatter.pdf
21 https://www.belgiuminspace.be/artikelen/belgen-in-de-sterrenkunde/belgen-in-desterrenkunde-paul-henri-stroobant

CHAPTER 2 – **The Elusive Planet Vulcan**

Astronomers have always paid close attention to the inner planets, Venus and Mercury, when they happen to cross the face of the sun, an event known as a solar transit. During the transit of Venus in 1769 measurements of the path of Venus across the sun's disc were made simultaneously, for the first time, by observers in places thousands of miles apart. The differences between the apparent paths, due to parallax, allowed the rough distance of the sun to be calculated reliably for the first time. Astronomers continued using transits to refine the exact size of the solar system, and also studied the tiny silhouettes of the planets through their telescopes in search of traces of atmosphere or other features that might be revealed.

But as well as the predicted transits of the known planets, many other shapes have drifted across the sun over the centuries in a tantalising shadow-play of odd blobs and spots, ranging from the weird (like the huge "spindle" seen by Swiss astronomers in 1762; see Chapter 3) to the more routine sightings of tiny moving spots, the greater part no doubt attributable to birds, balloons or airborne seeds (see Chapters 1, 3, 9, 12 and 14 of our first volume), others moving very slowly and believed to be unknown planets orbiting nearer the sun. Many early sightings languished unresolved and would have been forgotten were it not for the famous 19th century hunt for Vulcan, a small planet then believed to circle the sun inside the orbit of Mercury.

The origin of Vulcan lay in a calculation of the orbit of Mercury made by the renowned French mathematician Urbain Le Verrier, beginning in about 1840. Le Verrier's recent prediction of the existence of the planet Neptune from disturbances in the orbit of Uranus had been a triumphant validation of celestial mechanics based on Newton's theory of gravity. And after years of careful calculations based on measurements made during past transits of Mercury, Le Verrier finally determined in 1859 that that there was a tiny discrepancy – amounting to 43 seconds of arc per century – in the motion of Mercury, too. He declared the cause to be the gravity of an unknown small planet, which he called Vulcan, orbiting nearer the sun.

On the authority of "the man who discovered a world with the point of his pen" many astronomers searched for Vulcan, which was duly observed many times. But the motions never made sense. And not until 1915 did Einstein, and some while later the amazed world, realise that Le Verrier had unwittingly discovered something much more remarkable than another new planet: he had found the footprint of a wholly new theory of gravity – the Theory of General Relativity.

In a sense Le Verrier's infamous 43 seconds of arc, and indeed the whole Vulcan craze, was a sociological foreshadowing or premonition of 20th century physics. The shadow of curved spacetime with its bending light and gravitational black holes lay across the imagination of the 19th century like a strange and incomprehensible dream.

Charles Fort published *The Book of the Damned* in 1919. Isaac Newton figures largely, but Fort did not mention Einstein, relativity or quantum mechanics. Yet that same year Eddington's dramatic proof of starlight being bent by the sun's gravity during a solar eclipse, exactly as predicted by Einstein, catapulted General Relativity from an esoteric idea to an international sensation. Not until *Lo!* (1931) and *Wild Talents* (1932) did Fort refer to the new physics, in an abstract, philosophical way, expressing the same ironical contempt for "Einsteinism" that he had earlier expressed for Newton – and, indeed, for everybody and everything distinct enough to be thought about. So, we have only a vague idea of his opinion as to the meaning of the Vulcan affair, beyond his two essential points:

First, Le Verrier's theory-driven selection of a handful of "reliable" 19th-century observations from dozens of others that would not fit any sensible Vulcan orbit was, in retrospect, arbitrary and unscientific. And second, if Vulcan did not exist, what had been seen – or dreamed – drifting across the sun by so many astronomers?

Fort hinted at "vast things," "orbitless worlds . . . under navigable control," "dirigible worlds" or "dirigible super-constructions." Let's look briefly at the sightings he collected.

In the transit of 1799, which occurred in May, Schröter and Harding at Lilienthal, and Köhler at Dresden, saw a small luminous spot on the dark disk. The spot was not stationary, for Harding saw it change its position, and later in the day Schröter saw it sometimes on one part of the disk, sometimes on another. Other observers saw, not one, but two small spots of a greyish colour.

In the transit of May 1832 Professor Moll observed a spot, the periphery of which was not well defined, but was always situated in the same position, a little south of the centre of the planet, and preceding the centre.

Turning now to the November transits for further evidence of the luminous spot, we find that the transit of 1835 was not visible in this part of the world, and in the three previous ones of which we have some particulars, viz. those of 1736, 1789, and 1802, no mention is made of a luminous spot; but, as will be seen, it does not follow that it did not exist because it was not observed.

In November 1848 one spot was observed of a greyish colour, shading off on all sides from the centre.

In November 1861 Mr. J. W. Jeans saw a slight ashy light on the eastern limit or following the centre of the planet on its way to perihelion.

In November 1868 Mr. Huggins saw a point of light nearly in the centre which had no sensible diameter, but appeared as a luminous point. It was near the centre, a little south, and following the centre. It remained in the same position during the transit.

Mr. Browning, observing this transit, saw near the centre of the planet two bright grey spots close together, both a little south of the centre, one more conspicuous than the other.

So much for the luminous spot. Let us turn to the rings which have been observed round the planet during a transit.

In May 1707 the late Assistant of the then Astronomer Royal saw *Mercury* in transit encompassed by a thick haze or atmosphere.

In the transit of May 1753 a ring was observed round the planet; also in that of May 1786.

In May 1799 a dark or nebulous ring was observed, the tinge

Fig. 7. A page from B. G. Jenkins, "The luminous spot on Mercury in transit," *Monthly Notices of the Royal Astronomical Society*, 38 (April 1878), pp. 337-340[22]

---

22 http://mnras.oxfordjournals.org/content/38/6/337.full.pdf+html

He mentions a "luminous spot seen moving across the disk of Mercury, in 1799, by Harding and Schroeter"[23] while that planet was itself transiting the sun. In fact this phenomenon, also seen by Köhler at Dresden, is only one of half a dozen observations of Mercurial lights, blobs, and glows listed in Fort's source, in addition to other nebulosities and "rings" (see Fig. 7). Clearly an object on the near side of Mercury during a transit cannot be in an orbit closer to the sun than Mercury, so whatever it was it wasn't related to Vulcan.

Fort goes on to list numerous solar transits of suspected new planets from about 1762:

> Standacher, Feb., 1762; Lichtenberg, Nov. 19, 1762; Hoffman, May, 1764; Dangos, Jan. 18, 1798; Stark, Feb. 12, 1820. An observation by Schmidt, Oct. 11, 1847, is said to be doubtful: but, upon page 192, it is said that this doubt had arisen because of a mistaken translation, and two other observations by Schmidt are given: Oct. 14, 1849, and Feb. 18, 1850 -- also an observation by Lofft, Jan. 6, 1818. Observation by Steinheibel, at Vienna, April 27, 1820 (*Monthly Notices*, 1862).
>
> Haase had collected reports of twenty observations like Lescarbault's. The list was published in 1872, by Wolf.[24]

Another report concerns the "Observation, of June 26, 1819, by Gruithinson [sic] of two bodies that crossed the sun together."[25] This sighting, by Dutch astronomer Franz von Gruithuisen (Fig. 8), is widely quoted – and misquoted – both in the Vulcan literature and in the UFO literature, for reasons we cannot work out, unless it be that Fort mentions it. The Wikipedia page records Gruithuisen's sighting this day as one of the "most noteworthy" and, like Fort, mentions "two small spots...on the Sun" which it describes as "round, black and unequal in size."[26] Fort himself mentions the case again in *New Lands* (1923) where he says that "five unknown bodies were seen crossing the sun, upon June 26, 1819, according to Gruithuisen." [27] A major book of historical UFO mysteries records "three unknown bodies crossing the disk of the Sun, '...viz, one near the middle of the Sun, and two small ones without nebulosity near the western limb,'" which is somewhat more accurate. [28] However all of these versions and many like them are misleading.

Gruithuisen was actually looking for signs of a small comet expected to be crossing the sun. The comet was widely observed, and many astronomers attempted to spot its transit. There was disagreement as to whether anyone actually had done so. At least two of the spots noted by Gruithuisen were plainly stated by him to be sunspots. In his journal, as quoted in

---

23 Fort, *Damned*, p. 187, citing *Monthly Notices of the R. A. S.*, 38-338.
24 Fort, *Damned*, p. 193, citing *Monthly Notices of the R. A. S.*, 20-100. See also: R.C. Carrington, 'On some previous observations of supposed planetary bodies in transit over the Sun,' *Monthly Notices of the Royal Astronomical Society*, 20 (March 1860), p. 192; Rudolf Wolf, *Handbuch der Mathematik, Physik, Geodäsie und Astronomie*, Zurich, Bd. Ii (1869–1872), p. 327. Exhaustive references are given by "Mr. X" at www.resologist.net.
25 Fort, *Damned*, p. 190 source not given. However, see www.resologist.net citing: 'New planets,' *Annual of Scientific Discovery*, 1860, 410-11, at 411; Olbers, 'On the passage of the comet of 1819 across the disc of the sun,' *Philosophical Magazine*, s.1, 57 (1821), pp. 444-446.
26 http://en.wikipedia.org/wiki/Vulcan_(hypothetical_planet)
27 *The Complete Books of Charles Fort*, Dover Publications, New York, 1974, p. 393.
28 Vallée, J. & C. Aubeck, *Wonders In the Sky*, Tarcher, 2010, case #395, citing: 'New planets,' *Annual of Scientific Discovery* (1860), pp. 410-411, at 411.

1821 by German astronomer Heinrich Wilhelm Olbers (Fig. 9), he opined that a third faint spot *may* have been either the comet or a new sunspot appearing.

Fig. 8. Franz von Gruithuisen (1774–1852). [29]

Olbers quotes Gruithuisen's report among others as "incontestable proofs of the existence of the [sun]spots" at the time of the comet's passage. Olbers argues that since certain observers who saw no comet also reported no sunspots they might have missed the comet too, if it was fugitive – as was the "very small and undefined" spot seen by Gruithuisen ("as well as he can recollect"). Olbers noted that sometime around this date Wildt in Hanover had observed a spot that was "faint and so indeterminate that it appeared to me of little interest" and which he therefore did not bother to record. He thought nothing of it at the time but reflected, "if the calculations of M. Olbers were confirmed by my observations, I should be inclined to believe it was the comet." Olbers thought it likely but "doubts must remain". In any case, there never were "three unknown bodies crossing the disk of the sun" or "two bodies that crossed the sun together" – Gruithuisen saw some ordinary sunspots, and one other faint speck which might conceivably have been the nucleus of a suspected comet.[30]

It is rather hard to understand how Fort could have got hold of the story (even imprecisely) without knowing these facts. By the time of *New Lands* (1923) Fort certainly did know about the comet of 1819. There he writes that German astronomer Pastorff observed a solar spot on the same day as Gruithuisen which he thought might be the same comet. Fort mentions this sighting but is content to say that "according to Olbers [it] could not have been the comet." [31]

Privy Councillor J. W. Pastorff (1767–1838), an experienced solar observer who had made regular sunspot counts from 1819 to 1833, saw a number of other odd things. Fort mentions that "he had seen twice in 1836, and once in 1837, two round spots of unequal size moving across the sun, changing position relatively to each other, and taking a different

29 http://en.wikipedia.org/wiki/Franz_von_Gruithuisen
30 The authors of *Wonders in the Sky* (case #395) remark: "It is notable that this observation, initially published in Reverend Webb's well-known astronomy handbooks [*Celestial Objects for Common Telescopes*], has been deleted from recent editions!" – apparently implying some devious revisionism to suppress an anomaly. Most likely, the editors realised the vague observation was not clearly evidence of anything.
31 *The Complete Books of Charles Fort*, Dover Publications, New York, 1974, p. 393, citing Webb, *Celestial Objects*, p. 40.

course, if not orbit, each time: that, in 1834, he had seen similar bodies pass six times across the disk of the sun, looking very much like Mercury in his transits." [32]

[444]

LXXXIII. *On the Passage of the Comet of* 1819 *across the Disc of the Sun* *. *By* M. Olbers.

All the elements indicated this passage. According to those of Dirksen, the immersion was to take place at 17ʰ 30′ 34″, and the emersion at 21ʰ 5′ 37″ on the 25th June 1819; the hours were reckoned according to true time, Milan meridian. At 19ʰ 18′ 6″ the centre of the comet was only removed from that of the sun 2′ 8″. The aberration retards these phases 5′ 31″ and the parallax half a minute for the observatories of Germany.

In the Ephemeris of Berlin for 1822, I concluded (says M. Olbers) from the observation of M. de Lindener, confirmed by an observation made in Austria, that the comet had been invisible on the disc of the sun; but it is now proved that the sun was not without spots at that epoch; and if these spots were not remarked by the two observers to whom I have alluded, the comet, much more difficult to be seen, may also have escaped their notice, although a more attentive or more piercing eye might have been able to discern it. The following are incontestable proofs of the existence of the spots.

(1). M. Schumaker, then at Altona, had determined the collimation of his Troughton's sextant several times in the course of the month of June; and among others, on the 25th at 20ʰ. He recollects most positively of never having seen the sun without spots. The glass of the sextant multiplied nearly ten times; it is therefore not probable that one of these spots could be the comet.

(2.) Professor Brandes at Breslau viewed the sun on the 26th of June, a little before midday, with a glass of a thirty-four times multiplying power, and he perceived a spot distinctly visible, almost passing behind the disc, and precisely at the place where it ought to have been according to the preceding observations. This observation becomes important when compared with that of Dr. Gruithuisen inserted in the *Gazette Politique* of Munich, of the 12th of August 1819. According to the Meteorological Journal of Dr. Gruithuisen, there were on the 26th of June, at eight in the morning, two small spots without nebulosity near the west limb of the sun. One also was seen in the midst of the apparent disc. As well as he can recollect, the spot in the middle was very small and undefined; it is possible, therefore, that this philosopher might have seen the comet on the disc of the sun. Nevertheless doubts must still remain, until we learn that some other observer has seen this black point, either forward

* Extracted from a Memoir by M. Olbers in the Ephemeris of Berlin for 1823.

near the south limb, or behind near the north limb, considering that spots have never been seen in the neighbourhood of the poles of the sun. This spot in the middle appeared somewhat larger than double the size of the fourth satellite of Jupiter; it was not an old spot; indeed, four days before M. Gruithuisen had observed the following spots:

"Near the west limb a large spot with nebulosity.

"Towards the middle, but still a little to the west, three new spots rather large, and some smaller ones.

"And very near the east limb a small spot.

"The large spots in the middle were on the 26th of June near the west limb, and had greatly diminished; that on the east limb had disappeared; at least it is certain that it had not arrived at the middle of the sun in four days. It follows, that the small black spot in the middle of the disc on the 26th of June was a new spot, or the nucleus of the comet."

The observations of MM. Brandes and Gruithuisen appear to indicate that between the 23d and 28th of June none of the ordinary spots seen before or after that period had reached the middle of the solar disc; and the observation made at Hanover by Professor Wildt, appears to confirm that made on the 26th of June by M. Gruithuisen.

"I observed the sun," says M. Wildt, "about the 26th of June, one or two days sooner or later, and I saw an undefined spot, of which I still recollect the size and the situation. I believe it was the comet I saw upon the sun; my observation was made towards seven in the morning, and might have indicated the situation and the size of the comet. It is perhaps the only time that I did not commit my observation to writing; but the spot was so faint, and so indeterminate, that it appeared to me of little interest. It is truly to be regretted that the idea of a comet had not occurred to me. The fact of not having written down my observation leads me to think that it must have been on the 26th of June; for I am aware of circumstances which might have deprived me of the opportunity on that day. If then the calculations of M. Olbers were confirmed by my observations, I should be inclined to believe that it was the comet which I saw on the sun's disc."

"I will not decide," adds M. Olbers, "whether what MM. Gruithuisen and Wildt saw upon the sun (at the period of the passage) was really the comet, or an ordinary spot. However, none of the spots seen before the 26th of June could be on that day in the middle of the disc; and M. Brandes could not perceive at twelve o'clock the spot observed at eight by M. Gruithuisen: these two facts appear very remarkable. It is to be regretted, that there has not been any decisive observation of a phænomenon so interesting

interesting and so rare; but it has appeared to me proper, nevertheless, to collect here all the observations on the solar disc made on the 26th of June 1819, of which I have been able to receive an account."

Fig. 9. Heinrich Olbers, "On the passage of the comet of 1819 across the disc of the sun," *Philosophical Magazine*, Series 1, Vol. 57, 278 (1821), pp. 444-446 (extracted from a Memoir by Olbers in the *Ephemeris of Berlin* for 1823) [33]

---

32 Fort, *Damned*, p. 193, citing *Amer. Jour. Sci.*, 2-28-446. "Mr. X" at www.resologist.net amplifies: E. C. Herrick, 'Supposed new planet between Mercury and the Sun,' *American Journal of Science*, s. 2, 28 (1859), pp. 445-446.

33 tinyurl.com/1jh9yvqf

We have not located Fort's source in this case; however, we have found other, more nearly contemporary, accounts of Pastorff's observations, which clarify certain things but unfortunately also add to the confusion.

In 1841, the popular Austrian periodical *Jurende's Vaterländischen Pilger*, no doubt copying from another publication, reported that:

> Mr Pastorff from Buchholz near Berlin discovered in the year 1834 two small, black, completely round bodies, therefore differing completely from the ordinary sunspots, and which he saw moving across the sun's disc six times. Their relative distances from one another changed towards the end of 1836, and when Mr Pastorff observed them again on February 16, 1837, he found that the speed of their movement is very variable. [34]

It appears that Pastorff had already seen these objects in the years before 1834. We found the original source for those observations in *Astronomische Nachrichten*, whose editor in February 1835 reported in detail (Fig. 10) a communication from Mr Pastorff, describing how

> six times in the past years, he had seen two new bodies, which he calls asteroids, passing in front of the sun with different directions and different speeds. The bigger one was approximately 3" [seconds of arc] in diameter, the smaller one 1¼". He describes both as perfectly round. Sometimes the smaller one goes in front, sometimes the bigger one. The drawing for both cases, which he enclosed, gives their distance as 1'16", which is the biggest distance observed. Often, they were also very close together. The transit lasted a few hours. Both are said to have been as raven black as Mercury when it appears in front of the sun, and to have had a sharply rounded circular shape, which must have been difficult to determine for the smaller one.

This last comment reflects the fact that the 1¼ arc-second diameter of the smaller body would be smaller than the limiting angular resolution (Airy disk) of any telescope with an objective smaller than about 8.6-inches across. Therefore Pastorff could only be sure that this was a properly focused true image of a circular object – rather than a blur circle, due to an unresolved speck, whose shape was an artefact of the telescope's circular aperture – if his telescope had a significantly larger objective diameter than 8.6 inches. We have been unable to discover what instruments were at Pastorff's disposal; but although this would have been a fairly large aperture for a typical amateur at this date, mirrors of 10 or 12 inches were available from many makers, and larger instruments still were by no means unheard of.

The editor continues:

> [Pastorff] ends with the wish that astronomers with the strongest telescopes will want to pay attention to these irregular, sometimes brief, sometimes longer-lasting, and differently directed bodies in front of the sun. He says the bodies are definitely not

---

34 Translation Wim van Utrecht, from *Jurende's Vaterländischen Pilger*, Brunn, Austria, 28. Jahrgang (1841), p. 27; tinyurl.com/2fmcd9df

sunspots, because sunspots are far paler and have their regular movement. These bodies have often disappeared after 8 to 48 hours, entering the sun's limb raven black at this or that point and describing changing paths before the sun. Although I believe that the bodies observed by Mr Pastorff, as becomes clear from the information itself, are not what he seems to think they are, it is my duty as publisher of this journal, to honour the request of an honest man, and to make known what he saw. Incidentally, it is very regrettable that Mr Pastorff did not, on each occasion, compare his bodies, using the field of the telescope as a circle-micrometer, with the edges of the sun.[35]

Herr Geheimerrath *v. Pastorf* meldet mir unter dem 9. Januar, mit dem Ersuchen es in den A. N. anzuzeigen, daſs er 6mal im vergangenen Jahre zwei neue Körper, die er Asteroiden nennt, vor der Sonne in verschiedenen Richtungen und mit verschiedener Geschwindigkeit hat vorübergehen gesehen. Der gröſsere hat circa 3″ Durchmesser, der kleinere 1″ bis 1¼″. Beide beschreibt er als auf das deutlichste abgerundet. Bald geht der kleinere, bald der gröſsere vorauf. Die Zeichnung beider Fälle, die er beifügt, gibt ihren Abstand zu 1′ 16″ an, welches der gröſste beobachtete Abstand ist. Oft sind sie auch ganz nahe aneinander. Der Vorübergang währt wenige Stunden. Beide sollen ebenso rabenschwarz wie Mercur vor der Sonne erscheinen, und eine scharf abgerundete Kreisgestalt haben, was doch vorzüglich bei dem kleinern schwer zu bestimmen seyn muſs. Herr *v. Pastorf* schlieſst mit dem Wunsche, daſs Astronomen mit den stärksten Fernröhren versehen diese unregelmäſsig bald in kurzen bald in längeren Perioden in verschiedenen Richtungen vor der Sonne erscheinenden Körper ihrer Aufmerksamkeit würdigen mögen. Sonnenflecke, sagt er, sind diese Körper auf keinen Fall, denn Sonnenflecke sind weit blässer, und haben ihre regelmäſsige Bewegung. Diese Körper sind aber oft schon nach 8 bis 48 Stunden verschwunden, treten bald an diesem bald an jenem Puncte des Sonnenrandes mit Rabenschwärze ein, und beschreiben ihren Lauf verändert vor der Sonne.

Obgleich ich glaube, daſs bei diesen Beobachtungen des Herrn *v. Pastorff* wie schon aus den Angaben wahrscheinlich wird, die beobachteten Körper nicht das sind, wofür er sie zu halten scheint, so war es doch meine Pflicht als Herausgeber dieses Blattes, dem Verlangen eines unbescholtenen Mannes zu folgen, und das was er gesehen hat, bekannt zu machen.

Es ist übrigens sehr zu bedauern, daſs Herr *v. Pastorff* nicht jedesmal seine Körper auch nur durch das Feld des Fernrohrs, als Kreismicrometer gebraucht, mit den Sonnenrändern verglichen hat.

Fig. 10. *Astronomische Nachrichten*, Nr. 273 (11 February, 1835), pp. 150-151.[36]

---

35 Trans. Wim van Utrecht, from *Astronomische Nachrichten*, Nr. 273 (11 Feb. 1835), pp. 150-151.
36 tinyurl.cm/2snev8am

Even ignoring the issue of resolution, and neglecting their "sharply rounded circular appearance", these bodies moved far too slowly to have been birds or balloons in the atmosphere, taking hours to transit the sun. As for Pastorff's "asteroids", evidence of permanent asteroids inside the orbits of the inner planets has been sought assiduously in modern times without success. Transient Earth-crossing asteroids or comets passing sunward of the Earth may come and go, and occasional passing asteroids may be captured by Earth's gravity, becoming temporary "minimoons" for a few years or so. Astronomers suspect that there may be one or more of these visitors orbiting Earth at any given time; but they are very rarely seen, even now, because of their small diameter. Only two have been confidently identified, and both with 21st-century equipment: a 0.9 meter (3 ft) rock called 2006 RH120, which looped around the Earth for 18 months in 2006 and 2007; and most recently the slightly larger 2020 CD3, which appears to have been hanging around since 2017 and was expected to return to interplanetary space in April 2020.[37] But a repeated pattern of paired asteroids passing in changing configurations during several years seems very strange; and given that Pastorff's objects were apparently seen by no other observers we are entitled to be sceptical. As for what he did observe, we have no useful theory to offer.

In hindsight, the history of Vulcan proper begins after about 1840, when at the instigation of François Arago, of the Paris Observatory, Urbain Le Verrier began to calculate an exact orbit of the planet Mercury. Between then and the day in 1859 when Le Verrier finally published his refined orbit, with its famous unexplained discrepancy of 43 arc seconds, random sightings of the same type continued to accrue. Examples listed by Charles Fort include a terse note of "De Vico's observation of July 12, 1837,"[38] referring to the Italian astronomer Father Francesco de Vico (1805–1848), who at the time was Assistant Superintendent (later Director) of the Vatican Observatory, a planetary observer and discoverer of several comets.

In Fort's source (see Fig. 11) we find De Vico quoted (from *Memorie Dell Osservatorio del Collegio Romano*, 1838) as referring to the transits of "asteroids such as he had the fortune to observe in 1837" – specifically a "perfectly round spot" which crossed "a good part of the Sun's disk in the short space of 6 hours." In fact, 6 hours is not such a short space. Mercury typically crosses the entire disc of the sun in less than 6 hours,[39] whereas this spot only managed to cross "a good part" in that time. Clearly it was not an unknown inner planet because the orbit of a hypothetical Vulcan inside that of Mercury would have been faster, not slower. An asteroid, as assumed by De Vico, is possible, perhaps an Earth-crossing body on a highly eccentric orbit. It could even have been a balloon, although this is very unlikely.[40]

---

37   Brandon Specktor, 'Possible new 'minimoon' discovered orbiting Earth', *LiveScience*, 26 Feb. 2020; https://www.livescience.com/mini-moon-discovered.html. (As of the date of writing the asteroid is still around. See: https://theskylive.com/where-is-2020cd3.)

38   Fort, *Damned*, p. 190, citing *Observatory*, 2-424.

39   https://en.wikipedia.org/wiki/Transit_of_Mercury

40   Even assuming a low solar elevation and a slant range of 100 miles, a balloon would need to have been at high altitude and steadily moving transversely in the order of only 0.1 mph (0.04 m/sec), which seems improbable for 6 hours.

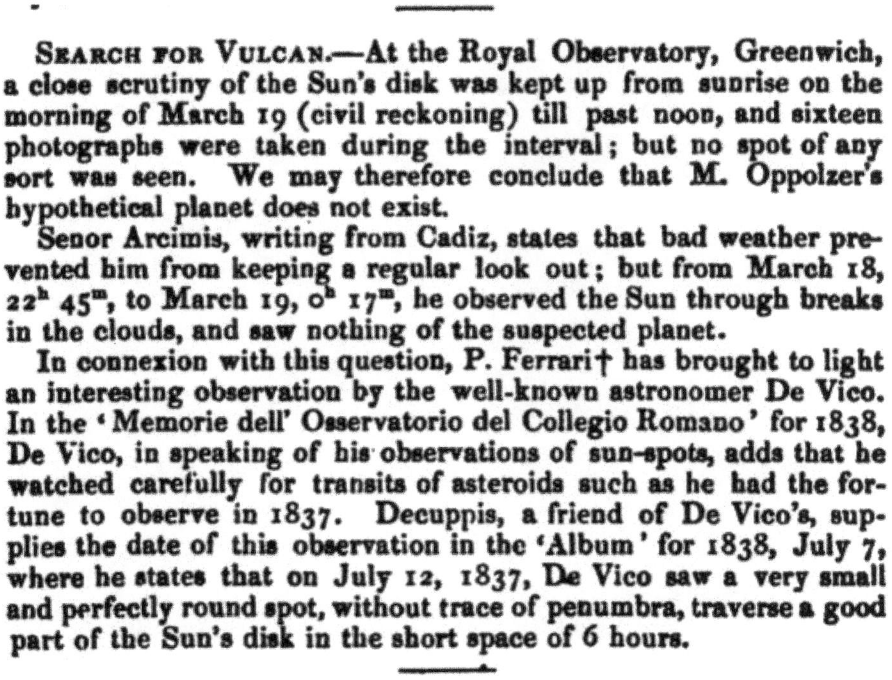

SEARCH FOR VULCAN.—At the Royal Observatory, Greenwich, a close scrutiny of the Sun's disk was kept up from sunrise on the morning of March 19 (civil reckoning) till past noon, and sixteen photographs were taken during the interval; but no spot of any sort was seen. We may therefore conclude that M. Oppolzer's hypothetical planet does not exist.

Senor Arcimis, writing from Cadiz, states that bad weather prevented him from keeping a regular look out; but from March 18, 22ʰ 45ᵐ, to March 19, 0ʰ 17ᵐ, he observed the Sun through breaks in the clouds, and saw nothing of the suspected planet.

In connexion with this question, P. Ferrari† has brought to light an interesting observation by the well-known astronomer De Vico. In the 'Memorie dell' Osservatorio del Collegio Romano' for 1838, De Vico, in speaking of his observations of sun-spots, adds that he watched carefully for transits of asteroids such as he had the fortune to observe in 1837. Decuppis, a friend of De Vico's, supplies the date of this observation in the 'Album' for 1838, July 7, where he states that on July 12, 1837, De Vico saw a very small and perfectly round spot, without trace of penumbra, traverse a good part of the Sun's disk in the short space of 6 hours.

Fig. 11. "Search for Vulcan," *Observatory,* 2 (1879), p. 424. [41]

A "balloon" – or thus it was characterised by the observer's 5-year-old son – did cross the sun in the summer of 1847. Fort tells us that one Benjamin Scott saw "a body that had seemed to be the size of Venus, crossing the sun. He says that, hardly believing the evidence of his sense of sight, he had looked for someone, whose hopes or ambitions would not make him so subject to illusion. He had told his little son, aged five years, to look through the telescope. The child had exclaimed that he had seen 'a little balloon' crossing the sun." [42]

Benjamin Scott (1814–1892) was at this time Chief Clerk to the Chamberlain of the City of London (he was elected Chamberlain himself in 1858).[43] He was a prominent social reformer and a Fellow of the Royal Astronomical Society.[44] It seems very unlikely that Scott, no doubt an observer with at least some knowledge and experience, did see a balloon; but we have no good information about times, angles and rates. Like a number of stories from this period it was not properly recorded at the time and only published years later, after the Vulcan enthusiasm had caused people to recollect past sightings.

41 https://archive.org/stream/observatory28unkngoog#page/n447/mode/2up
42 Fort, *Damned*, p. 194, citing the London *Times,* Jan. 10, 1860. "Mr. X" at www.resologist.net points out that Fort's account of the circumstances is a little confused, and gives these full references: 'New inferior planet,' London *Times,* Jan. 10, 1860, p. 11 c.1; 'New inferior planet,' London *Times,* Jan. 12, 1860, p. 11 c.5.
43 An ancient 13th-century post, but not merely ceremonial. The Chamberlain is Finance Director of the City of London Corporation.
44 https://en.wikipedia.org/wiki/Benjamin_Scott

Fig. 12. Benjamin Scott. Portrait photograph of the Chamberlain of the City of London in his finery, circa 1865 (Source Metropolitan Archive; Henry Maull[45])

As Fort mentions – apparently without realising it is the same story – Scott's sighting is referred to again in *Nature* in 1876 in an article[46] by J. R. Hind. Hind (1823–1895) was Superintendent of the British Nautical Almanac and discoverer in 1845 of the rare, deep-red, "carbon star" R Leporis in the constellation Lepus (the Hare), which is named in his honour as "Hind's Crimson Star." [47] According to another article in 1876, Hind himself, along with Lowe (possibly the astronomer, meteorologist and botanist Edward J. Lowe, 1825–1900), had himself seen a possible transit of Vulcan in March 1849.[48]

Such old observations, if known at all, had led to nothing but fruitless speculations at the time they were made, and many lacked detail or even credibility. But Le Verrier was able to select enough seemingly reliable data to define an orbit, and a March 1859 sighting by French country doctor Edmond Lescarbault led Le Verrier to publicly nail his colours to the mast.

Lescarbault saw a spot on the sun which he had assumed was merely a sunspot until it moved too quickly. Having heard of Le Verrier's work he wrote to the great man, who promptly rushed to Orgères-en-Beauce and came away convinced that the doctor had seen Vulcan exactly where and when it should have been, famously announcing to the Royal Academy in Paris in January 1860, "Gentlemen, I give you the planet Vulcan." Despite Le Verrier's reputation, not everyone was convinced even then.[49] But sightings increased.

---

45 https://commons.wikimedia.org/wiki/File:Benjamin_Scott_Chamberlain.jpg

46 J. R. Hind, 'The Intra-Mercurial planet or planets,' *Nature,* 14 (Sept. 28, 1876), pp. 469-470.

47 http://stars.astro.illinois.edu/sow/hinds.html

48   Fort, *Damned*, p. 190, citing *L'Année Scientifique,*1876–1879. Full reference per Mr.X: 'Les planètes entre le Soleil et Mercure...' *Année Scientifique et Industrielle,* 20 (1876), pp. 6-11, at 9. Hind saw what appeared to be Vulcan on at least one other occasion, in 1871, according to Fort (*Damned*, p. 195, citing London *Times,* Nov. 3, 1871).

49 Eminent astronomer Emmanuel Liais saw nothing whilst observing the sun at the same time as Lescaurbault (*Popular Science*, Vol. 13, 1878, pp. 732-735). Camille Flammarion was sceptical, believing the amateur Lescarbault had merely seen a sunspot and was innocently confused by the change in apparent orientation of the sun's north-south meridian as it moves across the sky. But there are conflicting sources and Flammarion's account of the affair is not without its discrepancies. According to James Lequeux, "Nothing is certain in this story" (James Lequeux, *Le Verrier—Magnificent and Detestable Astronomer*, Springer, 2013, p. 168).

SIR,—

During the total phase of the late solar eclipse, as observed at Denver, Colorado, I had a view of a celestial object not down in Argelander's charts, which to my mind, without any doubt, is the long-sought Vulcan.

It was in field with a star of the same magnitude, probably θ Cancri.

As soon as totality was over, I recorded in my notebook the following:—"Saw two stars, about 3° S.W. of Sun, apparently of the 5th mag., some 12′ apart, pointing towards Sun ; both red." I immediately acquainted Prof. Hough, formerly director of the Dudley Observatory, and my two assistants of the discovery, and, as soon as possible on the same evening, Mr. Burnham, the celebrated double-star observer, and many others. None of them knew of any star in that position answering the description.

On my way home the thought occurred to me that the distance between them was about equal, perhaps a little greater than half that between Mizar and Alcor. On arriving at home, I found Webb gives their distance as 11¼′, which would make the distance between θ Cancri and the new object some 6′ or 7′ instead of 12′, as estimated (hastily and roughly, of course) at the time.

The next morning I learned by telegraph that Prof. Watson, at Separation, Wyoming Territory, saw a star 2½° S.W. of the Sun and of 4½ mag., not down in any chart.

The two observations are therefore confirmatory each of the other.

162   *Notes.*   [No. 17.

As totality commenced some four minutes earlier with him than with me, of course he antedates me by that amount.

Telescope 4½-in. aperture ; comet eyepiece ; power 25 ; field 1½° ; periscopic and very superior.   I am, Sir, yours truly,

Rochester, N. Y., Aug. 13, 1878.   LEWIS SWIFT.

———————————————————————

NOTES

Fig. 13. 'Letter from Lewis Swift, relating to the discovery of Intra-Mercurial planets,' *American Journal of Science,* s. 3, 16 (1878), pp. 313-315.[50]

Less than a month after Le Verrier's announcement, a body "of apparent size of Mercury [was] seen, Jan. 29, 1860, by F. A. R. Russell and four other observers, crossing the sun."[51] Then a sighting in March 1865 of a moving black sunspot was reported to Le Verrier by "another amateur astronomer, M. Coumbray [sic, Coumbary[52]], of Constantinople," but this one, says Fort, was "disregarded by Le Verrier, because his formula required about four times that velocity. The point here is that these other observations are as authentic as those that Le

———————————————————————

50   http://articles.adsabs.harvard.edu/full/1878Obs.....2..161S

51   Fort, *Damned,* p. 190, citing *Nature,* 14-505. "Mr. X" at www.resologist.net points out that Russell was with three other observers, not four. F.A.R. Russell, 'An Intra-Mercurial planet,' *Nature,* 14 (Oct. 5, 1876), p. 505.

52   Aristide Coumbary was a French engineer in Constantinople overseeing maintenance of telegraph wires, who reported astronomical and weather observation in European journals and in 1868 was appointed administrator of the new Imperial Meteorological Observatory (Mehmet Alper Yalcinkaya, *Their Science, Our Values: Science, State, and Society in the 19th Century Ottoman Empire,* Doctoral dissertation, 2010, U. of CA, San Diego; http://escholarship.org/uc/item/4vq4w5k6?query=Coumbary;hitNum=1#page-234).

Verrier included."[53] Fort lists similar transits in 1871, 1873 and 1876 respectively by W. F. Denning, J. R. Hind (see above), and M. Weber.[54] Hind had invited astronomers around the world to look for a transit of Vulcan on March 24 1873, but received no positive reports except one doubtful claim in a telegram from a Mr Cowie in Shanghai.[55]

Over the years Le Verrier continued tinkering with refined orbits based on the many old and new sightings in order to explain away one failed transit prediction after another. By 1877, the year of his death, he had reduced the list to six reliable observations defining the orbit of the planet. No conclusive sighting was ever made but he died still believing in Vulcan.

Vulcan did not die with him. One of Fort's favourite Vulcan stories occurred ten months after Le Verrier's death, during the total eclipse of July 29, 1878 – "reports by Prof. Watson, from Rawlins, Wyoming, and by Prof. [sic] Swift, from Denver, Colorado: that they had seen two shining objects at a considerable distance from the sun." Fort derided "text-book systematists" who objected to discrepancies between these sightings, pointing out that Swift described his report as "a close approximation to that given by Prof. Watson" [56] and said they were "confirmatory each of the other."[57] Fort doubts that "Watson and Swift mistook stars for other bodies" because "Prof. Watson says that he had previously committed to memory all stars near the sun, down to the seventh magnitude."[58] He is contemptuous of Lockyer for cautiously defusing the explosiveness of his own statement – "There is little doubt, I think, that an Intra-Mercurial planet has been found by Prof. Watson" – with the qualifier, "If it will fit one of Le Verrier's orbits."[59] Apparently it did not fit,[60] despite which Prof. Swift protested: "I have never made a more valid observation, nor one more free from doubt."[61] Fort wanted his readers to be impressed by "how carefully and minutely these two sets of observations were made" as detailed in published letters by Prof. Swift (Fig. 13) and Prof. Watson (Fig. 14)

Fort's account is not quite accurate. He says that Swift and Watson were "hundreds of miles apart," but Swift was at Denver, Colorado, and Watson was at Separation Point near

53 Fort, *Damned*, pp. 192-193, citing *L'Année Scientifique,*1865–1866 ('La planète intramercurielle,'*Année Scientifique et Industrielle*, 10, 1865, p.16).

54 Fort, *Damned*, p. 193, citing: *L'Année Scientifique,* 1876–1877 ('Les planètes entre le Soleil et Mercure...,' *Année Scientifique et Industrielle*, 20, 1876, pp. 6-11); London *Times*, Nov. 3, 1871, and March 26, 1873 (W. F. Denning, 'Total eclipse in December next'); London *Times*, Nov. 3, 1871, p. 8, referring to an observation in 1869; 'Intra-Mercurial planet,' London *Times*, March 26, 1873, p. 5, in which J. R. Hind notes a sighting by Cowie, at Shanghai, in March 1873.

55 *L'Année Scientifique,* 1876–1877 ('Les planètes entre le Soleil et Mercure...,' *Année Scientifique et Industrielle,* 20, 1876, pp. 6-11). See also *N Y Times* (reprinted: *Rockhampton (Qld) Bulletin*, Sept. 18, 1873, p. 3): "Mr Cowie is not known as an astronomer, and in the opinion of most of the scientific journals he has made the common mistake of confounding an ordinary sun spot with a planet's disc" (http://trove.nla.gov.au/ndp/del/article/51805338).

56 Fort, *Damned*, p. 196, citing *Nature,* Sept. 19, 1878 (Lewis Swift, 'Discovery of Vulcan,' *Nature,* 18, Sept. 19, 1878, p. 539).

57 *Ibid.*, citing *Observatory*, 2-161 (Swift, 'Supposed discovery of Vulcan,' *Observatory,* 2, 1878, pp. 161-162).

58 *Ibid.*, citing *Observatory,* 2-193 ('The discovery of Vulcan,' *Observatory,* 2, 1878, pp. 193-195).

59 *Ibid.*, citing *Nature,* Aug. 20, 1878 (J. Norman Lockyer, 'The eclipse,' *Nature,* 18, Aug. 29, 1878, pp. 457-462.)

60 *Ibid.*, citing 'Watson's suspected planet,' *Nature,* 18 (Aug. 22, 1878), p. 433.

61 Fort, *Damned*, p. 197, citing *Nature,* 21-301 (Lewis Swift, 'The Intra-Mercurial planet question,' *Nature,* Jan. 29, 1880, pp. 299-301).

Rawlins, Wyoming, which lies only 185 miles NW of Denver. He also says that both men saw "two shining objects" ("Mr. X" at www.resologist.net says Watson saw one and Swift two). Actually, Swift saw one and Watson two, and the positions measured by Swift and Watson did not agree, bewilderingly suggesting *three* "new stars." It was also noted that no observers elsewhere had seen the same object(s) during the eclipse, or a transit on any nearby date, so most astronomers were sceptical. Flammarion believed the objects were familiar stars misidentified. Watson, at least, had been actively looking for Vulcan during the eclipse, and perhaps had been predisposed to see it.

Vulcan or not, people continued to be puzzled by spots on the sun, as Fort demonstrates: "Extract from a letter by Hicks Pashaw: that, in Egypt, Sept. 24, 1883, he had seen on the sun, through glasses, 'an immense black spot on the lower part of the sun.'"[62] This story has confused many plunderers of Fort who have blindly recycled his account of a sighting by one "Mr. Hicks Pashaw," no doubt thinking it an odd name.

Supp. 1878.   *Prof. Watson, Letter to Mr. Hind.*   525

Letter from Professor Watson to Mr. Hind, Superintendent of the "Nautical Almanac."

I doubt not that you will be interested to receive more precise information about the observations which I made on July 29 than has yet been published.

Upon my return from the Eclipse Expedition, in order to be able to answer numerous inquiries which were addressed to me, I made an approximate reading of the circles upon which I had marked the positions observed, and the resulting places of two new stars which I observed were immediately communicated to several astronomers in this country and in Europe, and also to the *American Journal of Science.* As soon as I had the leisure, I made a more careful determination, and I noticed, upon revolving the alidade of the reading-circle, that the circle to be read had a very considerable excentricity, as it had been hurriedly mounted. Since there would, in any event, be an error of excentricity to be determined in changing the hour-circle from the instrument to the reading-circle, I did not remount it, but determined the necessary corrections by means of the four readings upon the Sun.

I have made ten readings upon each mark, backward and forward, so that each reading is an independent determination. The results derived from the mean of these readings are shown by the following :—

Chronometer Times.						Washington M.T.			Object observed.	Circle Reading.	
By Newcomb's.			By Watson's.								
h	m	s	h	m	s	h	m	s		° ′	
			4	39	50	5	7	31	Sun	165 31·6	± 0·7
10	29	15				5	16	37	(a)	161 1·6	± 0·4
10	30	24				5	17	46	(b)	156 7·5	± 0·5
			4	55	10	5	22	51	Sun	161 38·3	± 0·5
			5	4	50	5	32	31	Sun	159 7·0	± 0·3
			5	46	55	6	14	36	Sun	148 21·7	± 0·7

By comparing the mean of the second and third readings upon the Sun with the extreme readings, I have obtained the following expression for the correction for excentricity :—

$$R_a = R + 103'\!\cdot\!7 \sin (R + 63°\!\cdot\!2);$$

so that we have

Washington M.T.			Object observed.	Corrected Circle Reading.	
h	m	s		° ′	
5	7	31	Sun	164	13·7
5	16	37	(a)	159	49·3
5	17	46	(b)	155	1·8
5	22	51	Sun	160	25·2
5	32	31	Sun	157	57·2
6	14	36	Sun	147	27·4

526   *Mr. Proctor, Note on Brightness.*   XXXVIII. 9,

From these I derive the following differences of right ascension between (a) and (b) and the Sun :—

From	(a) − ⊙ Δα		(b) − ⊙ Δα	
	m	s	m	s
S_1 =	− 8	31·6	− 26	32·6
S_2 =	− 8	37·6	− 26	38·2
S_3 =	− 8	25·6	− 26	26·6
S_4 =	− 8	31·5	− 26	32·4

The differences of declination previously determined were respectively −0° 22′ and −0° 35′; and hence we have

Washington M.T.				Planet−⊙ Δα	Δδ	Apparent α	δ
	h	m	s	m s	° ′	h m s	° ′
1878 July 29	5	16	37 (a)	− 8 32	−0 22	8 27 24	+18 16
	29	5	17 46 (b)	−26 32	−0 35	8 9 24	+18 3

The magnitude of (a) was 4 to $4\frac{1}{2}$; that of (b) about $3\frac{1}{2}$. They were probably really brighter because the illumination of the sky was not considered in the estimates.

Before I came to reduce the observations I thought that the star (b) might possibly have been ζ *Cancri*, because I did not see the latter also. The sweep was not extended beyond (b), and just as I had recorded its place, the Sun came out. The time available for the observations was so short that it was not possible to get more data than I have given above. I did see θ *Cancri* as well as (a), and the place of the latter is sure. I consider that of (b) to be also sure, and hence that it is a new star.

Ann Arbor, 1878, Sept. 3.

Fig. 14. 'Letter from Professor Watson to Mr. Hind, Superintendent of the *Nautical Almanac*,' *Monthly Notices of the Royal Astronomical Society*, 38 (1878), pp. 525-526.[63]

---

62 Fort, *Damned*, p. 199, citing London *Times*, Dec. 17, 1883, with an insignificant misquote (see Fig. 15).
63 http://mnras.oxfordjournals.org/content/38/9/525.full.pdf+html

Pasha or Pascha was an Ottoman Turkish political rank analogous to a peerage sometimes granted as an honorary title,[64] and Hicks Pasha became the universal form of address of Col. William Hicks who in the autumn of 1883 was in Khartoum, whence he was preparing to lead the doomed Egyptian expeditionary army against Mahdist forces during the Sudan Campaign. Hicks Pasha was killed along with most of his army at the Battle of El Obeid at the start of November 1883.[65] Around the time of the article quoted by Fort (Fig. 15) Reuters reports concerning the fate of William Hicks were breaking news around the world.[66]

A BLUE SUN IN THE SOUDAN.

TO THE EDITOR OF THE TIMES.

Sir,—It may be of interest to some of your readers to learn that in a letter dated "Daem, Sept. 24, 1883," Hicks Pasha wrote :—"By the way, have you in England noticed a large black spot on the sun? To-day, when it rose, it was of a pale green colour, and we saw through our glasses an immense black spot on the lower half of it. What does this portend? I feel sure there must be some notice of it in the papers in England."

Very faithfully yours,
L. D.
December 12.

Fig. 15. London *Times,* December 17, 1883, p. 6 (credit: Kay Massingill) with Col William Hicks, *aka* Hicks Pasha, in Egypt in 1883 (right[67]).

American readers, especially, could have seen "pascha" sometimes anglicised as pashaw or bashaw,[68] perhaps explaining why Fort has corrupted his own source which in fact gives "Hicks Pasha." That source quotes a letter datelined September 24, 1883, from Daem, whence, as we discovered, news of the campaign had been telegraphed to London only the previous day,[69] leaving no reasonable doubt as to the letter's author.

The short extract gives few clues to determine what Col. Hicks saw, but one major clue is the coloured sun. It appeared "pale green" (misleadingly labelled "blue" in the *Times* headline). A green colouration might be caused by particles like fine ash suspended in the atmosphere, scattering the red wavelengths out of the light as it passes through. It was at dawn and the sun was on the horizon, so could the cause of that "immense black spot" on the lower part of the sun have been a dense smoke plume hanging over a distant fire? Perhaps, but the date coincides with similar sunrise and sunset effects reported around the tropics in

---

64 https://en.wikipedia.org/wiki/Pasha#Honorific
65 https://en.wikipedia.org/wiki/William_Hicks
66 http://paperspast.natlib.govt.nz/cgi-bin/paperspast?a=d&d=ST18831218.2.9.1
67 http://www.nam.ac.uk/online-collection/detail.php?acc=1968-07-521-1
68 See, e.g.: 'Waiting with Warriors. English Government Alarmed About the Fate of Her Egyptian Army,' *El Paso International Daily Times*, Friday, Sept. 2, 1898.
69 "Sudanese Campaign. The *Daily News* has received the following telegram, dated Daem (*via* Khartoum), September 23: — 'To-day an advanced force, consisting of three battalions and six guns, have seized the first water station fifteen miles ahead, so...'" *St James's Gazette,* London, Sept. 29, 1883.

September 1883 suggesting a global rather than a local cause – specifically, the eruption of Krakatoa. See Fig. 16.

Krakatoa does not explain the black spot seen by Col. Hicks. Nothing similar appears to have been noticed elsewhere. But the surprising colour and dimmed brightness of the rising sun would have attracted attention and perhaps caused a person to notice things he might ordinarily have ignored. Very large sunspots do occur, and a non-astronomer might easily be startled to see them, especially at dawn, when the eye is drawn to the sun and when it is dim enough to stare at (even without volcanic ash). Also, mirage refraction close to the tropical horizon might distort and stretch a spot group, making it appear even stranger.

September 22.—The sun rose as a yellow ball, and showed distinct greenish-yellow afterwards. From ten minutes before till sunset the sun was greenish-yellow, but the sun was much brighter than on the 10th and 11th.

September 23.—The sun rose very green. At 5.37 p.m. the sun appeared from under clouds, very green; strong absorption in the red end of the spectrum to C; low-sun-bands weak. 5.45.—Clouds greyish-purple. There was only one bank of clouds which was near the horizon; above this was a peculiar greyish haze. At 6 the clouds were of a marked purple colour; breaks near the horizon were reddish-brown. During the night there was a great deal of sheet-lightning in the south.

September 24.—The sun rose bright yellow. The spectrum showed complete absorption up to B; the rain-bands α and β were very thick, and the low-sun-bands less marked than usual. There was lightning all night, beginning in the south and working round to the south-east. It consisted chiefly of sheet-lightning, with occasional zig-zag flashes, but no thunder; the stars were fairly clear except near the horizon. Saturn and the moon, when near the horizon, were both very dim.

September 25.—Sunrise golden-green. In the afternoon the shadows cast on white paper were still quite pink, but the sunset was bright yellow.

September 26.—Much the same as yesterday.

September 27.—Before sunrise C, β, α, the rain-band and the dry-air-band were very strong, but the dry-air-band was less than half as dark as the rain-band. The sun rose golden-red. The spectrum showed signs of clearing up; glimpses of A could be obtained. After dark there was very bright lightning in the west.

September 28.—Spectrum still showed great absorption. Lightning at night.

Fig. 16. From a paper read before the Royal Society of Edinburgh, July 7th, 1884, by Prof. Michie Smith, describing green suns seen after Krakatoa, in Madras, September 1883.[70]

The date was very close to the peak of Solar Cycle 12 (September 1878 – June 1890) which occurred in December 1883. The mean sunspot number was modest, but there had been a remarkable outbreak of spots that summer. "Everybody who watched the sun with a telescope," wrote Garrett Serviss, "must have wondered at the great belt of spots lying across the southern part of the disk," some "of extraordinary size" including "a monstrous spot of grotesque form surrounded by a crowd of smaller spots " and "a huge group, visible even to the unassisted eye." Serviss adds, "In the latter part of August and early in September a row of spots, principally in the southern hemisphere, was again seen upon the sun, but it was

---

70   Douglas Archibald, 'The Blue, Green and Otherwise Coloured Appearances of the Sun and Moon in 1883-84,' *Report of the Krakatoa Committee of the Royal Society* (ed. G. J. Symons, FRS), London, 1888, p. 211; https://archive.org/stream/eruptionkrakato00whipgoog#page/n318/mode/2up

shorter, more crooked, and composed of fewer spots and groups, than the great belt of July."[71] But by late September we find no record of exceptional sunspots.

According to the Greenwich Photoheliographic Results (GPR) sunspot catalogue September 24, 1883 was, together with the 25th, one of the rare days with no sunspots observed at all.[72] The NOAA daily sunspot table says the count for September 24 was 14 but agrees that on the 25th it was zero. Howsoever, it was evidently not a dramatic period for spots. From about the 20th of the month the count falls well below half the average daily count for September 1883.[73] We find no other anecdotal accounts of remarkable spots on this date.

If the date is correctly reported – and it seems likely – we can explain the green colour of the sun, but not the black spot. Since the latter appears to have been noticed nowhere else there is no reason to believe it had anything to do with Vulcan, or even with the sun. We tend to think it was an effect relatively local to Daem where Hicks was situated, noticed by chance owing to the unusual appearance of the sun – perhaps a silhouetted small cloud. But beyond that we have no clues.

Fort was withering in his criticism of "the method of the systematists" which he described as "slightingly to give a few instances of the unholy, and dispose of the few. If it were desirable to them to deny that there are mountains upon this earth, they would record a few observations upon some slight eminences near Orange, N.J., but say that commuters, though estimable persons in several ways, are likely to have their observations mixed. The text-books," he complains, "casually mention a few of the 'supposed' observations upon 'Vulcan,' and then pass on."[74]

There was some truth in this criticism. Post-Vulcan, most astronomers' rejections of the data were as unreasonable as Le Verrier's selective acceptance of them had been. But Fort's own method was not dissimilar. Just as he favoured Houzeau's similarly cherry-picked evidence for the hypothetical planet Neith in 1886 (see Chapter 1), Fort deliberately selected the anomalous, the ill-fitting, the odd, grouped them according to superficial similarities and exploited them to hint at outlandish theories, whilst closing his mind against the vast bulk of well-assimilated data and theory from which they stood apart.

Fort's fringe agit-prop probably had very little, if any, effect on the legacy of the Vulcan affair during the first half of the 20th century. Even as he was assembling *The Book of the Damned*, Einstein was explaining Le Verrier's famous 43 seconds of arc as a prediction of the General Theory of Relativity. At this point the search for Vulcan was effectively dead history, and, as far as the astronomical community was concerned, Fort's effort to revive interest in it was stillborn. But when flying saucers captured the world's imagination after the war they breathed new life into Fort's books. A new generation rediscovered many half-forgotten mysteries and looked at them with fresh eyes. In this way, at least, Fort may have played a part in keeping visible some of those dozens of sightings of unexplained telescopic

---

71 Garrett P. Serviss, 'A Belt of Sun-Spots,' *Popular Science Monthly*, Vol. 24 (Dec. 1883); https://en.wikisource.org/wiki/Popular_Science_Monthly/Volume_24/December_1883/A_Belt_of_Sun-Spots
72 http://fenyi.solarobs.unideb.hu/GPR/index.html
73 ftp://ftp.ngdc.noaa.gov/STP/space-weather/solar-data/solar-indices/sunspot-numbers/international/tables/daily-sunspot-numbers/daily-sunspot-numbers_1883.txt
74 Fort, *Damned*, p. 188.

blobs, keeping Vulcan from sliding utterly into obscurity; and his books may have helped encourage some curious scientists to look again at those old journals.

By about 1970 there was a renewed interest in the possibility of unknown small planetoids orbiting inside the orbit of Mercury, and the old 18th- and 19th-century accounts were studied again. But telescopic searches for what became known as "vulcanoid" asteroids yielded nothing. NASA probes scanned space near the sun but drew a blank. There could be objects barely large enough to detect, a few kilometers across or less, or transitory visitors like long-period comets or asteroids on eccentric and/or high-inclination orbits, or rare interstellar visitors like 2017's Oumuamua. But of the planet Vulcan, or the "super-constructions" beloved of Charles Fort, there is today no sign.

Part 2

Stigmata on the Sun & Moon

CHAPTER 3 – A "super-Zeppelin" Eclipses the Sun
CHAPTER 4 – Followed by a Moonshadow
CHAPTER 5 – Crows on the Moon

CHAPTER 3 – A "Super-Zeppelin" Eclipses the Sun

An amazing object silhouetted against the sun in 1762 was described by Fort as follows:

> upon the 9th of August, 1762, M. de Rostan, of Basle, France, was taking altitudes of the sun, at Lausanne. He saw a vast, spindle-shaped body, about three of the sun's digits in breadth and nine in length, advancing slowly across the disk of the sun, or "with no more than half the velocity with which ordinary solar spots move." It did not disappear until the 7th of September, when it reached the sun's limb. Because of the spindle-like form, I incline to think of a super-Zeppelin, but another observation, which seems to indicate that it was a world, is that, though it was opaque, and "eclipsed the sun," it had around it a kind of nebulosity -- or atmosphere? A penumbra would ordinarily be a datum of a sun spot, but there are observations that indicate that this object was at a considerable distance from the sun:
>
> It is recorded that another observer, at Paris, watching the sun, at this time, had not seen this object;
>
> But that M. Croste, at Sole, about forty-five German leagues northward of Lausanne, had seen it, describing the same spindle-form, but disagreeing a little as to breadth. Then comes the important point: that he and M. de Rostan did not see it upon the same part of the sun. This, then, is parallax, and compounded with invisibility at Paris, is great parallax -- or that, in the course of a month, in the summer of 1762, a large, opaque, spindle-shaped body traversed the disk of the sun, but at a great distance from the sun. The writer in the *Register* says: "In a word, we know of nothing to have recourse to, in the heavens, by which to explain this phenomenon." I suppose he was not a hopeless addict to explaining. Extraordinary -- we fear he must have been a man of loose habits in some other respects.
>
> As to us -- Monstrator.[75]

We find a few problems with this piece. First, from Fort's source, the *Annual Register* of 1766 (Fig. 17), we learn that the name of the second witness is "Coste", not "Croste", also that Sole is "in the bishopric of Basle". Basle, or Basel, is of course in Switzerland, not in France as Fort writes, and Sole evidently refers to the town south of Basel today known in French as Soleure, or as Solothurn in German.[76] But Solothurn is not "five and forty German leagues northward" of Lausanne, rather it is about fourteen German leagues northeast (see Fig. 19). A distance of 45 leagues could be nowhere near Basel, so this must be a mistake. However, it is in this case due neither to Fort nor to the editor of the *Annual Register*, for when we located the *Register*'s source – the original article published by the French Royal Academy of Sciences (Fig. 18) – we found that it, too, says "quarante-cinq lieues

---

75 Fort, *Damned* p. 190, citing *Annual Register,* 9-120.
76 It is so identified in Vallée and Aubeck, *Wonders In the Sky* (2010), Case #348, p. 313. We find no direct evidence that Solothurn/Soleure was called "Sole" but there is no other placename in the region that is even similar. See: https://fr.wikipedia.org/wiki/Soleure

d'Allemagne au nord de Lausane". Evidently the text should have read "quatorze lieues" instead of "quarante-cinq lieues", but in the end we cannot definitely explain this error. [77]

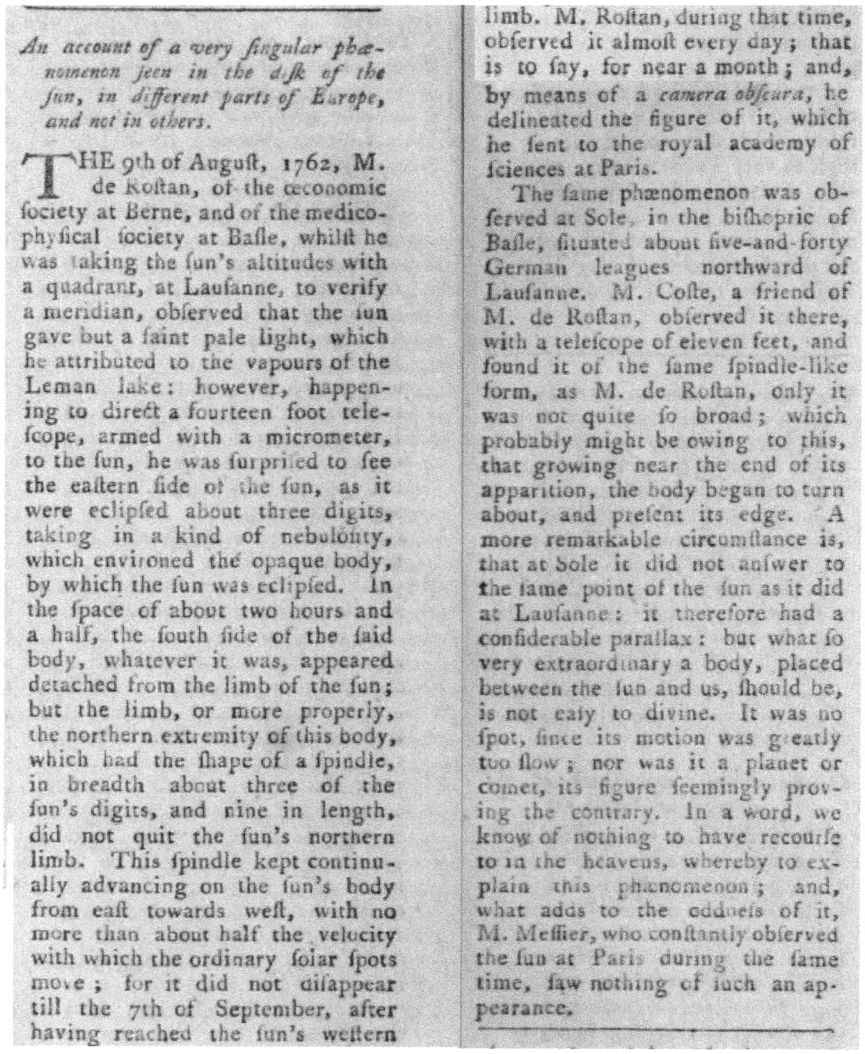

An account of a very singular phænomenon seen in the disk of the sun, in different parts of Europe, and not in others.

THE 9th of August, 1762, M. de Rostan, of the œconomic society at Berne, and of the medico-physical society at Basle, whilst he was taking the sun's altitudes with a quadrant, at Lausanne, to verify a meridian, observed that the sun gave but a faint pale light, which he attributed to the vapours of the Leman lake: however, happening to direct a fourteen foot telescope, armed with a micrometer, to the sun, he was surprised to see the eastern side of the sun, as it were eclipsed about three digits, taking in a kind of nebulosity, which environed the opaque body, by which the sun was eclipsed. In the space of about two hours and a half, the south side of the said body, whatever it was, appeared detached from the limb of the sun; but the limb, or more properly, the northern extremity of this body, which had the shape of a spindle, in breadth about three of the sun's digits, and nine in length, did not quit the sun's northern limb. This spindle kept continually advancing on the sun's body from east towards west, with no more than about half the velocity with which the ordinary solar spots move; for it did not disappear till the 7th of September, after having reached the sun's western limb. M. Rostan, during that time, observed it almost every day; that is to say, for near a month; and, by means of a camera obscura, he delineated the figure of it, which he sent to the royal academy of sciences at Paris.

The same phænomenon was observed at Sole, in the bishopric of Basle, situated about five-and-forty German leagues northward of Lausanne. M. Coste, a friend of M. de Rostan, observed it there, with a telescope of eleven feet, and found it of the same spindle-like form, as M. de Rostan, only it was not quite so broad; which probably might be owing to this, that growing near the end of its apparition, the body began to turn about, and present its edge. A more remarkable circumstance is, that at Sole it did not answer to the same point of the sun as it did at Lausanne: it therefore had a considerable parallax: but what so very extraordinary a body, placed between the sun and us, should be, is not easy to divine. It was no spot, since its motion was greatly too slow; nor was it a planet or comet, its figure seemingly proving the contrary. In a word, we know of nothing to have recourse to in the heavens, whereby to explain this phænomenon; and, what adds to the oddness of it, M. Messier, who constantly observed the sun at Paris during the same time, saw nothing of such an appearance.

Fig. 17. "An account of a very singular phænomenon seen in the disc of the sun, in different parts of Europe, and not in others." *Annual Register*, 1766, pt. 2, *Natural History*, pp. 120-121. [78]

---

77 One German league equalled approximately 4.6 English statute miles, therefore 45 German leagues = 207 miles, which, taken literally, would locate "Sole" somewhere near the French city of Metz in the Department of Moselle. Clearly this would not be "in the bishopric of Basle." Note that 1/45th of the true distance from Lausanne to Solothurn equals a little over 1.4 English statute miles; and it happens that this is approximately the length of the old Roman *leuga* or *leuca* that seeded the various "league" measures across Europe (see: *Webster's Revised Unabridged Dictionary*, 1828 & 1913 editions, p. 838). But this is presumably coincidence. One possible explanation is that de Rostan would have made his report in the form of a handwritten letter. We assume – but cannot prove – that de Rostan was a native French speaker, schooled in French orthography, although the dominant language of bilingual Basel and Berne in the late 18th century would have been German. We have found no evidence that a German language report exists (the German scientist Chladni in 1817 references only the French Academy report; see p. 44), suggesting that de Rostan reported only to the Royal Academy in Paris, presumably in French. Howsoever, it is common both in old German and in old French script for the numeral "1" to be written with an exaggerated diagonal ascending stroke, sometimes reaching the base of the numeral. If so, "15" might be mistaken for "45".

78 https://archive.org/stream/annualregisteror1766londuoft#page/120/mode/2up

OBSERVATION ASTRONOMIQUE.

LE 9 Août 1762, M. de Roftan, de la Société économique de Berne & de la Société Médico-Phyfique de Bâle, étant à Laufane, & prenant des hauteurs du Soleil avec un quart-de-cercle pour vérifier une méridienne, s'aperçut que cet Aftre ne donnoit qu'une lumière fort pâle ; il crut cet obfcurciffement caufé par les vapeurs du lac Léman : cependant ayant, à tout hafard, pointé au Soleil une lunette de 14

pieds, garnie d'un micromère, il aperçut avec furprife le côté oriental du Soleil comme éclipfé d'environ trois doigts, fi on y comprenoit une efpèce de nébulofité, dont le corps opaque qui éclipfoit le Soleil étoit environné : au bout de $2^h \frac{1}{2}$ le côté méridional de ce corps, quel qu'il fût, fe détacha du bord du Soleil, mais le bord, ou plutôt l'extrémité feptentrionale de ce corps, qui étoit fait comme un fufeau, ayant environ trois doigts du difque folaire de large, & neuf de longueur, ne quitta point le bord feptentrional du Soleil. Ce fufeau avança toujours fur le difque folaire d'orient en occident & avec environ moitié moins de vîteffe que les taches ordinaires, & il ne difparut que le 7 Septembre, après avoir atteint le bord occidental. M. de Roftan l'obferva pendant ce temps prefque tous les jours, c'eft-à-dire pendant près d'un mois, & il en tira à la chambre obfcure une figure exacte qu'il a envoyée à l'Académie.

Ce même phénomène fut obfervé à Sole, dans l'évêché de Bâle, fituée plus de quarante-cinq lieues d'Allemagne au nord de Laufane : M. Cofte, ami de M. de Roftan, l'y obferva avec une lunette de 11 pieds & lui trouva la même forme de fufeau qu'avoit remarquée M. de Roftan ; il étoit feulement un peu moins large, ce qui venoit probablement de ce qu'approchant de la fin de fon apparition, ce corps commençoit à tourner & à préfenter fon tranchant. Une circonftance plus remarquable, c'eft que ce corps ne paroiffoit pas à Sole répondre au même point du Soleil qu'à Laufane ; il avoit donc une parallaxe confidérable ; mais quel pouvoit être ce corps fingulier placé entre nous & le Soleil, c'eft ce qu'il n'eft pas aifé de deviner : ce n'étoit pas une tache, puifque fon mouvement étoit beaucoup plus lent : ce n'étoit ni une Planète ni une Comète, fa figure femble prouver le contraire, il étoit affez près de la Terre : en un mot, on ne connoît rien dans le Ciel à quoi on puiffe avoir recours pour expliquer ce phénomène ; & pour augmenter la fingularité de ce phénomène, M. Meffier, qui avoit obfervé conftamment le Soleil à Paris dans le même temps, n'y avoit aperçu rien de femblable.

O ij

Fig. 18. The original account, from *Histoire de l'Académie Royale de Sciences, Année M. DCCLXIII. – Avec les Mémoires de Mathématique & de Physique, pour la meme Année*, Paris, 1766, pp. 106-107.[79]

---

[79] https://gallica.bnf.fr/ark:/12148/bpt6k3561r/f114.item.r=108

Mr de Rostan, we are told, was a member both of the Medico-Philosophical Society at Basel and of the Berne Economic Society, the latter being one of a network of learned societies established to promote knowledge and expertise and to preserve records related to agriculture, mining, topography, meteorology, and the like. Mr Coste, observing from Sole, is described only as a "friend" of de Rostan. We were unable to develop any further information about either witness; however it is worth noting that the Berne Economic Society was the foremost such Society in Europe at this time with an international reputation.[80] Unfortunately, the *Mémoires* of the Society disclosed nothing of relevance to the observations.[81]

At the time of the first sighting de Rostan was "taking the sun's altitudes with a quadrant to verify a meridian." This means he was finding the compass direction of the sun when at its highest point, which defines true south or the longitude of the meridian (from Latin *meridies,* midday). Therefore, the time of the observation was around local noon. At noon on August 9, 1762 the altitude of the sun over the horizon from Lausanne[82] was 59° 19'. It was high in the sky, where the light path is much shorter through cleaner and less unstable air, and where image clarity is especially favourable for the eyepiece projection technique that de Rostan would have used to observe the sun. This matters because most things one can think of that might block or distort or degrade part of the image of the sun for a long period would intervene when it is near the horizon – a slow-moving distant cloud, seen side-on through its greatest optical thickness; a plume of smoke; a mirage; a tethered balloon, etc. The fact that the line of sight due south from Lausanne was across the lake, a body of water about 7 miles across, further limits various options of this sort. True, the first indication of anything unusual was that the light of the sun appeared dimmed, which de Rostan attributed to mist rising from the lake; but presumably this dimness was better explained when he used his telescope and found the object eclipsing part of the sun. It does not necessarily imply another atmospheric anomaly.

Any such local theory appears to be ruled out by the fact that, as day followed day, and as the sun moved across the sky, the blemish on its face shifted but didn't go away. And, of course, it could not have been something floating in the air near Lausanne if it was seen simultaneously at Solothurn. Crudely speaking, the baseline of 65 miles between Lausanne and Solothurn implies that the *minimum* distance d to the object is limited by parallax to approximately $d = 65/\mathrm{Tan}\ 0.5° = 65/0.00873 = 7445$ miles. This assumes that parallax displacement approached the full width of the sun's disc, which it probably did not – it "did not answer to the same point of the sun," but it was not said to be at the extreme opposite limb. Let's say it was displaced by half the disk, then the minimum distance would be about 15,000 miles. It would be conservative to infer a minimum distance in the order of 10,000 miles (16,000 km).

80 Emil Erne, 'Sociétés économiques', *Dictionnaire Historique de la Suisse*, 2017; https://hls-dhs-dss.ch/fr/articles/016420/2017-11-27/

81 *Mémoires et observations recueillies par la Société Oeconomique de Berne*, 1760–1773; https://www.e-periodica.ch/digbib/volumes?UID=soe-001

82 Note that de Rostan was not "in Basel" as stated in *Wonders In the Sky* (2010), Case #348, p. 313. Basel is about 85 miles (135 km) NE of Lausanne. De Rostan was a member of a learned society in Basel but was observing from Lausanne.

Spots on the sun famously occur, sometimes in large groups, especially near solar maxima,[83] and they drift as the sun rotates. De Rostan's object took more than 2 hours to detach perceptibly from the eastern limb, but its transit rate was less than half the rate at which fixed sunspots move with the synodic rotation of the sun.[84] A sunspot moves across the disc in about 13 days. The "spindle" took 29 days. It was not on the surface of the sun.

Neither was it even near the sun if, as reported in the original French source, it was not seen by Messier in Paris at any time even though he was observing the sun concurrently.[85] Paris is about 260 statute miles (419 km) away (Fig. 19), so the fact that it was not seen simultaneously against the 0.5° disc of the sun from both ends of this baseline allows us to say that the *maximum* distance d to the object is limited by parallax to approximately d = 260/Tan 0.5° = 29,782 statute miles. In other words, if it was a real object in the sky it was probably closer to the Earth than about 30,000 miles (48,280 km).

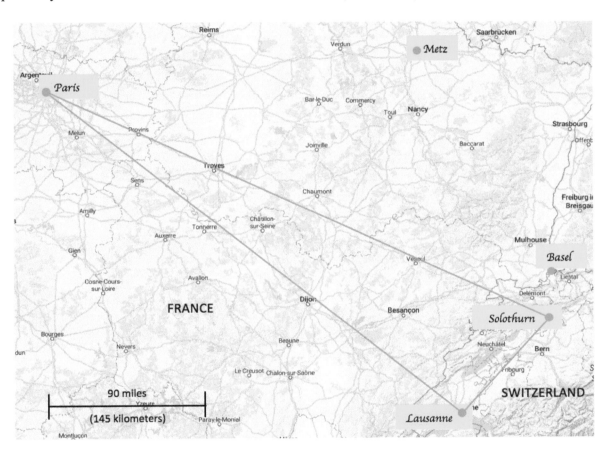

Fig. 19. Map showing sighting locations in relation to Messier's location at Paris
(adapted from: https://www.scribblemaps.com/).

---

83 The sunspot maximum of Solar Cycle 1 (August 1755 – March 1766) had occurred in June 1761.

84 The synodic rotation period of the sun, 26.24 days, is the time it takes for a sunspot to rotate all the way around the sun to the same *apparent* position as seen from Earth, which is not quite the same as the "true" or sidereal period because the Earth is moving around the sun at the same time.

85   De Rostan sent drawings the French Academy of Sciences in Paris, and these could have been received there during the month when the object continued to be visible; in which case it may be that Messier was alerted specifically to look for the object during the time de Rostan was observing it at Lausanne. However, this is not actually stated, and we note that although Messier was starting to become known as an observer and comet hunter, he was not elected a Fellow of the Academy until eight years later in 1770.

So, we can bracket the implied distance between about 10,000 and 30,000 miles (16,000-48,000 km), in space but quite near the Earth. As it happens, this range of altitudes is consistent with geosynchronous or geostationary orbit (as used for modern communications satellites). But this object clearly was not in such an orbit.[86] Rather, this object tracked the relative motion of the sun, remaining close to the Sun-Earth line. The object's apparent motion was in the same east-to-west direction as the sidereal motion of the sun and stars, but it had a small real velocity over and above the 0.25°/minute apparent motion of the sun. It was seen continually or intermittently from August 9 to September 7, taking 29 days to transit an angular distance equivalent, at d = 10,000 miles, to Tan 0.5°(10,000) = 87.3 miles (140 km). At the upper bracketed value of d (30,000 miles) this increases by a proportional factor, so assuming it was a real body in space at 10-30,000 miles distance its transverse real velocity relative to a point on Earth was between about 2600 and 7800 mph (4180 kph–12,550 kph), but its transverse real velocity relative to the Sun-Earth line was very small, almost zero in fact, in the order of 0.1 mph (in the range of about 0.07-0.2m/sec).

How big was this "spindle"? Its angular size was "in breadth about three of the sun's digits, and nine in length." A digit was an angular measure commonly used in eclipse observations, equal to 1/12 of the diameter of the sun,[87] therefore the spindle subtended 22.5 x 7.5 minutes of arc, which for the bracketed (inferred) distances corresponds to these physical dimensions: length 65-196 miles (105-315 km), width 22-65 miles (35-105 km). Of course, the true shape is unknown. We are told that it projected different silhouettes for observers at Lausanne and at Solothurn, showing a narrower aspect ratio than 3:1 at the latter place. No more detail is given, but it seems unlikely this could be explained completely by perspective foreshortening given that there has to be less than half a degree of parallax. The explanation offered – that "the body began to turn about and present its edge" – also seems unlikely if de Rostan and Coste were observing in the same time frame, because de Rostan, as far as one can tell from the report, saw no change in shape at all. So this is a puzzle.

It seems to have maintained the same orientation against the sun day by day, its long axis lying north-south, as it drifted very slowly to the west, while "its northern extremity . . . did not quit the sun's northern limb" (Fig. 20).

---

86   Obviously the sun would move behind a geostat at the sidereal rate, or 15°/hr, so the angular rate of drift against the sun would be the inverse of this and it would cross the sun from west to east in about 2 minutes, not from east to west in a month. In any case a geostat would orbit exactly above the equator (i.e., in the plane of the celestial equator) and could not have crossed the sun since the sun's path along the ecliptic was between 15° and 5° below this plane during the month of observation. It's true that in practice a "stationary" object in such an orbit actually describes a small closed curve called an analemma – an ellipse or figure-8, etc. – and this motion becomes quite large for 'geosynchronous' orbits that have a significant inclination relative to the equator, appearing larger still for observers at higher latitudes. An object in such an inclined orbit might wander across the sun but not in a fashion that would be relevant here.

87   See: Jacques Ozanam, *Recreations in Mathematics and Natural Philosophy*, recomposed by M. Montucla and trans. by C. Hutton (1803), revised edition Thomas Riddle, printed for Thomas Tegg, London, 1840, p. 434; tinyurl.com/45hqolad

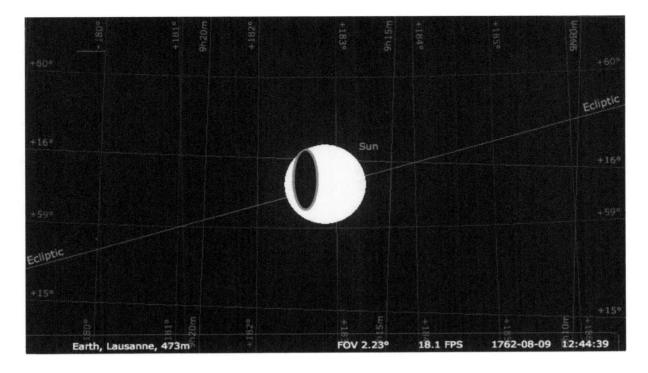

Fig. 20. Impression showing relative scale and proportions of the "spindle" limned by "a kind of nebulosity" against the disc of the sun (adapted from Stellarium image).

What could explain all this? Could it have been a near-Earth asteroid? And what would account for the fact that it was aligned with the Sun for so long?[88]

Clearly it was not an object in a near-circular orbit around the sun similar to that of the Earth, or it would have been detected often. An unknown Earth-crossing asteroid on an eccentric orbit could come in from the outer solar system on the far side of the sun, approaching perigee inside our own orbit and overtaking the Earth in the process. This is possible in principle and might explain why it appeared only temporarily without being seen by many observers, then and at other times. But staying within 0.5° of the Sun-Earth line for a month still requires an orbit closely matching Earth's along a path of at least 48 million miles (78 million km), not only in speed (real speed, not merely angular or apparent speed, because this object has to remain physically close to the Earth) but also in orbital inclination.

This is extremely unlikely for a transient approach by a body in an eccentric Earth-crossing orbit. A NASA list of hundreds of near-Earth asteroids shows relative velocities typically in the order of 10 km/sec (ranging from about 1.2 to over 30 km/sec).[89] Even at the rate of the slowest, de Rostan's object would have approached or receded from Earth by ten times its probable distance on the first day, either completely eclipsing the sun or dwindling to a speck. The same argument applies even more strongly to a visiting interstellar asteroid like Oumuamua, which crossed the ecliptic in October 2017 at 88 km/sec (Fig. 21). Yet the

---

88   One might think of a body in the L1 Lagrangian point. The Lagrangian points are islands of gravitational stability in free space which tend to "attract" objects (see also Chapter 1). L1 is a stable Lagrangian point on the Sun-Earth line. But if a large planetoid was at equilibrium with the L1 attractor, i.e. captured by it, why would it leave again? So this is not really helpful. Anyway, L1 is 1.5 million km from Earth, some 40 or 50 times too far away for our purposes – that is, it would have been seen against the sun by Messier from Paris at the same time.
89   http://neo.jpl.nasa.gov/risk/#legend; http://neo.jpl.nasa.gov/ca/

object seen by de Rostan and Coste was not substantially changed in appearance or position after 30 days, implying an object on an orbit which, if not precisely co-orbital with Earth, ought to have been regularly observed, if not before then certainly since.

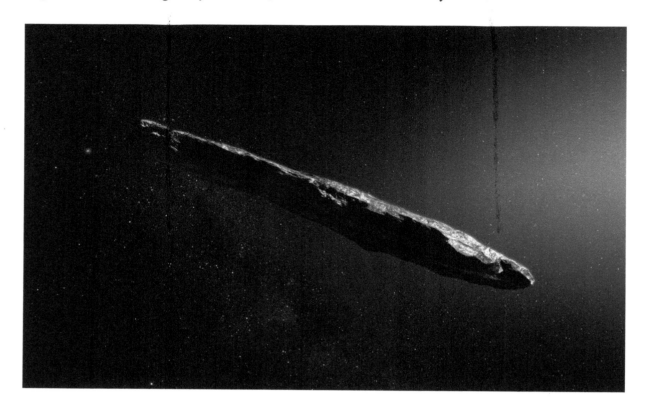

Fig. 21. Artist's impression of interstellar asteroid Oumuamua (ESO/M. Kommesser)

Secondly, we note the absence of rotation. If the object maintained essentially the same orientation with respect to celestial north for a month, then it was spinning exceedingly slowly, if at all. Asteroids over about a kilometer in size start to have a spin rate somewhat independent of size, and the larger they get the narrower the spread of rates becomes; until with asteroids a few tens of km in diameter or larger there is a fairly constant mean rotation period of about 10 hours with only "some minor variation."[90] A typical asteroid of the size indicated would have had the opportunity for about 70 rotations during the sighting period.

De Rostan's spindle might have rotated preferentially around its long axis, so that its spin would not have been seen; but there is no reason to expect this of an asteroid. The direction of spin of large asteroids is random with respect to axial orientation.[91] Highly asymmetrical asteroids tend to tumble (2017's Oumuamua being a good example of this, having an aspect ratio >5:1 and rotation period varying between about 7 and 8 hours), so it is hardly likely – to cover all possibilities – that its spin happened to coincide exactly with de Rostan's schedule of observing so that it was the same way up every time he looked; and one would expect that de Rostan (never mind Coste) might typically have observed about 30° of spin during any

90   A. W. Harris & P. Pravec, 'Rotational properties of asteroids, comets and TNOs,' in D. Lazzaro, S. Ferraz-Mello & J.A. Fernandez (eds.), *Asteroids, Comets, Meteors, Proceedings IAU Symposium*, No. 229 (2005), p. 439; tinyurl.com/v35x7hvx
91   *Ibid.*

given hour of observation. Yet for a month "its northern extremity . . . did not quit the sun's northern limb."

Thirdly, why would a passing asteroid be visible only from this small area of Switzerland for a whole month? It might potentially have been visible against the sun, at least in part, for other observers in a radius of (say) 100 miles (160 km). Granted, there were not that many solar observers in 1762; but if we assume a fairly constant rate of angular drift and extrapolate the E-W apparent motion back and forward in time at the same rate, the object's moving "shadow" should paint a band of potential visibility hundreds or thousands of miles long across central Europe during the course of months, so it is more than somewhat surprising that no other sighting reports exist, even given that communication and publication were slow and unreliable.

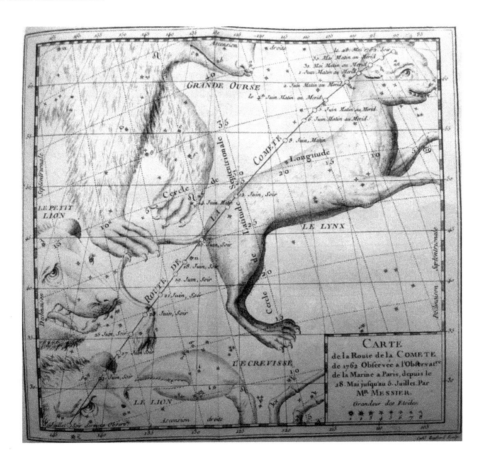

Fig. 22. Charles Messier's map of the path of Comet 1762 Klinkenberg, from
Savans étrangers, Vol. 5, 1768, p. 104.[92]

There is one more clue: de Rostan describes a "a kind of nebulosity which environed the opaque body." Could this have been simply blurring due to poor focus? Not if the object was beyond the minimum distance indicated by the <0.5° parallax between Lausanne and Solothurn. In de Rostan's telescope any object beyond about 100 miles or so (160 km) should

_____

92 Felice Stoppa: http://www.atlascoelestis.com/messier%201762%20pagina.htm

have been in the same focus as the sun for all practical purposes.[93] If the nebulosity was a real property of the object it suggests a halo of gas, dust or ice particles. It could not have been a permanent planetary atmosphere because no asteroid of the implied size has sufficient mass to retain one. The same applies to any kind of gaseous or particulate halo unless it was somehow recently acquired, or was constantly renewed by outgassing.

This happens to a frozen comet nucleus as it approaches the sun, producing a halo called the coma, and some of the coma material is driven out into a tail by the radiation pressure and particle wind from the sun. If the elongated core and nebulosity was a foreshortened view of a small cometary coma, with an incipient tail streaming away from the sun, this could go some way to explaining the fixed orientation of its long axis. And in the hypothetical situation where a comet nucleus is in line with the sun it is obviously not directly visible at night. The bulk of any tail would be pointing roughly towards the Earth at this time, so there would not be the unmistakable classic sight of a narrow, bright tail stretched across the sky. In fact, the Earth might be *inside* any tail (they can reach millions of miles in length), in which case it might have caused unusual effects in the night sky on the opposite side of the globe, or near dusk and dawn. We have not so far found any stories likely to be related to such effects in the same period.

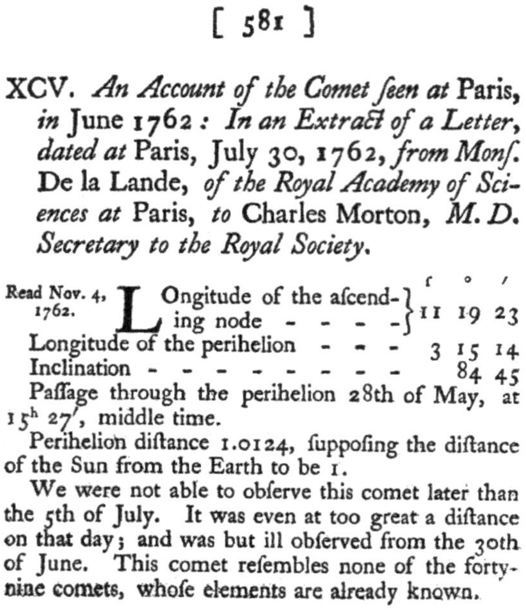

[581]

XCV. *An Account of the Comet seen at* Paris, *in* June 1762 : *In an Extract of a Letter, dated at* Paris, July 30, 1762, *from Monf.* De la Lande, *of the Royal Academy of Sciences at* Paris, *to* Charles Morton, M. D. *Secretary to the Royal Society.*

Read Nov. 4, 1762.

Ongitude of the ascending node - - - - 11 19 23
Longitude of the perihelion - - - 3 15 14
Inclination - - - - - - - - 84 45
Paſſage through the perihelion 28th of May, at 15ʰ 27′, middle time.
Perihelion diſtance 1.0124, ſuppoſing the diſtance of the Sun from the Earth to be 1.
We were not able to obſerve this comet later than the 5th of July. It was even at too great a diſtance on that day; and was but ill obſerved from the 30th of June. This comet reſembles none of the forty-nine comets, whoſe elements are already known.

Fig. 23. 'An Account of the Comet Seen at Paris, in June 1762' *Philosophical Transactions of the Royal Society*, 1761–1762, 52, p. 581.[94]

Interestingly, a new comet *was* discovered that summer. It is listed as #5 in Messier's catalogue of 44 comets[95] and known also as 1762 Klinkenberg (or C/1762 K1) after its

─────────────

93 With a focal length of 19 ft (5.8 m) light rays from beyond 130 miles (208 km) will be brought to a prime focus within a focal plane narrower than the wavelength of visible light (about 0.0005 mm) and thus are indistinguishable from parallel collimated rays from infinity. So all objects beyond this distance are "at infinity" for purposes of calculation. In practical observation the distance would be closer.
94 http://rstl.royalsocietypublishing.org/content/52/581.full.pdf+html
95 Messier's 'Notes on my comets,' handwritten original MS held by Paris Observatory; http://www.astrobril.nl/1762K1.html; http://messier.seds.org/xtra/history/44comets.html#1762

discoverer, who found it on May 17. It was first seen by Messier at Paris eleven days later on May 28, "surrounded by a nebulosity visible in the telescope," moving at an angle to the ecliptic from the constellation Lynx down through Leo (Fig. 22) at a mean angular rate equal to more than 3 sun diameters (~1.7°) every day until about July 5, by which time it was already faint in the telescope (Fig. 23). We are not able to reconstruct its path after passing through Leo. But the sun was travelling along the ecliptic through Leo towards Virgo during August-September when de Rostan's object was observed, so there is a chance that the apparent paths of the sun and of C/1762K1 converged to intersect at some point. When seen by Messier, C/1762K1 was very much smaller than de Rostan's object (Fig. 24);[96] but could it have been seen in front of the sun by de Rostan at Lausanne after Messier at Paris had lost it? Even if only briefly? No. According to the calculated orbit, as reported from Paris to the Royal Academy (Fig. 23), the comet's perihelion was outside the orbit of Earth, so it was never between the Earth and the sun; and it could not have approached closer than about 1.15 million miles, which is about 100 times too far away to explain the parallax.

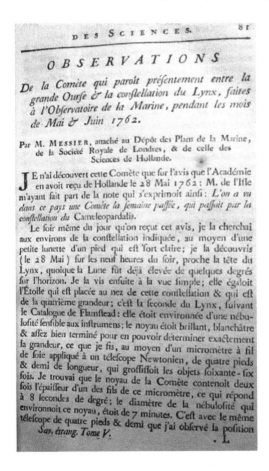

Fig. 24. Messier's description of the motion, appearance and angular size of the 1762 comet. *Histoire de l'Académie Royale des Sciences*, Année M.DCCLXII Mémoires de Mathématique et de Physique, Paris, 1762, p. 81[97]

---

96   "... the nucleus shone like a star, white and quite well-defined, enabling me to determine the exact size, which I did using a micrometer ... I found that the nucleus of the comet...[measured] 8 seconds of arc; the diameter of the nebulosity was 7 minutes."

97   http://www.atlascoelestis.com/messier%201762%20pagina.htm

It's probably worth emphasising that no sunward comet is likely to have remained within less than half a degree of the Earth-Sun line for even a day, never mind an entire month. Comets seen near perihelion sunward of the Earth are generally fast-moving and go from a faint telescopic spot at immense distance through maximum brightness and back in a few weeks. As already pointed out, the de Rostan/Coste object would have to be almost paralleling Earth's motion, pacing it on the sunward side at very similar speed, and very near Earth, for a month. This is even more unlikely for a comet than for an Earth-crossing asteroid because of the extreme eccentricity (elongation) of cometary orbits, which means their speeds at perihelion usually exceed Earth's by between about 10 and 70 km/sec (20,000-150,000 mph). A comet matching orbits with Earth is not just unlikely, it is physically impossible in terms of orbital mechanics.[98]

In summary, this is without doubt an intriguing observation; however, we find ourselves in agreement with the Editors of the London *Monthly Review*, who reflected thus five years after the event in 1767:

> [We] cannot help wishing that, for the conviction of the more incredulous, and the information of others, [the French Academy] had favoured the public with a more fully authenticated and circumstantial account of this very singular and stupendous phenomenon.[99]

The pioneer German meteoriticist Ernst Chladni discussed the event in 1817, predictably speculating that it could be meteoric in origin, specifically a persistent remnant of a meteor entering the upper atmosphere and leaving behind an "elongated mass, consisting mainly of dust or nebulous parts". He likens it to other accounts of meteors which "initially appeared as one or more streaks glowing at night, from which a fiery orb continued to build up afterwards". [100]

However, there is no way of explaining how a cloud of particles drifting in the upper atmosphere could track the Sun-Earth line across the sky for even a single day, never mind do this for nearly a month. And as shown above, the parallax implied by the baseline between

---

98   Because it implies a body with the same or very nearly the same "specific orbital energy" as the Earth. This is the energy per unit mass. For a given orbit this is a constant, related to velocity by Kepler's "equal areas" rule which means that the area swept out by the Sun-Earth line is always the same per unit time. Thus, if Earth and a comet sweep out the same orbital area in any given period then their orbits automatically have the same constant specific orbital energy. And as this value is totally determined by the period and the semimajor axis of the orbit, it specifies a cometary orbit with a semimajor axis of one Astronomical Unit (the same as the radius of Earth's orbit) and with a period of one Earth year. There are no comets like this in the solar system. See: https://en.wikipedia.org/wiki/Vis-viva_equation; http://astronomy.stackexchange.com/questions/6384/how-fast-is-a-comet-moving-when-it-crosses-earths-orbit

99   *The Monthly Review Or Literary Journal Enlarged*, Vol. XXXVII, R. Griffiths, London, 1767, pp. 172-174; https://books.google.co.uk/books?id=0_JdAAAAcAAJ&pg=PA172&lpg=PA172&dq=de+Rostan+Berne&source=bl&ots=3zM960IWqQ&sig=ACfU3U1vjBQCaCkSrPBIGcNmqHsbM7B_3g&hl=en&sa=X&ved=2ahUKEwiEp-a9j6bnAhU0SxUIHf3ICG4Q6AEwAHoECAYQAQ#v=onepage&q&f=false

100   E. F. F. Chladni, 'Ueber Dinge, die sich im Weltraume befinden, und von den bekannten Weltkörpern verschieden sind, und über noch einige kosmologische Merkwürdigkeiten', *Zeitschrift für Astronomie und verwandte Wissenschaften*, Vol. 4 (1817), pp. 304-306; https://books.google.be/books?id=K28wAAAAYAAJ&printsec=frontcover&source=gbs_book_other_versions_r&redir_esc=y#v=onepage&q&f=false

Lausanne and Solothurn would require a minimum slant range of well over 7000 miles, placing the object far beyond the atmosphere. It could not be meteoric.

It could still have been a cloud of particles. The object is described as an "opaque body", "environed" with a "nebulosity". How opaque or how well-defined this "body" may have been we do not know, but it appears very likely that it was not widely observable with the naked eye. Nothing in the account suggests that de Rostan saw it directly, at sunset or sunrise, for example, when large sunspots are often visible to the eye against the dull red solar disc; rather, he saw it in projected images *via* his telescope and a camera obscura. Before turning his telescope on it he noticed only that the ambient sunlight was dimmed, an effect which he put down initially to an unusual effect of mist from the lake. Is it possible that a nebulous obstruction could be imperceptible to the naked eye owing to low contrast and glare, even with the sun low in the sky, and yet have a dramatically greater apparent contrast suggesting an "opaque body" when seen by eyepiece projection?

Perhaps. Nevertheless, whether it was a cloud of particles, or a solid object with an aura of particles/gases around it, it was presumably in space, and behaving in a fashion which is hard to understand.

It's very unfortunate that so little information survives – or at least, little has emerged. At present we only have a second-hand account of de Rostan's sightings and what is probably a third-hand outline of Mr Coste's. But we know that contemporaneous evidence was sent to the French Royal Academy of Sciences – specifically, drawings made by de Rostan at the camera obscura – and records may exist somewhere. It's to be hoped that more will be found.

CHAPTER 4 – **Followed by a Moonshadow**

"One of the wickedest, or most preposterous, stories that we have so far exhumed," declared Charles Fort with relish, introducing the story of a "dark shade" seen on the moon by two Australian astronomers in 1878.[101]

The men, H. C. Russell of Sydney Observatory and experienced amateur G. D. Hirst, were testing observing conditions at altitude in the Blue Mountains of New South Wales west of Sydney. They set up instruments at their camp and made measurements over several days, testing the clarity and stability of the air by observing stars at high magnification and detecting the fine lines in the spectrum of the sun. It was on the morning of October 21 when, at about 9:00 am, Hirst noticed what Russell later called "one of those remarkable facts, which being seen should be recorded, although no explanation can at present be offered."

Russell's notes (Fig. 25) describe how Hirst happened to look at the moon and "found that a large part of it was covered with a dark shade quite as dark as the shadow of the earth during an eclipse of the moon; its outline was generally circular and it appeared to be fainter near the edges." They inferred rather than saw the outline of this circle, since only a part of the apparent shadow was visible where it crossed the terminator between bright and dark segments of the moon, the rest assumed to be falling in the dark part. It was huge. Russell estimated the diameter of that circle to be about ¾ of the diameter of the moon itself. "Conspicuous bright spots of the moon's surface could be seen through it," whilst it "quite obliterated the view of about half of the moon's terminator." Most significantly, it did not change its position on the surface of the moon during three hours of watching.

"One could hardly resist the conviction that it was a shadow," said Russell – tantalising Fort with the hope of "a beautiful positivism" – "yet it could not be the shadow of any known body," he finished, leaving Fort to lament the astronomer's "intermediateness." Fort's own interpretation: the shadow cast on the moon by "a vast dark body."

Fort seems not to have known who Russell was – "Mr. H. C. Russell . . . was as orthodox as anybody I suppose – at least he wrote 'F.R.A.S.' after his name." In fact, Henry Chamberlain Russell CMG FRAS FMS FRS (1836–1907) was Director of Sydney Observatory and Government Astronomer from 1870 for over 35 years. He organised notable expeditions to observe eclipses and transits, pioneered astrophotography in Australia and is credited with discovering 500 double stars, his special interest. He was also a pioneer in Australian meteorology, for which he invented a number of auto-recording instruments, built the first statewide network of weather stations linked by telegraph, and played a big part in the development of accurate forecasting in the Southern hemisphere. He is reckoned one of the most eminent scientists in 19th-century Australia.[102]

---

101 Fort, *Damned*, pp. 216-217, citing *Observatory, 2-374.*
102 He was the first graduate of the University of Sydney to be elected a Fellow of the Royal Society of London. He became President of the Australasian Association for the Advancement of Science in 1888 and Vice Chancellor of the University of Sydney in 1891. See: G. P. Walsh, 'Russell, Henry Chamberlain (1836–1907),' *Australian Dictionary of Biography*, National Centre of Biography, Australian National University, http://adb.anu.edu.au/biography/russell-henry-chamberlain-4525/text7409 ; University of Sydney Archives, http://sydney.edu.au/arms/archives/history/FUO/VC_Russell.shtml

Russell's companion and assistant, George Denton Hirst, of Sydney, was a member of the observing sections of Jupiter and Mars of the British Astronomical Association, and several of his drawings appeared in the Memoirs of the BAA. At the time of the sighting he was 32 years old and an eminent amateur, a member of the Royal Society of New South Wales, "noted for his remarkable skill in astronomical drawings." He was commended by the illustrious Mars observer Antoniadi for exceptionally faithful work.[103] Over a period of 40 years Hirst observed planets, comets and double stars and published numerous studies in various journals. He was elected a Fellow of the Royal Astronomical Society in 1895, and when he died in May 1915, at the age of 69 years, his *MNRAS* obituary stated that he had "no equal in Australia as an astronomical draughtsman." [104, 105]

> On the afternoon of Oct. 20 the third satellite of Jupiter was seen in transit as a black body, small and well defined ; as it neared Jupiter's limb the blackness seemed to get hazy as if it were seen through a mist ; and at $7^h 27^m$ P.M., Sydney mean time, I lost sight of it. Four minutes later it was detected as a small bright bulge on the limb of Jupiter, which looked brighter than the surface of the planet. At $7^h 36^m 40^s$ egress was complete, and there was nothing about the appearance of the satellite then that would have given rise to the suspicion that it was black a few minutes before.
>
> During the daylight hours Mr. Hirst employed a part of his time looking up Venus near the Sun, the Sun itself, and many other objects, of which very fine views were obtained ; but the only observation that I would here place on record was made on the morning of the 21st October at 9 A.M., when, on looking at the Moon, he found that a large part of it was covered with a dark shade quite as dark as the shadow of the earth during an eclipse of the Moon ; its outline was generally circular and it seemed to be fainter near its edges ; conspicuous bright spots on the Moon could be seen through it, but it quite obliterated the view of about half of the Moon's terminator (or that part where the sunlight ends), while those parts of the terminator not in the shadow could be very distinctly seen. I should estimate the diameter of the shadow from the part we could see on the Moon as about $\frac{3}{4}$ that of the Moon.
>
> This is one of those remarkable facts which being seen should be recorded, although no explanation can at present be offered. One could hardly resist the conviction that it was a shadow ; yet it could not be the shadow of any known body, and if produced by a comet it must be one of more than ordinary density, although dark bodies have been seen crossing the Sun which were doubtless comets. No change in the position of the shade could be detected after three hours watching.
>
> 1878, Nov. 26. H. C. RUSSELL.

Fig. 25. Extract from Russell's 'Notes of an Astronomical Experiment made on the Blue Mountains, near Sydney, N.S.W.,' *The Observatory*, No. 23 (1879), p. 375.[106]

The witnesses appear to have been more than averagely sophisticated observers of the sky. But not everyone was impressed. Readers of an article[107] in a London newspaper by the well-

---

103 *Memoirs* B.A.A., Vol. XVII (1905), Part II.
104 Pietro Baracchi, F.R.A.S., *Astronomy & Geodesy in Australia : Part 4. Ch. VIII(c) Amateur Astronomy*. Commonwealth of Australia Federal Handbook, prepared in connection with the 84th meeting of the British Association for the Advancement of Science, Australia, Ed. George Handley Knibbs, Commonwealth Bureau of Census and Statistics, Aug. 1914, pp. 326-390; http://www.southastrodel.com/Page032003.htm
105 Virginia Trimble, et al., *Biographical Encyclopedia of Astronomers*, Springer Science & Business Media, 2007, p. 515.
106 http://adsabs.harvard.edu/full/1879Obs.....2..370R
107 Richard A. Proctor, 'A startling astronomical discovery,' *London Echo*, March 14, 1879, p. 1.

known science writer Richard A. Proctor could have been forgiven for thinking Russell and Hirst were a couple of wide-eyed innocents. Proctor's flippant tone verged on the derisory, claiming that the observers had been fooled by mistaking the ordinary lunar mare Oceanus Procellarum (Ocean of Storms; see Fig. 28) for the shadow of an impossible space object, which could scarcely have cast a fixed shadow on the moving moon for three hours.

Fig. 26. Henry Chamberlain Russell, from the *Sydney Mail,* Saturday, 12 January 1895.

Proctor (1837–1888) trained as a lawyer but instead of the bar chose writing and science. He was not a practical observer of any note, but wrote books and magazine articles on a huge range of topics, becoming one of the most famous and prolific popularisers of his generation, second only to the French astronomer Camille Flammarion in his output.[108] He was not an unopinionated man. His obituary in *The Observatory* noted his reputation for being "quarrelsome" but said that in his private life he had been "feminine in his abhorrence of inflicting pain," even though to "the imposter or self-advertising quack" he showed "no mercy; and there were few more scathing writers than he when he had to lay on the lash."[109]

On this occasion the recipient of the lash did not much appreciate it. Russell reacted through the pages of *The Observatory* (Fig. 27), complaining, "one would have expected a writer who has had so much to do with the observations of other people" – a subtle thrust – "and who knows the danger of twisting them to suit a theory, to hesitate before doing so in this instance." He was "at a loss to conceive" how Proctor could "charge me with ignorance of the commonplace fact he offers as the explanation of the dark shade," unless it was done merely to be sensational and in the expectation that Russell, in Australia, would never see it.[110] He wished to be clear that he had *not* proposed the "shade" *was* a shadow cast on the

---

108 He has been called "an armchair astronomer," a little unfairly. He was elected FRAS, for a while becoming Honorary Secretary and editing the *Monthly Notices*. He had a special interest in charting, compiling star charts and making one of the earliest maps of Mars, from others' drawings, which allowed him to make one of the first accurate determinations of the length of the Martian day. In later life he moved to America where he continued his writing career and gave public lectures. See: https://en.wikipedia.org/wiki/Richard_A._Proctor; John Fraser, 'Richard Anthony Proctor,' *Scribners Monthly, an Illustrated Magazine for the People*, Vol. 7, Issue 2 (Dec. 1873), pp. 172-175; http://todayinsci.com/P/Proctor_RichardA/ProctorRichardA-BioScribners.htm
109 http://adsabs.harvard.edu/full/1888Obs....11..366N
110 Yet see it he did. The story spread and appeared in American papers too - for example, a faux-scandalised and inaccurate piece in the *Cincinatti Enquirer* based on a tip-off by an anonymous "Fellow of the Royal Astronomical Society" by whom the names of the culprits had been "in charity suppressed." The author relishes the "gross ignorance of the bare rudiments of selenography" demonstrated by these "English astronomers,"

moon, only that it resembled one, and that he was perfectly aware of the location and ordinary appearance of the relatively dark Mare Procellarum.

"A startling Astronomical Discovery."

Sir,—

In the 'Echo' of March 14, 1879, there appeared an article by Mr. R. A. Proctor under the above heading, and in it my name was freely used. I ask space for a few words in reply to the groundless charges made against me in that article; at the same time I feel that I do so at a disadvantage, because what I have to say cannot be published probably for five or six months after the charges were made.

With the tone of Mr. Proctor's article I have nothing to do; he no doubt has a good reason for writing thus about astronomical matters; but when he deliberately puts a construction upon what I have written, which the words were not intended to convey, it is perhaps worth while to say a few words in reply.

The words in question are:—"One could hardly resist the conviction that it was a shadow: yet it could not be the shadow of any known body; and if produced by a comet, it must be one of more than ordinary density, although dark bodies have been seen crossing the Sun which were doubtless comets. No change in the position of the shade could be detected after three hours' watching"*.

These words, I think, clearly express, and they certainly were intended to convey the idea, that I had effectually resisted the conviction that what I saw was a shadow, and that I knew it could not be the shadow of any known body; and to place this beyond doubt I added the words, "No change in the position of the shade could be detected after three hours' watching." Yet Mr. Proctor, in an absurd argument, endeavours to prove that I thought this dark shade on the Moon was the shadow of some body nearly as large as the Moon; and, in the effort to make the facts suit his shallow explanation, he even goes so far as to tell me that I exaggerated what I did see, although he had no means, except from my description, of knowing what I saw, and was for that reason incompetent to correct me. One would have expected a writer who has had so much to do with the observations of other people, and who knows the danger of twisting them to suit a theory, to hesitate before doing so in this instance.

* 'Observatory,' No. 23, p. 375. "Notes of an Astronomical Experiment made on the Blue Mountains, near Sydney, N.S.W."

How Mr. Proctor could venture to charge me with ignorance of the commonplace fact he offers as the explanation of the dark shade, I am at a loss to conceive, unless it was because the article had to be written in keeping with its heading, and the probability amounted almost to a certainty that any such statement published in an evening paper in London would never be seen by me in this out-of-the-way place, and therefore would not be contradicted.

In order to clear the way for any future attempt of his to explain the dark shade, I may here say that for nearly twenty years I have been familiar with the fact that there was an apparent shade over part of the old Moon, and with its appearance as seen through a telescope; and since 1864 I have known its effect upon the photographic plate, which is so well marked in every good set of lunar photographs.

Further, what I saw when on the mountains was darker and remarkably different from any thing of the sort I had seen before; and when I mentioned the fact as one of those observed at Woodford, I carefully avoided any attempt to explain the cause of what I saw, and I did not think it necessary to tell the readers of an astronomical paper that I knew there was a slight shade over part of the old Moon. It did, however, occur to me that the shade in question might vary in intensity, and that therefore what I saw should be recorded.

Mr. Proctor says "the phenomenon is one in which we terrestrials are very considerably interested, for what happens on the Moon in this way may at any time happen to the Earth."

Precisely so; and I am sure he does not need to be reminded that such phenomena have happened on the Earth—witness the dry fogs of 1783, 1831, and others which might be mentioned, quite thick enough to hide all terrestrial features under them from an observer outside the Earth, and these remained stationary not for hours only but for weeks in spite of strong winds. Whether they would all have appeared from outside the earth dark as a shadow is doubtful, for they may have reflected light as clouds do; but it is certain they were thick enough to hide all terrestrial features under them, and in some cases there seems to be no doubt that they were like dark shadows over parts of the Earth.

I am, Sir, yours faithfully,

H. C. Russell.

Sydney Observatory,
1879, July 17.

Fig. 27. Russell's follow-up letter, *The Observatory*, No. 30 (1879), pp. 178-180.[111]

Maybe we cannot absolve Russell entirely from a suspicion of something slightly mealy-mouthed in his response? If he had really thought it might be a "varying in intensity" of the well-known dark mare (due to a lunar cloud, eruption, soil chemistry, or whatever imagined cause), would he not have hinted more clearly at this in his original report, if only to identify its position? On the other hand, is it really credible that astronomers as experienced as Hirst and Russell, who had been observing the sky for many years, could have looked at the moon for fully three hours without recognising one of the most prominent familiar features on it?[112]

which "would be laughable if it were not really pitiable," passing on his informant's suggestion that the Government should provide them with a copy of a Moon atlas. See: 'A Shady Discovery by British Astronomers,' *Cincinnati Enquirer*, Friday, May 23, 1879, p. 4.

111 https://ia600408.us.archive.org/7/items/observatoryvolu04servgoog/observatoryvolu04servgoog.pdf

112 At least Russell knew a sunspot from a planet at this time, unlike some of his Vulcan-hunting contemporaries in Europe: "A careful watch has been kept up at the Observatory by Mr. H. C. Russell, the astronomer, ever since the morning of the 20th [March 1877], for the planet Vulcan [see Chapter 2], which was expected, by the astronomers of the world, to pass over the disc of the sun . . . No sign of Vulcan appeared all through the 20th and 21st. But in watching for this planet several interesting observations were made on the sun's spots." ('The Planet Vulcan,' *Sydney Evening News*, Friday, March 23, 1877, p. 2; http://trove.nla.gov.au/newspaper/article/108201398)

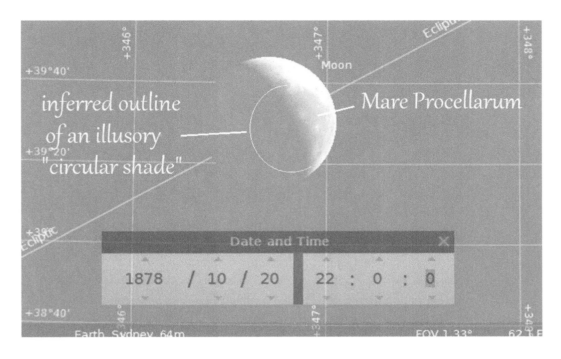

Fig. 28. The appearance of the moon that morning (time/date shown is UTC, Sydney -11hrs) illustrating R. A. Proctor's theory (Stellarium image).

A handwritten letter preserved in the archive of Sydney Observatory shows Russell writing, a decade later on May 30, 1889, to a Mr L. Kingsmill, evidently a regular weather observer well-known to Russell. [113] Kingsmill's measurements or methods had been exposed to what he considered unreasonable criticism in a local newspaper and he had sent the offending piece with a complaint to Russell, who replied with reassurance: "I would advise you to take no notice whatever of what anyone may say either in the newspaper or out of it, so long as you know that you do your duty." He was perfectly satisfied with Kingsmill's data. "If you knew," he finished wearily, perhaps recalling his savaging by the pen of Richard Proctor, "how often people who know nothing of the subject undertake to teach me in matters which I have spent my life in studying, you would not be much surprised at your own experiences."[114]

It would be interesting to know Russell's thoughts in later years about his own 1878 observation with George Hirst. He was not averse to pursuing unconventional ideas, such as a supposed influence of the Moon on Earth's weather; and a few months after his letter to Kingsmill he made – if the Australian press is to be believed – observations of at least one other lunar anomaly, namely the apparent disappearance of two mountains and their replacement by fresh "conspicuous craters" (see Fig. 29). But we have found nothing more about the strange "shade" on the moon.

---

113 https://maas.museum/observations/2009/05/30/letter-by-h-c-russell-30-may-1889/
114 The newspaper was the *Braidwood Dispatch and Mining Journal*. published in Braidwood, N.S.W. We have not found the item referred to, but we found L. Kingsmill mentioned therein several times in public notices as the Post Master and Telegraph Station Master for the town of Braidwood. See: Saturday, Sept. 15, 1888, p. 2; Wednesday, Jan. 9, 1889, p. 1 (http://trove.nla.gov.au/newspaper/).

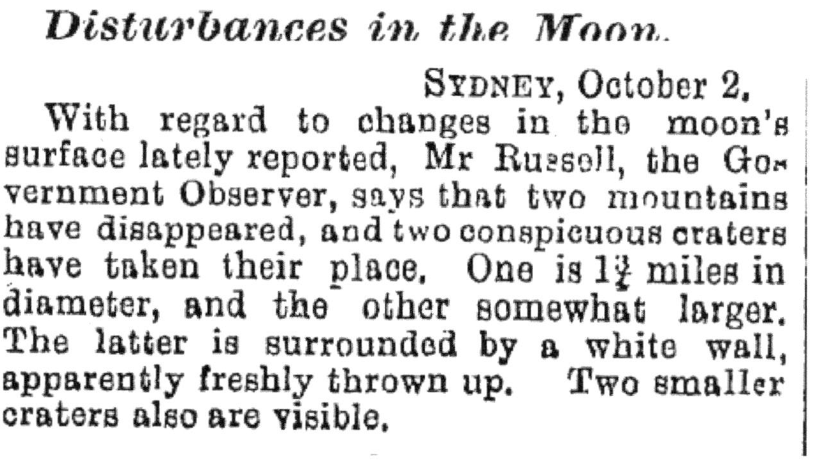

Disturbances in the Moon.

SYDNEY, October 2,

With regard to changes in the moon's surface lately reported, Mr Russell, the Government Observer, says that two mountains have disappeared, and two conspicuous craters have taken their place. One is 1½ miles in diameter, and the other somewhat larger. The latter is surrounded by a white wall, apparently freshly thrown up. Two smaller craters also are visible.

Fig. 29. The *Nelson Evening Mail*, October 2, 1889.[115]

Many other writers since Fort have picked up the story, for example Morris K. Jessup whose scientifically-literate and influential 1955 book *The Case For the UFO* called it "an important observation . . . almost without recorded precedent" which indicated that "things were going on in space near the earth." Jessup pointed out that Russell's description of the dark patch as getting fainter towards its edge is typical of a shadow's dense umbra and lighter penumbra, and he calculated that the responsible object would probably have been over 1400 miles in diameter[116] and less than 100,000 miles from the moon. "We cannot tell," he said, "whether it was solid or a dense cloud," but because it maintained its position on the moon despite the relative motions of the moon and the sun this indicated "control – firm, steady, calculated and maintained control of position. It implies purposefulness, persistence, delicacy and … intelligence." On the other hand, had it been not a shadow, but rather some obscuring phenomenon like a nearby cloud interposed between the observers and the moon, then in this case "the manipulation of this object was even more complex" because the Earth "was rotating rapidly while the moon was revolving around it."

Given that the "object" was in space between the moon and the sun, Jessup suggested, it could have been "well within the intense glare of sunlight and difficult to see." Of course it had to arrive and depart at some time without being seen by astronomers anywhere else on Earth – could it have done so without ever leaving the sun's glare? Jessup might have said that this adds yet another order of deliberation.

Another might say, it adds another order of unlikelihood. Richard Proctor in 1879 had reasoned similarly about the static "shadow" but came to a very different conclusion. Jessup – who had an astronomical degree and some observatory experience[117] – dismissed Proctor as an "armchair astronomer." Nevertheless, Proctor had a point, although Russell himself would

---

115 https://paperspast.natlib.govt.nz/newspapers/NEM18891002.2.8.4?items_per_page=10&page=3&query=russell+moon&snippet=true

116 Of course, a "circular" shadow would not imply a circular or spherical obstruction because the circle lay across the terminator. As will be evident from the phase shown in Fig. 28, the sun would be in the zenith of an observer on the lunar farside. There is no source of illumination radially above the "shadow".

117 He did his BSc with the University of Michigan while working at the University's Lamont-Hussey Observatory in South Africa.

have said it was aimed at a straw man, claiming that he had never believed it was really a shadow in the first place.

In response to Proctor, Russell implied that it might be similar to certain obscuring "dry fogs" on Earth that "remained stationary not for hours only but for weeks in spite of strong winds." Even here, Jessup argues that Russell was suggesting "something purposeful in the behaviour;" but there isn't the least evidence in Russell's letter, or in his other work and writings, that would support this impression.

In the end, however, Jessup's summing up of Russell's position is probably accurate enough: "At best he was thoroughly but honestly puzzled." [118]

If Russell and Hirst were reliable, and if they were not fooled by an almost childish failure to recognise the Mare Procellarum, what unusual phenomenon could have stayed put for three hours? The simplest explanation would clearly be something on the surface of the moon, or else close to it and gravitationally bound to the moon. A huge debris cloud from a meteor impact, even slow-falling in the 1/6th lunar gravity, would change extent and transparency in three hours, and would presumably change the surface reflectivity permanently when it fell out. No such change, let alone any evidence of new massive cratering, was reported by astronomers around the world.

We should mention that recent mapping of gravitational anomalies on the moon has revealed that the Mare Procellarum basin is not an ancient asteroid impact basin as once assumed. Rather, it is an ancient volcanic rift feature caused by upwelling of a vast magma plume within the once-active moon. [119] Is it a coincidence that in historical times this same huge mare happens to contain the highest frequency of Transient Lunar Phenomena or TLP – those odd lights, glows, smudges and shadows that have been reported for centuries, notably in and around its central triad of craters, Copernicus, Kepler and Aristarchus? Perhaps. But, as pointed out in Chapter 6 ("Lights on the Moon" [120]), selenologists have found evidence of "recent" (~10 million years ago) vulcanism on the moon, indicating that even today the interior is probably not quite cold. Occasional future eruptions are predicted to occur. But as for Russell's enormous "shade" of 1878, not even the most optimistic experts would suspect outgassing on such a scale and so recently.

All of which leaves us, perhaps like Henry Chamberlain Russell, "honestly puzzled." But there is no good reason to believe in Charles Fort's "vast dark body" in space.

118   Morris K Jessup, *The Case for the UFO*, Bantam Books, New York, 1955 (Part 4: Astronomy Speaks); http://www.bibliotecapleyades.net/ciencia/ciencia_flyingobjects03h1.htm
119   http://www.eurekalert.org/multimedia/pub/80224.php?from=278493
120   With reference to the claimed correlation between TLP frequency and sunspot number mentioned in Chapter 6, we should point out that the date of Russell's sighting was at the *minimum* between Solar Cycles 11 and 12, when sunspot number and geomagnetic activity were low.

CHAPTER 5 – **Crows on the Moon**

Two triangular, luminous appearances reported by several observers in Lebanon, Conn., evening of July 3, 1882, on the moon's upper limb. They disappeared, and two dark triangular appearances that looked like notches were seen three minutes later upon the lower limb. They approached each other, met and instantly disappeared . . . [They] were vast upon the moon -- "seemed to be cutting off or obliterating nearly a quarter of its surface." [121]

This extraordinary story, culled from the pages of *Scientific American,* inspired Charles Fort to imagine "vast black things, poised like crows over the moon . . . upon, or over, the moon." When we examined the original (Fig. 30) we found more information, but discovered two confusing errors.

A Curious Appearance of the Moon.

A singular appearance of the moon was observed by several residents of Lebanon, Conn., on the evening of July 3. The moon, almost full, was about three-quarters of an hour high. An observer says: " Two pyramidal luminous protuberances appeared on the moon's upper limb. They were not large, but gave the moon a look strikingly like that of a horned owl or the head of an English bull terrier. These points were a little darker than the rest of the moon's face. They slowly faded away a few moments after their appearance, the one on the right and southeasterly quarter disappearing first. About three minutes after their disappearance two black triangular notches were seen on the edge of the lower half of the moon. These points gradually moved toward each other along the moon's edge, and seemed to be cutting off or obliterating nearly a quarter of its surface, until they finally met, when the moon's face instantly assumed its normal appearance. When the notches were nearing each other the part of the moon seen between them was in the form of a dove's tail."

Fig. 30. "A Curious Appearance of the Moon,"
Scientific American, n.s., 46 (January 28, 1882), p. 49.[122]

---

121 Fort, *Damned,* p. 255 citing *Scientific American,* 46-49.
122 https://archive.org/stream/scientific-american-1882-01-28/scientific-american-v46-n04-1882-01-28#page/n2/mode/1up

The first error is Fort's. His date, July 3, 1882, can't be right because his own source was published 6 months before that, in January 1882. "July 3" is correctly quoted from *Sci. Am.*, therefore one might assume the true date was probably the previous July 3, 1881. But this implies another error, either in the publication or in the original report: On the evening of July 3, 1881 the moon would have been setting in the west; but if the moon is in the west in the evening it can never be "almost full." In fact, on that date it was in its first quarter, not "almost full". So, nothing fits.

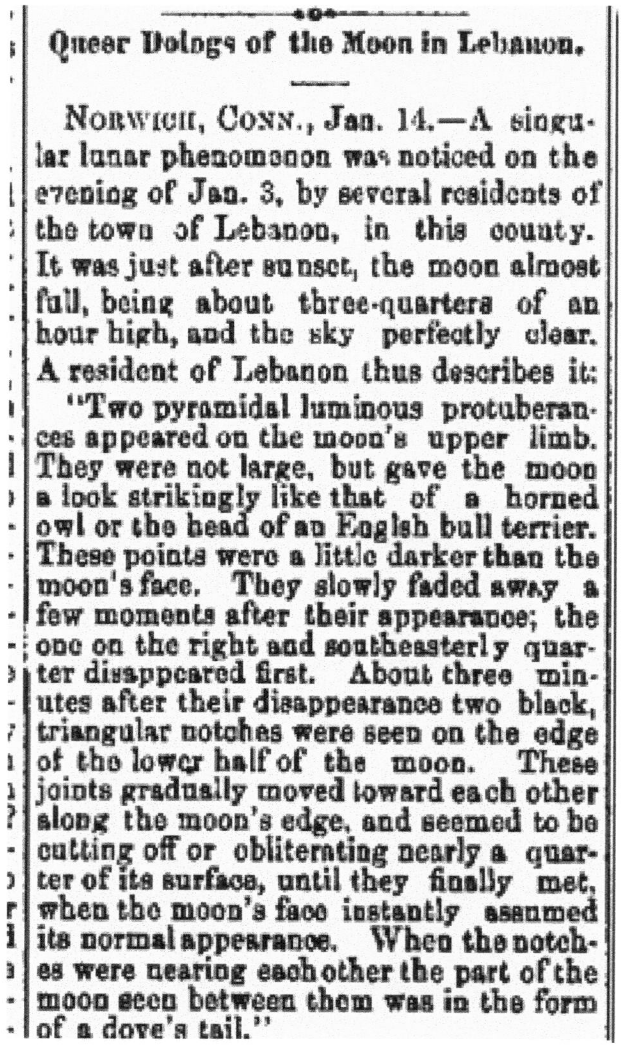

Queer Doings of the Moon in Lebanon.

NORWICH, CONN., Jan. 14.—A singular lunar phenomenon was noticed on the evening of Jan. 3, by several residents of the town of Lebanon, in this county. It was just after sunset, the moon almost full, being about three-quarters of an hour high, and the sky perfectly clear. A resident of Lebanon thus describes it:

"Two pyramidal luminous protuberances appeared on the moon's upper limb. They were not large, but gave the moon a look strikingly like that of a horned owl or the head of an English bull terrier. These points were a little darker than the moon's face. They slowly faded away a few moments after their appearance; the one on the right and southeasterly quarter disappeared first. About three minutes after their disappearance two black, triangular notches were seen on the edge of the lower half of the moon. These joints gradually moved toward each other along the moon's edge, and seemed to be cutting off or obliterating nearly a quarter of its surface, until they finally met, when the moon's face instantly assumed its normal appearance. When the notches were nearing each other the part of the moon seen between them was in the form of a dove's tail."

Fig. 31. *New Philadelphia, Ohio Democrat*, January 26, 1882, p. 1.[123]

The mystery was solved when we discovered another piece, published two days before the *Sci. Am.* article, in the *New Philadelphia, Ohio Democrat* (Fig. 31), containing an identical description but with one major difference: we now have the sighting occurring on "Jan. 3", "just after sunset", and that of course makes for an entirely different story. On January 3, 1882, the moon was rising in the East around sunset as required and was indeed "near full" (phase 99.7%, see Fig. 31). *Scientific American* plainly misprinted "July" instead of January.

---

123 Credit: Kay Coggin; https://newspaperarchive.com/new-philadelphia-ohio-democrat-jan-26-1882-p-1/

Sunset on January 3, 1882, at Norwich, CT, was at 4:34 p.m. If the moon was literally "three quarters of an hour high" at the time of the sighting it was only about 8° above the horizon. It reached this altitude at azimuth 70° at 5:04 p.m.,[124] which is acceptably "just after sunset". Therefore, everything now fits.

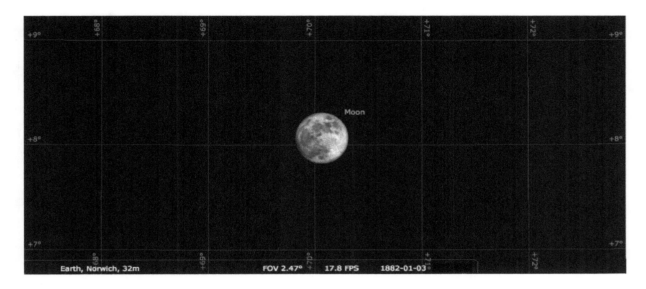

Fig. 32. The near-full moon rising after sunset on the evening of January 3, 1882 (Stellarium).

A third source, *The Willimantic Chronicle* of Wednesday, January <u>11</u>, 1882, confirms the date as "Tuesday evening Jan. 3d" and offers the added provenance of being evidently the original text of a letter written by one of the observers, [125] from which the later newspapers took their stories, almost – but not quite – verbatim:

> Lebanon. A remarkable and unaccountable phenomenon in connection with the moon was witnessed by at least three persons on Tuesday evening Jan. 3d. It occurred just after sunset, the moon being near its full and about three quarters of an hour high; the atmosphere being perfectly clear at the time. The appearance at first consisted of two pyramidal protuberances upon the moon's upper limb, and which apparently, were a part of the moon itself. This singular illusion, or whatever it might be termed, gave the moon a striking semblance as described by one, of a horned owl, but which to your correspondent more nearly resembled the head of an English bull terrier. The projections in a few minutes after they were discovered, gradually faded away; the one on the right and southeasterly quarter disappearing first. Some two or three minutes after, two black triangular spot[s] or notches were seen upon the edge of the lower half of the moon in the same relative position as were the projections upon the upper half, and apparently of the same size. These notches gradually moved towards each other along the moon's edge and seemed to be cutting off, or obliterating nearly a quarter of its surface, until they finally met, when the moon instantaneously assumed its usual proportions. When the notches were nearing each other, the part of the moon

---

124 https://www.timeanddate.com/moon/@4839843?month=1&year=1882

125 In typical 19th-century style the phrase "your correspondent" is used here by the writer to refer formally to him- or herself.

seen between them was in the form of a dove's tail and altogether presenting an appearance that will be long remembered by those who were fortunate enough to see it. [126]

So, what was seen that evening by those "at least three persons" from Lebanon?

Given that there were several observers, we can probably rule out a freak optical illusion, delusion, or instrument defect. We should add the caveat that these observers may, for all we know, have been together, confabulating, rather than reporting independently. However, the quoted description seems careful and articulate, and tends to suggest some astronomical knowledge. [127]

Fort's vast black crows poised over the moon make a spectacular image; but presumably something that was noticed only by a few people in the town of Lebanon (as far as we can discover) was not on or near the moon. We suppose it was in the local sky of Lebanon.

We made a search for relevant stories concerning Lebanon, CT, January 3, 1882, but nothing came up. No other witnesses, and no festivities or scientific experiments in the area which may have involved balloons or kites. But, of course, hot-air balloons could have ascended from many miles away.

The objects' downward change of position relative to the moon suggests the moon may have been rising behind them. They were first seen bright against the upper limb, then, about 3 minutes later, dark against the lower limb. That rough rate of ~0.5° in ~3 minutes is acceptably close to the sidereal rate (4 minutes per degree) suggesting the object(s) may have been, more or less, stationary relative to the ground. And the moon was low enough that they might have been something flown from the ground, possibly tethered – like kites or balloons. The "triangular" shapes reported could be interpreted as kite-like. An object that was only, say, ¼ of a mile away would need to be only 2 or 3 ft across to "obliterate nearly a quarter" of the moon, and at 8° altitude it would have been only about 150-200 ft above the ground – an altitude that could easily be exaggerated because most observers overestimate angles.

On the other hand, this implies something holding station against the moon, within a fraction of a degree, for several minutes – something too steady, perhaps, to be nearby kites or toy balloons at the mercy of the wind? Arguably the same could be said for hovering hawks, and the change from bright or pale shapes to dark ones is hard to interpret. It is possible to see some resemblance to a pair of large hot-air balloons at higher altitude, perhaps initially illuminated by the last rays of the sun, then descending or receding into shadow and finally appearing silhouetted as "black notches" against the bright moon. The "instantaneous" merging and vanishing of the shapes, at a point where they eclipsed "nearly a quarter" of the moon's area, is a problem for this theory, however.

Mirage distortions of the rising moon can occasionally be extreme when it is on the horizon, and perhaps if parts of the lower limb were obscured by (say) distant mountain peaks its mirage image might look extraordinary and change in surprising ways. The sudden vanishing of the dark triangles at the moment they came together perhaps hints at some sort

---

126   We are still searching for a scan or a physical copy of this paper; however we have no reason to distrust our source: http://www.ctgenweb.org/county/cowindham/records/newspaper/willimanticchronicle/jan1882.html
127   For example, the reference to the moon's "limb", and the phrase "right and southeasterly quarter". The latter could suggest someone used to using the moon's own coordinates.

of optical cause. But what? The undulating skyline is fairly featureless E of Lebanon and the shapes and changes reported here do not resemble any common mirage distortion. And in any case the story indicates that the moon was many times its own diameter above the skyline, not on it (presumably well clear of, for example, distant roof peaks or boat sails[128]) and therefore much too high for natural mirage. Any refraction effects caused by plumes of hot air from factory chimneys or the like would be turbulent and unstable, and surely recognisable over the course of several minutes.

Small clouds might occur, "perfectly clear" weather not withstanding; and lenticular clouds triggered by airflow over hilltops may remain stationary and well-defined for an extended period. But that is not an attractive explanation given the absence of prominent hills, the oddly angular shapes, and the instantaneous vanishing of the notches.

In short: given the information we've got, we're stumped.

---

128 Apart from small ponds the nearest river would have been the Thames at Norwich, about 10 miles away.

Part 3

Transient Lunar & Martian Phenomena

CHAPTER 6 – Lights on the Moon
CHAPTER 7 – The Case of the Missing Eclipse
CHAPTER 8 – Martian Lights and Clouds

CHAPTER 6 – **Lights on the Moon**

Lights that may have been seen upon – or near – the moon . . . A new aspect of interplanetary inhabitancy or occupancy – Worlds in hordes – or beings – winged beings perhaps – wouldn't astonish me if we should end up by discovering angels – or beings in machines – argosies of celestial voyagers – *The Book of the Damned*

Fort lists numerous accounts of anomalous lunar lights and glows – what we would today classify as Transient Lunar Phenomena, or TLP – between about 1780 and 1860.[129] Among the earliest are sightings by William (or Wilhelm) Herschel, one of the true giants of astronomy with discoveries too numerous to mention. But as Fort complained, "in divergences from the orthodox" even Herschel's word had no weight. "These observations are of the disregarded."

230   *Dr.* HERSCHEL's *Account of*

how far we have been authorized to ufe the mental eye. This being premifed, I may fafely proceed to give my obfervations.

April 19, 1787, 10 h. 36′ fidereal time.

I perceive three volcanos in different places of the dark part of the new moon. Two of them are either already nearly extinct, or otherwife in a ftate of going to break out; which perhaps may be decided next lunation. The third fhews an actual eruption of fire, or luminous matter. I meafured the diftance of the crater from the northern limb of the moon, and found it 3′ 57″,3. Its light is much brighter than the nucleus of the comet which M. MÉCHAIN difcovered at Paris the 10th of this month.

April 20, 1787, 10 h. 2′ fidereal time.

The volcano burns with greater violence than laft night. I believe its diameter cannot be lefs than 3″, by comparing it with that of the Georgian planet; as Jupiter was near at hand, I turned the telefcope to his third fatellite, and eftimated the diameter of the burning part of the volcano to be equal to at leaft twice that of the fatellite. Hence we may compute that the fhining or burning matter muft be above three miles in diameter. It is of an irregular round figure, and very fharply defined on the edges. The other two volcanos are much farther towards the center of the moon, and refemble large, pretty faint nebulæ, that are gradually much brighter in the middle; but no well defined luminous fpot can be difcerned in them. Thefe three fpots are plainly to be diftinguifhed from the reft of the marks upon the moon; for the reflection of the

4   fun's

---

129 Fort *Damned*, p. 198 *et seq.*, citing various sources.

63

fun's rays from the earth is, in its prefent fituation, fufficiently bright, with a ten-feet reflector, to fhew the moon's fpots, even the darkeft of them: nor did I perceive any fimilar phænomena laft lunation, though I then viewed the fame places with the fame inftrument.

The appearance of what I have called the actual fire or eruption of a volcano, exactly refembled a fmall piece of burning charcoal, when it is covered by a very thin coat of white afhes, which frequently adhere to it when it has been fome time ignited; and it had a degree of brightnefs, about as ftrong as that with which fuch a coal would be feen to glow in faint daylight.

All the adjacent parts of the volcanic mountain feemed to be faintly illuminated by the eruption, and were gradually more obfcure as they lay at a greater diftance from the crater.

This eruption refembled much that which I faw on the 4th of May, in the year 1783; an account of which, with many remarkable particulars relating to volcanic mountains in the moon, I fhall take an early opportunity of communicating to this Society. It differed, however, confiderably in magnitude and brightnefs; for the volcano of the year 1783, though much brighter than that which is now burning, was not nearly

much brighter than that which is now burning, was not nearly fo large in the dimenfions of its eruption: The former feen in the telefcope refembled a ftar of the fourth magnitude as it appears to the natural eye; this, on the contrary, fhews a vifible difk of luminous matter, very different from the fparkling brightnefs of ftar-light.

WILLIAM HERSCHEL.

Slough near Windfor,
April 21, 1787.

Fig. 33. "An Account of Three Volcanoes in the Moon. By William Herschel, LL.D. F.R.S.; communicated by Sir Joseph banks, Bart. P.R.S. Read April 26, 1787." *Philosophical Transactions of the Royal Society of London*, 77, 229.[130]

Herschel was in no doubt that the lights he saw on the moon twice in 1783 and twice in 1787 (and again in 1790; see below), were erupting volcanoes. His descriptions (see Fig. 33) are vivid and specific:

an actual eruption of fire, or luminous matter . . . of an irregular round figure, and very sharply defined on the edges . . . exactly resembled a small piece of burning charcoal, when it is covered by a very thin coat of white ashes . . . All the adjacent parts of the volcanic mountain seemed to be faintly illuminated . . . more obscure as they lay at a greater distance from the crater.

---

130 http://rstl.royalsocietypublishing.org/content/77/229.full.pdf+html

It is usually assumed this was in the region of Aristarchus, which has indeed been the location of some of the most interesting TLPs ever since.

Actually, Herschel's report was not "disregarded." His impressive reputation ensured that his volcanoes were taken seriously at the time. They were a powerful inspiration to Johann Heironymous Schröter (1745–1816) who began a major effort to map the moon, and himself observed a number of TLPs, one of which is Fort's next topic.

Fig. 34. William Herschel (1738–1822).[131]

Fort takes this from an account by "Prof. Serviss" [132] in the magazine *Popular Science Monthly* (Fig. 35) where "Serviss tells of a shadow that Schroeter saw, in 1788, in the lunar Alps. First he saw a light. But then, when this region was illuminated, he saw a round shadow where the light had been.... Prof. Serviss thinks that what Schroeter saw was the 'round' shadow of a mountain – in the region that had become lighted." Fort asks rhetorically why Serviss "disregards the light in the first place" and he is sceptical that a mountain could cast a "round" shadow. "Our own expression," he says, is that Schröter "saw a luminous object near the moon: that that part of the moon became illuminated, and the object was lost to view; but that then its shadow underneath was seen." [133]

Fort misunderstands Serviss's theory (which was that of most astronomers) to the effect that Schröter's light had been the illuminated tip of a mountain in the dark part of the moon just inside the shadow terminator, high enough to catch the first rays of the sun. When the area became fully sunlit the presence of the round mountain – perhaps of a darker material than the surrounding plain – was then disclosed, its prominence accentuated by its early-morning shadow.

---

131 https://commons.wikimedia.org/wiki/File:William_Herschel,_from_p6_of_Hector_Macpherson_-_Herschel_(1919).jpg
132 Garrett Putnam Serviss (1851–1929) was not a professional educator and not a professor at any academic institution. He was a journalist, trained in science and law, who became one of the most influential popular science writers of his day and was funded by Andrew Carnegie to tour the US giving lectures on his main enthusiasm, which was astronomy.
133 Fort, *Damned*, p. 214, citing *Popular Science,* 34-158.

Prof. Holden then refers to a similar, though less brilliant, display that was witnessed in 1843 by Dr. Gerling, of Marburg, apparently at the same spot on the moon.

I may add that there are at least two other recorded apparitions of this sort which were seen in that neighborhood, but evidently not in exactly the same place. The first was observed by Schroeter, the German selenographer, in 1788. He saw in the shadow of the great range of the lunar Alps, at the eastern foot of the mountains, a bright point, as brilliant as a fifth-magnitude star, which disappeared after he had watched it for fifteen minutes. Subsequently, when the region where this light appeared had become fully illuminated by the rising sun, Schroeter perceived, where the light had been, a round shadow on the surface of the moon, which was sometimes gray and sometimes black. Nothing more was ever seen of the light, so far as any record informs us, until 1865, when Grover, an English observer, caught sight of it again, under circumstances similar to those of its first apparition, and watched it for half an hour, when it once more disappeared. It should be said that, in the case of Dr. Gerling's observation, referred to by Prof. Holden, a "small, round, isolated, conical mountain" was found in the place where the light had been, on the evening following its appearance. It is altogether probable that the gray or black spot perceived by Schroeter was the shadow of a similar mountain, for it is well known that some of the lunar mountains and hills are hardly visible at all except when lateral illumination indicates their position and form by means of the shadows.

Herschel thought he had seen three active volcanoes. If

Fig. 35. Garrett P. Serviss, "New light on a lunar mystery," *Popular Science Monthly*, 34 (December 1888), pp. 158-161.

Of Johann Schröter, it has been said, "Never had such a powerful telescope or so keen an eye been trained so systematically and indefatigably on the moon." One example of his acuity was his observation of faint extensions of the horns of the new moon, which he deduced (incorrectly of course) were caused by a thin lunar atmosphere. The claim was dismissed rather severely by critics such as Maedler (1794–1824) who failed to see the effect with a better telescope. But this is now known to be a real effect of libration seen in certain circumstances close to new moon, a fact which "ought to make one wary of dismissing Schroeter's observations out of hand," according to the authors of a modern paper on his influence. "Though unskilled as a draughtsman he rarely made a serious mistake."[134]

In fact we find no less than nine separate TLPs observed by Schröter in 1788, but the one in question is clearly that seen on September 26, 1788, which he described as a whitish bright spot of about 5th magnitude, somewhat "hazy", SE of the crater Plato in the mountains

---

134 William Sheehan & Richard Baum, 'Observations and inference: Johann Heironymous Schroeter, 1745–1816,' *J. Br. Astron. Assoc.*, 105, 43, 1995, p. 172;
http://adsbit.harvard.edu/cgi-bin/nph-iarticle_query?1995JBAA..105..171S

(Montes Alpes) bounding the NE edge of the Mare Imbrium.[135] Thomas W. Webb's influential *Celestial Objects* of 1859 described the light as "close beneath the eastern foot of Mont Blanc" – one of the highest peaks in the Montes Alpes mountains – and said that Schröter "kept [it] in view for fully 15 minutes." Webb concluded that Schröter's grey/black "shadow," at least, was "probably nothing new," but added, "Strange to say, 1865, January the 1st, Grover recovered this bright spot, or one very near its site, with only 2 Inch of aperture, and saw it unchanged like a 4 Magnitude star to the naked eye, but rather larger, for fully 30 minutes." [136]

If Schröter's TLP and others like it were only sunlit mountain tops, the difficulty that astronomers had in reproducing many observations of this type seems at first a little surprising. Mountains do not move, and the motions of the sun are regular and predictable. In some cases, too (though not in this case), the lights seen were irregular or intermittent in brightness. But in chaotic mountain terrain the changing angles of the setting or rising sun on different dates might cause effects that are difficult to predict and might surprise even experienced observers.

However, in October 1790 William Herschel again saw unexplained lights, this time during a total lunar eclipse. Fort describes them as follows: "many luminous points, which he saw upon -- or near? -- the moon, during an eclipse," musing that to ask why they were luminous when the moon itself was dark "would get us into a lot of trouble." Fort hinted that they were "luminous objects close to this Earth,"[137] although it's very hard to imagine how or why nearby objects would have followed the true motion of the moon (15 seconds of arc per second, seen with an enormous magnification of 360x; see Fig. 36) so exactly as to appear fixed on its surface. The "sunlit mountain" theory had never been a good explanation for all TLPs, and now, in the absence of any direct sunlight at all, it became unsupportable. Yet Herschel was now more cautious about these "bright, red, luminous points" and there is no mention of volcanoes. He declines to "venture a surmise of the cause," but he does say their relative brightness "did not much exceed that of Mons Porphyrites Hevelii" which is the old name for the crater today known as Aristarchus,[138] where (it is generally inferred) Herschel had seen his "actual eruption of fire" in April 1787. Even when not a source of TLPs Aristarchus is one of the brightest of all large features visible on the moon, so the brightness of the luminous points was not insignificant; but there are many very small, bright craters and other features that might have appeared prominent with a magnification of 360x. Herschel was prudent to demur, saying "we know too little of the surface of the moon."

135 Middlehurst, Burley, Moore & Welther, *Chronological Catalogue of Reported Lunar Events*, NASA Technical Report TR R-277, July 1968.
136 T.W.Webb, *Celestial Objects for Common Telescopes*, Volume 1: The Solar System (1859), pp. 113-114.
137 Fort, *Damned*, p. 198 citing *Philosophical Transactions, 82-27.*
138 Johann Hevelius (1611–1687), a Polish astronomer regarded as the "father of lunar topography," named it Mons Porphyrites. He believed it to be "without doubt" a sulfurous volcano "in the midst of continuous eruption" with a red appearance he likened to "those known to us as Aetna, Hekjla, Vesuvius etc."

Remarkable Phænomena in an Eclipse of the Moon.

The 22d of October, 1790, when the moon was totally eclipsed, I viewed the disk of it with a twenty-feet reflector, carrying a magnifying power of 360. In several parts of it I perceived many bright, red, luminous points. Most of them were small and round. The brightness of the moon, notwithstanding the great defalcation of light occasioned by the eclipse, would not permit me to view it long enough to take the places of these points. They were, indeed, very numerous ; as I suppose that I saw, at least, one hundred and fifty of them. Their light did not much exceed that of Mons Porphyrites HEVELII.

We know too little of the surface of the moon to venture at a surmise of the cause from whence the great brightness, similarity, and remarkable colour of these points could arise.

Slough, Dec. 17, 1791.

E 2

Fig. 36. William Herschel, 'Remarkable Phaenomena in an Eclipse of the Moon,' Miscellaneous observations, *Philosophical Transactions of the Royal Society of London,* 82 (1792), p. 27.[139]

A hundred years later, experienced observers could still be surprised. When Edward Holden, at Lick Observatory in July 1888, saw a spectacular light near the lunar Alps, on the dark side of the terminator, he was first thunderstruck, then amazed to realise that it was a mountain ridge catching the sun. He wrote in *The Observatory* that he now understood how even Herschel could have been deceived.[140] This prompted A. Stanley Williams to point out that Herschel's "volcanoes" had been far inside the dark part of the moon's disc and could not possibly have been sunlit peaks. "The explanation usually given seems amply sufficient," he said, quoting Webb: "It is now well known that the volcanoes . . . were only the brighter spots reflecting back to us the earth-shine of the lunar night."[141]

At first blush this theory, too, seems incredible, given the experience and stature of an astronomer like Herschel. Already at the time of his first "volcano" sighting in 1783 he had been a systematic observer and telescope builder for a decade, and would have been familiar with the moon's major features in different conditions. Four years later, could he really have imagined "an actual eruption of fire" like "burning charcoal" whilst failing to notice that his three "volcanoes" coincided with the positions of the three most reflective large craters on the face of the moon? Yet this explanation became the most popular one during the early 19th century and remains common among modern writers: "As we now know, Herschel had made

---

139 http://rstl.royalsocietypublishing.org/content/82/23.full.pdf+html
140 Holden, E. S., 'Regarding Sir William Herschel's Observations of Volcanoes in the Moon,' *The Observatory*, Vol. 11, 1888, pp. 334-335.
http://articles.adsabs.harvard.edu//full/1888Obs....11..334H/0000334.000.html
141 Williams, A. S., 'Sir William Herschel's observations of volcanoes on the Moon,' *The Observatory*, Vol. 11 (1888), pp. 378-379 http://adsabs.harvard.edu/full/1888Obs....11..378W

one of his rare mistakes; he was only seeing the bright rayed craters Aristarchus, Copernicus and Kepler illuminated by earthshine." [142]

Similar observations continued to be made by other astronomers in the 19th century. Charles Fort mentions "Bright spots seen in the moon, Nov., 1821," [143] which we traced to the short account by Rev. Fallows in Fig. 37. Without some idea of where these "luminous spots" were located in relation to the day-night terminator, or how long they were seen etc., they are impossible to evaluate.

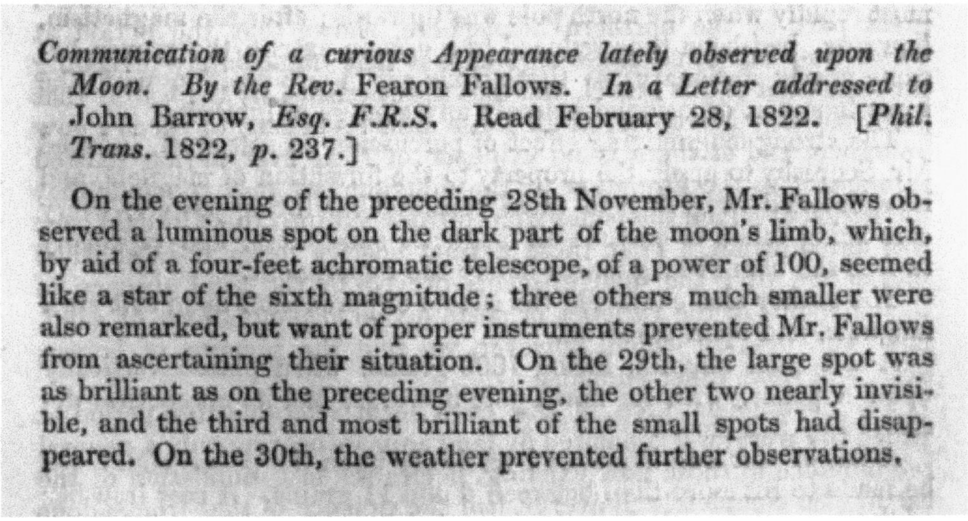

Communication of a curious Appearance lately observed upon the Moon. By the Rev. Fearon Fallows. In a Letter addressed to John Barrow, Esq. F.R.S. Read February 28, 1822. [Phil. Trans. 1822, p. 237.]

On the evening of the preceding 28th November, Mr. Fallows observed a luminous spot on the dark part of the moon's limb, which, by aid of a four-feet achromatic telescope, of a power of 100, seemed like a star of the sixth magnitude; three others much smaller were also remarked, but want of proper instruments prevented Mr. Fallows from ascertaining their situation. On the 29th, the large spot was as brilliant as on the preceding evening, the other two nearly invisible, and the third and most brilliant of the small spots had disappeared. On the 30th, the weather prevented further observations.

Fig. 37. Fearon Fallows, "Communication of a curious Appearance lately observed upon the Moon," *Proceedings of the Royal Society of London*, Vol. 2, p. 167.[144]

Referring in passing to four other cases mentioned in a book by American mathematician Elias Loomis[145] Fort then focuses on a case which sounds a little different: a light on the moon which was "moving" and therefore, presumably, was neither a reflection nor a volcano:

A moving light is reported in *Phil. Trans.*, 84-429. To the writer, it looked like a star passing over the moon – "which, on the next moment's consideration I knew to be impossible." "It was a fixed, steady light upon the dark part of the moon." I suppose "fixed" applies to luster.[146]

---

142   William Sheehan & Richard Baum, 'Observations and inference: Johann Heironymous Schroeter, 1745–1816,' *op.cit.*
143   Fort, *Damned*, p. 198 citing *Proc. London Roy. Soc.*, 2-167.
144   https://archive.org/stream/proceedings02royauoft#page/166/mode/2up
145   Elias Loomis, *A Treatise on Astronomy*, Harper & Brothers, New York, 1881, pp. 174-175. These observations were all made during solar eclipses in 1778, 1836, 1842, 1860, from Europe and North Africa.
146   Fort, *Damned*, pp. 198-199.

XXVI. *An Account of an Appearance of Light, like a Star, seen in the dark Part of the Moon, on Friday the 7th of March,* 1794, *by* William Wilkins, *Esq. at Norwich. In Extracts of a Letter to the Rev.* Samuel Vince, *F. R. S. and of three Letters to the Rev.* Nevil Maskelyne, *D. D. F. R. S. and Astronomer Royal; and communicated by the latter.*

Read July 10, 1794.

LETTER I.

REVEREND SIR, Norwich, 17th April, 1794.

I RECEIVED your letter yesterday ; and I am extremely happy in giving you the best description in my power respecting the phænomenon I saw in the moon, on Friday the 7th of March, a few minutes before eight o'clock in the evening. I was in hopes, as it was a bright evening, that some astronomer might observe it, who would have described it in a more *scientific* manner than I can. The few observations I made were merely to compare with some account I expected and wished to meet in some periodical publication.

My friend Mr. BECKWITH having the day before told me that I might see Mercury soon after sun-set, I had been looking for that planet from the Castle-hill in Norwich, but was disappointed by a clouded horizon. I mention this merely as the reason of my being led to a more particular notice of the moon also in this evening, having lost the first object of that evening's attention.

When I saw the light speck, as shewn in the sketch, (see Tab. XXI. fig. 1.) I was very much surprised ; for, at the instant of discovery I believed a star was passing over the moon, which on the next moment's consideration I knew to be impossible. I remembered having seen, at some periods of the moon, detached lights from the serrated edge of light, through a telescope ; but this spot was considerably too far distant from the enlightened part of the moon ; besides, this was seen with the naked eye. I was, as it were, rivetted to the spot where I stood, during the time it continued, and took every method I could imagine to convince myself that it was not an error of sight ; and two persons, strangers, passed me at the same time, whom I requested to look, and they (may be, a little more ignorant than myself) said it was a star. I am confident I saw it five minutes at least ; but as the time is only conjectural, it might not, possibly, be so long.

The spot appeared rather brighter than any other enlightened part of the moon. IT WAS THERE WHEN I FIRST LOOKED. The whole time I saw it, it was a FIXED, STEADY LIGHT, except the moment before it disappeared, when its brightness INCREASED ; but that appearance was instantaneous.

I have a reflecting telescope, and as I was very near home, I had determined to return and use it on this occasion ; for it was so fixed, I had scarcely a doubt but its appearance would continue ; but almost at the instant, and whilst I was looking, it totally disappeared. You can tell, by the age of the moon at that time, the apparent breadth of light upon the surface of that body, which, as near as I can judge, determines the distance of the spot from two points, B and C, on the periphery of the circle, (see fig. 1.) in which A is the enlightened spot ; B A = A D = D C ; B A D is supposed a right angle.

I mentioned this soon afterwards to a gentleman of my acquaintance, who sometimes amuses himself in the study of astronomy ; he was extremely inquisitive about it, and conjectured this phænomenon to be some great volcanic convulsion in the moon, which induced me at that time to assist my memory with a sketch like what I have here sent you. I shall be obliged to you, Sir, if you will favour me with Dr. MASKELYNE's opinion, if what I have related is sufficient ground for him to form an opinion upon ; and whether any such phænomenon has ever before been observed. When I was lately in town, I mentioned the particulars to my worthy friend Mr. H. REPTON, and if my engagements would have permitted, he was desirous I should call with him upon Dr. HERSCHEL, with whom he has some acquaintance.

I am, &c.

Norwich,   WILLIAM WILKINS.
17th April, 1794.
To the Rev. SAMUEL VINCE.

LETTER II.

REVEREND SIR, Norwich, 2d May, 1794.

I am favoured with your letter of the 1st instant, respecting the description of the light spot observed by me in the moon.

I am certain as to the evening I saw the phænomenon, because I made the memorandum in a pocket journal I keep ; besides, another local circumstance convinces me of its being on a Friday, and not on any other day than the 7th of March.

You are undoubtedly right in supposing I had forgot how near the moon was to a half moon ; and when I wrote to Mr. VINCE, I answered him in haste ; for his letter to me requested

an immediate answer, on account of his engagement to leave Cambridge in a short time. If you will please to refer to my letter, I think you will find I was somehow aware of my not describing the age of the moon properly in the sketch ; for I said, " *you will be able to tell* by the age of the moon at that " time, *the apparent breadth of light*, which may, in some mea- " sure, determine the situation of the spot according to my " idea."

The sketch I made at first was in pencil, without the assistance of compasses.

It appeared like a small star, without changing its form or situation ; and its distance was as far from the enlightened edge D as from the dark edge B.

I am, &c.

WILLIAM WILKINS.
To the Rev. Dr. MASKELYNE.

LETTER III.

REVEREND SIR, Norwich, 8th May, 1794.

I am again favoured with yours of the 6th instant. The evening I saw the bright spot on the moon, I had been looking for Mercury soon after sun-set, and walked more than an hour ; and having been disappointed by a clouded horizon, I returned home (my house is within 50 yards of the Castle-hill) ; and after staying some time, set out again to the coffee-house to look at the papers, as I usually do about that time, *i. e.* eight o'clock. I took the Castle-hill again in my way, when I was surprised with the appearance I have already described. After the disappearance of the phænomenon, I was very

particular in my inquiries respecting the time, and called pur-
posely on a neighbour* to ascertain it with certainty ; and
found it a few minutes before eight o'clock, which time I entered in my pocket journal ; and on inquiry of Mrs. WILKINS,
she says I left home at that time.

I am in my 44th year, and have a strong, good sight, not in
the least short sighted. About two years since, I purchased a
pair of spectacles in town, because I did not, in pointing a pen,
see the nib so distinctly as formerly ; but notwithstanding,
they lay in my drawer totally useless.

My profession has lately carried me frequently to Or-
fordness, where I have been constructing a lighthouse for
Lord HOWARD, upon the new principle, with ARGAND lamps
and reflectors ; and the goodness of my sight has often been
remarked, in discovering vessels with the *naked eye*, which
my companions could not discover but with the telescope. I
find that by looking some time at an object, my left eye
waters, I suppose from weakness ; but if I shut it, my other
eye still remains strong sighted. When the moon is young, I
do perfectly see the whole circumference, from the faint light
which surrounds it ; and on that evening the moon appeared a
well defined crescent.

I remember seeing the star you mention that evening ; but
I think it was between nine and ten o'clock that I observed it ;
and it was in appearance, may be, two of the moon's diameters
distance to the west ; but I did not particularly notice it.

I am very certain of this spot appearing WITHIN the circumference of the moon's circle.

I am, &c. WILLIAM WILKINS.

Castle Meadow.
To the Rev. Dr. MASKELYNE.

* Mr. R. BACON, who is publisher of one of the Norwich papers.

LETTER IV.

SIR, Hare-street, by Romford, 26th May, 1794.

Having been some days from Norwich, I received your favour of the 23d instant only this morning. The clocks at
Norwich are regulated by mean time, in the same manner as
in London. I have herewith given the figure you request,
copying the moon's appearance from your scheme, not having
any of my former sketches with me (see fig. 2.) ; I have placed
the spot of light to the best of my recollection ; and I hope it is
such as will be the means of satisfying your curious inquiries.

I am, &c.

WILLIAM WILKINS.

To the Rev. Dr. MASKELYNE.

Fig. 38. "An account of an appearance of light, like a star, seen in the dark part of the Moon,
on Friday the 7th of March, 1794, by William Wilkins, Esq. at Norwich," *Philosophical
Transactions of the Royal Society of London,* 84, pp. 429-434.[147]

But Fort is wrong here. "Fixed" applies to position. The original account, shown in Fig.
38, reveals that the light did *not* move across the moon but remained in place "without
changing its form or situation", as though on the lunar surface, for an estimated 5 minutes
before "instantaneously" brightening and then suddenly vanishing. Nevertheless, this is an
interesting observation because the light appeared like a star, was seen with the naked eye, by
three people, and therefore could not have been reflection of earthlight. It was also too far
removed from the day-night terminator to be a sunlit mountain peak, even supposing such a
thing could be visible without a telescope. The observer's original diagram of the light's
position is the upper drawing in Fig. 39.

147 https://archive.org/stream/jstor-106912/106912#page/n1/mode/2up

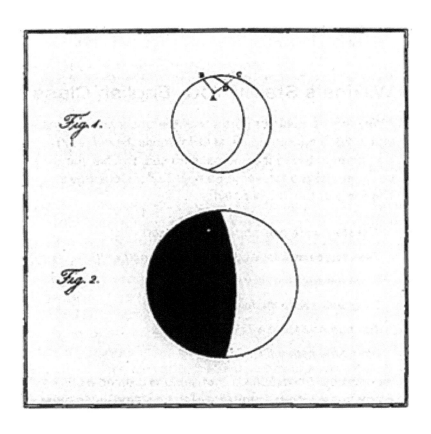

Fig. 39. Two drawings by William Wilkins showing the position of the light on the moon, the first (top) accompanying his original letter to Rev. Samuel Vince, FRS, the second sent a month later to Rev. Dr. Nevil Maskelyne, FRS, showing the remembered position on a diagram with the corrected lunar phase.

The main observer's age in 1794 identifies him as William Wilkins the elder (1751–1815), a prominent Norfolk architect and builder.[148] He was responsible for the restoration of Norwich Castle and Norwich Cathedral, and built a museum at York. Among other works he designed a major extension to the Master's Lodge at Gonville and Caius College, Cambridge, and left a bequest to the college (beginning a close connection with Cambridge which was continued by his nationally-famous son[149]). He also built lighthouses, including – as mentioned in his letter – the Orford Ness light made famous in ufological literature by the 1980 Rendlesham Forest incident.[150] Wilkins gives every indication of being a cautious and well-intentioned witness. Nevertheless, there are signs of possible error.

---

148   Norfolk   Architects   (http://www.heritage.norfolk.gov.uk/record-details?TNF2318-Norfolk-Architects-(Article)); Ian Atherton, *Norwich Cathedral: Church, City, and Diocese, 1096–1996*, A&C Black, 1996, p. 714; Christopher Nugent Lawrence Brooke, *A History of Gonville and Caius College*, Boydell & Brewer Ltd, 1985, p. 188; https://en.wikipedia.org/wiki/William_Wilkins_(architect)

149   William Wilkins the younger, designer of the National Gallery, of University College, London, and of several Cambridge college buildings among numerous other buildings and monuments.

150   A series of sightings of UFOs by US airmen, including a supposed landing, near RAF Woodbridge, in Suffolk. The Orford Ness beacon has been identified as one major cause of mysterious lights. See: http://www.ianridpath.com/ufo/rendlesham.htm

His reply dated May 8, 1794, to Nevil Maskelyne, the Astronomer Royal, discloses that Maskelyne had mentioned the presence near the moon of a certain bright star, and had probed Wilkins' confidence about the time of the sighting. Wilkins expressed great confidence in the time, adducing circumstantial evidence. But in a subsequent letter on 23rd May, Maskelyne returned to the issue. The probable reason for the Astronomer Royal's curiosity is revealed when we look at the view of the moon from Norwich on the evening in question and discover there was an unusual "occultation" of the prominent star Aldebaran by the moon (see Fig. 40a).[151]

Aldebaran, the brightest star in the constellation Taurus and at magnitude 0.85 the 14th brightest star in the sky, was on the point of vanishing behind the dark limb of the moon a few minutes before 19:00 GMT on that evening. But Wilkins recalled that the sighting occurred "a few minutes before eight o'clock," or 20:00 hrs, and wrote this in his journal shortly afterwards. Maskelyne evidently queried Wilkins about local Norwich timekeeping in order to be sure of the positions of the moon and Aldebaran.[152] Wilkins replies that Norwich clocks used local mean time "in the same manner as in London," which would mean that the time should be corrected by a few minutes in converting to Greenwich Mean Time; but as the sighting time is not precise this is not very material. If Wilkins recorded the time even approximately correctly, it seems the light could not have been Aldebaran because that star would have been west of the moon, nowhere near its dark eastern limb. "I am very certain of this spot appearing within the circumference of the moon's circle," insisted Wilkins.

Whilst what a witness describes seeing can obviously be a clue, sometimes the obvious thing that a witness does *not* see provides an even stronger one – for example, when a witness describes seeing a light where Venus is known to have been, but does not mention seeing Venus too, then we suspect that Venus may have been the culprit. And it's noticeable that Wilkins does not mention seeing Aldebaran close to the moon at the time of his sighting, although – if the time he gave was accurate – Aldebaran would have been quite prominent at that time just a little to the west of the moon, as in Fig. 40b. Instead he tells Maskelyne, "I remember seeing the star you mention that evening; but I think it was between nine and ten o'clock" (between 1 ½ and 2 hours later) and perhaps a degree or so west of the moon.

Consider Fig. 40c which shows the position of Aldebaran two hours after the moment of occultation, appearing very much as Wilkins describes seeing it one or two hours after his sighting. So, this is latent evidence, provided unwittingly by Wilkins, tending to support a sighting time closer to the occultation time of 18:55 than to his claimed time of nearer 19:55.

---

151 It was a discrepancy in the record of a similar occultation of Aldebaran by the moon observed from Athens in the 6th century which led to the discovery by Edmund Halley in 1718 of the proper motions of the stars relative to the solar system.

152 At this date most towns across England still used their own local noon meridian and corrections needed to be applied. It was only the practical necessity of coordinating railway timetables half a century later that drove the standardisation of Greenwich Mean Time or "railway time" across the nation.

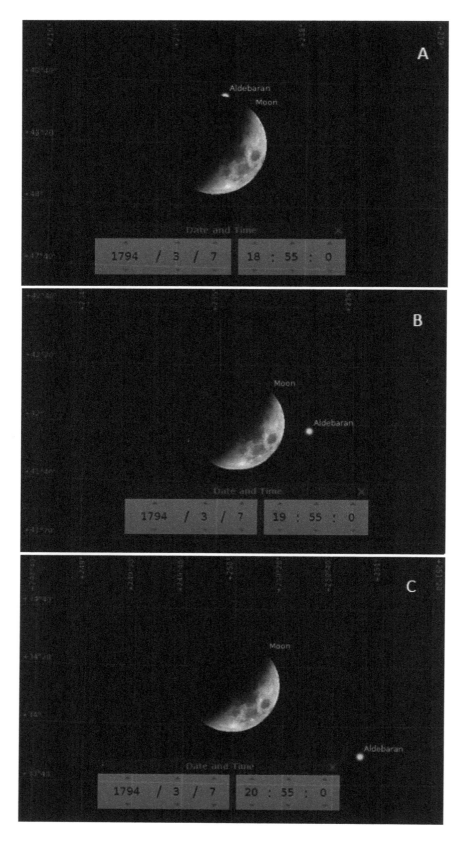

Fig. 40. An unusual occultation of the star Aldebaran by the moon on March 7, 1794 (Stellarium images).

Did Wilkins and his two companions see the occultation of Aldebaran? It is a fact that no comparable occultation of another bright naked-eye star could have been seen by Wilkins at any time on any other evening near this date. Given this rather striking coincidence it is reasonable to suspect Aldebaran, and theorise a one-hour clock error, even if the reason for it is obscure. But could his impression of the light's position "within the circumference of the moon's circle" have been mistaken? Wilkins was "very certain" of this fact, and it would indeed seem an extravagant mistake for an experienced observer. Nevertheless, the evolution of his drawings (Fig. 39) shows that the depicted position of the light cannot be regarded as precise; and it may be that, as suggested by the astronomer Thomas William Webb in 1860, ocular glare and a near-sighted eye made the illuminated phase of the moon seem larger than it really was, fostering the illusion that a star lay within the dark phase.[153] Wilkins' remark that the light brightened instantaneously on the point of vanishing could fit Aldeberan because a similar effect is observed when the light of an occulted star is diffracted by the edge of the moon.[154] It is impossible to prove the theory, but bearing in mind the fact that Wilkins' two companions were not impressed and "said it was a star" it seems a reasonable theory.

Fort's next example takes us to February 1821, "a light not referable to a star – because it moved with the moon: was seen three nights in succession; reported by Capt. Kater." He cites two secondary sources,[155] but in Fig. 42 we give the original from *Philosophical Transactions*.

Fig. 41. Captain Henry Kater FRS (1777–1835). [156]

Captain Henry Kater FRS (Fig. 39) was a significant scientific figure in his day, closely associated with Thomas Young, Joseph Banks, Humphrey Davy and other luminaries of the Royal Society; well-known for his contributions to metrology, geodesy, and astronomy. He was also an instrument maker, inventor of a new type of pendulum for measuring gravity and

153   https://introtocybersecurity.wordpress.com/2017/12/25/volcano-on-the-moon/
154   See, e.g., http://tdc-www.harvard.edu/occultations/moon/movie.html ; http://articles.adsabs.harvard.edu//full/1939ApJ....89..467W/0000467.000.html. Also, Fig. 38 shows that it was almost what is called a grazing occultation, when the star passes behind the moon at such a shallow angle that mountains and valleys on the limb of the moon can cause momentary fluctuations in brightness, see https://solarsystem.nasa.gov/docs/IOTA_Observers_Manual_all_pages.pdf
155   Fort, *Damned,* p. 209, citing *Annual Register,* 1821-687. Full reference: "Volcanic appearance in the Moon." *Annual Register,* 1821, pp. 687-688. Fort also cites *Quar. Jour. Roy. Inst.,* 12-133.
156   http://sydney.edu.au/museums/exhibitions-events/kater.shtml

of the azimuth compass, a forerunner of the modern prismatic compass.[157] His interest in precision measurement suggests a careful observer.

[130]

XI. *Notice respecting a volcanic appearance in the Moon, in a Letter addressed to the President. By Captain* HENRY KATER *F. R. S.*

Read February 8, 1821.

DEAR SIR,

London, February 5th, 1821.

IT may perhaps be interesting to the Royal Society to be informed, that on Sunday evening, the 4th instant, I observed a luminous spot in the dark part of the moon, which I was inclined to ascribe to the eruption of a volcano.

The telescope used was an excellent Newtonian of 6¼ inches aperture, with a power of 74. The moon was exactly two days old, and the evening so clear, that I was able to discern the general outlines in the dark part of her disk. Her western azimuth was about 70°, and her altitude about 10 degrees.

In this position at 6 hours 30 minutes, the volcano was situated (estimating by the eye) as in the accompanying sketch. [See Plate X.] Its appearance was that of a small nebula subtending an angle of about 3 or 4 seconds.

Its brightness was very variable; a luminous point, like a small star of the 6th or 7th magnitude, would suddenly appear in its centre, and as suddenly disappear, and these changes would sometimes take place in the course of a few seconds.

On the evening of the 5th, having an engagement which prevented my observing it myself, I arranged the telescope

Captain KATER *on a lunar volcano.* 131

for two friends, who remarked the same phenomena as the night before, but in an inferior degree, partly perhaps in consequence of the evening not being so favourable.

On the 6th I again observed it; it had certainly become more faint, and the star-like appearance less frequent. I could see it very distinctly with a power of 40. As the moon approached the horizon, it was visible only at intervals when the star-like appearance took place. On the same evening I had the pleasure of showing it to Mr. HENRY BROWNE, F. R. S.

I regret that I had no micrometer adapted to my telescope; but I have reason to believe the distance of the volcano from the edge of the moon was about one tenth of her diameter, and the angle it formed this evening with a line joining the cusps was about 50°.

I remarked near the edge of the moon, a well known dark spot, from which the volcano was distant, as nearly as I could estimate, three times its distance from the edge of the moon.

In a map of the moon published by Dr. KITCHENER (and which is the best small map with which I am acquainted), there is a mountain sufficiently near the situation of the volcano, to authorize the supposition that they may be identical.

On the 7th I could still see the volcano, and the occasional star-like appearance; but I do not think it was sufficiently perceptible to have been discovered by a person ignorant of its precise situation. I am inclined however to think, that the difficulty of seeing it is rather to be attributed to the

132 *Captain* KATER *on a lunar volcano.*

increased light of the moon, than to the diminished action of the volcano.

I have the honour to be,

Dear Sir, &c. &c.

HENRY KATER

To Sir Humphry Davy, Bart.
P. R. S. &c.

P. S. Since the preceding letter was written, I have ascertained that the spot in which I observed the volcanic appearance is that named ARISTARCHUS. This spot was particularly examined by HEVELIUS, who calls it Mons Porphyrites, and who considers it to be volcanic. If his drawings are to be relied upon, it has undergone a considerable change in its appearance since his time.

Sir WILLIAM HERSCHEL has recorded in the Philosophical Transactions an observation of three volcanoes, which he perceived in the moon, April 19th, 1787, at 10ʰ. 36ᵐ, sidereal time. One of these, which he says showed " an actual eruption of fire or luminous matter," was distant from the northern limb of the moon 3'. 57".3, the diameter of the burning part being not less than 3". I find that this observation was made about 9 o'clock in the evening, when the moon was not quite two days old; and from the situation of the spot described by Sir WILLIAM HERSCHEL, I have no doubt of its being the same that I have noticed.

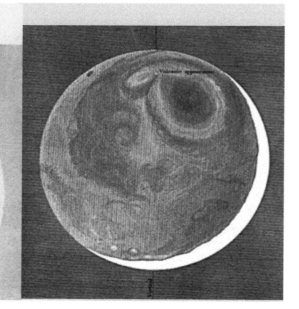

Fig. 42. Henry Kater, "Notice respecting a volcanic appearance in the Moon, in a letter addressed to the President," *Philosophical Transactions of the Royal Society of London*, 111 (1821), pp. 130-133, plate X.[158]

---

157 *Ibid.*
158 http://babel.hathitrust.org/cgi/pt?id=njp.32101076185303;view=1up;seq=163

Kater believed he saw an eruption. Being later made aware of the "volcano" reported by Herschel and, before him, Hevelius, Kater concluded, "I have no doubt of its being the same as I have observed" and he identified the location as the crater Aristarchus.[159] The light was "a luminous point, like a small star" which would appear and disappear, either "suddenly" or sometimes over a period of "a few seconds," suggesting an erratic eruption. But the earthlight-reflection theory suggests a different interpretation. These changes could have been due to fluctuations in "seeing" (the unsteadiness of Earth's atmosphere, like heat shimmer) causing the central bright peak of Aristarchus to pop out and then fade away. Also, the moon was a crescent only two days old, and over the next days, as the phase of the moon waxed, the "volcano" became fainter. This would fit the theory since the phase of Earth as seen from the moon would be waning reciprocally, and thus the brightness of earthshine on the moon would be decreasing, causing reflections to fade.

XVII. *Communication of a curious appearance lately observed upon the Moon. By the Rev.* FEARON FALLOWS. *In a Letter addressed to* JOHN BARROW, *Esq. F. R. S.*

Read February 28, 1822.

Cape Town, Cape of Good Hope,
December 13, 1821.

DEAR SIR,

I TAKE the earliest opportunity of communicating to you a curious appearance which I lately observed upon the moon. My present means of making observations of this kind are indeed very limited, as the large telescopes, destined for the Cape Observatory, have not yet arrived. Still, however, it is right to have phenomena of this kind recorded, though the description may, from the want of proper instruments, be imperfect.

About eight o'clock in the evening of the 28th of November last, the sky being extremely clear, and the moon shining with a brilliancy which I never observed in England, my attention was drawn to a whitish spot on the dark part of the moon's limb, sufficiently luminous to be seen with the naked eye. Lest I might be mistaken, I requested Mr. FAYROR, the assistant astronomer, to look at the moon attentively, and inform me whether he could observe any bright appearance upon the dark part of it. We both agreed in the identity of the spot, and remarked that now and then it seemed to flash with considerable lustre. Mr. FAYROR having in his possession a good achromatic telescope, which Mr. TROUGHTON had given him previous to our departure from England, I requested the loan of it for a few nights, so that I might be able to examine this appearance more minutely. Having directed the telescope to the moon, I immediately recognised the luminous spot, which seemed like a star of the sixth magnitude, and *three others* much smaller, but *one* of these more brilliant than the one we had seen with the naked eye. The largest spot was surrounded by a nebulous appearance. I could not perceive any thing of the kind about the small brilliant spot. The two others were similar to faint nebulæ, increasing in intensity towards the middle, but without any defined luminous point. As I am not yet in possession of a micrometer, by means of which the situation of these spots might be ascertained, you must rest satisfied with this imperfect description. On the evening of the 29th, the sky being equally favourable for observation as on the former one, I found that the large spot was, at the least, as bright as before, two others were nearly invisible, and the small brilliant spot had disappeared. I was unable to make any farther observations, as a strong south-east wind began to blow with great violence on the 30th, accompanied with rain, and which lasted several days. I wait with great anxiety for the next new moon, when, if the sky be clear, I shall not fail to examine it as carefully as my means at present will permit.

The telescope which I used is 4 feet long, and at the time of observation its magnifying power was 100.

Fig. 43. Fearon Fallows, "Communication of a curious appearance lately observed upon the Moon," *Philosophical Transactions of the Royal Society of London*, 112 (1822), pp. 237-238.[160]

---

159 Aristarchus does not abut the "northern limb of the moon," being rather in the west-southwest of the moon. But Herschel himself had written that his main volcano was close to "the northern limb of the moon" although the same lunar map conventions applied in Herschel's day (see e.g. the Dunn/Riccioli map of 1787, http://www.davidrumsey.com/luna/servlet/detail/RUMSEY~8~1~3627~420002). Kater appears to be following Herschel in using terrestrial equatorial coordinates to define North on the moon.
160 http://rstl.royalsocietypublishing.org/content/112/237.full.pdf+html

Just a few months later, on November 28, 1821, came a sighting from Cape Town, South Africa, described by Fort as "a whitish spot on the dark part of the moon's limb. Three smaller lights were seen." [161] The letter, from Fearon Fallows FRAS, FRS, is shown in Fig. 41. Fallows, who was appointed Astronomer Royal to George IV, had lately arrived in Cape Town to direct the new observatory at the colony, but construction did not begin until 1822 and at the time of the sighting no instruments had yet arrived.[162] Fallows obtained a borrowed telescope, but the phenomenon he first saw with the naked eye is in some respects reminiscent of the William Wilkins sighting of 1794.

The time was "about eight o'clock in the evening" when Fallows happened to glance at the moon. He makes a point of noting the unusual clarity of the sky, and the brightness of the moon. But one thing he does not mention is Venus. That evening, as seen from Cape Town, Venus was in a rare close conjunction with the moon, so close in fact that it was actually occulted by it. This happens for an observer somewhere on Earth on average about once every 177 days, between zero and a handful of times in any calendar year;[163] but for any particular location it is extremely rare, and in 1821 when conjunctions and occultations were still closely observed by professional and amateur alike for important scientific reasons it would have been reckoned a major astronomical event.

At "about eight o'clock in the evening" local solar time Venus was approaching the moon, less than one degree away, and at magnitude -3.78, high (>28°) in a dark sky, beside a moon which, however distinct in the clear air, was only a thin crescent, it would have been a very striking sight. The pair would have looked like Fig. 44. So it is a little odd, perhaps, that Fallows does not mention Venus but instead says, "my attention was drawn to a whitish spot on the dark part of the moon's limb," i.e. *on the rim* or the perimeter of the dark part of the moon's disc. Clearly Venus was not on the moon's limb at this time. But an hour and a half later it *was* on the limb – poised to vanish behind it as shown in Fig. 45. And the time of this event happens to be "about eight o'clock in the evening" – *if* one reckons by Greenwich Mean Time.

We have to wonder about this extraordinary coincidence. Is it possible that Fallows was using GMT rather than local time? Is it likely that the Astronomer Royal *a*) did not know that a lunar occultation of Venus was expected and *b*) failed to recognise it when it occurred? It seems unlikely.

It is conceivable that a colonial observatory in 1821 might have run on GMT,[164] but there was no functioning observatory building until at least 1822. Fallows had been in Cape Town since August and presumably had his own clocks and pocket watches adjusted to local time. And although the observatory was not yet established he was there on observatory business, not on holiday; he doubtless kept in touch with astronomical colleagues and had every reason to become familiar with the South African sky by means of study and observation (the assistant astronomer had a 48-inch refractor and Fallows knew it). Moreover the theory requires that the assistant astronomer also was misled, and implies that when Fallows resorted

---

161 Fort, *Damned*, p. 209, citing *Phil. Trans.*, 112–237.
162 http://www.sahistory.org.za/dated-event/fearon-fallows-first-astronomer-royal-cape-born-england; https://en.wikipedia.org/wiki/Fearon_Fallows
163 http://climate.gi.alaska.edu/Curtis/graf/MoVo.gif
164 It has proved surprisingly difficult to pin this down.

to the telescope (Venus presumably having vanished completely behind the moon in the interim) he must have transferred his attention to earthshine reflections of Aristarchus or the like without realising – and similarly on the next evening (when Venus would have been nowhere near the moon). It is a strained theory. And yet, it is undeniably odd that Fallows did not comment on the striking conjunction of Venus, and the coincidence of times remains thought-provoking.

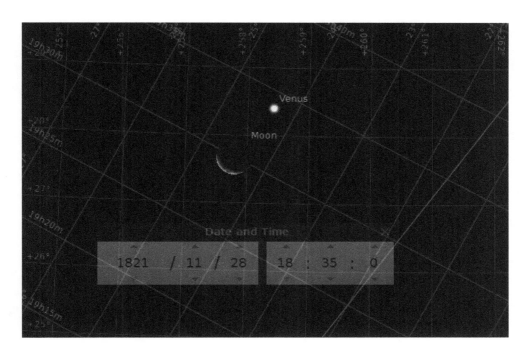

Fig. 44. The moon and Venus at 8:00 pm Cape Town solar time (6:35 pm GMT).

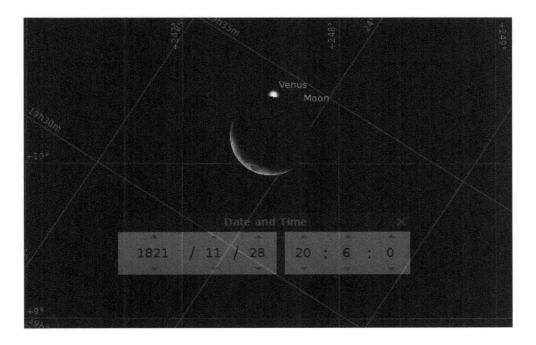

Fig. 45. The moon and Venus at 8:06 pm GMT (Stellarium).

79

According to Fort there were more "luminous points seen on the shaded part of the moon, during an eclipse" in 1847, by T. Rankin.[165] Other than the fact that Rankin describes the lights as looking like "reflections of stars" Fort gives no details, although his own later book *New Lands* reveals a little more. Here he talks of light displays "like carnivals on the moon" or "like signals on the moon" and he remarks:

> Upon the nights of March 18 and 19, 1847, large luminous spots were seen upon the dark part of the moon, and a general glow upon the upper limb, by the Rev T. Rankin and Prof. Chevalier (Rept. B.A., 1847-18). The whole shaded part of the disc seemed to be a mixture of lights and shades. Upon the night of the 19th, there was a similar appearance on this earth, an aurora, according to the London newspapers. It looks as if both the moon and this earth were affected by the same illumination, said to have been auroral. I offer this occurrence as indication that the moon is nearby, if moon and earth could be so affected in common. [166]

On Phosphoric Meteors. By the Rev. T. Rankin.

Over a pond at Huggate, in the Wolds of Yorkshire, richly charged with phosphoric matter from putrescent sources, Mr. Rankin saw, a few years since, in the evening, a large globular meteor. It was about two feet in diameter, rose from the leeward side of the pond like a balloon to a height of twenty feet, and then gradually decreased in size till it disappeared. ⎯⎯⎯⎯

On a singular appearance of the shaded part of the Moon on the Evening of March 18, 1847. By the Rev. T. Rankin.

The appearance was of large luminous spots on the shaded part of the lunar disc; indeed the whole shaded part appeared a mixture of light and shade, but the upper part was like the luminous broad top of a mountain. The author imagined these appearances were due to reflection of the light of Sirius, Procyon and other stars, these having suitable positions. ⎯⎯⎯⎯

Meteorological Observations at Huggate. By the Rev. T. Rankin.

The author presented the results of twelve months' observation with the usual instruments, and mentioned the occurrence of Aurora Borealis on Sept. 13 and 22, 1846.
P.S. Professor Chevallier observed the same appearance of the moon, through his telescope, on the evening of March 19th. ⎯⎯⎯⎯

Fig. 46. 'On a singular appearance of the shaded part of the Moon on the Evening of March 18, 1847'.[167]

---

165 Fort, *Damned*, p. 208, citing *Report of the Brit. Assoc.,* 1847-18.
166 *The Complete books of Charles Fort*, Dover, New York, 1974, p. 398.
167 Rev. T. Rankin, 'On a singular appearance of the shaded part of the Moon on the Evening of March 18, 1847,' *Notices and Abstracts of Communications to the British Association for the Advancement of Science at the Oxford Meeting, June 1847*, p. 18.

Fort's original source (Fig. 46) names the Rev. T. Rankin from Huggate, Yorkshire, whom we are able to identify as the Reverend Thomas Rankin (1783–1863), curate of Huggate and North Dalton (1821–1863), a member of the Yorkshire Philosophical Society and the Yorkshire Antiquarian Club, "noted for his meteorological and antiquarian researches".[168]

We find the Rev. Rankin's name occasionally in periodicals like the *Gentleman's Magazine* and the *Evangelical Magazine and Missionary Chronicle*. In addition to accounts of astronomical, meteorological and other noteworthy phenomena[169] he recorded routine daily weather observations[170] for the Yorkshire Philosophical Society (whose museum coincidentally was built by Norwich architect William Wilkins, our witness to that light on the moon in 1794). The Rev. Prof. Chevalier appears in (e.g.) the *Monthly Notices of the RAS*[171] describing an observation of the solar eclipse of July 1841 from Durham; but we have little information about him.

Rev. Rankin's account in the *Report of the B.A.* confirms Fort's claim that Prof. Chevalier saw the same luminosity on the moon,[172] but only on the second night, March 19; whilst also making it clear that Rankin himself only saw this phenomenon on the 18th. Thus, it would seem the observations were never concurrent. Moreover, Fort is mistaken to say that these events occurred during a lunar eclipse – as is, indeed, obvious from the fact that they were observed over two successive nights. A (total) lunar eclipse can never last more than a few hours, and in fact the nearest (partial) lunar eclipse was not until March 31, 1847.[173]

A "general glow" and "large luminous spots" sound less like the sort of point-source lights that might be likened to "reflections of stars" – a notion that makes no physical or even geometrical-optical sense – than like reflections caused by earthshine. But details are too vague for comment (and see p. 84 below).

Herschel's observations in the 1780s remained the classic and defining example of this type of TLP throughout the controversies of the 19th century. As mentioned already, Herschel was an experienced observer and his description of the "volcano" in Aristarchus shows him to have been aware of the effects of earthshine at the time. The glow he saw was "plainly to be distinguished from the rest of the marks upon the moon," he said, "for the reflection of the sun's rays from the earth is, in its present situation, sufficiently bright, with a ten-feet reflector, to shew the moon's spots, even the darkest of them." And he added, "nor did I perceive any similar phenomena last lunation, though I then viewed the same places with the same instrument." Before dismissing his observation as simply terrain reflecting earthshine,

168 Harrison, S., 'The Yorkshire Antiquarian Club 1849–c.1860,' *Bulletin of the History of Archaeology*, 20(1), 2010, pp.38–48; https://www.archaeologybulletin.org/articles/10.5334/bha.20105/
169 Though not related, the first entry in Fig. 46 (describing Rankin's sighting of a "large globular meteor" of "phosphoric matter" rising from a pond "like a balloon") is quite unusual too! What's even stranger, Rankin witnessed something similar two years later, on June 11, 1849: 'a violent explosion of flammable gas . . ., accompanied with smoke, great noise, and a rumbling concussion [which] was propagated across the [Huggate] pond from NW to SE.' According to Rankin the pond had been a long-time receptacle for refuse and animal carcasses. See: https://archive.org/details/report36sciegoog/page/n288/mode/2up/search/pond+at+huggate
170 See, e.g., *Ann Rep York Phil Soc.*, 1830.
171 Dec. 10, 1841, Vol. V, No. 18, p. 125.
172 Note that the 'P.S.' underneath the third entry in Fig. 43 refers to Prof. Chevalier's sighting, and should have been placed underneath the second entry.
173 https://eclipse.gsfc.nasa.gov/LEcat5/LE1801-1900.html

these factors should be borne in mind, as should the persistent history of TLPs in the region of Aristarchus into the 20th century.

Recent literature surveys have found that fully one third of all TLPs are reported in the region of Aristarchus and its adjacent plateau.[174] Most modern planetary scientists remain very cautious about TLPs for two reasons: lunar geological models which indicate that the moon ought to be long dead, with no active volcanoes; and the fact that the evidence is mostly eyewitness testimony, suffering a paucity of photographic and other instrumental support. But modern observations from Earth and from lunar orbit have produced some photographic, photometric and other hard data on TLPs, as well as revising some ideas about lunar geology.

Fig. 47. Transient Lunar Phenomenon (TLP) near the terminator. A "lunar flare" 8 seconds in duration, photographed on November 15, 1953, by Dr Leon H. Stuart in Tulsa, Oklahoma. A recent NASA study suggests this may have been a meteorite impact.[175]

---

174 The list of astronomers to have observed TLPs in Aristarchus since the 18th century includes: Schröter, Bode, Von Brühl, Kater, Olbers, Browne, Ward, Baily, Struve, Ruppell, Göbel, Gruithuisen, Argelander, Tempel, Elger, Flammarion, Klein, Johnson, Hislop, Jackson, d'Adjuda, Molesworth, Pickering, Kruger, Stuyvaert, Rey, Moye, Ward, Joulia, Goodacre, Douillet, Andrenko, Barcroft, Favarger, Wilkins, Brown, Hare, Bartlett, Firsoff, Kozyrev, Stynskaya, Argentiere, Haas, Dachille, Alter, Rule, Sartory, Grainger, Ring, Adams, Scarfe, Greenacre, Barr, Jacobs, Fisher, Doherty, Budine, Lecuona, Earl, Titulaer, Genatt, Reid, Crowe, Cross, farrell, Emmanuel, Welch, Bornhurst, Presson, L.Johnson, Harris, Cragg, M.Brown, Patterson, Moore, Farrant, Classen, Darnell, Anderson, Delano. See: Middlehurst, Burley, Moore & Welther, *Chronological Catalogue of Reported Lunar Events*, NASA Technical Report TR R-277, July 1968;
http://www.astrosurf.com/lunascan/papers/R-277.pdf
175 https://www.thelivingmoon.com/43ancients/02files/Transient_Lunar_Stuart.html;
https://www.nasa.gov/vision/universe/watchtheskies/old_moon_mystery.html

Is the moon really geologically dead? It seems less sure than it once did. In October 2014 NASA's Lunar Reconnaissance Orbiter detected new evidence of "recent" lunar vulcanism which, it was said, will "rewrite the text books."[176] Of course, recent in geological terms means possibly as young as 10 million years, and the features concerned are much smaller than the scale of the eruption apparently seen by Herschel. But never say never. According to selenologists it is still not quite cold after all, and occasional future volcanic activity is likely.[177] So some lingering activity in recent centuries is not ruled out, possibly explaining occasional odd sightings of vapour-like obscurations. Howsoever there may be different explanations for some of those lights on the moon.

On October 29, 1963, two cartographers, James Clarke Greenacre and Edward M. Barr, working at Lowell Observatory, Flagstaff, Arizona, observed bright red, orange, and pink phenomena on a hill southeast of the lunar valley Vallis Schröteri (named for 18th-century selenographer and TLP observer Johann Schröter; see above) and inside the rim of the crater Aristarchus. These observers' reputations for precision sparked a change in attitude towards TLPs, aided by the fact that only a few days later astronomers Zdeněk Kopal and Thomas Rackham, at Pic-du-Midi observatory in the French Pyrenees, photographed what was called "wide area lunar luminescence" around the craters Aristarchus, Kepler and Copernicus – the very craters identified by convention as the cause of Herschel's illusory "volcanoes."[178]

The fact that this occurred soon after the eruption of a large flare on the sun suggested to Kopal that they had detected fluorescence of lunar rocks caused by the impact of energetic solar particles. The sun connection seemed confirmed when Kopal discovered that Herschel's 1787 TLPs had themselves coincided with a display of aurora borealis, seen as far south as the latitude of Padua, Italy, and that both events occurred shortly before a peak in the number of sunspots.[179]

Which reminds us of the "mixture of lights and shades" or "general glow" and "large luminous spots" seen on the moon by Rankin and Chevalier from the north of England on March 18-19, 1847. According to Charles Fort, the London newspapers recorded a display of northern lights on the same night. We confirmed that this was so.

In fact, the display was well observed all over the south of England, in Europe and in the US. According to the *Journal of the Society of Telegraph Engineers* (1873) all telegraph lines in Britain were rendered inoperable on that date, and it was probably the first time that the disruptive effect of induced electric currents caused by space weather got the full attention of scientists and engineers.[180] It led to the first systematic study by W. H. Barlow, who observed

---

176 https://www.nasa.gov/press/2014/october/nasa-mission-finds-widespread-evidence-of-young-lunar-volcanism/

177 See: Eric Hand, "Recent volcanic eruptions on the moon," *Science*, Oct. 2014 (http://www.sciencemag.org/news/2014/10/recent-volcanic-eruptions-moon); S. E. Braden, *et al.*, "Evidence for basaltic volcanism on the Moon within the past 100 million years," *Nature Geoscience*, 7 (2014), pp. 787-791 (http://www.nature.com/ngeo/journal/v7/n11/full/ngeo2252.html); http://www.skyandtelescope.com/astronomy-news/volcanoes-on-the-moon-10142014/; http://lroc.sese.asu.edu/posts/818

178 Kopal, Z., "The luminescence of the moon," *Scientific American*, 212, 5 (May 1965), p. 28; see also https://en.wikipedia.org/wiki/Transient_lunar_phenomenon

179 http://www.daviddarling.info/encyclopedia/T/TLP.html; *Kopal, Z. (December 1966), "Lunar flares," Astronomical Society of the Pacific Leaflets, 9, pp. 401-408.*

180 Varley, C. F., 'Discussion of a few papers on earth currents,' *J. Soc. Telegraph Engineers*, 2 (1873), pp. 111-114; see also http://www.spaceweather.gc.ca/tech/se-chr-en.php

the "brilliant aurora" on the evening of March 19, 1847, and "strong alternating deflections on all instruments during the whole time of its remaining visible."[181] Interestingly, Alexander von Humboldt speaks of this very aurora having been measured "by Professors Challis, of Cambridge, and Chevalier, of Durham," [182] the latter being also an observer of the concurrent TLP on the moon (see the report by Rev. Rankin discussed on p. 81 above; we do not know if Chevalier made any speculative connection at the time). The aurora was observed by Morgan and Barber at Cambridge, who published drawings of the spectacular arch (Fig. 48). And, as in London, "magnetic perturbations" were recorded in Belgium and the Netherlands simultaneously with the display.[183] Indeed, the display was recorded widely across the northern hemisphere – as witness the "great extent of the illumination" described in a New York publication, referring to "numerous records of observations made in Great Britain, and in the northern parts of the United states . . . over a surface of 4,000 miles in extent" (Fig. 49). We have found other anecdotal reports of strange blue lights in the UK that same night which may conceivably be related.[184]

Fig. 48. The brilliant aurora of March 19, 1847, as observed by Morgan and Barber at Cambridge.[185]

181   Barlow, W. H., 'On the spontaneous electrical currents observed in wires of the electric telegraph,' *Phil.Trans. Roy. Soc.*, London, 139 (1849), pp. 61-72; http://www.jstor.org/stable/108470
182   Alexander von Humboldt, *Cosmos: A Sketch of the Physical Description of the Universe* (1845), Harper & Brothers edition, NY, 1858–1859, p. 199.
183   A. Quetelet, *Sur le climat de la Belgique*, Tome Second (1857), Brussels, p. 43.
184   Blue, flame-like lights illuminating the sea were seen by crew and passengers of the Stornoway mail boat in the Minch; and in Islington, London, strange moving lights cast a bright bluish light on the houses. See: Aubeck, C., & Shough, M., *Return to Magonia*, Anomalist Books, 2015, p. 56.
185   https://www.repository.cam.ac.uk/handle/1810/244592

*This meteor began to be visible a little before the close of twilight: the day had been quite cloudless from sunrise, and the barometer, as also on the preceding day, falling rapidly: about six o'clock in the evening, a bank of clouds (cumulo-stratus) appeared in the western horizon, and gradually rose higher, till they reached an altitude of 20° the wind being then S.S.E.; at 6h. 35m. P.M., this cloud was separated into several smaller parts, assuming the character of cirro-stratus, and all of them moved towards the North, where they disappeared; a bank of cumulo-stratus still remaining on the horizon in the S.W. the whole evening.

As early as 6h. 50m. P.M., it was observed that the sky from W. by S. to N.N.E round by N. was more than usually bright; this was first attributed to the moon and the strong twilight at that hour, but as the brightness of the sky still continued without much diminution, attention was especially directed to this quarter of the heavens for the expected Aurora. At 7h. 26m. the first decisive appearance of this phenomenon was seen in the form of a very black circular segment, each corner of which rested upon the horizon, one in the N.W. by W. the other in the N.E., while the vertex of this dark arc was situated about 7° W. of the astronomical meridian, with an altitude of about 8¼°; at first sight it seemed to be a hazy fog or light cloud, but as two stars, α Lyræ, and α Cygni, were soon after seen in the midst of it, there no longer remained any doubt as to its nature: at 7h. 44m. two concentric luminous arcs were formed round this black segment, being most perfect towards the N.E.; in another minute, and almost instantaneously, several streamers shot up to an altitude of 38°, each being at right angles to the parts of the arcs from whence they proceeded; after this, or about 7h. 50m. the black segment below the arcs vanished, but streamers still continued to dart up in great numbers, being mostly of a white colour, a few were pink, and one, which appeared like a sheet of light, had a pulsating motion: those streamers which proceeded from the N.W. and W., after attaining an altitude of about 45° curved towards the South: after 8h. 10m. the streamers were much less numerous, and the arc was no longer seen in the N.W.

8h. 35m. At this hour, there seemed to be an arch forming N. of the astronomical zenith, having the appearance of a faint band, nearly perpendicular to the plane of the magnetic meridian; it remained like this until 8h. 45m., when it appeared to shoot up very suddenly from the W.S.W., passing close to Capella, and through part of the Great Bear. In a few minutes it soon extended across the entire sky to the N.E. by E., passing close to the star Arcturus. "At 8h. 50½m., the lower border passed a very little above γ Orionis, and about as much below Pollux, the upper border passed through Castor: its axis passed also between the stars γ and μ on the feet of the Twins,

rather nearer to the former than to the other. It terminated at a point between Arcturus and β Andromedæ, distant from the former by about 4-10ths of the interval between the stars. At 8h. 57m. α and γ Orionis were equi-distant from its axis on opposite sides. At 9h. 0m. its upper border was a little below α Orionis, and its lower border as much above δ Orionis. At 9h. 13m. its upper border was as much above δ Orionis, as the lower was below ε Orionis, and the lower border passed midway between ι and ζ Orionis."

"At 9h. 10½m., the lower border just covered δ Orionis, and passed a little above β Canis Minoris. Near the meridian, two stars, γ and δ Cancri, were one on the upper, and the other on the lower border; the breadth measured by the positions of these two stars was 3° 20', which was nearly the maximum apparent breadth at the time; at 9h. 14½m. it passed entirely below γ and δ Cancri; at 9h. 15½m., it covered the belt of Orion."* The whole arch had a progressive motion to the S.S.E., and appeared to move in such a manner that its vertex was always on the magnetic meridian, or nearly so, the direction of the motion being perpendicular to that meridian: the portion to the S.W. appeared to move more quickly than the remaining part, but it did not extend to the horizon towards the N.E. after 8h. 50m., whereas it appeared to sink below in the S.W. at the time the clouds rose and obscured it, at 9h. 16m. At 9h. 49m., there was a slight break in the clouds, but the bow could not be distinguished. The mean height of this Auroral arch, as determined by Professors Challis and Chevallier, was 177 miles above the surface of the earth. The following are the meteorological observations taken at the Cambridge Observatory, just before and after the appearance of this meteor.

DAY.	BAROM. 9 A.M.	THERM.			BAROM. 3 P.M.	THERM.			Min. Ther.	Max. Ther.
		Att.	Ext.	Wet.		Att.	Ext.	Wet.		
	in.	deg.	deg.	deg.	in.	deg.	deg.	deg.	deg.	deg.
March 18.	29·897.	45·2	48·3	42·4	29·889.	49·9	59·7	46·3	34·3	64·0
„ 19	29·718.	45·1	47·4	41·8	29·660.	50·2	56·9	45·9	33·9	58·0
„ 20	29·548.	48·8	48·9	46·8	29·566.	50·2	56·8	48·6	45·0	61·9

* Communicated by Professor Challis to the *Cambridge Chronicle*, March 27.

Fig. 49. 'An Account of the Aurora Borealis seen near Cambridge, October the 24th, 1847'.[186]

AURORA BOREALIS OF MARCH 19, 1847.

In a report made by the Regents of the University of the State of New York, to the State Legislature in 1848, and recently published by order of that body, are numerous records of observations made in Great Britain, and in the northern parts of the United States upon the aurora borealis, seen on the night of March 19th, 1847, over a surface of 4,000 miles in extent.— On examining the records and noticing the great extent of the illumination, I was led to refer to my own records of that particular period, as made up from observations made by myself, at my place of observation on Long Island, and the observations made upon the mountains of South-Western Virginia, by an associate observer, and other observations made at various localities by my correspondents. From the mountains of South-Western Virginia, near the line of the States of Tennessee and Kentucky, the aurora borealis is rarely seen. On the 19th of March, 1847, the temperature at that locality, altitude 1882 above the sea, was as follows:

Fig. 50. The "great extent" of the March 19, 1847, aurora seen across the northern US.[187]

186 'An Account of the Aurora Borealis seen near Cambridge, October the 24th, 1847; together with those of September 21, 1846, and March 19, 1847, seen at the Cambridge Observatory. With twelve coloured engravings. By John H. Morgan, of Jesus College and late of the Cambridge Observatory, and John T. Barber, of Trinity College, Cambridge,' Macmillan, Barclay, and Macmillan, London, 1848.

Since the game-changing photographs of luminescence on the moon obtained by Kopal and Rackham in 1963 there has been some further photometric, photographic, polarimetric and spectroscopic evidence – much of it, as it happens, relating to Aristarchus – suggesting that the "dark" surface of the moon emits, at times and in certain places, more light than can be explained by refracted sunlight, earthshine etc. The cumulative evidence is said to prove that the radiation concerned is non-thermal, and that the effect may be correlated with the solar cycle, as would be expected of mineral fluorescence caused by solar particle bombardment.[188] In addition, radioactive radon gas emissions have been detected by Apollo and Lunar Prospector missions, and after a ruthless winnowing of the anecdotal database, removing errors and correcting for selection effects, it is claimed that Aristarchus remains a significant locale for TLP observations.[189]

Whilst some lights on the moon are explainable, easily or otherwise – as earthshine, stellar occultations, meteor impacts, and the like – some may indicate effects of remnant active geology, and there appears to be little doubt that other transient physical phenomena, possibly involving new science, do occur.[190] By assembling a large number of stories in one place, however uncritically, and making them accessible to the general reader, Fort's efforts may have helped to keep the fringe topic of TLPs visible during the early 20th century, thereby encouraging amateur astronomers to be aware of them.

In parallel, and to an even greater extent of course, Fort's work has encouraged ufologists and others keen to find evidence of alien visitation in our solar system. Many of Fort's ideas were prophetic of those which have become popular today in these fields. But of his "argosies of celestial voyagers" and habitations on the moon built by "beings in machines" there is, as yet, no sign.

---

187   E. Meriam (Ed.), 'Aurora Borealis of March 19, 1847', *New York Municipal Gazette*, Volume 1, Issues 41-63, p. 1020;
https://books.google.co.uk/books?id=h2ZMAAAAYAAJ&pg=PA1020&dq=march+19+1847+aurora+london&hl=en&sa=X&ved=0ahUKEwjD1P_y0dvnAhXZUhUIHXmjDGMQ6AEIOjAC#v=onepage&q&f=false

188   Zdenek Kopal, *The Moon*, Reidel, Dordrecht, 1969, pp. 425-437, and Note p. 487-488, Ch. 22.;
https://books.google.co.uk/books?id=wrPvCAAAQBAJ&pg=PA9&dq=herschel+moon+volcano&source=gbs_toc_r&cad=4#v=onepage&q&f=false

189   Arlin P. S. Crotts, "Lunar Outgassing, Transient Phenomena and The Return to The Moon, I: Existing Data," (2007); http://arxiv.org/pdf/0706.3949v1.pdf

190   http://www.armaghplanet.com/blog/whatever-happened-to-transient-lunar-phenomena.html

CHAPTER 7 – **The Case of the Missing Eclipse**

In Chapter 6 we heard how Rev. Rankin and Prof. Chevalier saw odd lights and glows on the moon whilst a spectacular aurora was disrupting telegraph wires across England on March 19, 1847. Charles Fort believed that a lunar eclipse was in progress at the time, too. He was mistaken. But exactly one year to the day later, on March 19, 1848, an eclipse of the moon did occur – or rather, should have occurred. It went missing. And again an aurora was in progress.

Charles Fort cites "an extract from a letter from Mr. Forster, of Bruges . . . and another letter, from another astronomer, Walkey, who had made observations at Clyst St. Lawrence" concerning the extraordinary brightness and redness of the moon for an hour or so during the height of the total eclipse, when it should have been completely in the shadow of the Earth.[191] Fort hinted at an explanation – that the moon was really much further away than supposed, so that the Earth's shadow had "fallen short" – remarking correctly that this would make "much trouble for astronomers", whilst, amusingly, failing to notice the trouble it made for his own theory, based on the Rankin/Chevalier observation of the previous year, that the moon was much *nearer* than supposed.

The article Fort quoted (Fig. 51) was headed "Remarkable Appearances during the total Eclipse of the Moon," and with good reason. According to Forster the moon was 3 times as bright as it ought to be and "of a deep red colour," and he had received a letter from the British Consul in Ghent asking for an explanation of the "blood-red" moon. Walkey compared it to the light from a furnace, "tinged a deep red," and thought it was "as perfect with light as if there had been no eclipse whatever" – an expression which Fort chose to take literally.[192] Indeed Walkey remarked that in observations of several lunar eclipses "never before did my eyes behold the moon positively giving *good* light."

The astronomer Walkey was Rev. C. E. Walkey, Rector of Clyst St. Lawrence, a village in East Devon, England. We find his eclipse observations reported occasionally in *Monthly Notices*.[193] But he is not much known.

---

191 Fort, *Damned*, p. 219, citing *Monthly Notices of the R. A. S.,* 8-132.

192 This is as good a place as any to mention Fort's missing *solar* eclipse of 1903. He quotes from Capt. Robert Falcon Scott's record of the event in Antarctica: "'There may have been an eclipse of the sun [on] Sept. 21, 1903, as the almanac said, but we should, none of us, have liked to swear to the fact.' This eclipse had been set down at nine-tenths of totality. The sky was overcast at the time." (Fort, *Damned*, pp. 219-220, citing *Voyage of the Discovery,* Macmillan, London, Vol. II, 1905, p. 215.) Now clearly this eclipse was seen, as scheduled, elsewhere on Earth (https://en.wikipedia.org/wiki/Solar_eclipse_of_September_21,_1903), therefore logically we should be looking for local circumstances that caused the effect reported by Scott. The first is that all day "a thick stratus cloud hung over our heads, and as the hours went by we were forced to abandon all hope of a clearance" (Robert Falcon Scott, *The Voyage of the Discovery*, Charles Scribner's sons, NY; Smith Elder & Co. London, Vol. II, p. 155). Add to this the fact that whilst 9/10th of totality sounds almost complete, the sun is very bright and 1/10th of full sunlight is a lot of light. A 90% eclipsed sun is still 40,000 times as bright as the full moon, for example. The time of maximum eclipse on July 21, 1903 was 04:40 UTC. Stellarium shows the maximum occurring only an hour before local sunset at White Island, Antarctica (the location of Scott's ship). The sun was only about 2.5° above the horizon at that moment and would have emerged completely from eclipse just as it was sinking below the horizon. Therefore, it isn't surprising they saw no clear sign of the eclipse. The effect under a thick overcast would be merely to bring on a slightly early dusk.

193 See, e.g., *MNRAS*, Vol. 8 (1847), 11.

Remarkable Appearances during the total Eclipse of the Moon on March 19, 1848.

Extract of a Letter from Mr. Forster, Bruges.

" I wish to call your attention to the fact which I have clearly ascertained, that during the whole of the late lunar eclipse of March 19, the shaded surface presented a luminosity quite unusual, probably about three times the intensity of the mean illumination of an eclipsed lunar disc. The light was of a deep red colour. During the totality of the eclipse, the light and dark places on the face of the moon could be almost as well made out as in an ordinary, dull moonlight night, and the deep red colour, when the sky was clearest, was very remarkable from the contrasted whiteness of the stars. My observations were made with different telescopes, but all presented the same appearance, and the remarkable luminosity struck every one. The British consul of Ghent, *who did not know that there was an eclipse*, wrote to me for an explanation of the blood-red colour of the moon at 9 o'clock.

" The sky was of unusual brilliancy, as often occurs between showers ; there was a bright aurora in the north, and a most magnificent meteor descended obliquely towards the north-west horizon about the time of the central eclipse. The western margin of the disc presented a rough, uneven appearance at this time. What would be the effect on the dark surface of the moon of extensive aurora borealis on our earth ?"

Mr. Walkey, who observed the eclipse at Clyst-St. Lawrence, near Collumpton, says the appearances were as usual till 20 minutes to 9. " At that period, and for the space of the next hour, instead of an eclipse, or the umbra of the earth being the cause of the *total* obscurity of the moon, the whole phase of that body became very quickly and *most beautifully illuminated*, and assumed the appearance of the glowing heat of fire from the furnace, rather tinged with a deep red. The above description I gave to the editor of one of the Exeter papers, and some one has attempted to solve the peculiarity of the appearance by speaking of the umbra and penumbra, which might have been the cause of it. But such a solution has nothing to do with the appearance, the whole disk of the moon being as perfect *with light* as if there had been *no eclipse whatever*.

" Having spoken of this appearance, I was informed by one or two individuals that they had seen, between twenty minutes to nine and twenty minutes to ten, a very luminous appearance of the aurora borealis. Now, it strikes me that the light reflected from this northern effulgence might have caused the *luminous appearance* of the moon in this part of the country at the time when it was under the perfect umbra of the earth in other portions of England.

" Many more than threescore years have passed with myself,

and during that period I have several times beheld an eclipse of the moon, but never before did my eyes behold the moon positively giving *good* light from its disk during a total eclipse. The phases of the moon perfectly corresponded with the authorised diagram up to the period of 8ʰ 40ᵐ and after 9ʰ 40ᵐ to the end of the eclipse."

Fig. 51. Forster, "Remarkable appearances during the total eclipse of the Moon on March 19, 1848," *Monthly Notices of the Royal Astronomical Society*, 8, pp. 132-133.[194]

Dr Thomas Forster of Bruges (1789–1860) is a different matter. He wrote numerous books on anatomy, medicine, meteorology, astronomy, philosophy and poetry.[195] He was also an educational theorist and pioneer animal rights advocate, serving as a Foreign Secretary (in Bruges) of the Animals' Friend Society, in between his "pursuits of the physical sciences." He had been a student at Cambridge with Herschel, Babbage, and Whewell, where he became convinced from an early age of "the sinfulness of invading unnecessarily the rights of animals".[196] He was modern, a progressive reformer, and yet a man of his time. He was a supporter of Francis Gall's phrenology (which even in its early-19thC hay-day was regarded

---

194 http://mnras.oxfordjournals.org/content/8/5/132.full.pdf+html
195 http://onlinebooks.library.upenn.edu/search.html
196 "Every species of cruelty and injustice towards them entails a vitious retaliation on ourselves, which is manifested in the social crimes by which we are surrounded; and that in fact, the neglect of our duties towards animals has been the cause of the principal evils suffered by man; according to that constant law of reaction which we call vindictive Justice." He argued that redressing this cruelty should be at the heart of public education, hoping thereby to "tame the destructive passions of man and give a new stability to the fabric of society." *A Collection of Letters on Early Education and its Influence in the Prevention of Crime*, by T. Forster, MB. FRAS. FLS., Hon. M. Med. Chir. Soc. Corresponding Memb. of the Acad. Sciences. Phil., Corr. Memb. of the Academie Royale etc. Honorary Foreign Secretary of the Animals Friend Society. 2nd Edition, Sherwood & Bowyer, London and Bruges, 1844.

with suspicion in some parts of Europe as a materialistic, atheistic novelty), and believed that the phases of the moon and the days of the week influenced the weather.[197]

Fort could actually have quoted numerous other contemporary sources about the lunar eclipse of March 19, 1848, many telling similar stories. And he could have quoted many more late 19th-century and early 20th-century discussions of it than the one book he mentioned.[198] All agree that it was a remarkable event. But the volume of material would have tended to undermine the sense of oddity, showing it less like an isolated fortean freak and more like what it was, an unusually ruddy eclipse belonging on a continuum of ecliptic ruddiness.

Today it is still widely cited as one of the best instances of this effect. The late Patrick Moore's *Data Book of Astronomy*, for example, confirms that it was "so 'bright' that lay observers refused to believe that an eclipse had happened at all."[199] But the phenomenon occurs regularly, in different degrees, and there are few astronomers today who believe that it is not well understood.

The cause is said to be analogous to the familiar reddening of the terrestrial atmosphere at sunset due to scattering out of the blue wavelengths. During a total lunar eclipse the moon "sees" the entire Earth with the sun hidden behind it, surrounded in effect by a ring of red sunset, the brightness of which varies from point to point and from time to time depending on two main factors: the cloudiness and dustiness of the atmosphere, affected mainly by things like volcanic eruptions and weather, perhaps also meteoric dust; and the refractivity of the atmosphere, which is controlled by the way its temperature varies with height. [200] If conditions are just right the amount of reddened light reaching the surface of the moon may be significant (see Fig. 52). The brightness and depth of red colouration is now measured by what is called the Danjon scale, proposed by the French astronomer André-Louis Danjon in 1921, which uses descriptors like "deep red," "brick-red" and "very bright copper-red."[201] There is no reason to believe that the March 1848 lunar eclipse was qualitatively different.

---

197 "Dr. Forster, of Bruges, well known as a meteorologist, declares that by the Journal kept by his grandfather, father, and self, ever since 1767, to the present time, whenever the new moon has fallen on a Saturday, the following twenty days have been wet and windy, in nineteen cases out of twenty." Timothy Harley, *Moon Lore*, 1885, p. 185, citing: *Folk-Lore; or, Manners and Customs of the North of England*, by M.A.D. Novo-Castro-sup, Tynan, 1850–1851, p.11; http://www.sacred-texts.com/astro/ml/ml18.htm.
198 George Frederick Chambers, *The Story of Eclipses,* George Newnes, London, 1902, pp. 192-193.
199 Patrick Moore & Robin Rees, *Patrick Moore's Data Book of Astronomy*, Cambridge University Press, Jan. 16, 2014, p. 44.
200 http://earthsky.org/space/why-does-the-moon-look-red-during-a-total-lunar-eclipse; http://www.timeanddate.com/eclipse/why-does-moon-look-red-lunar-eclipse.html
201 L=0: Very dark eclipse. Moon almost invisible, especially at mid-totality.
    L=1: Dark Eclipse, gray or brownish in coloration. Details distinguishable only with difficulty.
    L=2: Deep red or rust-colored eclipse. Very dark central shadow, outer edge of umbra relatively bright.
    L=3: Brick-red eclipse. Umbral shadow usually has a bright or yellow rim.
    L=4: Very bright copper-red or orange eclipse. Umbral shadow has a bluish, very bright rim.
Danjon, A., 'Relation entre l'éclairement de la Lune éclipsée et l'activité solaire,' *L'Astronomie*, Vol. 35 (1921), pp. 261-265; http://adsabs.harvard.edu/abs/1921LAstr..35..261D

Fig. 52. Total lunar eclipse imaged by Giuseppe Donatiello from Oria, Italy on January 21, 2019. Direct sunlight is being blocked by the Earth, and the only light reaching the moon is sunlight refracted by Earth's atmosphere, producing a reddish colour. [202]

However, this may not be the whole story. It is worth noting that part of Danjon's motivation for devising his scale in the first place had been to investigate a correlation which he believed to exist between eclipse brightness (measured by the sensitive new "cat's-eye photometer" of his own invention) and the ~11-year solar activity cycle – a correlation which, if real, could not be explained in the same way. And this brings us to Transient Lunar Phenomena (TLP).

In Chapter 6, "Lights on the Moon", we referred to modern photometric and polarimetric measurements of a small but unexplained light emission from the lunar surface which some studies have suggested may be caused by impact of high-energy particles from the sun. The Czech-born astronomer Zdeněk Kopal (1914–1993), a leading lunar expert,[203] was a champion of this research, having photographed anomalous glows himself from Pic-du-Midi Observatory in 1963. According to Kopal the correlation between eclipse brightness and solar activity detected by Danjon was confirmed and extended in later studies by De Vaucouleurs and Link between 1944 and 1965; moreover, other studies showed that the brightness even of the *un*eclipsed moon varied by as much as 10-20% over the cycle of solar activity, even though the change in solar luminosity is within only 1%.[204] Other studies by Fisher, Yamaguchi and Sekiguchi did not find a significant correlation. According to a recent overview the status of all this evidence "is not clear" because the statistical sample size is still too small, although the result of a comparison between the Earth's geomagnetic index (a global measure of disturbances correlated with solar activity) and eclipse brightness was positive.[205]

---

202 https://commons.wikimedia.org/wiki/File:Total_lunar_eclipse_on_January_21,_2019_(39862040333).jpg
203 Kopal held posts at Cambridge, Harvard and MIT, and as Professor of Astronomy at Manchester University he headed NASA's moon mapping effort for the Apollo program from 1958.
204 Zdenek Kopal, *An Introduction to the Study of the Moon*, Springer, 2013 (1966), Ch. 22, 'Luminescence of the Lunar Surface', p. 388.
205 John Westfall, William Sheehan, *Celestial Shadows: Eclipses, Transits, and Occultations*, Astrophysics and Space Science Library, Springer, Vol. 410 (2014), pp. 68-69.

So, it is interesting that both Walkey and Forster in 1848 commented independently on a vivid display of aurora borealis that was visible at the time of the eclipse – auroral glows being of course caused by the arrival of energetic particles from the sun. It would be fair to say that this display was somewhat unusual owing to the rather low latitudes of the observers, in Devon and Belgium respectively, consistent with the fact that the date was near the peak of Solar Cycle 9 (1843–1855), the maximum sunspot number occurring just a couple of weeks later in February 1848.[206] This is a suggestive coincidence. We are reminded of Herschel and the glowing "volcanoes" of 1787 which coincided with a low-latitude aurora, just a few days before a sunspot maximum;[207] and of the lunar glows seen by Rankin and Chevalier during the intense solar storm of March 1847.

A correlation between bright/red lunar eclipses and terrestrial aurorae had been noted long before Danjon conceived his eclipse scale. Ahead of a total eclipse in 1906, S. J. Johnson[208] advised readers of *The Observatory* to be alert for unusual effects because it was expected to coincide with the peak activity of Solar cycle 14 (1902–1913; sunspot maximum February 1906). Looking back at previous red eclipses, Johnson singled out as the "best authenticated" examples those in "April 1623, December 1703, and 19 March, 1848," and argued that auroral displays were either reported or were at least likely on each date, adding to his list the total lunar eclipse of December 1898 which was "of a somewhat bright character, far more so than usual," on a date coinciding with one of only four nights in that year when an aurora was seen (although "faint").[209]

Fort could have been aware of this issue when writing *The Book of the Damned*, yet seems not to have been. His mention of the eclipse aurora of 1848 presumes the unlikely idea that the terrestrial aurora itself illuminated the moon; but he was dismissive of this: "It is said that at the time there had been an aurora borealis, which might have caused the luminosity, without a datum that such an effect, by an aurora, had ever been observed upon the moon."

The anecdotal data are at least intriguing coincidences, given some force by the statistical analyses of Danjon, De Vaucouleurs and others, and by a few modern observations including some instrument measurements and photographs.

It has yet to be proved, but in this case perhaps Fort missed a trick.

---

206   There were some exceptional displays later that year: in Lancashire in October "the most magnificent for many years" was seen; and notably on November 17 the Virgin Islands experienced a rare "lurid" show at the very low latitude of 17° 44' 32" simultaneous with "an aurora of extraordinary brilliancy" in the north of the British Isles. See: Rev. A. Weld, 'Account of the aurora borealis as seen at Stonyhurst Observatory, October 1848,' *Philosophical Magazine*, Series 3, Vol. 33 (1848), Issue 223; Sir Andrew Lang, 'On the aurora borealis of Nov. 17, 1848,' *Monthly Notices of the Royal Astronomical Society*, Vol. 9, p. 148.

207   http://www.daviddarling.info/encyclopedia/T/TLP.html; *Kopal, Z. (December 1966), "Lunar flares," Astronomical Society of the Pacific Leaflets 9: 401-408.*

208   Rev. S. J. Johnson, FRAS, was Vicar of Melplash, near Bridport, Dorset. He was an active meteor observer and contributed many observations to the BAA; http://www.britastro.org/vss/JBAA%20124-2%20Shears%20Astbury.pdf.

209   Johnson, S. J., 'Bright lunar eclipses,' *The Observatory*, Vol. 26 (1903), pp. 358-359; http://adsabs.harvard.edu/full/1903Obs....26..358J

CHAPTER 8 – **Martian Lights and Clouds**

A light-reflecting body, or a bright spot near Mars: seen Nov. 25, 1894, by Prof. Pickering and others, at the Lowell Observatory, above an unilluminated part of Mars – self-luminous, it would seem – thought to have been a cloud – but estimated to have been about twenty miles away from the planet. [210]

Actually, the bright blob or streak was seen twice, on two successive days, November 25 & 26. And there is no reason to think that it was self-luminous. A. E. Douglass' article in the *Astrophysical Journal* (the source referred to by Fort and reproduced here as Fig. 53), tabulates heights and distances on the basis that it was illuminated by the sun.

Andrew Ellicott Douglass (1867–1962) was an assistant to the MIT-educated astronomer William Henry Pickering (1858–1938), who had been lured away from an assistant professorship at Harvard by wealthy amateur enthusiast Percival Lowell with the offer to found an observatory. Pickering and Douglas together designed and established the eponymous Lowell Observatory at Flagstaff, equipped initially with 18-inch and 12-inch refractors. In 1894 the operation was brand new, but both men were very experienced, having built other observatories and amassed years at the telescope eyepiece studying nebulae, the sun and planets. [211]

Everything about the Martian blob seen that November suggests that Pickering and Douglass were correct to interpret it as a cloud. On each sighting it was close to, and aligned with, the sunrise terminator or the line between night and day. This is exactly the position in which a high cloud would be expected to be revealed against the dark surface, catching the sunlight just before the Martian dawn. The intermittent fading on the second night further suggests a cloud. Both ice clouds and sand clouds are now well-known features of the Martian sky. If a point of interest remains concerning the 1894 events it is perhaps the unusual height of the cloud measured by Douglass and Pickering.

---

210 Fort, *Damned*, p. 187, citing *Astrophysical Journal*, 1, 127.
211 Pickering was also a pioneer astrophotographer – he would later discover the 9th moon of Saturn by means of photography – and he produced some of the earliest pictures of Mars, a planet with which he became especially identified at Lowell Observatory as a result of the supposed *canali* of Mars earlier championed by himself, Douglass, Schiaparelli and others. Douglass later became sceptical of the Martian canals. He left for a professorship at the University of Arizona where he pursued his 1894 discovery of a correlation between sunspots and tree rings, founding the new discipline of dendrochronology. See: *New International Encyclopedia*, Vol. 18 (1918), p. 605; Martz, E. P., Jr., "Professor William H. Pickering – An Appreciation," *Popular Astronomy*, 46 (1938), p. 299;
http://adsabs.harvard.edu/full/1938PA.....46..299M ; https://en.wikipedia.org/wiki/A._E._Douglass

A CLOUD-LIKE SPOT ON THE TERMINATOR OF MARS.

By A. E. Douglass.

On November 25 and 26 a bright spot was seen in the unilluminated portion of Mars, to which, in my opinion, no other name than cloud can be applied. Its great height, size, and brilliancy, and, on the second evening, its singular fluctuations, render it of importance in the study of the Martian atmosphere.

I first saw it at $16^h 35^m$, G. M. T. of November 25, and made an estimate of its height. It seemed to be rapidly increasing in length in a direction parallel to the terminator at that point. Subsequent estimates of its height gave a different and greater value than at first, until its sudden disappearance at $17^h 6^m$ or perhaps a minute later. After once attaining its size, it seemed to remain with little change, presenting the appearance of a line 140 miles long by 40 miles wide at the center and lying parallel to the terminator, but separated from it by an apparent space of over 100 miles. It was generally yellowish in color, like the limb, but of less brilliancy than the center of the disk, though distinctly surpassing in that respect the adjacent terminator. I estimated it to have the brilliancy of the light areas of the disk at a distance of 9° from the terminator. In one view it appeared to be a very small whitish point (Observation 2, below), and I am inclined to think that there may have been a real diminution in its size at that moment. This idea is partly sustained by the following night's observations. At $16^h 54^m$ it was observed by Professor Pickering, whose estimate of its height is found in Observation 6, below. At $17^h 5^m$, after obtaining two readings of the micrometer screw for latitude, the seeing, which had been quite steadily at the figure 7 (on a scale of 10), dropped to 4, and in attempting the next setting I could not find the "cloud," although once before it had remained visible when the seeing dropped instantaneously to that figure. Nor did it reappear in the next half hour. This

127

with reference to a glass thread in the micrometer, whose diameter is $0''.9$. One-tenth of the thread, therefore, represented on Mars a little less than twenty-four miles. In Table I below the observed dimensions are given directly in miles. Column S gives the separation of the cloud from the terminator; W gives its width; H, its total height, and L, its length along the terminator. In the two final columns the longitude and latitude of the nearest point of the terminator are given. Table II gives various computed quantities.

TABLE I.

Date	Obser.	Time (G. M. T.)	S	W	H	L	Long. Term.	Lat.
Nov. 25	1	16^h 37.5^m	71	48	119		43.6	−32.5
"	2	39.0				142	44.0	"
"	3	41±	143		143		44.4	"
"	4	47.0	119	58	177		45.9	"
"	5	49.1			166	142	46.3	"
"	6	55.0	119				47.9	"
Nov. 26	7	17 23.0	96	24	120		43.0	−23.3
"	8	43.0			118		47.8	"
"	9	49.3	49	48	97		49.4	"

TABLE II.

Obser.	Min. Ht. Bottom	Long.	Dist. Term.	Vert. Ht. Top	Min. Ht. Top	Long.	Dist. Term.	Lat.
1	6	48.7	159	58	17	51.9	263	−30.3
2								"
3	24	54.5	323	24	24	54.5	323	"
4	17	54.2	263	79	38	58.2	399	"
5					34	58.0	376	"
6	17	56.2	263					"
7	11	49.1	211	37	16	50.5	263	−21.5
8					16	55.2	259	"
9	3	52.6	107	56	11	55.5	211	"

In Table II, column 1 gives the number of the observation, column 2, the height at which the shadow of the planet will strike a cloud presenting the observed separation; column 3 gives the surface longitude for such a point; column 4 gives the tangential distance in miles of such a point from the terminator;

sudden disappearance without any previous lessening of its height above the terminator or of its size, made its cloud character unmistakable, since a mountain beyond the sunrise terminator must either constantly decrease in height, or soon join to the illuminated disk.

A subsequent computation showed that this phenomenon took place over the southern part of Schiaparelli's Protei Regio. Other reasons lead me to think, however, that he has placed that island some 5° too far south.

On November 26 the cloud promptly appeared at $17^h 15^m$ G. M. T., but nearly 9° farther north. Instead of remaining continuously visible it dissipated and re-formed at irregular intervals. The first appearance lasted sixteen minutes. After somewhat over four minutes had passed it reappeared momentarily, and six minutes elapsed before it appeared again, lasting then but two and one-half minutes. Then followed an absence of three minutes, presence for two minutes, absence for three minutes, presence one minute, and a final brief appearance eight minutes later at $18^h 1^m$. Its presence was suspected five minutes before that hour, and again at $18^h 11^m$, but with great uncertainty.

At this time it presented in general the same characteristics as the night before, though its appearances were too brief to permit such careful observations as were hoped for. The seeing, too, was not so good as before, varying from 4 to 7, and if the cloud happened to appear under the former figure, its observation was difficult. It is needless to remark that under such conditions it was impossible to observe its appearance or disappearance to the second. In general, it seemed to exhibit a less elevation than the night before. A careful estimate of its latitude placed it precisely at the center of the terminator. I believe these latitude observations, though made rapidly, cannot be subject to an error greater than 2°, and probably less than 1°. On November 27 at 18^h I searched for the cloud, but was not rewarded by finding any trace of it.

Estimates of the size and height of this cloud were made

130   A. E. DOUGLASS

column 5 gives the total height the cloud would have if all its apparent height were extended vertically over this point; column 6 gives the least possible height the top could have and still be illuminated by the Sun; columns 7 and 8 give the longitude of this point and distance from the terminator, and column 9 gives the latitude.

In order to get an idea of the mean height of this cloud, we may take the mean of column 4 and average it with the mean of column 8, obtaining 260 miles. This gives us an elevation above the surface of between 16 and 17 miles. In this process we have taken the apparent center of the cloud, and have assumed the seeing to have no influence. We obtain, therefore, the smallest possible mean height of the center of the cloud. If we assume that the seeing was not perfect, its effect would be to lessen the separation, but not to change the total height. Supposing, for example, that the apparent extension of the cloud was due to poor seeing enlarging a point, then our terminator distance would be 299 miles, and our minimum elevation 22 miles. Therefore we can assume 20 miles to be the smallest probable mean elevation of this cloud. The average height of our cirrus clouds is five and one-half miles.

One more idea requires mention, namely, the movement of this cloud in latitude. From the extreme rarity of such an occurrence I am inclined to connect intimately the appearances of the two evenings, and consider them as due to one source, presumably a large body of air moving northward. Such an advance would be at the rate of 13.1 miles per hour.

Lowell Observatory,
December 10, 1894.

Fig. 53. A. E. Douglass, "A cloud-like spot on the terminator of Mars," *Astrophysical Journal*, 1 (1895), pp. 127-130. [212]

---

[212] http://articles.adsabs.harvard.edu/full/1895ApJ.....1..127D

Nine years later in 1903 we have another, quite similar "cloud" seen on Mars, again from the Lowell Observatory, this time by Lowell himself and the notable astronomer Vesto Melvin Slipher (1875–1969), whose important spectroscopic discoveries included planetary periods, planetary atmospheres, the rotation of spiral galaxies, and (before Hubble) the redshifts revealing that most of the galaxies are flying away from us.[213] Fort writes:

> In the first *Bulletin* issued by the Lowell Observatory, in 1903, Prof. Lowell describes a body that was seen on the terminator of Mars, May 20, 1903. On May 27, it was "suspected." If still there, it had moved, we are told, about 300 miles – "probably a dust cloud."

PROJECTION ON MARS.

On May 25th at 15ʰ 34ᵐ G. M. T., Mr. V. M. Slipher noticed a large projection about half way down the terminator of the planet. He at once notified me and we then proceeded to observe it by turns.

What first impressed me was its size. This, both in length and height, was excessive. The projection consisted of a long band of light, a little north of the centre of the arc of the phase ellipse, lying parallel to the terminator but parted from it by a dark line half the band's own width. To this effect I made a sketch of it at 15ʰ 37ᵐ. The next thing to strike the eye was its color. This was not white nor whiteish but ochre-orange, closely assimilated in tint to the subjacent parts of the disk, the region to the north and west of the western end of the Deuteronilus. Such distinctive complexion it kept throughout the time it was visible. Coincidentally Baltia, then close on the terminator and north of the projection, showed white. The seeing was 5 on a scale of 10—sufficiently good to disclose the Phison and Euphrates double—the power 310 and the aperture that of the 24-inch.

As soon as possible micrometric measures were begun of its position and length, the position angle taken being that of the tangent to the terminator at the point directly under the projection. For such tangent, together with the projection's distance from the disk, furnishes all the data necessary to determine its location. Measures of this angle were repeated at intervals during the time of visibility.

At 15ʰ 41ᵐ the separation of the projection from the terminator seemed to have sensibly lessened and I recorded it in another sketch. The whole projection appeared to have moved bodily in. At 51ᵐ, however, it seemed higher again but then advanced rapidly toward the disk, for by 55ᵐ only the tip of it could be seen. Thus it showed for some minutes, being last seen for certain at 16ʰ 8ᵐ and vanishing completely after 16ʰ 10ᵐ.

My measures and notes were as follows, where P. A. denotes the position angle of the tangent to the terminator as above described:

15ʰ 37ᵐ Projection on terminator—found about five minutes before by Mr. Slipher. The projection is long and is separated from the terminator by a dark line. (Drawing.)

41 P. A. 200.°4 along terminator.
44 Projection less separated from terminator. (Drawing.)
48 P. A. Projection 199.°9.
51 Length projection .0.″92; now seems higher again.
55 Just about gone; only the tip showing apparently. No striking separation now.

16ʰ 10ᵐ P. A. Projection 199.°8; only suspected by glimpses; surely seen last at 16ʰ 8ᵐ.

Impression that projection had moved toward north as regards Deuteronilus.

During the course of the observation a 12-in. diaphragm was tried once but in this case without gain. At the same time Mr. Slipher's measures were these:

15ʰ 42ᵐ (?) P. A. Projection 203.°7.
45 P. A. Projection 204.°0.
Length 1.″58.
52 P. A. Projection 201.°0.

Of the apparent perpendicular distance of the top of the projection from the terminator our respective estimates were:

By Mr. Slipher, 0.067 of the radius of the disk.
By me, 0.075 of the radius of the disk.

These estimates were got from measurements of our drawings and from remembrance of the

---

213 John A. Peacock, "Slipher, galaxies, and cosmological velocity fields," in: M. J. Way & D. Hunter (eds), *Origins of the Expanding Universe:1912–1932*, Proceedings of Centenary meeting (2012), ASP Conf. Ser., Vol. 471 http://arxiv.org/abs/1301.7286 ; http://www.roe.ac.uk/~jap/slipher/; https://en.wikipedia.org/wiki/Vesto_Slipher

size of the projection as compared with the size of the disk.

To find from these data the position of the projection upon the planet we may proceed as follows: We shall first determine the height of the highest point of the projection above the planet's surface.

Taking the centre of the disk for origin and the minor axis of the phase ellipse for the axis of x,

let d=perpendicular from the projection upon the terminator.

d_1=distance to the terminator perpendicular to the phase axis.

r=distance from the centre of the disk to the foot of the perpendicular d.

t=equal distance of the projection from the centre.

ψ=angle between r and t.

χ=exterior angle between d and r.

A=phase latitude of the tip, or its latitude in the auxiliary circle to the phase ellipse.

ϕ=angle between the tangent to the terminator under the projection and the major axis of the ellipse.

a=radius of the disk, in seconds of arc.

a_0=radius of the disk in miles.

h_1=height of the projection in the plane of the circle of its phase latitude.

h=its true height.

ξ_1=angle in the plane of the phase latitude circle between the tip of the projection and the point on the terminator.

ξ=same in the plane passing through the origin, the observer and the tip.

θ=angle between r and the axis of x.

x and y the coordinates of the foot of d.

x_1 and y_1 those of the foot of d_1.

E=angle of the phase.

P=position angle of the polar axis.

Q=position angle of the phase equator.

B=latitude of the centre of the disk.

λ=longitude of the centre of the disk.

By a property of the ellipse we have

$$\tan\theta = -\frac{\tan\phi}{\cos^2 E}$$

also

$$r^2 = \frac{1}{\sin^2\theta + \sec^2 E \cos^2\theta}$$

Then in the triangle made by r, d and t we have

$$t^2 = d^2 + r^2 + 2dr\cos\chi$$

and

$$\chi = \theta - \phi$$

whence we can find y_1, d_1 and then A since

$$\sin A = \frac{y_1}{a}$$

Now

$$\tan\xi_1 = \frac{d_1}{\sin E . a \cos A}$$

and

$$h_1 = (\sec\xi_1 - 1) \, a_0 . \cos A$$

then since

$$a^2 = (a+h)^2 + h_1^2 - 2(a+h) h_1 \cos A$$

we find h.

Since the height of the projection is always small with regard to the radius of the disk we may take

$$d_1 = \frac{d}{\cos\phi} \quad \text{approx.}$$

and

$$\tan\xi_1 = \frac{d}{\cos\phi \sin E . a . \cos A} \quad \text{approx.}$$

and

$$h = (\sec\xi_1 - 1) \, a_0 . \cos^2 A \quad \text{approx.}$$

If, as in the present case the projection is nearly on the phase equator, the process admits of still greater simplification. For then both ϕ and A become small and

$$\tan\xi = \frac{d}{a \sin E} \quad \text{approx.}$$

and

$$h = (\sec\xi - 1) a_0 \quad \text{approx.}$$

In the present instance the height distance from my estimate is

$$h = 17 \text{ miles.}$$

From Mr. Slipher's

$$h = 14 \text{ miles.}$$

We can now find the position. Were the body causing the projection upon the surface of the sphere, with radius unity, we should have t equal to the sine of the angle from the centre of the disk to the tip of the projection. Since in reality the projection is raised above the surface it may be considered to be upon the surface of another sphere concentric with the first and of radius $a+h$. The point directly under it will not, therefore, be where the tip appears. But since codirectional lines from the same point, in this case the common centre of the two spheres, are altered in the ratio of their length, however projected, we have for the point upon the planet's surface directly under the projection a distance which we will call p.

$$p = \frac{a}{a+h} t$$

The angle between its direction and that to the planet's pole or γ is

$$\gamma = Q - P - \theta + \psi$$

while the distance in angular measure to that pole

is the colatitude of the centre. We thus have two sides and the included angle of a spherical triangle given from which to find the colatitude of the point or the third side and the lower angle or the longitude of the point from the centre of the disk.

Thus calculated the positions of the projection at the several moments when the measures were taken prove to be as subjoined.

G. M. Time	Latitude	Longitude
May 26, 15ʰ 41ᵐ	18° 31' N	39° 45'
48	19 44 "	39 59
16 10	21 24 "	40 33

From the successive positions of the centre of the projection it appears that that centre changed its place during the time of its visibility. It was three degrees farther north and three-quarters of a degree farther west at the end of the observations than it had been at their beginning. Such shift could be due to either of two causes. Bodily transference over the planet's surface would account for it; or obliquity of tilt of the projection's medial line to the terminator would produce a like effect. To which of the two possible causes the result was to be attributed was conclusively shown by the observations of the next day. It is worth noticing that the shift was recorded in the notes as impressing itself upon the eye apart from the measures and confirmatory of them.

At 15ʰ 51ᵐ I measured the length of the projection along the terminator and found it to be 0.″92. If we allow 0.″15 for irradiation this makes it 0.″77. Now the diameter of the disk at the time was 10.″76 according to Mr. Crommelin's ephemeris which takes the value to be 9.″30 at distance unity. Mr. Slipher's measure makes it greater, but as his estimates from his drawing makes it less we may, perhaps, consider the above as a fair measure. We have, then, for its value in degrees upon the planet's surface and in miles respectively:

Length of projection = 8.°2 = 300 miles.

On the next evening, May 27th, the return of the projection's longitudes off the terminator was duly awaited. They were due about 38ᵐ later than on the preceding night, but in order that if the projection had moved to the eastward in the interval it might also be caught, observations were begun some time beforehand. My notes and measures read as follows:

15ʰ 40ᵐ Cannot certainly see anything on terminator, though I can suspect at times something at its centre but cannot be sure. Seeing 3.

44½ Suspect something just below centre of terminator.

52 Distinctly suspicious.

58 Certainly have seen a small projection. P. A. 195.°8. Seeing 4.

16 3 Thought to see it again.

5 P. A. 196.°6, had previously thought it higher (up terminator). Were it anything like that of last night it must certainly have been seen.

17 Can see nothing on terminator. Seeing a good 5.

27 Suspect projection again but cannot be sure. P. A. 196.°2. Have been observing about half the time.

16 39 No projection visible. Seeing 3.

40 No projection visible. Seeing 4.

41 No projection visible. Seeing 4.

44 No projection visible.

At 16ʰ 15ᵐ I made a drawing of the whole planet under seeing as good as on the night before, using an 18-inch diaphragm upon the 24-inch objective, which diaphragm was also employed throughout the observations recorded above.

Mr. Slipher, who observed with me by turns, could not detect any projection.

From these observations it is at once evident that the something which caused the projection of May 26th, had ceased to exist in situ and in size on May 27th. It had changed its place as the position angles show and had greatly diminished in extent during the twenty-four hours elapsed. For the position of the terminator with regard to the surface was substantially the same as on the day before. Q-P having changed in the interval only +0.°13, B−0.°02 and E+0.°29. The chief effect of these slight alterations of phase aspect would have been to delay the advent of the projection by about one minute of time.

If we take now the mean of the two measures of the position angle at 15ʰ 58ᵐ and 16ʰ 5ᵐ, we find for the position of the tip of the projection at 16ʰ 3ᵐ.

G. M. T.	Latitude	Longitude
May 27, 16ʰ 3ᵐ	25° 29' N	31° 43'
and 16 27	25 45 "	36 51

Comparing these positions with those of May 26th, we see that the object causing the projection shifted its place over the surface of the planet from

latitude 18° 31' N longitude 39° 45' on May 26th, to latitude 25° 29' N longitude 31° 43' on May 27th,

taking the time, of greatest apparition on both occasions. It, therefore, moved 7° in latitude and 8° in longitude in the twenty-four hours, or 390 miles, at the rate of sixteen miles an hour. From this we infer: First, that it was not a mountain or mountains illuminated by the sun; and, second, that it was what alone fits the observations, an enormous cloud travelling northeast and dissipating as it went.

Turning now from the observations of May 27th to those of May 26th, with the recognition of the rate of shift deduced from this comparison of the two sets, we see that the change of place recorded by the first night's observations is to be ascribed to the second of the two possible suppositions mentioned in their discussion, or to the form and orientation of the cloud. Its longer axis lay E by S and W by N. Its axis lay, then, roughly speaking, at right angles to the direction of its motion. This is further made evident by the measures of May 27th in which the same tilt of the cloud's axis to the meridians is disclosed.

We shall now see that Mr. Slipher's observations tell the same tale. If we deduce from his measures, as has been done by Mr. Lampland, the resulting positions of the apparent centre of the projection at different times on May 26th, we find as follows:

G. M. T.	Latitude	Longitude
15^h 42^m	14° 52′ N	38° 2′
45	14 58 "	36 55
52	19 8 "	38 21

Here again is evident a tilt of the axis of the projection to the meridians, such that the following end lay farther north and farther west than the preceding end.

It is of interest to inquire under what conditions, diurnal and seasonal, the cloud came into being. As to the time of day, the terminator in question was the sunrise one. The cloud, therefore, was first seen when it was half an hour before sunrise upon its part of the planet, and continued to be visible up to the rising of the sun. The place was within the tropics, in the desert region to the south of the Lacus Niliacus. With regard to the Martian season of the year it was, in this the northern hemisphere of the planet, at the time, according to the data of Crommelin's excellent ephemeris, what corresponds to the first of August with us and the sun was overhead in latitude 18.°7′ N. The cloud, then, when first seen was almost exactly under the sun. It then travelled north, dissipating as it went, and was practically dissolved again by the time it had reached 25° N latitude.

Finally its color leads me to believe it not a cloud of water-vapor but a cloud of dust. Other phenomena of the planet bear out this supposition.

On May 28th no trace of it could be perceived by Mr. Slipher.

PERCIVAL LOWELL.

Flagstaff, Arizona, June, 1903.

Fig. 54. Percival Lowell, "Projection on Mars," *Lowell Observatory Bulletin,* No.1 (1903), pp. 1-4.[214]

Again, Fort makes a mistake with the date. The "projection" was not first seen on May 20, 1903. Annotator "Mr. X"[215] corrects this to "May 25, 1903," but in so doing inadvertently passes on another error, this time from Lowell's own article which does indeed give May 25 in the introduction but has May 26 everywhere else. May 26 appears to be correct (see Fig. 54). Fort also gives 300 miles as the distance moved, but this was actually the length of the blob, which moved an estimated 390 miles.

The blob seen by Pickering and Douglass in 1894, and this one in 1903, were described by Fort as, respectively, "a body" and "a light-reflecting body." But both were clearly clouds in the Martian atmosphere. Both were close to the morning terminator, in a position to suggest a high cloud illuminated by the sun a little before local sunrise. Both moved and dissipated at a speed and in a manner suggesting a cloud driven by Martian winds, and both were identified by the observers as clouds. The 1894 cloud had a mean height of over 20 miles and was "yellowish in colour, like the limb." The 1903 cloud also had the same ochre colouration as the Martian surface, rising up to 17 miles in height, and Lowell concluded it was an enormous dust storm.

Neither event would be considered abnormal today. Observations from Mars orbiters have confirmed the common presence of dust clouds and carbon dioxide/water ice clouds at much greater heights, up to 80 km (50 miles) and sometimes even 100 km (60 miles).[216, 217] These

214 http://babel.hathitrust.org/cgi/pt?id=coo.31924093073454;view=1up;seq=9
215 www.resologist.net
216 http://hirise.lpl.arizona.edu/ESP_034342_1315

are much higher than clouds on Earth. The reason for this is the low Martian gravity, which allows the thin atmosphere to expand to a much greater depth.

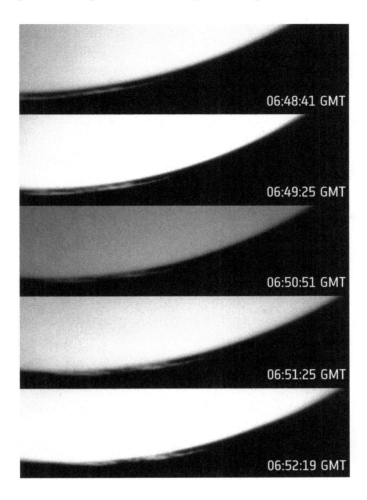

Fig. 55. A limb-cloud event photographed by Mars Express on December 15, 2009, above the Martian equator. The cloud reached an altitude of 25 miles (40 kilometres) and was 516 miles (830 km) across. The date, close to the northern spring equinox, suggests the cloud was a condensate of water-ice particles (image credit: ESA, CC BY-SA 3.0 IGO).[218]

On the other hand, this doesn't mean all cloud-like effects in the Martian atmosphere are understood or that all historical observations by Earth-based telescopes can be dumped as antiquated and irrelevant. Far from it.

In March 2012 a mysterious "cloud" that puzzled experts was observed blooming high into the atmosphere of the red planet – not by NASA spacecraft but by amateur astronomers on Earth who collaborated to obtain series of photographs of the event. Like the clouds of 1894 and 1903 this one, too, was seen close to the morning terminator, but it recurred for 10 days. And when the data were analysed by planetary scientists it was found that the plume

217 https://www.dailymail.co.uk/sciencetech/article-6330033/Mysterious-900-MILE-long-plume-cloud-spotted-surface-Mars-near-giant-volcano.html ; https://www.space.com/38556-martian-clouds-mars-express-photos.html ; https://planete-mars.com/la-webcam-de-mars-express/
218 https://www.space.com/38556-martian-clouds-mars-express-photos.html

rose about 200-250 km (125-155 miles) above the surface, well over twice the height of any previously known clouds.

Archived images taken by the Hubble space telescope were searched, and similar phenomena were found, dating from 1997. Finally reporting in 2014, the experts admitted they were puzzled. The brightness pattern and spectral properties might be consistent with ice crystals, or a bright aurora; but ice crystals should not have been able to form anywhere near such a height, and an aurora would need to be 1000 times as intense as any on Earth to account for the brightness. These hypotheses are the "most plausible," they concluded, but still "seem impossible insofar as they challenge our current knowledge."[219]

Then in early 2015 came news that the Mars orbiter spacecraft MAVEN had discovered more mysteries. Over Christmas 2014 an unprecedented auroral glow spread around Mars' northern hemisphere for several days, coinciding with the arrival of a solar particle burst. The surprise was how deep this aurora – naturally dubbed the Christmas Lights – penetrated into the thin atmosphere, and the brightness of the ultraviolet emission detected by MAVEN. But that was not all. MAVEN also detected a huge dust plume at a height never suspected before – so high, in fact, as to reach into space, the bulk lying between 90 and 185 miles (150-300 km) but rising even above 620 miles (1,000 km). With space sources including Mars' moons ruled unlikely, its probable origin was thought to be the planet's surface. But how it got into space was unexplained.[220]

Neither of these phenomena was thought at the time to be related to the unexplained plume detected in 2012. However, in 2016 a paper reporting on plasma and solar wind measurements collected in 2012 by the Mars Express orbiter found evidence that the plume had coincided with a large coronal mass ejection (CME) from the Sun impacting the Martian atmosphere. The report's authors conjectured that the hurtling CME perturbed the plasma and magnetic fields in the planet's ionosphere, causing electrically charged dust and ice grains in the upper atmosphere to be lofted even higher and ultimately into space. [221] Such events ought to be quite rare. It is suggestive that the only previous such plume, seen by the Hubble Space Telescope in May 1997, had occurred at the time another CME was striking the Earth (unfortunately information about concurrent space weather effects on Mars was not available). [222]

The last and most recent Mars phenomenon in *The Book of the Damned* concerns "Very conspicuous and brilliant spots seen on the disk of Mars, Oct. and Nov., 1911." [223] We checked the original source and this precis is accurate enough. Latimer J. Wilson describes[224] "numerous light spots" seen during that opposition of Mars; but when he says that "certain

---

219 Numerous sources, see e.g., http://scitechdaily.com/extremely-high-altitude-plume-mars/; http://www.popularmechanics.com/space/moon-mars/a14107/what-is-this-mystery-cloud-on-mars/

220 http://news.nationalgeographic.com/2015/03/150318-mars-maven-dust-aurora-cloud-space-astronomy/; http://astronomynow.com/2015/03/19/mysterious-martian-dust-cloud-and-aurora-detected-by-nasa-spacecraft/

221 D. J. Andrews, *et al.*, 'Plasma observations during the Mars atmospheric "plume" event of March–April 2012', *JGR Space Physics*, Vol. 121, No. 4, April 2016, pp. 3139-3154; https://agupubs.onlinelibrary.wiley.com/doi/10.1002/2015JA022023

222 https://www.universetoday.com/129106/space-weather-causing-martian-atmospherics/

223 Fort *Damned*, p. 187, citing *Popular Astronomy*, Vol. 19, No. 10.

224 Latimer J. Wilson, 'Mars as seen with an 11-inch reflector,' *Popular Astronomy*, 19 (1911), p. 627; http://articles.adsabs.harvard.edu//full/1911PA.....19..627W/0000627.000.html

parts of the disc of Mars seem to be subject to the formation of very conspicuous and brilliant white spots" it does not suggest anything more remarkable than changing reflectivity of certain regions of the planet's surface. Of the four examples of "extraordinary white spots" specified in Latimer's letter, one was the unusual extent of a white area "on the northern cap" and another was a fringe of white bordering "the southern part of the dark strip from the Primus Lucus to the Lucus Lucrinun." These are plainly not objects or bodies of any kind, but simply patches of carbon dioxide frost. Semi-permanent frost coats the poles, but transient frosts and ice fogs may form and dissipate daily at any latitude in deep valleys or on high peaks; and ice clouds of frozen carbon dioxide and/or water form high in the atmosphere. These are routinely observed from Earth in amateur and professional telescopes.[225] In Fort's day there was still much room for speculation about the nature of markings on Mars, but even then the presence of surface ice and reflective clouds was understood.

So there are still mysteries on Mars; and perhaps, somewhere among the thousands of historical records collected by Fort[226] and added to by his followers, lie clues to their cause, even if most of his anomalies, like those discussed here, will inevitably turn out to be blind alleys.

225 http://www.alpo-astronomy.org/mars/whiteareas.html
226 Many of which remain unpublished. See http://www.resologist.net/notes/

Part 4

Fire from the Deep

CHAPTER 9 – The Blue Fireball
CHAPTER 10 – *Victoria's* Secret
CHAPTER 11 – Vast Luminous Wheels
CHAPTER 12 – Paced by a Fireball off Cape Race

CHAPTER 9 – **The Blue Fireball**

Charles Fort imagined that things like vast luminous machines not only sailed our skies but also prowled beneath our oceans, sometimes bursting forth to terrify ship crews and damage their vessels.

The earliest of these oceanic extrusions in *The Book of the Damned* is an undated story he found in the London science and literature journal *The Athenæum*, published in 1848. At a meeting of the British Association for the Advancement of Science that summer, Fort reports, "Sir W. S. Harris said that he had recorded an account sent to him of a vessel toward which had whirled 'two wheels of fire, which the men described as rolling millstones of fire.' 'When they came near, an awful crash took place, the topmasts were shivered to pieces.' It is said that there was a strong sulphurous odor." [227]

Going to Fort's original source (Fig. 56) we find that he commits one error: W. S. Harris did not say it was "an account sent to him," only that he had "recorded a fact" from somewhere. He gives no hint as to where. There is little else to amplify Fort's brief account. No date, time, place or ship's name, no clue to help track down the story. And yet, the few details seem suspiciously familiar.

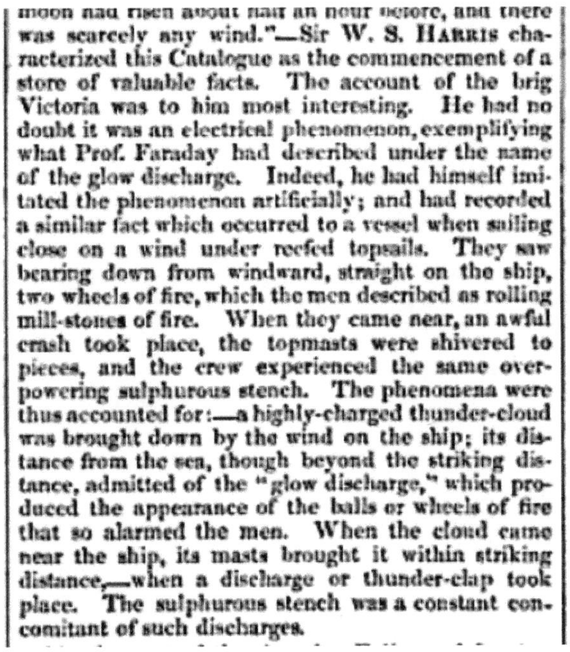

moon had risen about half an hour before, and there was scarcely any wind."—Sir W. S. HARRIS characterized this Catalogue as the commencement of a store of valuable facts. The account of the brig *Victoria* was to him most interesting. He had no doubt it was an electrical phenomenon, exemplifying what Prof. Faraday had described under the name of the glow discharge. Indeed, he had himself imitated the phenomenon artificially; and had recorded a similar fact which occurred to a vessel when sailing close on a wind under reefed topsails. They saw bearing down from windward, straight on the ship, two wheels of fire, which the men described as rolling mill-stones of fire. When they came near, an awful crash took place, the topmasts were shivered to pieces, and the crew experienced the same overpowering sulphurous stench. The phenomena were thus accounted for:—a highly-charged thunder-cloud was brought down by the wind on the ship; its distance from the sea, though beyond the striking distance, admitted of the "glow discharge," which produced the appearance of the balls or wheels of fire that so alarmed the men. When the cloud came near the ship, its masts brought it within striking distance,—when a discharge or thunder-clap took place. The sulphurous stench was a constant concomitant of such discharges.

Fig. 56. From "Eighteenth meeting of the British Association for the Advancement of Science," *The Athenæum*, #1086 (August 19, 1848), p. 833.

Already in 1752, the *Philosophical Transactions*, the journal of the Royal Society, had published an account of an incident that happened aboard a Royal Navy ship in 1749 (Fig. 57). All the details are similar: the reefed topsails; the approach from windward; the "rolling"

---

227 Fort, *Damned*, p. 265, citing *The Athenæum*, 1848-833.

motion; the likeness to a "millstone"; the explosion; the shattered topmast; and the stench of "sulphur". The only difference is that, according to the *Athenæum*, Harris recalled two "wheels" or "rolling mill-stones of fire" whereas in the 1749 case it was a single "Ball of blue Fire rolling . . . of the Bigness of a large Millstone".

Sir William Snow Harris FRS (1791–1867) was a Plymouth doctor who was nicknamed "Thunder & Lightning Harris" thanks to his research into electricity and his long battle to persuade the Admiralty to install lightning conductors on ships at sea.[228] He published in the *Philosophical Transactions* on this issue and spoke several times before the Royal Society, in whose library he, or a colleague, could well have encountered the 1749 report. Indeed, we found that very report detailed – accurately – in his book *Thunder Storms*, published 5 years earlier in 1843.[229] It seems likely that the erroneous "two wheels of fire" were introduced by the *Athenæum* writer.

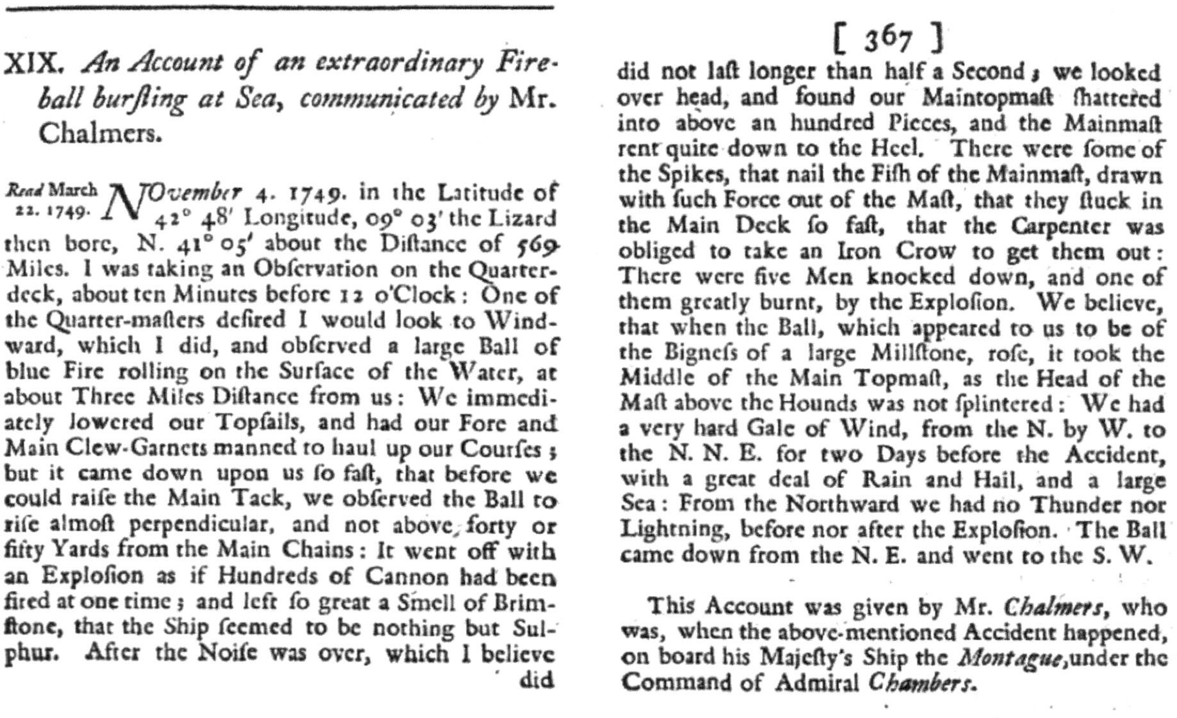

XIX. *An Account of an extraordinary Fire-ball bursting at Sea, communicated by* Mr. Chalmers.

Read March 22. 1749. NOvember 4. 1749. in the Latitude of 42° 48′ Longitude, 09° 03′ the Lizard then bore, N. 41° 05′ about the Distance of 569 Miles. I was taking an Observation on the Quarter-deck, about ten Minutes before 12 o'Clock: One of the Quarter-masters desired I would look to Wind-ward, which I did, and observed a large Ball of blue Fire rolling on the Surface of the Water, at about Three Miles Distance from us: We immediately lowered our Topsails, and had our Fore and Main Clew-Garnets manned to haul up our Courses; but it came down upon us so fast, that before we could raise the Main Tack, we observed the Ball to rise almost perpendicular, and not above forty or fifty Yards from the Main Chains: It went off with an Explosion as if Hundreds of Cannon had been fired at one time; and left so great a Smell of Brim-stone, that the Ship seemed to be nothing but Sul-phur. After the Noise was over, which I believe did

[367]

did not last longer than half a Second; we looked over head, and found our Maintopmast shattered into above an hundred Pieces, and the Mainmast rent quite down to the Heel. There were some of the Spikes, that nail the Fish of the Mainmast, drawn with such Force out of the Mast, that they stuck in the Main Deck so fast, that the Carpenter was obliged to take an Iron Crow to get them out: There were five Men knocked down, and one of them greatly burnt, by the Explosion. We believe, that when the Ball, which appeared to us to be of the Bigness of a large Millstone, rose, it took the Middle of the Main Topmast, as the Head of the Mast above the Hounds was not splintered: We had a very hard Gale of Wind, from the N. by W. to the N. N. E. for two Days before the Accident, with a great deal of Rain and Hail, and a large Sea: From the Northward we had no Thunder nor Lightning, before nor after the Explosion. The Ball came down from the N. E. and went to the S. W.

This Account was given by Mr. *Chalmers*, who was, when the above-mentioned Accident happened, on board his Majesty's Ship the *Montague*, under the Command of Admiral *Chambers*.

Fig. 57. *Philosophical Transactions* Vol. XLVI (1752), pp. 366-367.

Thanks in part to Charles Fort, this story is well known today and has been requoted in many books over the years. But until research in 2014 for the book *Return to Magonia* (co-authored by Martin Shough and Chris Aubeck) little real work had been done to verify provenance, check the facts and seek an explanation.[230]

The first problem was the ship's name. Most accounts gave it as HMS *Lizard*. But we could find no suitable ship called the *Lizard*. This is almost certainly a misinterpretation of

228 https://en.wikipedia.org/wiki/William_Snow_Harris

229 W. Snow Harris, *On the Nature of Thunderstorms*, J. W. Parker, London, 1843, pp. 36-37. Thanks to Kay Coggin, Magonia Exchange email group, for the lead.

230 *Return to Magonia*, Anomalist Books, 2015, Ch. 4, pp. 67-82.

Lizard Point (often referred to as "the Lizard"), a navigational seamark on the coast of Southwest England; and the only ship involved was HMS *Montague*, a 920-ton, 144-ft (43.9 m), 60-gun ship of the line, rebuilt from HMS *Lyme* in 1716,[231] which, we confirmed, had indeed been commanded during the 1740s by a Captain (presumably later Admiral) Chambers, as mentioned in the end note of the article in *Philosophical Transactions*.

A second problem is in the title of the report: "*An account of an extraordinary Fire ball bursting at Sea, communicated by* Mr. Chalmers, *Read* March 22, 1749." In the absence of a time machine, how could an account relating events from November 4, 1749 have been read to the Royal Society on March 22, 1749?

On finding that HMS *Montague* was broken up before the end of 1749, it is natural to suspect that the November 1749 date of the incident must be in error. But the solution lies in the change from the Julian calendar to the Gregorian calendar in 1752, the year in which the Society's *Transactions* was printed. Before that date, the English year began and ended on Lady Day, March 25, instead of January 1. Thus, the "March 22, 1749" Royal Society meeting was, in fact, on March 22, 1750, by our present reckoning, over four months after the date of the event.[232]

Mystery solved. But now we have a third problem: Where did this take place? The report says: "In the Latitude of 42° 48' Longitude, 09° 03' the Lizard then bore, N 41° 05' about the distance of 569 Miles," which sounds very clear. But the coordinates are ambiguous because we don't know if they are given in degrees S or N, E or W, and the bearing is not consistent.

The stated bearing and distance of the Lizard Point landmark in Cornwall evidently imply a N latitude, and, if taken as degrees measured clockwise, east of north, in the accustomed way, place the ship in the North Atlantic off the Iberian coast. However, the longitude of this position is nowhere near 09° 03', whether E or W of the Greenwich Meridian. Indeed, 09° 03'W is on land in Spain, and 09° 03'E is in the Mediterranean, about 10 km off the north coast of Corsica. The latter is at least in water; but measuring a bearing in degrees west of north (anticlockwise) is not conventional, and the use of the Lizard as a navigational mark – natural in the Channel Approaches of the North Atlantic – would be unintelligible in the Mediterranean.

We found the solution in a survey of pre-1850 Royal Navy logbooks compiled by Dr Clive Wilkinson of the Climatic Research Unit, University of East Anglia. Before the 1790s it was usual for noon longitudes to be logged in terms of degrees west of the last prominent landmark. "The meridian used is most often, though not always, the landmark recorded in the column following 'longitude'. This is the 'bearings and distance' column . . . The officer would often keep a daily record in this column of the bearing and distance to some landmark whose position was well established. This was often the most recent sighting of land and this landmark would provide a zero meridian."[233] When sailing out of the English Channel this

---

231 https://en.wikipedia.org/wiki/HMS_Montagu_(1660)

232 https://www.nottingham.ac.uk/manuscriptsandspecialcollections/researchguidance/introduction.aspx

233 Clive Wilkinson, *British Logbooks in UK Archives, 17th–19th Centuries – a survey of the range, selection and suitability of British logbooks and related documents for climatic research*, '2.1 The Early Royal Navy Logbook – Pre 1850', CRU Research Publication 12, University of East Anglia, 2012, p. 28; http://www.cru.uea.ac.uk/documents/421974/1301877/CRU_RP12.pdf/0eb44edd-b085-4617-a5dd-5a32e44b1e9a

would often be Lizard Point. Thus Mr Chalmers' report that "the Lizard then bore, N 41° 05' about the distance of 569 Miles", evidently taken from the ship's log, identifies a longitude equal to that of the Lizard, 5° 12'W, plus 9° 3'W = 14° 15' west of Greenwich, shown as position A in Fig. 58.

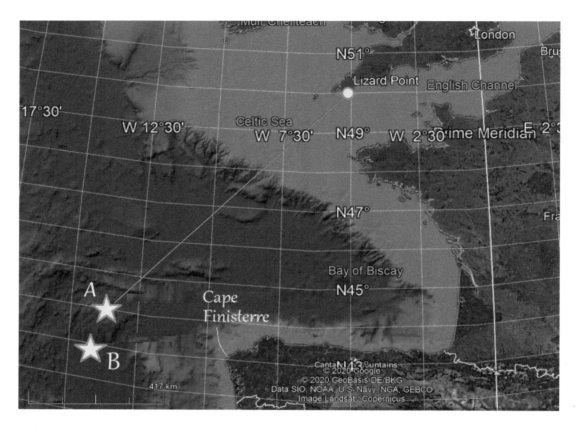

Fig. 58. The position of HMS *Montague* as indicated by: *A*, calculated distance and bearing from Lizard Point; *B*, latitude & longitude coordinates (map © 2020, Google Earth).

Making allowance for inaccuracies in dead reckoning,[234] common in these days before John Harrison's revolutionary "sea clock" had its first successful trials,[235] the discrepancy of about 90 miles between position A and position B – the latter identified by latitude/longitude coordinates, and arguably the least inaccurate since the latitude was probably determined by Mr Chalmers' noon "Observation" – is acceptable. So, we say with confidence that the blue

---

234 Dead reckoning is the process of calculating one's current position by using a previously determined position, and advancing that position based upon known or estimated speeds over elapsed time and course.
235 See Wilkinson, *op. cit.*, p. 28. At this date, even latitude 'could either be an estimate, by account or dead reckoning, or by observation', and 'until the last decades of the 18th century it can be assumed that all longitudes are an estimate based on dead reckoning.' The log showed 'the bearing and distance of some landmark from the vessel at noon…. If the landmark was not in sight, the bearing was taken from a chart and was therefore a true bearing. In this instance the bearing would be expressed very precisely in degrees…. As a general rule, bearings expressed as compass points are likely to be magnetic, those expressed in degrees are almost always true.' The North point used by Google Earth as in Fig. 58 is understood to be True.

fireball struck HMS *Montague* in the North Atlantic some 240 miles west of Cape Finisterre, northern Spain.

The location of the ship could be significant when it comes to working out what was seen.

Writers both lay and scientific often refer to "ball lightning" in similar cases, and of course in 1848 Sir William "Thunder and Lightning" Harris assumed without question that it was something electrical. He suggested they had first seen "glow discharge" – otherwise known as corona discharge, or St. Elmo's fire, which is typically bluish in colour – caused by the electric field beneath an approaching "highly charged thunder cloud", which then came near enough for a lightning strike to hit the ship. But there are problems with this idea.

Corona discharge does not occur in isolation in the free atmosphere. The steep field gradients needed to cause electrical breakdown of the air only occur where charge is concentrated on conductive objects – usually on points and corners thereof, like the wet mast-tops and spars of ships, hence the phenomenon's other name of "point discharge". In this case, what conductive object on the open ocean could have been glowing whilst approaching the ship faster than they could raise sail? Another ship? If so, what happened to it?

Could an approaching ship have been destroyed by a near-simultaneous lightning strike? This in turn suggests a different interpretation of a fiery ball appearing to "rise almost perpendicular" – the fireball of a powder keg explosion.[236] The sulphur, charcoal and saltpetre composition of 18th century "black powder" might explain the smell of "brimstone" or "sulphur".

But could the wreckage of this hypothetical ship have escaped detection? Even in conditions of darkness and confusion it would seem unlikely. And although the time of the event – approaching "12 o'clock" – is ambiguously stated, being either noon or midnight, the fact that Mr Chalmers was "taking an Observation on the Quarterdeck"[237] tells us that it was noon, then the start of the nautical day, which was the routine time for a "sun sight" to determine solar elevation,[238] and thus the ship's latitude. So, it was probably broad daylight, making it still harder to imagine how another ship could approach unrecognised before being destroyed completely with all hands, leaving no visible wreckage.

Perhaps Sir William's "highly charged thundercloud" might itself have seemed aglow, in a gloomy sky, due to near-continuous internal lightning. However, neither the scale nor the altitude of thunder clouds – rising tens of thousands of feet high – sits easily with the image of a ball the apparent size of a millstone rolling on the sea nearby before exploding, especially given that there was "no thunder nor lightning, before nor after." And a sulphurous stink is not characteristic of electrical phenomena in the atmosphere, which are rather associated with the peppery tang of ozone – although in the 19th century, and earlier, it was not uncommon for the odour of a lightning strike to be described as "sulphurous", probably because of its devilish connotations.

---

236 Shipboard powder magazines were sometimes protected from canon fire with copper-sheeted walls. It is well known that copper salts burn with a blue flame.

237 Using perhaps quadrant, back-staff, or the then state-of-the-art sextant, see: https://www.mat.uc.pt/~helios/Mestre/Novemb00/H61iflan.htm

238 An observation at midnight would not have been normal. Star sightings were taken morning and evening during nautical twilight, whilst the horizon remained visible; https://en.wikipedia.org/wiki/Sailing_ship

miles in a minute. Fire-balls, in appearance fimilar to
thefe, though vaftly inferior in fize, have been fometimes obferved at the furface of the earth. Of this
kind Dr. Prieftley mentions one feen on board the
Montague, 4th November 1749, which appeared as
big as a large millftone, and broke with a violent explofion.

From analogical reafoning, it feems very probable,
that the meteors which appear at fuch great heights
in the air are not effentially different from thofe which,
like the fire-ball juft mentioned, are met with on the
furface of the earth. The perplexing circumftances
with regard to the former are, that at the great
heights above-mentioned, the atmofphere ought not to
have any denfity fufficient to fupport flame, or to propagate found ; yet thefe meteors are commonly fuc-
ceeded by one or more explofions, nay are fometimes
faid to be accompanied with a hiffing noife as they
pafs over our heads. The meteor of 1719 was not

Fig. 59. *Encyclopædia Britannica*, Vol. 2 (1791), 'Atmosphere', p. 615.

from them ; when it left their faces, hands,
and cloaths, with the earth, and all the neighbouring objects, fuddenly illuminated, with
a diffufed and lambent light, attended with
no noife at all. While they were ftarting up,
ftanding, and looking at one another, fur-
prifed at the appearance, a fervant came running to them out of a neighbouring garden,
and afked them if they had feen nothing ; for
that he had feen a light fhine fuddenly in the
garden, and efpecially upon the ftreams which
he was throwing to water it *.

ALL thefe appearances were evidently electrical ; and Signior Beccaria was confirmed in
his conjecture, that electricity was the caufe
of them, by the quantity of electric matter
which, as was mentioned before, he had feen
gradually advancing towards his kite ; for
that, he fays, had very much the appearance
of a falling ftar. Sometimes alfo he faw a
kind of *glory* round the kite, which followed
it when it changed its place, but left fome
light, for a fmall fpace of time, in the place
which it had quitted †.

THAT appearances, which bear evident
marks of electricity, have a very fenfible pro-
greffive motion, is demonftrated from a variety
of meteorological obfervations. I fhall relate
one made by Mr. Chalmers, when he was on
board the Montague under the command
of Admiral Chambers. The account of it

* Lettere dell' eletricifmo, p. 111.
† Ibid. p. 130.

7   was

was read at the Royal Society, March the 22d,
1749.

ON the 4th of November 1749, in lat.
42° 48' long. 9° 3' he was taking an ob-
fervation on the quarter-deck, about ten minutes before twelve, when one of the quarter-
mafters defired he would look to the wind-
ward ; upon which he obferved a large ball of
blue fire rolling on the furface of the water, at
about three miles diftance from them. They
immediately lowered their top-fails, &c. but
it came down upon them fo faft, that before
they could raife the main-tack, they obferved
the ball to raife almoft perpendicular, and not
above forty or fifty yards from the main-
chains ; when it went off with an explofion as
if hundreds of cannon had been fired at one
time, and left fo great a fmell of brimftone,
that the fhip feemed to be nothing but ful-
phur. After the noife was over, which, he
believed, did not laft longer than half a fecond,
they found their main top-maft fhattered into
above a hundred pieces, and the main maft
rent quite down to the heel. There were fome
of the fpikes which nail the fifh of the main-
maft drawn with fuch force out of the maft,
and they ftuck fo faft in the main-deck, that
the carpenter was obliged to take an iron
crow to get them out. There were five men
knocked down, and one of them greatly
burnt by the explofion. They believed, that
when the ball, which appeared to them to be
of the bignefs of a large mill-ftone, rofe, it
took the middle of the main top-maft, as the

F f 2   head

Fig. 60. Joseph Priestley, *The History and Present State of Electricity*, Vol. 1, Sect. 12, 'THE
ATTEMPTS THAT HAVE BEEN MADE TO EXPLAIN SOME OF THE MORE UNUSUAL APPEARANCES IN
THE EARTH AND HEAVENS BY ELECTRICITY – The Theory of Meteors', London, 1775, pp. 434-436. [239]

239 https://archive.org/details/historyandprese00priegoog/page/n478/mode/2up/search/fire+ball

On the other hand, the smell *is* suggestive of sulphur dioxide and hydrogen sulphide gases emitted from active volcanic vents; and methane, another volcanic gas, might burn blue. In a superficially similar case (see Chapter 10) the crew of a brig sailing south of Sicily encountered an "overpowering stench of sulphur" when glowing objects appeared to emerge from the sea in June 1845, and in that case the cause may well have been an eruption from a submarine volcano. However, there is no evidence of active volcanic vents on the deep seabed off Spain – at least 4 or even 5 km (2.5 or 3 miles) down – where HMS *Montague* was struck.

Another vast source of methane is in seabed deposits, often bound in icy clathrates, which might bubble to the surface – as happened when a 20 m geyser of methane and mud erupted from the shallow waters of the Tyrrhenian Sea east of Corsica in 2017.[240] But again, HMS *Montague* was in water thousands of metres deep, far beyond the continental shelf on which organic methane hydrate deposits are concentrated. Abiotic methane does occur in deep ocean floor rocks;[241] but without the diphosphane (P_2H_4) of microbial origin thought (possibly) to provide the spontaneous ignition in the case of "marsh gas" combustion[242] – which might conceivably be a factor also in the case of methane in coastal ocean sediments – an abiotic deep-water methane plume should not ignite. Autoignition of simple methane/air mixtures can occur without flame, but only in contact with a heat source of about 600°C.[243]

And even if a ball of ignited gas could remain stable (perhaps because of annular vortex spin), it is hard to imagine it drifting on or near the water surface for an estimated three miles before rising; and it seems equally unlikely that chemical combustion could sustain the sort of energy density implied by the destruction wrought.

There is one more idea worth considering: a daylight fireball meteor. Before doing so we should note that in the *Encyclopædia Britannica* of 1791 the author of the article 'Atmosphere' mentions this case in passing as an example of a "meteor . . . observed at the surface of the Earth", which was to be distinguished from those observed moving rapidly "at great heights in the air" only by circumstance, being "not essentially different" in nature (Fig. 59). In this he was not saying that the crew of HMS *Montague* encountered a space rock, but that all such aerial meteors were – as was widely believed at that date – "meteorological", i.e., some kind of electrical effect in the atmosphere, like lightning.

The article credits the story to "Dr. Priestley", without doubt the famous natural philosopher, chemist, and teacher Joseph Priestley (1733–1804),[244] discoverer of oxygen, and author between 1767 and 1770 of five papers delivered to the Royal Society on coronal discharge and related electrical phenomena.[245] Priestley's "mention" of the incident may have

---

240 *Corse Net Infos*, March 24, 2017; https://www.corsenetinfos.corsica/Geyser-entre-Pianosa-et-la-Corse-L-hypothese-d-un-volcan-de-boue-_a26538.html
241 https://www.whoi.edu/press-room/news-release/origin-of-massive-methane-reservoir-identified/
242 https://en.wikipedia.org/wiki/Will-o%27-the-wisp;
https://userpages.umbc.edu/~frizzell/SwampGas.html#_ftn3
243 https://www.newcastle.edu.au/__data/assets/pdf_file/0007/382948/Kundu-2016-JLPP.pdf
244 On the previous page (p. 614) of the same *Encyclopædia Britannica* article, the author cites "Dr. Priestley" in the same style in connection with "dephlogisticated air" – or what we now know as oxygen – identifying him unambiguously.
245 https://en.wikipedia.org/wiki/Joseph_Priestley

been in person to the *Britannica* author[246] or, most likely, in his 1775 book *The History and Present State of Electricity* (Fig. 60). In the latter, under the heading 'The Theory of Meteors', Priestley paraphrases Mr Chalmers' account to the Royal Society, offering it as evidence "That appearances, which bear evident marks of electricity, have a very sensible progressive motion." Thus Priestley, also, had been advocating a meteor in the older 18thC sense, rather than in the modern sense of a rock from the sky, which would remain an out-of-favour superstition until opinion began to shift after the publication of Ernst Chladni's famous book in 1794.[247]

Looking at the case today, with our modern knowledge of fireball meteors, and experience of how they are reported, the idea raises different questions. How could a meteor falling from space and hurtling through the upper atmosphere have been perceived as a millstone of fire rolling on the sea, then ascending, close enough to HMS *Montague* to cause explosive damage?

This might in part be explained by a very large, slow fireball, with a trajectory perhaps many hundreds of miles long, approaching the ship in line of sight and growing brighter, but so far beyond the curve of the horizon that despite its great altitude – probably 20 miles (30 km) or more – it remained for many seconds apparently near the surface of the sea. Even though it was gradually descending, as it came nearer the ship its angular elevation would begin to increase, slowly at first but then more rapidly (see *Vol. 1, Aerial Phenomena*, Ch. 22, for a detailed presentation of this theory in another case), until it broke up with a thunderous detonation, apparently over the ship although no doubt still at great height and range.

This is not a completely satisfactory explanation, however. The blue colour of the light would tend to indicate the higher ionisation energy of a fast fireball, whereas slow, long-duration ones of the type required *tend* to emit light towards the red end of the spectrum. This might not be the case if, for example, the slow bolide is rich in blue-emitting copper; but in any case, slow bolides are, awkwardly for the theory, not those that tend to break up explosively. And more significantly, whilst the suggested illusion is plausible – it being quite common for very remote meteors seen from ships on the open sea to be perceived as falling nearby – in this case a mere illusion of proximity seems insufficient. The chance of an actual meteor impact is implausibly tiny, [248] but barring an unbelievable coincidence, there still

---

246 The author is unknown. But Priestley was in London from August of 1791, having left Birmingham – where he had worked closely with Wedgwood, Boulton, Watt and other scientists – after his house and laboratory were burned down by rioters incensed by his support for the French and American Revolutions. He taught science in London until emigrating to Pennsylvania in 1794.

247 *Über den Ursprung der von Pallas gefundenen und anderer ihr ähnlicher Eisenmassen und über einige damit in Verbindung stehende Naturerscheinungen* ('On the Origin of the Iron Masses Found by Pallas and Others Similar to it, and on Some Associated Natural Phenomena');
https://digital.slub-dresden.de/werkansicht/dlf/79533/5/

248 Houses and even people have from time to time been struck by small stones believed to be meteorites – falling cool to Earth at terminal velocity after burning out at the end of their bright flight. However, these typically cause little damage. Large meteorites are relatively extremely rare. Rather arbitrarily adapting one published analysis (Daniel M. Byrd, C. Richard Cothern, *Introduction to Risk Analysis: A Systematic Approach to Science-based Decision Making*, Rowman & Littlefield, 2000, pp. 94-95) concerning intact meteorites weighing a pound or more – which might cause more significant damage to a ship's masts, perhaps comparable to small cannon shot – the probability of one of these actually hitting a ship the size of HMS *Montague* would be

needs to be a causal connection between, on the one hand, the detonation of the meteor at altitude and, on the other hand, the physical damage incurred to the ship and its crew.

Mr Chalmers gives the impression that the sound, as of "Hundreds of Cannon fired at one time", was simultaneous with the explosion when the ball was visually "observed to rise almost perpendicular, and not above forty or fifty Yards from the Main Chains". Of course, sight and sound would not be simultaneous if a meteor detonated tens of miles away[249] – another argument for unlikely proximity, perhaps? On the other hand, the story does not rule out a short delay. A shockwave, travelling faster than the local speed of sound like a "sonic boom", could arrive within only a few seconds, and the abrupt detonation described by Chalmers "which I believe did not last longer than half a second" is consistent with a shockwave.[250] Shockwaves can do damage.

Bolides with airburst energies in the few-kiloton range occur above some spot on Earth once every few years, typically terminating at altitudes around 100,000 ft (30 km; 19 mi). Even with an unlikely "near miss" the slant range of one of these from the ship would probably have been some tens of kilometres; so, effects like splintered masts, and burned and thrown-down crewmen, would be highly unlikely. The shockwave from a 500 kiloton airburst at a similar altitude, like the spectacular Chelyabinsk superbolide of 2013, can cause surface damage such as broken windows and the like at distances of tens of kilometres, and a few cases of UV "sunburn" were reported in that case. But these events occur very rarely, perhaps once or twice in a century somewhere on the globe;[251] whilst larger megaton airbursts from superbolides able to penetrate down to altitudes in the order of 10,000 ft (3 km) – without doubt capable of inflicting major mechanical and thermal damage – are expected to occur about once every 2000 years.[252]

So, the theory has attractive aspects and isn't impossible. Nevertheless, these figures give us a flavour of how unlikely it is that such a rare object would chance to fall near a lone ship in the middle of the open Atlantic. And it still doesn't remove the need for other remarkable coincidences.

The explosion "left so great a Smell of Brimstone, that the Ship seemed to be nothing but Sulphur." Whilst a faint odour like sulphur has sometimes been associated with certain

---

in the order 10^{-10} per year, or only about 1 in 10 million per millennium. But this is a very slippery problem depending on guesstimates of frequency and with many variables of mass and velocity etc., becoming almost impossible to quantify when fragmentation of larger objects is considered also.

249   So-called electrophonic sounds, believed to be directly transduced from electromagnetic waves by conductive structures in, or near, an observer's ear, may be heard simultaneously; but these are faint hissing sounds, not percussive detonations.

250   Arguably, it is even more consistent with a sonic boom caused by the meteoroid's velocity than with a fragmentation shock. But a boom's shock cone trails its source and would in this case be extremely narrow proportionally to the meteoroid's hypersonic velocity; meaning that the delay between the burn-out of the still far-off fireball and the boom would be significant. The shock cone, itself expanding only at the speed of sound, would intercept the ship much later than any supersonic fragmentation shock running ahead of the detonation. The force of the damage presumably implies (ex hypothesi) that fragmentation did occur.

251   JPL's Center for Near-Earth Object Studies keeps records of all fireballs detected by US Government instrumented sensors since 1988. This objective resource shows that Chelyabinsk was the only event of anything like its size detected anywhere on Earth in 32 years, and only one other impact with an energy of >100 kilotons occurred during the same period; https://cneos.jpl.nasa.gov/fireballs/

252   https://en.wikipedia.org/wiki/List_of_meteor_air_bursts

recovered meteorites,[253] it's very hard to imagine a stink suddenly enveloping the ship from a meteorite blowing up many miles away and tens of thousands of feet in the air. If we wished to blame a bolide for that, it would imply the most unlikely bull's-eye targeting of the ship within tens of meters rather than of tens of kilometres. Furthermore, the damage caused was not only mechanical and thermal; there was also a strange magnet-like effect: "some of the Spikes that nail the Fish of the Mainmast [were] drawn with such Force out of the Mast, that they stuck in the Main Deck so fast that the Carpenter was obliged to take an Iron Crow to get them out." Nothing about this resembles anything in the meteor catalogues. If accurate, it strongly suggests an electromagnetic effect of the type sometimes reported of "ball lightning".

Should we say it was ball lightning, then? Since nobody really understands quite what ball lightning is, this is difficult to answer. None of the reported behavioural or circumstantial characteristics is near the median for reports of ball lightning; but each of them has a counterpart somewhere in the unfiltered literature. The type of damage incurred to the mast is fairly typical of lightning running to ground. Yet there was no electrical storm in progress, "before, nor after".

Perhaps there is justification for speculating about a rare link between large meteors and atmospheric electrical phenomena near sea-level? Queensland University physicist Stephen Hughes has proposed controversially that by tribocharging (friction charging), and fracturing, meteoroids in flight can accumulate significant charge, which might then discharge to ground along ionisation tracks, causing electrical effects near the surface – essentially, meteoric lightning (see also Chapter 13).[254]

We searched the internet for other mentions of a fireball (bola de fuego/bola fogo) seen from the west coast of Spain or Portugal in November 1749. We found nothing. This means there is no evidence for our hypothetical meteor; at the same time, it means we have no corroboration of Mr Chalmers' story. Is the glass half empty? Or half full?

It would be easy to dismiss Chalmers' account as a mere seaman's anecdote, but that would be to risk ignoring a first-hand eyewitness account of an extraordinary phenomenon.

---

253 California State University meteorite recovery expert Robert Verish: "Maybe a little like ozone, but with a more smoky, sulfurous aroma. The phrase 'burnt gunpowder' came into my mind. And ... the Apollo astronauts reported that moondust had the strong smell of 'spent gunpowder'." Robert Verish, 'Planetary Body Odors', *Meteorite-Times Magazine*, Sept. 2010, p. 19;
https://www.meteorite.com/meteorite-times/meteorite-times_2010_9.pdf
254 Hughes, S., 'Green fireballs and ball lightning', *Proceedings of the Royal Society A*;
http://eprints.qut.edu.au/38939/25/38939_2.pdf

CHAPTER 10 – *Victoria*'s Secret

On a June night in 1845 three separate reports came from different regions around the Mediterranean, describing glowing objects in the sky and sulphurous fireballs that burst upwards from the sea. Fort writes:

> That, upon June 18, 1845, according to the Malta *Times,* from the brig V*ictoria,* about 900 miles east of Adalia, Asia Minor (36 40' 56", N. Lat: 13 44' 36" E. Long.) three luminous bodies were seen to issue from the sea, at about half a mile from the vessel. They were visible about ten minutes.
>
> The story was never investigated, but other accounts that seem acceptably to be other observations upon this same sensational spectacle came in, as if of their own accord, and were published by Prof. Baden-Powell.[255]

These stories are well known and retold in many modern UFO books as though they relate to the same event. Fort thought they did, and had some justification based on reputable 19th century sources. The British Association for the Advancement of Science (BAAS) publication which he cites (Fig. 61)[256] treated them as sightings of the same "extraordinary appearance," and an article in *The Athenæum*[257] stated they all occurred "at the same time." If Fort had properly visualised the geography he might have thought twice about these claims, but his confusion shows that he did not. The coordinates which Fort quotes – accurately[258] – are in the Mediterranean, not far from Malta, approximately 900 miles *west* of Adalia, not east of it, as he says.

---

255 Fort, *Damned*, p. 261, citing *Rept. Brit. Assoc.,* 1861-30.

256 *BAAS Reports on the State of Science*, 31st Meeting (1861), 'A Catalogue of Observations of Luminous Meteors,' Appendix 2, pp. 30-31. "Accounts of the remarkable meteor of June 11th, 1845, from Adalia, Asia Minor; the brig 'Victoria'; Amab [sic] on Mount Lebanon."

257 *The Athenæum*, #1086 (August 19, 1848), p. 833.

258 There is some garbling in various other sources. According to the *Sydney Morning Herald*, "The position of the ship, as well as [the captain] could judge from observations taken at noon was – latitude 30 deg., 40 min., 56 sec., longitude 13 deg., 44 min., 36 sec., by two chronometers." (*Sydney Morning Herald* , Nov. 17, 1845; see https://molegenealogy.blogspot.com/2014/02/captain-george-caithness-and-undersea.html). However, the figures are incoherent, indicating a position either on land deep inside Africa (if the longitude is degrees W) or near the Canaries (if degrees E). A ship trading from Newcastle to Malta is not likely to be anywhere near the Canaries, and even if it had been there on June 18 it could not arrive in Malta 1,884 miles (3,032.66 km) away on June 20, as recorded, without making a continuous 40 knots! Clearly the latitude of 30° is wrong; and the longitude should be degrees East as given in the *Malta Times* and related secondary sources. Moreover, both times given here are 30 minutes adrift from the other accounts (9:00 and 11:00 instead of 9:30 and 11:30). However, the *Sydney Morning Herald* does add the interesting detail that the coordinates were calculated by dead reckoning from a noon position, which is probably correct based on standard navigational procedure of taking a sun shot at noon. Meanwhile, one of the earliest known sources – the *Glasgow Herald* of July 7, 1845, p. 4 (see Fig. 68) – says the latitude *it* quotes was the measured value seven hours earlier *at noon*. However, that latitude – "36.44.36" – looks like a mangled version of the complete coordinates given in the *Malta Times* - lat. 36° 40' 56" long. 13° 44' 36". All a little confusing, as usual.

The *Athenæum* quotes this extract from the *Malta Mail Times*,[259] August 18, 1845:

> On June 18th, at 9h. 30m. p.m. the brig Victoria, from Newcastle to Malta, in lat. 36°
> 40' 56," long. 13° 44' 36," was becalmed, with no appearance of bad weather; when
> her top-gallant and royal masts suddenly went over the side as if carried away by a
> squall. Two hours it blew very hard from the east; and whilst all hands were aloft
> reefing topsails, it suddenly fell calm again, and they felt an overpowering heat and
> stench of sulphur. At this moment three luminous bodies issued from the sea, about
> half a mile from the vessel, and remained visible for ten minutes (it is not said what
> became of them). Soon after it began to blow hard again, and the vessel got into a
> current of cold fresh air.

The other sightings were from Ainab, on Mount Lebanon, and from Adalia (Antalya),
Turkey. At Ainab "two large bodies, each apparently at least five times larger than the moon"
were seen in the west for an hour, connected by "streamers or appendages" resembling "large
flags blown out by a gentle breeze." The Adalia sighting, confirmed also from Philadelphia
(modern-day Alasehir), was described in the BAAS report as "a remarkable meteor" whose
persistent trail remained glowing in the sky for about half an hour.

In the book *Return to Magonia*[260] one of the present authors (Martin Shough, with co-
author Chris Aubeck) examined these stories in depth to determine if, despite the distance
between the events, they might relate to the same cause. Both the Turkish sightings and the
one at Ainab, Lebanon, occurred soon after sunset. No precise times are given. But the times
of sunset would differ by only about 20 minutes between these locations, so they could be
sightings of the same event, even though the descriptions are not identical. (When the BAAS
article says "very nearly the same time" it may be referring specifically to these two
sightings.) Most likely, witnesses at these places did see the same fireball and its persistent
trail in the western sky, composed of sunlit smoke and/or glowing plasma, deformed into
sinuous "streamers" by high-altitude winds.

On the other hand, the third sighting from the *Victoria* sounds very different. She was near
the islands of Malta and Gozo off the south coast of Sicily (Fig. 62), 1,200 miles from
Lebanon. The long trail of a large Earth-grazing fireball or superbolide might conceivably be
visible from all locations nearly simultaneously; however, the *time* of the *Victoria*'s sighting
was also very different.

---

259 Actually, the name of the newspaper isn't clear. The *Athenæum* extract, #1086 (August 19, 1848), pp. 831-
846, at 833) is from "Malta Mail Times", whilst the version in BAAS *Reports on the State of Science* (Volume
31, 186), says "Malta Mail", which Fort incorrectly cites secondarily as "Malta Times". The National Archives
(http://discovery.nationalarchives.gov.uk/details/r/C2227067) records a *Malta Times* publishing between 1853–
1855, and a *Malta Mail* publishing 1842–1846 (http://discovery.nationalarchives.gov.uk/details/r/C2227068)).
We do not find a record of a *Malta Mail Times*. Given the dates, the *Malta Mail* would appear to be the likely
source. However, there was an explosion of mostly short-lived Maltese titles after British granting of press
freedom in 1839 (http://www.independent.com.mt/articles/2011-06-26/local-news/New-Cassola-Book-on-
Maltese-19th-century-newspapers-294646) so a *Mail Times* may have been printed in 1845.
260 *Return to Magonia*, Anomalist Books, 2015, Ch. 9, pp. 139-152.

No. 2.—The following accounts of the remarkable meteor of June 11th, 1845, of which some descriptions have already been published in preceding Reports, have been forwarded to us, as first seen by the Rev. F. Hawlett, F.R.A.S., near Adalia, Asia Minor :—

1. Towards the close of the 18th we started, after one of the sultriest days I almost ever experienced; at 11 A.M. the thermometer was 98° in the coolest part of Mr. Purdie's house, whilst not a breath of wind was astir. I know not whether the stagnant heat may have contributed to the occurrence of a very splendid meteor which we witnessed that evening. We had entered the mountainous district north-west of Adalia, the sun had recently set in a perfectly cloudless sky, and the twilight was coming on, when there suddenly burst out in the north a meteor that resembled in appearance a bright but permanent flash of lightning, whose upper extremity lay a little to the east of the pole-star. The length of the flash, as near as I could judge, was about 50°— certainly more than half the space between the zenith and the horizon (sloping downwards towards the west of north) ; and that which I presumed was the vapour resulting from the explosion presented for several minutes the same shape as the original flash, and being strongly illumined (as I took it) by the upslanting rays of the vanished sun, appeared about the brightness of the rising moon, which was then about at the full. Absorbed as we all were by the magnificence of the spectacle, which elicited from the Turks repeated cries of " Allah, Allah," I forgot to note by my watch the time which might elapse until an explosion should be audible, and was only reminded of the omission upon hearing a dull heavy report like that of a distant piece of ordnance boom on my ear, after an interval we then judged of some 7 or 8 minutes. According to this estimate, the sound, if it came to us from the meteor, and which (it was so peculiar) I think was the case, must have travelled to us from a distance of 90 miles (sound travelling 1140 feet per second), and owing to the altitude of the meteor must have had its origin in the highest and rarest regions of our atmosphere.

This brilliant visitant gradually appeared to grow larger and more diffuse, as to breadth more particularly, and at last to break up into detached portions, which were beautifully decked in luminous colours of red, orange, and silvery green. Finally the coloured portions, having taken meanwhile a slightly westerly course, by degrees faded away, having continued visible at least 20 minutes to half an hour. We were informed that the meteor was seen at Philadelphia (160 miles west).

2. From ' Malta Mail.'

The brig ' Victoria ' saw this extraordinary appearance when in latitude 36° 40′ 56″ north, and longitude 13° 44′ 36″ east, being becalmed and without any appearance of bad weather; her topgallant and royal masts suddenly went over the side, as if carried away by a sudden squall; and two hours after' it blew very hard from south and east, but suddenly again fell calm, with an overpowering stench of sulphur and an unbearable heat. At this moment three luminous bodies were seen to issue from the sea at the distance of about half a mile from the vessel, which remained visible for about 10 minutes ; soon after it came on to blow hard from the south-east, and the vessel ran into a current of air the reverse of that just experienced (900 miles west of Adalia).

3. Letter from Amab, on Mount Lebanon.

On the same day, about half an hour after sunset (very nearly the same time), the heavens presented an extraordinary and beautiful appearance. A fiery meteor, composed of two luminous bodies, each appearing at least five times larger than the moon, with streamers and appendages to each, joining the two, and looking like large flags blown out by a gentle breeze, appeared in

A CATALOGUE OF OBSERVATIONS OF LUMINOUS METEORS. 31

the west, remained visible for an hour, and taking an easterly course gradually disappeared. The appendages appeared to shine from the reflected light of the main bodies, which it was painful to look at for any length of time. The moon had risen half an hour before, and there was scarcely any wind (350 miles south-east of Adalia).

Fig. 61. From *BAAS Reports on the State of Science*, 31st Meeting (1861).[261]

---

261 "Accounts of the remarkable meteor of June 11th, 1845, from Adalia, Asia Minor; the brig 'Victoria'; Amab [sic] on Mount Lebanon," *BAAS Reports on the State of Science*, 31st Meeting (1861), 'A Catalogue of Observations of Luminous Meteors,' Appendix 2, pp. 30-31. Note: The introductory text erroneously gives the date as "June 11, 1845". https://www.biodiversitylibrary.org/item/93052#page/5/mode/1up

After the first sudden gust of wind at 9:30 p.m., we are told, it blew hard for two hours before the sudden calm when the objects appeared around 11:30. Was this Malta time, or ship time? Local, or GMT? We can't be sure, but the uncertainty is only in the order of one hour; [262] whereas the sighting in Lebanon, half an hour after local sunset, would have been about 5:15 p.m. GMT. So, unless the time of the *Victoria* sighting is badly mistaken, there must have been a discrepancy of several hours between the two sightings, tending to rule out a common natural cause.

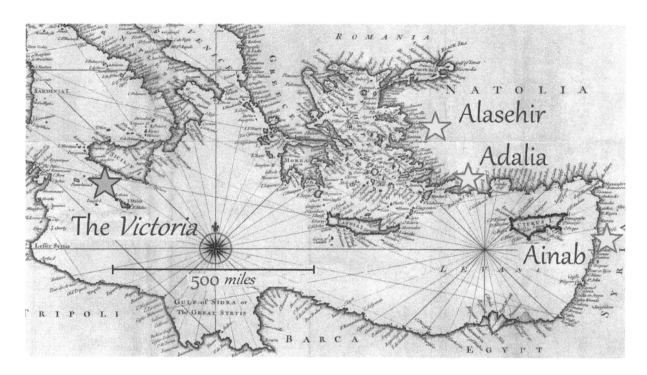

Fig. 62. Map of sighting locations around the Mediterranean, June 18, 1845.

This leaves the sighting from the *Victoria* to be considered on its own. *Victoria* was a popular name for British vessels at this time, but we can now identify the ship concerned thanks to the blog of a South African genealogist[263] where we find the entry from Lloyd's Register shown in Fig. 63 recording the Newcastle-Malta route of a 252-ton "snow" (or "snauw", abbr. "Sw", a type of brig with an extra trysail) under ship's Master "Catness", evidently the same Captain Caithness identified elsewhere (see Fig. 64) as Master of the ship we are seeking, which sailed "laden with patent fuel, from Newcastle, bound to Malta" [264] in June 1845.

---

262 At this date, long before the 1884 Meridian Conference, the longitude of Greenwich was already in widespread use as the prime meridian, especially by Navy ships; but on passenger and merchant ships like the *Victoria* time would usually be either the local time in the port of departure (Newcastle in this case, meaning GMT) or at the port of arrival (Valetta, the capital of Malta). The captain generally made the transition somewhere *en route*.

263 https://molegenealogy.blogspot.com/2014/02/tracing-master-mariners-career.html

264 *Glasgow Herald*, Monday, July 7, 1845, p. 4. See Fig. 68.

118

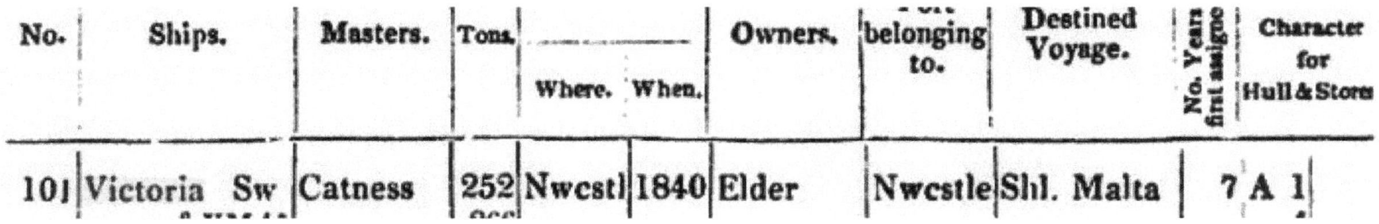

No.	Ships.	Masters.	Tons.	Where.	When.	Owners.	belonging to.	Destined Voyage.	No. Years first assigned	Character for Hull & Stores
101	Victoria Sw	Catness	252	Nwcstl	1840	Elder	Nwcstle	Shl. Malta	7	A 1

Fig. 63. Entry in Lloyd's Register recording the ship *Victoria*. [265]

George Henry Caithness, Master of the *Victoria*, was born July 5, 1818, according to a school document signed by his mother.[266] Thus, at the time of the sighting he was still a young man of 27, but already very experienced. According to his Master's Certificate (Fig. 64) he had risen since 1830 from Apprentice, to Seaman, and then to Mate, on ships out of London and Southampton, and had then served as Master of two vessels, *Rosebud* and *Schiedam*, before taking over the *Victoria* on trade to the Mediterranean and South America from March 1845 to December 1846.

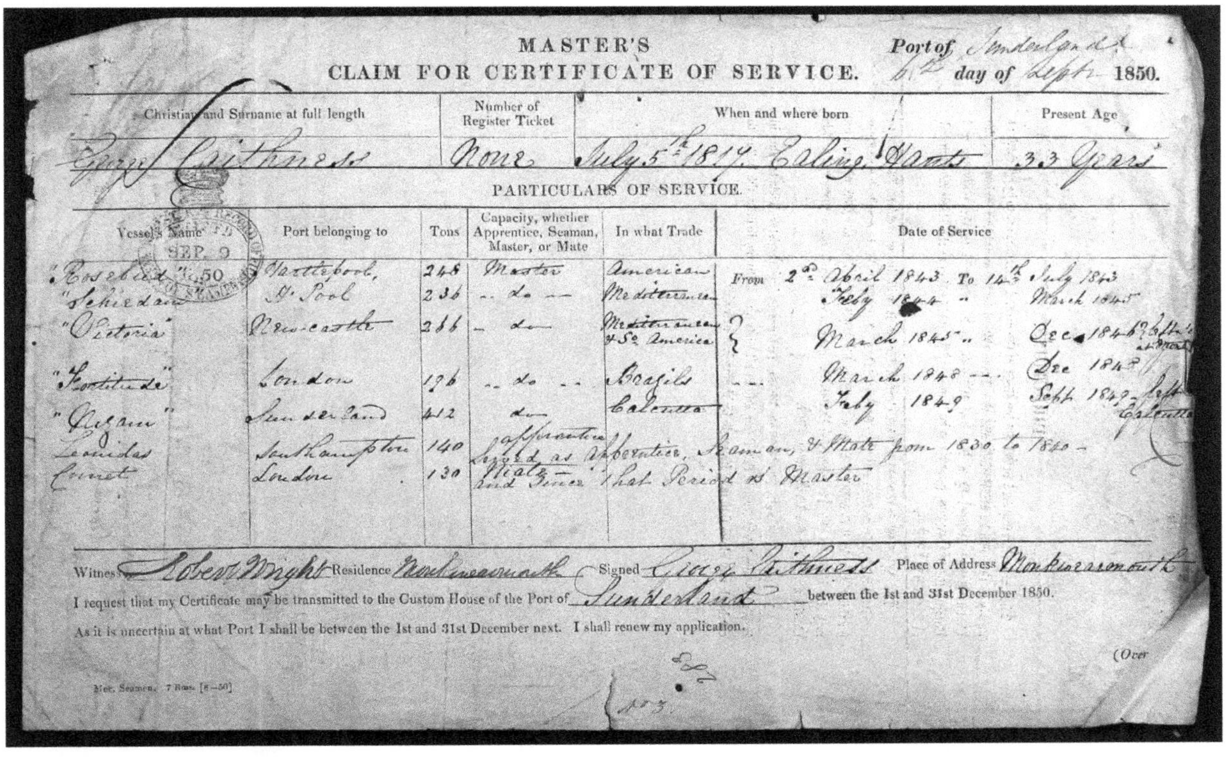

MASTER'S CLAIM FOR CERTIFICATE OF SERVICE. Port of Sunderland 6th day of Septr 1850.

Christian and Surname at full length	Number of Register Ticket	When and where born	Present Age
George Caithness	None	July 5th 1817. Ealing Hants	33 Years

PARTICULARS OF SERVICE.

Vessel's Name	Port belonging to	Tons	Capacity, whether Apprentice, Seaman, Master, or Mate	In what Trade	Date of Service
"Rosebud"	Hartlepool,	248	Master	American	From 2d April 1843 To 14th July 1843
"Schiedam"	H. Pool	236	do	Mediterranean	Feby 1844 – March 1845
"Victoria"	Newcastle	266	do	Mediterranean & So. America	March 1845 – Dec 1846
"Fortitude"	London	196	do	Brazils	March 1848 – Dec 1848
"Pegasus"	Sunderland	412	do	Calcutta	Feby 1849 – Sept 1849
Leonidas	Southampton	140	Served as Apprentice, Seaman, & Mate from 1830 to 1840 – and since that Period as Master		
Comet	London	130			

Witness Robert Wright Residence Monkwearmouth Signed George Caithness Place of Address Monkwearmouth

I request that my Certificate may be transmitted to the Custom House of the Port of Sunderland between the 1st and 31st December 1850.

As it is uncertain at what Port I shall be between the 1st and 31st December next. I shall renew my application.

(Over

Fig. 64. Captain Caithness' Master's Certificate issued in September 1850. [267]

265 *Ibid.*

266 https://molegenealogy.blogspot.com/2014/02/tracing-master-mariners-career.html. The birth date of '1817' on his Master's Certificate (Fig. 64) is presumably in error.

267 *Ibid.*

There appears to be no reason to doubt the authenticity or, broadly, the reliability of the story.

Turning then to the question of what happened, an obvious clue is the heat and stench of sulphur. One natural source of a smell of sulphur is a volcanic eruption. After water vapour, the main volcanic gases are the pungent irritants hydrogen sulphide, or "sewer gas," and sulphur dioxide. But the recorded active dates of the major volcanoes around Sicily and southern Italy, their distances from the ship's position, and the probable wind direction, together make this an unpromising theory at first blush.

However, an eruption from an underwater volcanic vent might explain sulphurous gas and heat, and could at the same time explain luminosities emerging from the sea. The seafloor between Malta and the Strait of Sicily is an active volcanic zone known as the Campi Flegrei Mar Sicilia (Phlegraean Fields of the Sea of Sicily) containing numerous volcanic seamounts rising near the surface. Eruptions here are recorded as far back as 200BC. Several vents have erupted in more recent historical times, including some in the 19th century quite near the location of the brig *Victoria*.

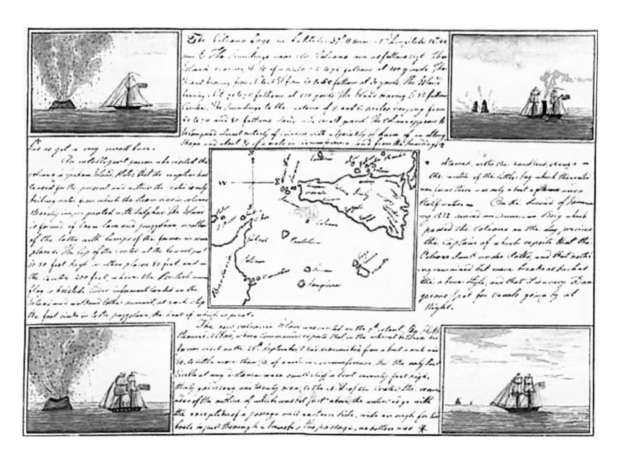

Fig. 65. The emergence and disappearance of Ferdinandea, or Graham Island, in August 1831. From the journal of French geologist Constant Prévost.[268]

In August, 1831, a seamount west of the Strait of Malta erupted, creating a new island and, with it, an international incident, as several nations claimed sovereignty. It was called, in Italian, Isola Ferdinandea, but known more widely as Graham Island (Fig. 65). The value of this small atoll of cooling slag was hardly even strategic, more symbolic; but there was also a proposal for a hotel allowing tourists to overlook its steaming crater lake. Such was its fame that it received a visit from Sir Walter Scott and inspired the writers Jules Verne and James Fennimore Cooper.[269] After a brief spell the island was eroded away and it sank back beneath the waves in December 1831, its smoking vent briefly reappearing in 1863, and again in 1984.

Fig. 66. A contemporary painting of the eruption of Ferdinandea (Graham Island).[270]

There appears to be no record of activity in the area during June 1845, other than the experience of the *Victoria*; but it is very possible that one of the many vents erupted briefly on the night of June 18, with gouts of flame and smoke giving the appearance of luminous bodies emerging from the ocean – perhaps resembling the picture of Graham Island's emergence in Fig. 66. The Madrepore Bank vent, at 36.7°N 13.7°E, is the closest known vent to *Victoria's* reported position (Fig. 67); and the distance from it of the ship's position (23 km; 14 mi) might be explained – in conditions of intermittent wind "from the east" or "from

---

269 Cooper's 1847 novel *The Crater, or Vulcan's Peak* is said to have been based on Ferdinandea's appearance. In Jules Verne's *Twenty Thousand Leagues Under the Sea* (1870), Capt. Nemo brings the *Nautilus* close to the island of Santorini to experience the "unbearable heat [and] insupportable smell of sulphur" of a submarine eruption.

270 https://medium.com/through-the-optic-glass/ferdinandea-lisola-che-non-c-è-c69981ce5483

south and east" – by drift after the position was logged, and/or by a small longitudinal error due to an inaccurate chronometer. [271] If the cinder cone broke the surface it could have been broken down again quickly by wave action, sinking back into the sea without any other vessels passing near enough to see it.

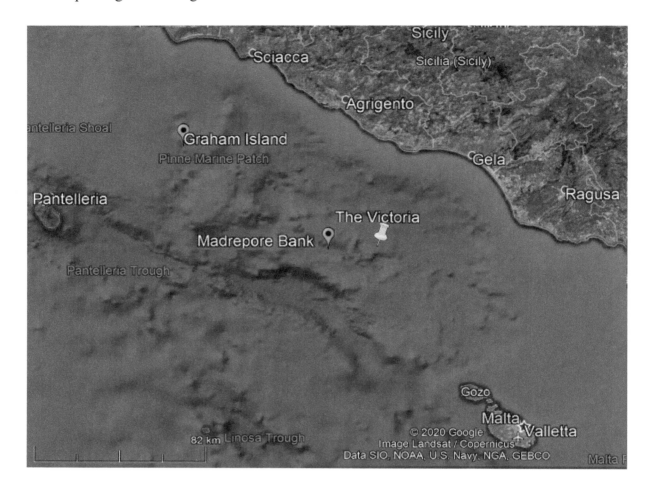

Fig. 67. Showing volcanic seamounts Graham Island (Ferdinandea) and Madrepore, in the Campi Flegrei Mar Sicilia, in relation to the brig *Victoria* (Google Earth).

We found a report of light in the sea below a ship in 1839, close to Nerita Bank, another seamount in between Graham Island and Madrepore Bank (see *Return to Magonia*, p. 151) – only one of several accounts of fire from the sea pointing to ongoing activity in the area, as we will see. In fact, the volcanic nature of the fireballs was suspected by many writers from the start. For example, Fig. 68 shows one of the earliest published sources, an article in the *Glasgow Daily Herald* less than three weeks after the event, headed "Volcanic eruption in the Mediterranean".

---

271 As mentioned in an earlier note, the *Glasgow Herald* says that the ship's latitude (which it quotes in mangled form – "36.44.36") was measured seven hours earlier at noon. But this is likely to be a misunderstanding. It was standard navigational procedure to take a sun shot at noon; however, all other accounts appear to indicate that the coordinates were given for the start of the event – when the damage was incurred, 2 hours before the appearance of the fireballs. The *Sydney Morning Herald*'s account that these coordinates were calculated by dead reckoning from a noon position is probably correct based on standard practice.

In this source the name of the ship is given erroneously as *Victory*, not *Victoria,* as was the case in most American, European, and British papers, excepting notably the London *Times*.[272] The narrative in some papers is slightly different, although not very materially. Interesting details are occasionally added, such as the *Glasgow Herald*'s comment that the ship's cargo was "patent fuel" (basically coal dust bound with pitch into small blocks or briquettes), or the report in the Austrian *Wiener Zeitschrift*, July 17, 1845, that "The ship 'Victory', Captain Caithness, felt in the middle of the open sea, suddenly, a violent jolt, as if it had struck a Sand bank"[273] before the glowing objects appeared – presumably either the shockwave of an explosive eruption that damaged the masts[274] or, perhaps, an impact with the hitherto submerged cinder cone of Madrepore breaking the surface.

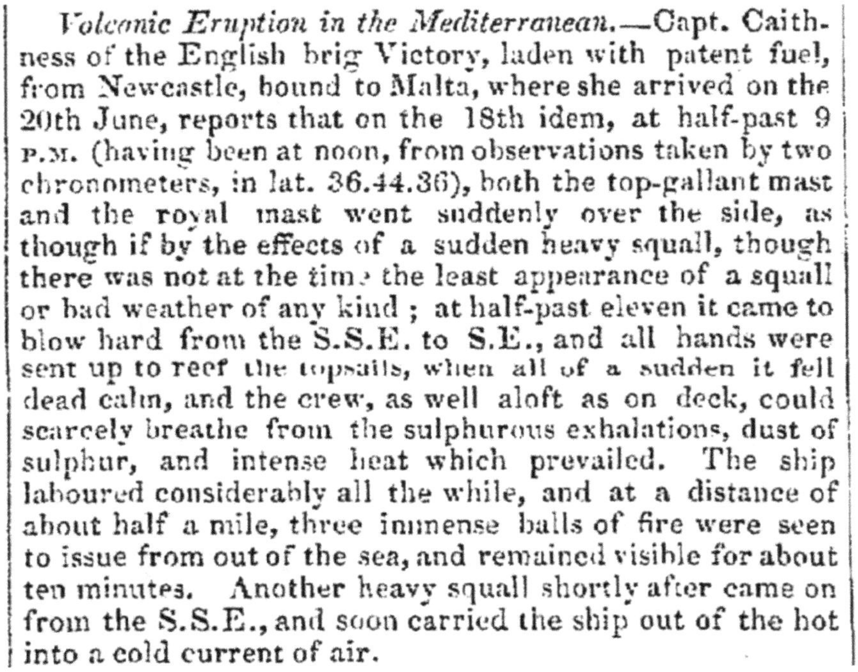

> *Volcanic Eruption in the Mediterranean.*—Capt. Caithness of the English brig Victory, laden with patent fuel, from Newcastle, bound to Malta, where she arrived on the 20th June, reports that on the 18th idem, at half-past 9 P.M. (having been at noon, from observations taken by two chronometers, in lat. 36.44.36), both the top-gallant mast and the royal mast went suddenly over the side, as though if by the effects of a sudden heavy squall, though there was not at the time the least appearance of a squall or bad weather of any kind ; at half-past eleven it came to blow hard from the S.S.E. to S.E., and all hands were sent up to reef the topsails, when all of a sudden it fell dead calm, and the crew, as well aloft as on deck, could scarcely breathe from the sulphurous exhalations, dust of sulphur, and intense heat which prevailed. The ship laboured considerably all the while, and at a distance of about half a mile, three immense balls of fire were seen to issue from out of the sea, and remained visible for about ten minutes. Another heavy squall shortly after came on from the S.S.E., and soon carried the ship out of the hot into a cold current of air.

Fig. 68. *Glasgow Herald*, Monday July 7, 1845, p. 4.[275]

We looked for other independent local newspaper sources but found none. However, a number of academic references from the 19th and 20th centuries are worth mentioning, a

---

272 Theo Paijmans, Magonia Exchange email group, July 3, 2018. A preliminary international publication history of the incident compiled by Theo Paijmans already lists 30 newspaper stories dated between July 4 and August 27.

273 http://anno.onb.ac.at/cgi-content/anno?aid=wzz&datum=18450717&seite=4&zoom=33
Credit: Kay Massingill, Magonia Exchange, June 29, 2018.

274 We confirmed from several sources that the expression "the masts suddenly went over the side" does mean that the ship was dismasted, not that it merely heeled over. See, e.g.: A glossary of 18th and 19thC nautical terms, https://www.mq.edu.au/macquarie-archive/lema/glossaries/nautical.html;
Commodore S. B. Luce, U.S.Navy, *Text-Book of Seamanship*, Van Nostrand, 1891, p. 494;
https://www.hnsa.org/manuals-documents/age-of-sail/textbook-of-seamanship/losing-spars/

275 Credit: Theo Paijmans, Magonia Exchange email group.

couple of which hint at the existence of other sources containing more information about the *Victoria* – and not just about her June 18, 1845 encounter.

Geologist Leonardo Ricciardi, writing in 1911, records a series of submarine volcanic events among which we find listed *another* case of erupting marine fireballs, seen from the *same ship*, in the *same area* south of Sicily, the previous year!

According to Ricciardi (Fig. 69), on July 17, 1844, when at a position to the west of Madrepore Bank, "during a storm, the English captain commanding the *Vittoria* saw balls of fire coming out of the sea and spreading sulphurous odor, ash and sand at a great distance." The similarity of the coordinates might fuel suspicion that this is a garbled version of the same incident listed with the wrong date; however, the "ash and sand" and the sighting "at a great distance" are not mentioned in the 1845 report. And there are other reasons for moderating our scepticism, such as Ricciardi's rather specific report that the 1845 event lasted "6 minutes", an apparent refinement of the widely-requoted "about 10 minutes" that suggests access to another source of information. Furthermore, given the number of submarine vents and the frequency of eruptions recorded in the Campi Flegrei Mar Sicilia, it isn't so unlikely that a ship passing through on a regular trade route from Newcastle to Malta would be treated to a repeat performance.

> Il 17 luglio 1844 nel Mediterraneo, a 36° 40' 36" di lat. *N* ed a 13° 14' 36" lung. *E* da Greenwich, il capitano inglese comandante la *Vittoria*, vide, durante una burrasca, globi di fuoco che uscivano dal mare e spandevano a grande distanza odore solfureo, cenere e sabbia.
>
> Alle 9,30 p. del 18 giugno 1845 nel Mediterraneo, a 36° 40' 56" lat. *N* ed a 13° 44' 36" long. (da *G*) la nave inglese Vittoria provò una violenta scossa, sebbene in quel momento il tempo fosse perfettamente calmo. Bentosto si sparsero nell'aria emanazioni solforose talmente forti che a malapena la gente dell'equipaggio poteva respirare. La nave riportò qualche avaria in seguito all'inatteso urto; e dopo aver preso il largo, l'equipaggio vide tre immensi globi di fuoco lanciati dal seno delle acque e visibili per 6 minuti.
>
> Nel 1846 dal 4 al 5 ottobre un capitano mercantile, trovandosi nel mare di Seculiana (Girgenti) a 7 miglia dalla costa, osservò da lungi un grande splendore, che a tutta prima giudicò proveniente da qualche battello incendiato.

Fig. 69. Leonardo Ricciardi, 'Su le Relazioni delle Reali Accademie di Scienze di Napoli e dei Lincei di Roma suiterremoti Calabro-Siculi del 1783 e 1908', *Bolletino della Societa di Naturalisti*, Napoli, 1911.[276]

The next item on Ricciardi's list is from the following year, dated 4-5 October 1846, at which time the captain of a merchant vessel 7 miles off the southwest Sicilian coast near

---

276 https://archive.org/details/bollettinodellas24soci/page/n7/mode/2up/search/18+giugno

Agrigento "observed from afar a great splendor, which at first he judged to be coming from some burning boat". This was probably the same October 1846 submarine eruption mentioned by Italian seismologist Mario Baratta (1868–1935) in 1901 as being accompanied by "very localized, but very intense earthquakes which . . . shook Sciacca" [277] further up the coast. The same 1846 event was mentioned in 1907 by Giuseppe Mercalli (1850–1914), the eminent volcanologist (and catholic priest) best remembered today for the Mercalli scale of earthquake intensity, who listed the case, alongside the *Victoria*'s July 18, 1845 sighting, as one of two "fleeting submarine eruptions" in those years.[278] And it was another work by Mercalli that may have been the source for Ricciardi's report that the Victoria event lasted "6 minuti".

Domenico Macaluso, a diver and Inspector of Sicilian Cultural Riches[279] from Sciacca, the town shaken by that eruption of October 1846, notes that the *Victoria* incident "is particularly interesting for the registration of the coordinates of the place". Macaluso assesses Giuseppe Mercalli's work as "qualified and reliable" and quotes him as describing the *Victoria*'s sighting as "three huge globes of fire, visible for 6 minutes".[280] Macaluso's reference for this is "Negri et al., 1883". We were able to identify this source; [281] unfortunately we have not been able to verify whether or not it contains other information on the *Victoria* sighting unavailable elsewhere.

Another aspect of Macaluso's article emphasises the big picture within which an incident like the *Victoria*'s encounter recedes to a somewhat commonplace detail. In the church of Santa Maria dell'Itria (aka the Badia Grande), in Sciacca, an old oil painting is to this day displayed above the altar. A detail from this painting (Fig. 70) shows a huge plume of flame emanating from the sea. According to Macaluso, the painting's purpose is not to illustrate any specific event, but rather to be "a votive offering [on behalf] of sailors who (like those of the British [ship] *Victoria*) escaped an underwater explosion". As such it nicely dramatizes how often eruptions in the area must have alarmed the seamen of southern Sicily. We doubt that such an altarpiece is likely to be found anywhere else in the world.

277 Mario Baratta, *Sulle aree sismiche Italiane*, Voghera, 1901, p. 19;
https://archive.org/details/sulleareesismic00baragoog/page/n11/mode/2up/search/1846
278 G. Mercalli, *Vulcani Attivi Della Terra*, Milan, 1907, p. 268;
https://archive.org/details/MercalliVulcaniAttivi/page/n329/mode/2up/search/18+giugno
279 In Feb. 2000 Macaluso was tasked by the Sicilian government to monitor events off-shore where volcanic events promised an imminent re-emergence of sunken Ferdinandea. The presence of British Navy ships, and a newspaper article entitled "A Long-vanished Piece of the British Empire is About to Resurface", had awakened anxious memories of the international territorial fracas of 1831.
See: 'The Island that Time Remembered' *The Independent*, 26 Sept. 2001;
https://www.independent.co.uk/news/world/europe/the-island-that-time-remembered-5364331.html
280 Domenico Macaluso, 'Vulcanesimo sedimentario e ricerca di idrocarburi in mare. La scoperta di un grande pockmark nello stretto di Sicilia', *Geologia dell'Ambiente*, Società Italiana di Geologia Ambientale (IGEA), 2/2016, April–June 2016, p. 2; https://www.sigeaweb.it/documenti/gda/gda-2-2016.pdf
281 G. Mercalli, 'Vulcani e fenomeni Vulcanici' in: Gaetano Negri, Antonio Stoppani, and Giuseppe Mercalli (Eds), *Geologia d'Italia,* Vallardi, Milan, 1883. Republished as *Vulcani e Fenomeni Vulcanici in Italia*, Sala Bolognese: A. Forni, 1981.

Fig. 70. detail of a painting from an altarpiece in the church of Santa Maria dell'Itria in Sciacca, a coastal town in the southwest of Sicily, which was shaken by a simultaneous earthquake at the time of a submarine eruption on October 4-5, 1846.

To sum up: For Charles Fort those "luminous bodies" from the sea fit into a pattern of "submerged constructions" lurking below Earth's oceans (see Chapter 11). But by and large, the story told everywhere fits the theory that the crew of *Victoria* witnessed fiery plumes erupting from the Madrepore subsea vent.

CHAPTER 11 – **Vast Luminous Wheels**

Night on the ocean. Regularly spaced lines of light move steadily by, one after another, sometimes in the water, sometimes seeming suspended in the air. Their glow illuminates the mist, lighting the hulls and decks of ships. Sometimes the lines are parallel, travelling from horizon to horizon like some vast rolling road; or they rotate like the spokes of a great wheel. Sometimes smaller glowing wheels cluster around ships, spinning above the waves. They have been recorded by sailors for over 140 years. What are they?

To Charles Fort it was "obvious" (in an intermediatist sort of way) that these were the lights of great wheel-shaped "constructions" gliding underwater, presumably controlled by the same agencies responsible for those predatory hordes of vast space machines roaming the solar system, shepherding their "property" (us) and in the process filling the environment of Earth with their weird detritus of raining frogs and anachronistic buried artifacts. He collected seven of these accounts in *The Book of the Damned*, the earliest – to this day, one of the oldest known – supposedly dating from 1875. In fact, it turns out to be somewhat older.

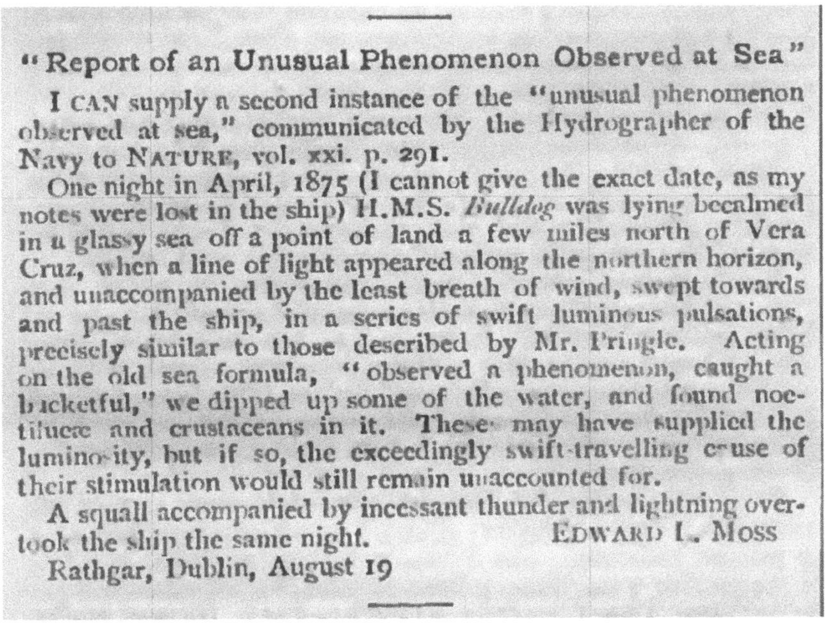

> **"Report of an Unusual Phenomenon Observed at Sea"**
>
> I CAN supply a second instance of the "unusual phenomenon observed at sea," communicated by the Hydrographer of the Navy to NATURE, vol. xxi. p. 291.
>
> One night in April, 1875 (I cannot give the exact date, as my notes were lost in the ship) H.M.S. *Bulldog* was lying becalmed in a glassy sea off a point of land a few miles north of Vera Cruz, when a line of light appeared along the northern horizon, and unaccompanied by the least breath of wind, swept towards and past the ship, in a series of swift luminous pulsations, precisely similar to those described by Mr. Pringle. Acting on the old sea formula, "observed a phenomenon, caught a bucketful," we dipped up some of the water, and found noctilucæ and crustaceans in it. These may have supplied the luminosity, but if so, the exceedingly swift-travelling cause of their stimulation would still remain unaccounted for.
>
> A squall accompanied by incessant thunder and lightning overtook the ship the same night.　　　　EDWARD L. MOSS
>
> Rathgar, Dublin, August 19

Fig. 71. Edward L. Moss, "Report of an unusual phenomenon observed at sea," *Nature,* 20, #513 (August 28, 1879), p. 428[282]

A correspondent of *Nature* signing himself Edward L. Moss wrote that sometime in April 1875 he had seen what Fort called "a series of swift lines of light" from the deck of HMS *Bulldog* a few miles north of Vera Cruz. Moss says that they found organisms in the water that might have explained luminosity, but Fort opined that this "could not account for

---

[282] http://www.dbc.wroc.pl/dlibra/plain-content?id=15498

phenomena of geometric formation and high velocity," adding, "If he means Vera Cruz, Mexico,[283] this is the only instance we have out[side] of oriental waters."[284]

The original letter from Edward Moss is shown in Fig. 71. It does not clarify the location; but a little research proved that Vera Cruz, or Veracruz, Mexico, is indeed the right place, although 1875 turns out not to be the right year.

Cdr Edward Lawton Moss, R.N. (1843–1880) was an Irish doctor who became a Royal Navy surgeon and spent most of his short life at sea. HMS *Bulldog,* a 1,124-ton wood-built steam paddle sloop launched at Chatham Dockyard and commissioned in 1847, was his first ship. It saw action in the Baltic during the Crimean War in 1854, was recommissioned in 1860 to survey the route of the proposed transatlantic telegraph cable,[285] then in 1864 was sent to the North America Station where it finished its service. A prolific watercolourist, Edward Moss himself painted the last heroic action of the *Bulldog* before she was stranded on a reef, abandoned and blown up by her crew off Haiti in 1865.[286]

Fig. 72. "HMS Bulldog Shelling the Forts at Cap Haiti on 9-11-1865 after sinking the rebel vessel Valdrogue" by Edward Lawton Moss.[287]

283 Other coastal places called Vera Cruz are a former district in the county of Aveiro, Portugal (https://pt.wikipedia.org/wiki/Vera_Cruz_(Aveiro)) and a district of East Timor in Indonesia containing the national capital Dili (https://en.wikipedia.org/wiki/Dili_District#/media/File:Dili_cities_rivers.png).
284 Fort, *Damned*, p. 264, citing *Nature*, 20 (August 28, 1879), p. 428.
285 G. C. Wallich MD, FLS, FGS, *The North-Atlantic Sea-bed, comprising a diary of the voyage on board HMS Bulldog in 1860 . . . to survey the proposed North Atlantic telegraph route between Great Britain and America*, Van Voorst, London, 1862; https://archive.org/stream/northatlanticse00wallgoog#page/n9/mode/2up
286 http://collections.rmg.co.uk/collections/objects/18774.html
287 http://www.the-saleroom.com/en-us/auction-catalogues/mallams-ltd-oxford/catalogue-id-srmalla10038/lot-35048604-1f5a-4eee-878d-a4c601152a3e

Moss survived the loss of the *Bulldog* to join the crew of HMS *Alert* as Staff Surgeon for the British Arctic Expedition of 1875–1876, a voyage he also documented in dozens of watercolours.[288] He later returned to American waters in HMS *Atalanta*. This proved to be his last voyage, the *Atalanta* and all hands being lost without trace off Bermuda in 1880 just months after his letter to *Nature*.[289]

It is obvious from this history that Moss was not on HMS *Bulldog*, at Veracruz or anywhere else, in April 1875. The simplest explanation is a single-digit date error by Moss or – perhaps more likely – by the editors or printers of *Nature*.[290] If "April 1865" was intended, then *Bulldog* could very well have been at Veracruz, preparatory to her fatal engagement at Haiti a few months later. If so, that would make the "swift luminous pulsations" observed by her crew probably the oldest known case of this type – as well as a rare geographical outlier, as Fort correctly observed back in 1919.

REPORT OF AN UNUSUAL PHENOMENON OBSERVED AT SEA

THE following Report to the Admiralty has been communicated to us for publication by Capt. Evans, C.B., F.R.S., the Hydrographer to the Navy :—

H.M.S. *Vulture*, Bahrein, May 17, 1879

SIR,—I have the honour to inform you that, at about 9.40 P.M. on May 15, when in lat. 26° 26′ N. and long. 53° 11′ E., a clear, unclouded, starlight night, Arcturus being within some 7° of zenith, and Venus about to set; wind north-west, force 3, sea smooth, with slight swell from the same direction; ship on starboard tack, heading west-south-west and going three knots, an unusual phenomenon was seen from the vessel.

I noticed luminous waves or pulsations in the water, moving at great speed and passing under the ship from the south-south-west. On looking towards the east, the appearance was that of a revolving wheel with centre on that bearing, and whose spokes were illuminated, and looking towards the west a similar wheel appeared to be revolving, but in the opposite direction. I then went to the mizen top (fifty feet above water) with the first lieutenant, and saw that the luminous waves or pulsations were really travelling parallel to each other, and that their apparently rotatory motion, as seen from the deck, was caused by their high speed and the greater angular motion of the nearer than the more remote part of the waves. The light of these waves looked homogeneous, and lighter, but not so sparkling, as phosphorescent appearances at sea usually are, and extended from the surface well under water; they lit up the white bottoms of the quarter-boats in passing. I judged them to be twenty-five feet broad, with dark intervals of about seventy-five between each, or 100 from crest to crest, and their period was seventy-four to seventy-five per minute, giving a speed roughly of eighty-four English miles an hour.

From this height of fifty feet, looking with or against their direction, I could only distinguish six or seven waves; but, looking along them as they passed under the ship, the luminosity showed much further.

The phenomenon was beautiful and striking, commencing at about 6h. 3m. Greenwich mean time, and lasting some thirty-five minutes. The direction from which the luminous waves travelled changed from south-south-west by degrees to south-east and to east. During the last five minutes concentric waves appeared to emanate from a spot about 200 yards east, and these meeting the parallel waves from south-east did not cross, but appeared to obliterate each other at the moving point of contact, and approached the ship, inclosing an angle about 90°. Soundings were taken in twenty-nine fathoms; Stiffe's Bank, with fifteen to twenty fathoms, being west about one mile. The barometer was already at 29·25 from 8 to 12 P.M.

	At 8 P.M.	10.15 P.M.	Midnight.
Temperature of air ...	84	83	83
Temperature of sea-water ...	84	82	82

I observed no kind of change in the wind, the swell, or in any part of the heavens, nor were the compasses disturbed. A bucket of water was drawn, but was unfortunately capsized before daylight. The ship passed through oily-looking fish spawn on the evening of the 15th and morning of the 16th inst.—I have the honour to be, Sir, your obedient servant,

J. ELIOT PRINGLE, Commander

Fig. 73. J. Eliot Pringle, "Report of an unusual phenomenon observed at sea," *Nature,* 20 (July 24, 1879), p. 291.[291]

---

288 http://www.spri.cam.ac.uk/museum/catalogue/polarart/artists/moss,+edward+lawton/

289 http://www.invaluable.com/auction-lot/edward-lawton-moss-irish,-1843-1880-hms-bulldog-29-c-5c0eee38fd

290 Another error in the letter is the reference to "vol. xxi. p.291" (letter concerning the HMS *Vulture* case) which should read "vol. xx." But whether Moss or *Nature* is to blame we can't say.

291 https://archive.org/stream/naturejournal20londuoft#page/290/mode/2up

In a study based on "almost 230 reports" of so-called "phosphorescent wheels"[292] British marine biologist Peter Herring[293] and colleague Paul Horsman wrote: "Consideration of the positions of the various reports . . . shows that there is a restriction to tropical regions, between 35°N and 25°S and that it is a predominantly Indo Pacific phenomenon, 95 per cent of the observations occurring in this area."[294] In short, observations of the 'line' or 'wheel' type are limited almost exclusively to the Indian Ocean and the China Sea. It is therefore curious that the earliest case on record[295] constitutes one of the very few exceptions.[296]

The next on Fort's list[297] is a sighting in the Persian Gulf in May 1879 reported to *Nature* by Commander J. Elliot Pringle of HMS *Vulture*. This is the incident to which Cdr Edward Lawton Moss referred in his letter to *Nature* concerning his own earlier sighting from HMS *Bulldog*. HMS *Vulture* (Fig. 74) was certainly in the Indian Ocean for most of that decade, as claimed, running patrols in suppression of the slave trade; and in 1873 she had been called upon to take the mummified body of explorer Dr David Livingstone to Zanzibar for the

---

292 "Luminous wheels" would be strictly preferable; but the phrase "phosphorescent wheels" has been (mis)used for so long that, like other authors, we retain it here, even though true phosphorescence – slow emission of light from a substance such as zinc sulphide or strontium aluminate after excitation by energy from another source, as in cathode ray TVs and radar screens – is not suspected.

293 Dr Peter John Herring joined the National Institute of Oceanography in 1966. Herring authored and co-authored over 250 papers on marine zoology, and in particular on the colouration, camouflage and bioluminescence of deep-sea animals. Often cited in connection with luminous wheels is his 1985 paper 'Phosphorescent Wheels: Fact or Fiction?', a study co-authored with Paul V. Horsman of the London Marine Society. Herring is especially praised for his textbook *The Biology of the Deep Ocean*, published by Oxford University Press in 2002.

294 P. J. Herring & P. Horsman, "Phosphorescent wheels: fact or fiction?" *Marine Observer*, Vol. 55 (1985), pp. 194-201; https://eeuwen.home.xs4all.nl/Download/Herring1985.pdf

295 Another candidate for the very earliest case, found in various Russian publications (e.g.: Col. Pravdivtsev, V. L. and Capt. Litvinov E. P., *On the history of the study of anomalous phenomena by reconnaissance of the USSR Navy*), is believed to be a modern hoax, worth mentioning here in order to drive home the need to check sources. Allegedly, on the night of July 16, 1864, in the Gulf of Thailand, the Russian clipper *Vestnik* passed among counter-rotating glowing wheels hundreds of meters in diameter for about 20 minutes. We attempted to identify a clipper *Vestnik* of the right date, without success, finally seeking assistance from our Russian colleague Mikhail Gershtein. Gershtein had checked every 1864 edition of the Russian Navy journal *Morskoi sbornik* (*Marine Collection*), which records all foreign voyages, including extracts from the logs and notes about unusual phenomena, finding that it lists no such vessel and no such voyage. A Russian UFO magazine which appears to be the original source of this story (*NLO* [UFO], St. Petersburg, 2006, #18) confuses the issue with alternative possible ship names, none of which are listed in *Morskoi sbornik* either. Only two clipper voyages are recorded in July 1864, neither anywhere near the Gulf of Thailand (Mikhail Gershtein, *Magonia Exchange* email list, May 14 & May 15, 2020).

296 In his *Lightning, Auroras, Nocturnal Lights, and Related Luminous Phenomena* (Sourcebook project, Glen Arm, MD, 1982), William Corliss writes (p. 193): "It appears that wheel displays outside the usual habitat (Indian Ocean and China Sea) are rather degenerate forms." Three examples are given:
- May 3, 1954: report of a "A stationary wheel" seen in Atlantic equatorial waters (*Marine Observer*, 25:93, 1955);
- September 10, 1960: report of "Lines spinning in a circular movement" observed in the South Pacific off Tocopilla, Chile (*Marine Observer*, 31:123, 1961);
- January 3, 1976: report of "Rotating circles with radii of 3 nautical miles" seen in the Southern North Pacific (*Nature*, 104:563, 1920 [sic]).
https://archive.org/details/GeophysicalAnomalies/page/n185/mode/2up

297 Fort, *Damned*, p. 264, citing *Nature* 20-291.

onward voyage home to England.[298] The vessel was a 664-ton, screw-driven gunboat launched in 1869, and she is recorded as being in the East Indies in 1879.[299] The story appears to check out.

Fig. 74. HMS *Vulture* 1869–1885.[300]

Commander Pringle's letter to *Nature* is shown in Fig. 73. The most interesting thing about it is that the impression of vast, counter-rotating, spoked wheels of light, one each side of the ship, was in this case revealed to be an illusion of perspective. When looked down on from the top of the mizzen mast the apparent radial spokes turned out to be parallel lines, receding like railway tracks towards a vanishing point near the horizon, passing the ship regularly from bow to stern.

A similar phenomenon was seen some seven months later off the coast of Malabar, and this is Fort's next offering.[301] On the calm, cloudless morning of January 5, 1880[302] R. E. Harris, Commander of the steamship *Shahjehan,* saw a display so strange that he stopped the ship to observe it. Lines of light swept past the ship, "wave succeeded wave in rapid succession, one of the most grand, and brilliant, yet solemn, spectacles that one could ever think of."[303]

That May, another sighting was made in the Persian Gulf, from the steamer *Patna.* Fort's version[304] of the letter originally published under a pseudonym in *Knowledge* has been requoted in many UFO books, perpetuating some errors. The correct text follows:

---

298   Clare Pettitt, *Dr Livingstone I Presume? Missionaries, Journalists, Explorers And Empires*, Harvard University Press, 2007; see also http://www.worldnavalships.com/forums/showthread.php?t=1022

299   "machinery notes: 847 hpi 160 hp". See: https://sites.rootsweb.com/~pbtyc/18-1900/U/05124.html

300   http://www.the-weatherings.co.uk/pccship0318.htm

301   Fort, *Damned*, p. 263, citing *Nature*, 21-410, reprinting a letter from the Calcutta *Englishman*, Jan. 21, 1880.

302   Fort gives "June" but corrects this in a marginal note as pointed out by "Mr. X" at www.resologist.net

303   "A strange phenomenon," *Nature*, 21 (Feb. 26, 1880), pp. 409-410.

304   Fort, *Damned*, p. 278-279, citing *Knowledge*, Dec. 28, 1883.

. . . on a dark calm night, about 11:30 p. m., there suddenly appeared on each side of the ship an enormous luminous wheel, whirling round, the spokes of which seemed to brush the ship along. The spokes would be 200 or 300 yards long, and resembled the birch rods of the dames' schools. Each wheel contained about sixteen spokes, and made the revolution in about twelve seconds. One could almost fancy one heard the swish as the spokes whizzed past the ship, and, although the wheels must have been some 500 or 600 yards in diameter, the spokes could be distinctly seen all the way around. The phosphorescent gleam seemed to glide along flat on the surface of the sea, no light being visible in the air above the water. The appearance of the spokes could be almost exactly represented by standing in a boat and flashing a bull's-eye lantern horizontally along the surface of the water, round and round. I may mention that the phenomenon was also seen by Captain Avern, commander of the *Patna*, and Mr. Manning, third officer.[305]

The SS *Patna* certainly existed. She was a 3-masted, single-screw, sail-and-steam-powered passenger vessel of 1,764 tons built in Dumbarton, Scotland, in 1871 (possibly a model for the fictional SS *Patna* in Joseph Conrad's novel *Lord Jim*).[306] She was owned and operated by the British India Steam Navigation Company, and her commander in 1880 was indeed Captain J. Avern.[307] The letter was signed by "Lee Fore Brace," revealed in a later letter to be the pseudonym of one J. W. Robinson. We were able to confirm that J. W. Robinson was employed as an officer of the British India Company. We could not find his status on board SS *Patna* in 1880 but he reappears as Commander of the SS *Itola*, SS *Itinda* and SS *Santhia* in the years 1904, 1906, and 1914 respectively.[308]

The significant statement that "the spokes could be distinctly seen all the way around" makes explicit that the apparent axis of rotation was not on the horizon, as had been the case in the illusion observed by HMS *Vulture* the previous year, but only "200 or 300 yards" away (the sea horizon being several miles distant). The "spokes" could be seen sweeping through a complete circle 500-600 yards in diameter, as if some nearby object in the sea was really revolving. (The natural suspicion that this was the same illusion, misreported, should be evaluated in the light of several yet-more-explicit modern reports. See below.) Fort wondered "how vast luminous wheels, each the size of a village, ever got under the surface of the Persian Gulf" and "what they were doing there."

Another "wheel" with curved "spokes" about 300 yards long that "seemed to move round a center" was seen in the Malacca Strait in 1907, reported by the 2nd Officer of the P&O steamship *Delta*.[309]

---

305 J. W. Robertson, "Strange phenomenon," *Knowledge,* 4 (Dec. 28, 1883), p. 396. See also: http://www.resologist.net/damn21.htm

306 http://www.theshipslist.com/ships/lines/bisn.shtml; https://en.wikipedia.org/wiki/SS_Patna

307 http://www.biship.com/people/commanders1.htm

308 http://www.biship.com/people/commanders2.htm

309 Fort, *Damned*, p. 264, citing *Journal of the Royal Meteorological Society,* 33-294 (Title: 'Display of phosphorescence').

Curious Light Phenomena of the Indian Seas

QUEER things still happen at sea. Every now and then a vessel-master reports the observation of some phenomenon that defies explanation in the light of our present knowledge, and forcibly reminds us of the uncanny inventions of writers such as Poe, who have found the sea a particularly available theater for mysterious happenings.

In the *Nautical-Meteorological Annual*, published by the Danish Meteorological Institute, appears a report from the master of the Danish East Asiatic Company's steamer "Bintang," Captain Gabe, of a singular luminous phenomenon observed on the surface of the water when the ship was passing through the Strait of Malacca in June, 1909. At 3 A. M., June 19th, he was roused by the second mate, and went on the bridge, where the mate had been watching the phenomenon for some minutes. The latter reported that he first saw light-waves traveling in the water from west to east. Gradually the light-waves took the form of long arms issuing from a center, around which the whole system appeared to rotate. The center, which seemed to lie on the horizon —the other half of the system not being visible—moved from right astern to the starboard beam. When the captain came on deck the phenomenon resembled the beams from a revolving light, with a pretty fast rotation; the light itself not being visible.

The system moved forward, decreasing in brilliancy and in speed of rotation, and at last disappeared when the center was right ahead. The phenomenon lasted about fifteen minutes.

The system was perfectly regular, the breadth of the rays along the side of the ship being about six feet, and that of the intervening spaces twice as much. The light was evidently in the water, as it did not light up the deck nor the side of the ship more than the common phosphorescence of the sea, of which there was a good deal. The rays were curved with their concavity in the direction of the rotation.

(*Concluded on page 58.*)

Curious light phenomenon, redrawn from sketch by Capt. Gabe.

Curious Light Phenomena of the Indian Seas

(*Concluded from page 51.*)

The captain was especially struck by the fact that the larger spots of phosphorescence in the sea appeared to light up more brightly as the rays reached them, and to fade out in the dark intervals. When the center was right abeam the rotation was so fast that the rays passed about once a second. When the rays were no longer visible the bigger spots of phosphorescence for some time lighted up at regular intervals, as if they were still passed by the rays. Gradually this decreased, and the phosphorescence shone as usual in the bow-water and along the vessel's side. The lookout and the helmsman also observed the phenomenon.

The Danish Meteorological Institute has collected a few reports of other observations somewhat similar to the above. A similar case was reported in the *Annalen der Hydrographie und maritimen Meteorologie*, 1899, p. 483, as follows: On November 21st, 1897, the German ship "Arethusa" encountered a curious illumination of the sea after midnight, when in the Bay of Bengal, lat. 14.2 degrees N., long. 96.5 degrees E. As far as the eye could reach the surface of the water shone with myriads of lights, which the officers declared had the effect of searchlights in a hazy atmosphere. The ship's log says: "It was a splendid but also an uncomfortable sight." At 2 A. M. it began to rain, and the phenomenon suddenly disappeared. The wind was south-southeast and east-southeast, its force 4, and the weather cloudy.

A more recent case was reported by Captain Breyer, of the Dutch steamer "Valentijn." At midnight August 12th, 1910, this vessel was near the Natuna Islands, in the South China Sea. The course was magnetic south, the speed eight knots. Suddenly the easterly horizon became illuminated with a light which commenced to oscillate rapidly and regularly. The phenomenon soon passed into a rotation of flashes above the water. It looked like a horizontal wheel, turning rapidly, the spokes being the rays of light running over the water. The rotation was against the sun and very regular, one ray passing every half second. The bundles of rays diverged very little and were not curved. The center could not be discerned as an isolated point. Gradually the rays grew clearer and somewhat narrower, until the source of light appeared to be beneath the ship. The water around the ship seemed to be in rapid oscillating motion, and it was as bright as at full moon (the moon had set at 10 P. M.). This lasted about five minutes; then the rotation recommenced with the center on the opposite side of the ship. The rotating rays gradually decreased in brilliancy and breadth, and at 12:40 A. M. the phenomenon had quite disappeared in the northwest to west.

In this case the ordinary phosphorescence of the water was not observed. The sea was rather smooth and the air clear. The phenomenon was observed by the captain, first and second mates, and first engineer, and on all of them it made a somewhat uncomfortable impression.

Similar observations have occasionally been reported to the Meteorological Office at London by the captains and officers of British ships.

No complete explanation of the phenomenon can be given. It is well known that in many marine organisms the capacity to produce light is awakened by sudden movement. Thus disturbance by the blade of an oar produces luminescence in the seat—commonly called "phosphorescence," though phosphorus has nothing to do with it. Also the wind rippling the surface of the water evokes the same luminosity from myriads of minute protozoa and crustacea, and the crests of the ripples are marked with light. The luminous rays seen in the cases above described appear to have marked lines of disturbance in a sea abounding in organisms capable of phosphorescence; in other words, long and regular waves, having a systematic movement of rotation. Such waves, however, appear to be altogether anomalous.

Fig. 75. "Curious light phenomena of the Indian seas," *Scientific American*, 106 (new series, January 13, 1912), pp. 51, 58. [310]

---

310 http://babel.hathitrust.org/cgi/pt?id=umn.31951001389800v;view=1up;seq=68;size=200

In the same region, in June 1909, Capt. Gabe of the steamship *Bintang* reported a "singular luminous phenomenon" with "long arms issuing from a center around which the whole system appeared to rotate." (Fig. 75) But this time the revolving wheel was so vast that its centre lay on the horizon. In other words, the further half of it was not seen, merely inferred from the appearance of rotation – suggesting the same perspective illusion observed from HMS *Vulture* in the Persian Gulf 30 years before.[311]

Fort argued that the apparent motions of the supposed "wheels" in general "do not synchronize with a vessel's motions" and so presumably could not be caused by the ships. He suggested that in the *Bintang* case the dimming of the spokes and slowing of their apparent rotation occurred because "the source of light was submerging deeper and deeper and slowing down because meeting more and more resistance."

The same article (Fig. 75) provides Fort with his last example. In August 1910 the crew of the Dutch steamer *Valentijn* in the South China Sea saw a glow on the midnight horizon which "commenced to oscillate rapidly and regularly" then "soon passed into a rotation of flashes above the water" that "looked like a horizontal wheel, turning rapidly," although "the center could not be discerned." As the effect crossed from one side of the ship to the other the illuminated water below appeared to be disturbed for several minutes.

The favoured explanation has always been a type of bioluminescence due to small marine organisms called *noctiluca scintillans*. The theory lacks detail, but *noctiluca* has long been known to react to ships' bow waves and propeller wakes, and might be triggered by cyclical pressure waves in the water, due perhaps to ships' engines, or, on a larger scale, to seabed quakes, or subsidence. Whenever waves interfere with each other – for example, if there are multiple sources, or if internal waves in the water column are reflected from the seabed – unexpected secondary patterns can form.

There is much persuasive evidence consistent with this general idea. Ships have pulled up buckets of water from the vicinity of "wheels", often finding these organisms present. Almost all known cases of wheels or lines of light occur in the organism-rich Persian Gulf, Indian Ocean and China Sea regions, around coastal shelves[312] where the water depth is shallow, which is what the reflection-interference theory would predict. However, there is no convincing correlation with known earthquakes either in space or in time.

It has often been noted that there appear to be few if any cases from the days of sail. Indeed, we are not sure there are any. There is an intriguing early description by the eminent French naturalist Michel Adanson (1727–1806)[313] of bioluminescence off the coast of Senegal, West Africa, in March, 1750: "we sailed in a luminous inclosure, which surrounded us like a large circle of rays" (see Fig. 76). But it is doubtful if this should be taken literally. We also found an account of "geometrical" luminous patterns including a barred circle dating from September 1851; but the explanation in this case is probably tubular or string-like

---

311 Fort, *Damned*, p. 265, citing *Scientific American,* 106-51 (Title: "Curious light phenomena of the Indian seas").

312 Robert F. Staples, *The Distribution and Characteristics of Surface Bioluminescence in the Oceans*, Technical report TR-184, US Navy Oceanographic Office, Washington, March 1966.

313 Adanson, the son of an exiled Scottish Jacobite family, has been compared in stature with the great Swedish naturalist Linnaeus. See: Joseph Thomas, *The Universal Dictionary of Biography and Mythology*, Vol. 1, London, 1887, p. 49.

colonial organisms called pyrosomes and siphonophores, not a phosphorescent wheel proper (see p. 145). In their 1985 article, marine scientists Herring and Horsman list the HMS *Bulldog* and HMS *Vulture* cases (see pp. 129-132 above) as among "a very few observations by sailing vessels" which if true would argue against the theory of engine vibration.[314] But this is not quite correct. Both were steam powered, although both also carried sail. It is true, however, that HMS *Vulture* was "on a starboard tack" and making only 3 kt when the lights appeared, which implies she was under sail at the time; whilst *Bulldog* was "lying becalmed", implying that her engines were not functional. In fact we discovered that in 1862 *Bulldog*'s engines had been "almost condemned" and she was laid up on Rum Cay, near Bermuda, to determine if she was repairable or should be sent home.[315] That she was not sent home implies a repair. It is conceivable that she was kept on, reduced to sail; however, Cdr Moss's painting (Fig. 72) shows *Bulldog* in her final action off Haiti a few months later with all sails furled, which seems most unlikely if manoeuvering power was not available. Otherwise, our review of Fort's cases is generally consistent with the claim that most, if not all, cases have involved steamships.

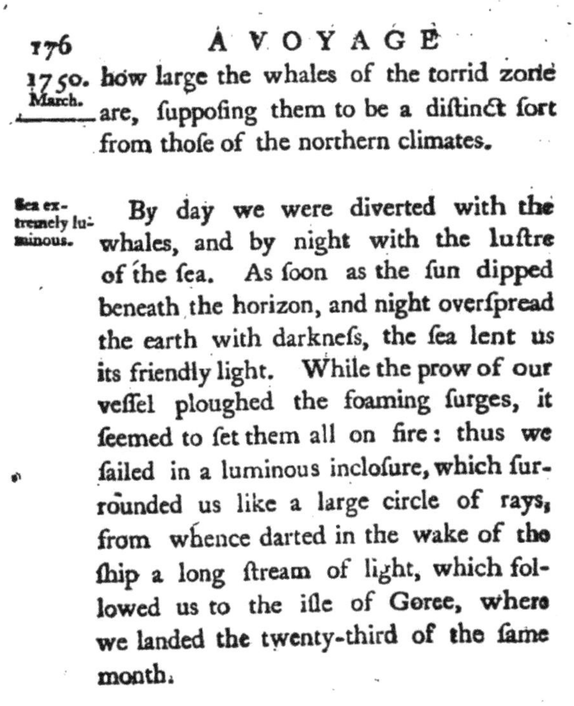

176   A V O Y A G E

1750. how large the whales of the torrid zone
March. are, suppofing them to be a diftinct fort
from thofe of the northern climates.

Sea ex- By day we were diverted with the
tremely lu-
minous. whales, and by night with the luftre of the fea. As foon as the fun dipped beneath the horizon, and night overfpread the earth with darknefs, the fea lent us its friendly light. While the prow of our veffel ploughed the foaming furges, it feemed to fet them all on fire: thus we failed in a luminous inclofure, which furrounded us like a large circle of rays, from whence darted in the wake of the fhip a long ftream of light, which followed us to the ifle of Goree, where we landed the twenty-third of the fame month.

Fig. 76. M. Adanson, *A Voyage to Senegal, the Isle of Goree, and the River Gambia*, London, 1759, p. 176 (credit: Mikhail Gershtein, Magonia Exchange).

This appears to favour the theory that engine vibrations might be the source of the waves. The mechanism is not clear, but in some reports the lights do appear to react to a ship's

314 P. J. Herring & P. Horsman, "Phosphorescent wheels: fact or fiction?" *Marine Observer*, Vol. 55 (1985), pp. 194-201; https://eeuwen.home.xs4all.nl/Download/Herring1985.pdf
315 John Beeler, *The Milne Papers: Vol II: The Royal Navy and the Outbreak of the American Civil War 1860–1862*, Ashgate, 2015 (Milne Mss MLN/116/3 [9]; https://books.google.co.uk/books?isbn=1472402251).

engines, as happens to be the case in the earliest definitely dated report we have (notwithstanding that the HMS *Bulldog* case may be the earliest date*able*), from April 1870, shown in Fig. 77 : "We took in sail and set the engines going. I *then noticed* in the water large white flakes which I had at first taken to be reflections of the moon . . . . After steaming further forward for six or seven knots, a most wonderful spectacle presented itself. On both sides obliquely in front of us, long white waves of light were seen floating towards the ship, increasing in brightness and rapidity . . . [emphasis added]"

ILLUMINATION OF THE SEA

THE following is derived from the *Kölnische Zeitung* of June 19 :—

"Gulf of Siam, April 11

" Last night, between two and three o'clock, I had the opportunity of witnessing an illumination of the sea of the most peculiar kind. It had become quite calm, after a sharp breeze which had sprung up from the N.N.W., caused by a passing storm in the distance. Heat-lightning was still very frequent in the west horizon, and the sky was covered with light clouds, through which the moon shone rather brightly. We took in sail and set the engines going. I then noticed in the water large white flakes which I had at first taken to be reflections of the moon ; they were about a fathom in diameter, apparently lustreless, and of no particular shape, like objects seen lying deep in the water. By the rising and falling of the sea's surface these flakes floated off to a short distance from the ship without imparting any noticeable increase of brightness to the water illuminated by the moon's rays. After steaming further forward for six or seven knots, a most wonderful spectacle presented itself. On both sides obliquely in front of us, long white waves of light were seen floating towards the ship, increasing in brightness and rapidity till at last they almost disappeared, and nothing was observed but a white lustreless, whirling (*schwirrendes*) light upon the water. After gazing for some time it was impossible to distinguish between water, sky, and atmosphere, all which were but just now clearly distinguishable, and a thick fog in long streaks appeared to be driving upon the ship with furious swiftness. The phenomenon of light was somewhat similar to that which would be produced by the whirling round of a ball striped black and white so rapidly that the white stripes seem to be lost and blended with the dark ones. The light was just as if we were enveloped in a thick white fog. The direction of the waves of light upon the ship was always on both sides obliquely from the front. The phenomenon lasted about five minutes, and repeated itself once more afterwards for about two minutes. Without doubt, therefore, shoals of small creatures in the water were the cause

Fig. 77. 'Illumination of the Sea', *Nature*, June 30, 1870, p. 165.

136

Furthermore, whilst many huge "wheels", such as those with spokes apparently radiating from the horizon, can be readily explained with simple linear wave patterns and a perspective illusion, there is a significant number of cases where multiple small, discrete wheels are seen close to a ship, as in the SS *Patna* case of 1880 (see pp. 131-2 above). In fact, these reports tend to be more recent and better documented. In these and similar cases the geophysical shock wave theory – with or without interference effects – and the perspective illusion theory, both seem to fail.[316]

For example, in April 1995 the Master and Second Officer of m.v. *British Alliance* in the Strait of Hormuz, Persian Gulf, saw "phosphorescent cartwheels of bright-blue light" form all around the vessel. The wheels were 15-18 m (50-60 ft) in diameter and with shafts or spokes 30 cm (1 ft) thick. "Their direction of movement seemed random and they were spinning at high speed, some chasing each other, others spinning in opposite directions next to each other . . . Whole groups dumbbelled around each other, all spinning in apparently random directions. The display lasted for about 18 minutes before petering out."[317]

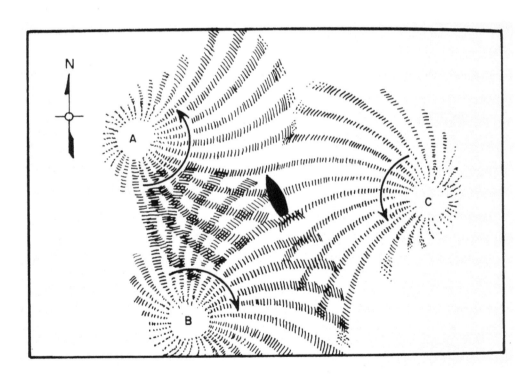

Fig. 78. Three phosphorescent wheels rotating simultaneously, Gulf of Thailand, April 24, 1953. W. Corliss, citing: Naysmith, A., 'Phosphorescence,' *Marine Observer*, 24:137, 1954.

316 P. J. Herring, "Bioluminescent Phenomena in the Ocean," in: J. F. Case *et al* (eds) *Bioluminescence and Chemoluminescence*, World Scientific, 2001, p. 72.
317 Greig, N. J., "Bioluminescence," *Marine Observer*, 66 (1996), p. 62.

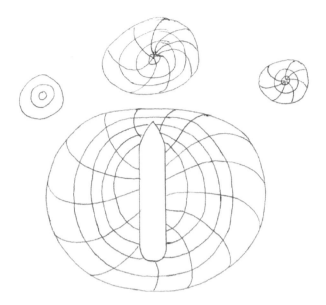

Fig. 79. Sketch of light wheels observed on board the ship ms *Dione*, from: Stijn Naus,
An analysis of marine light patterns, Institute of Marine and Atmospheric Research
Utrecht, University of Utrecht, 2014 (citing J. P. Molenaar, 1978).

In the Gulf of Aden in October 1991, in conditions where bioluminescence was known to be occurring, a collection of bright wheels of similar size clustered round the m.v. *Wiltshire* for about half an hour, coming within 12 m (40 ft) of the ship and all turning with "a slow clockwise motion."[318] Other similar displays observed in the modern era are shown in Figures 78 and 79.

Presumably, interference between waves propagating from multiple vessels at great distances from one another, or between incident and reflected waves reaching the shore or seabed, might cause unexpected second-order effects. But in cases of multiple small wheels with complex movements it is very hard to explain them as due either to engine vibration or to seismic pressure waves. Other speculative ideas have been considered, such as electromagnetic energy from radars[319] and the like, or the magnetic fields of iron ships' hulls.[320] But no one theory seems able to account for all different types and scales of wheel effects.

And the phenomenology is even more complicated than may be apparent from the cases collected by Charles Fort. Whilst Fort, like most commentators, was exercised by glowing wheels on or under the surface, the strangest of the reports concern "aerial luminescence" – wheels or lines appearing in the air some meters *above* the sea surface.

---

318 Marsh, C. H., "Bioluminescence," *Marine Observer*, 62 (1992), p. 177.

319 Hilder, B., 'Radar and Phosphorescence at Sea', *Nature* 176 (1955), pp. 174-175;
https://www.nature.com/articles/176174a0

320 Stijn Naus, *An analysis of marine light patterns*, Institute of Marine and Atmospheric Research Utrecht, University of Utrecht, 2014;
https://www.staff.science.uu.nl/~maas0131/files/marine%20lights%20bachelor%20scriptie%20Stijn%20Naus2014.pdf

We saw a hint of this in Fort's last case, the 1910 *Valentijn* observation mentioned previously in which a horizontal wheel rapidly rotated "above the water". To be fair to Fort, the description in the *Valentijn* case is not very clear and perhaps leaves room for doubt; and as it was the only example of aerial wheels in his 1919 collection he cannot be faulted for neglecting this aspect. But in more modern sources – in particular, *The Marine Observer*, a quarterly journal devoted to marine meteorology published by the British Meteorological Office, whose dozens of first-hand reports were an indispensable research resource from 1923 to 2003 – there are enough explicit accounts to argue that the effect really is (sometimes) in the air above the surface. In one case the effect appeared "about 30 feet above the sea surface", in others "many degrees above the water", or "higher than the hull". One wheel appeared "on the underside of a thin layer of mist 30-35 feet above the water", and on another occasion waves of light "passed across the well deck, starboard to port, at about 6 knots".[321]

Consider this report of a wheel seen in March 1961 in the Gulf of Thailand, which we have translated from an account sent by P. De Hullu, First Mate of the ship *Royal Rotterdam Lloyd*, to the Dutch maritime journal *De Blauwe Wimpel*. One wheel display had just degenerated, when another began, rotating in the opposite direction:

> . . . the entire process repeated itself, but this time the spokes turned counter-sunwise, the axis was now at 4 strokes from the bow[322] and at about 3 or 4 meters above the sea surface as it were. The spokes, too, seemed to rotate at that height. The axis didn't seem further away than 500 meters, and again it consisted of a darker centre with a luminous edge, from where the spokes emerged. There was no wind before the observation, only a little afterwards. The barometer slowly dropped during the watch; there was no sea or swell, and humidity was quite high. [323]

Another display, observed by Chief Officer Peter Newton of the m.v. *Mahsuri* on May 9, 1983, in the Gulf of Oman, has been the subject of an excellent article by our publisher Patrick Huyghe. On that dark, "moonless" evening[324] Newton was on the bridge when "parallel bands of blue-green light" swept towards the ship every few seconds, making him instinctively want to duck. "Each light band was about 10 to 15 feet wide and at least 500 feet long and appeared to be some 15 feet above the water." After 10 minutes "the bands gave way to expanding circles of light" whose "diameter ranged from ten feet to more than 600 feet." Some of the circles travelled with the ship; others fell behind. Newton was emphatic

321 William R. Corliss, *Lightning Auroras Nocturnal Lights And Related Luminous Phenomena*: *Marine Phosphorescent Displays*, Sourcebook Project, Glen Arm, 1982, p. 180 *et seq.* (https://archive.org/details/LightningAurorasNocturnalLightsAndRelatedLuminousPhenome/mode/2up); R. J. Turner, *Notes on the Nature and Occurrence of Marine Bioluminescent Phenomena*, National Institute of Oceanography, Internal Report No. B4, July 1965, p. 10 (https://eprints.soton.ac.uk/392084/1/00473569.pdf).
322 Presumably referring to oar strokes in a ship's boat, an approximate measure of short distances at sea not much used since the 17th century. See: Roel Nicolai, *The Enigma of the Origin of Portolan Charts: A Geodetic Analysis of the Hypothesis of a Medieval Origin*, Brill, Leiden, 2016, p. 396.
323 'Lichtende wielen' (Luminous wheels), *De Blauwe Wimpel,* Vol. 16, No. 10 (Oct. 1961).
324 We confirmed that the evening of May 9-10, 1983 was indeed moonless. The waning crescent moon didn't rise in the Gulf of Oman until after midnight.

that all these phenomena were located *above the water*, and that there was no mist in the air. "The whole lot was out of the water," he said. "I was looking out from the bridge, rather than looking down. Some of the effects were almost parallel with my line of sight."[325]

Are these aerial wheels optical illusions? Mirages? Or are they real? If – as most marine scientists *au fait* with the problem accept – they are real, are they and the aquatic wheels multiple aspects of a single phenomenon? Or are there multiple different phenomena? The aerial patterns are perhaps the most mystifying, but could be the key to understanding their aquatic cousins also. What is the relationship?

One might suspect a layer of mist illuminated from below by lights in the sea, and one or two cases are at first sight suggestive of this; the presence of "mist", or luminosity resembling mist, is sometimes reported. But other cases are like the 1983 Gulf of Oman case just mentioned in specifically reporting "no mist". And in general, reflection from light in the sea isn't a good explanation of most aerial luminescence because, as R. J. Turner says in a report for the UK's National Institute of Oceanography, "if a 'wheel' were distinct enough to be thus projected, it would be easily visible to people looking over the side", yet "similar luminescence in the sea is definitely stated in all reports to be absent." Indeed, in some cases sampling of the ocean has also revealed the absence of *noctiluca*. Turner goes on to say that even though the waves in the air seem to share a "common origin" with those in the sea, the former are, he thinks, "fundamentally different from the normal phosphorescent wheel". The idea of tiny organisms suspended in droplets in a moist layer of air is possible, but "it's difficult to account for the stimulation of the organisms in waves."[326]

Some of the simpler aerial effects might be compared to wind-driven waves on a shallow layer of stable air – a fine-scale relative of the process that causes mountain wave clouds, or higher wave clouds like mackerel sky. In the right conditions – such as a strong wind blowing over some landscape obstruction when the layer is sandwiched between unstable regions; or in the presence of wind shear – standing waves may form on such a stable layer, marked by a regular pattern of condensation in their peaks, travelling rapidly, slowly, or not at all. (A related phenomenon occurring over the sea, albeit on a colossal scale, is the famous 'Morning Glory' effect on the coast of the Gulf of Carpentaria, North Australia, in which ranks of parallel, cylindrical, roll clouds form due to waves on an inversion that caps a shallow stable layer over the sea. See Fig. 80) The air motion through the standing waves is rapid even if the waves are not, so there could be the opportunity for *noctiluca* organisms hypothetically suspended in such a layer to be agitated in a regular periodic pattern of bioluminescence.[327]

---

325 Patrick Huyghe, "Wheels of Light; Sea of Fire," *Oceans*, 20:20, Dec. 1987. See also: Patrick Huyghe, 'Reports of Luminous Seas', *Edge Science*, #3, April–June 2010, pp. 13-17.

326 R. J. Turner, *Notes on the Nature and Occurrence of Marine Bioluminescent Phenomena*, National Institute of Oceanography, July 1965, p. 10 (https://eprints.soton.ac.uk/392084/1/00473569.pdf).

327 Always assuming that *noctiluca* in suspended droplets would encounter shear stresses similar to those that mechanically deform the organism when in the sea, as this is the only known trigger of luminescence.

When wave clouds form, moisture condenses in the peaks of the waves, where the lifted air is cooled adiabatically below the dew point. Condensation of water vapour droplets, on which the tiny airborne organisms could collect, might conceivably be a factor in stimulating an inert airborne population to glow in narrow bands. But we don't know of any evidence for this.

It's true that increased temperature is a driver of *noctiluca*'s luminescence, and for higher temperature we need to look in the wave troughs, not the peaks. So instead of wondering how bright rays are produced on a dark

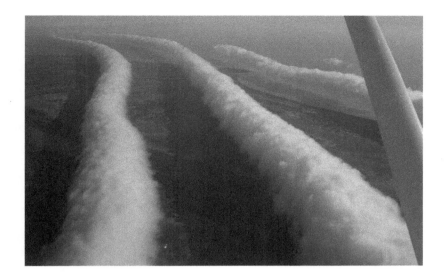

Fig. 80. 'Morning Glory' roll cloud, captured from an aircraft over the Gulf of Carpenteria, Australia (Mick Petroff, https://en.wikipedia.org/wiki/Morning_Glory_cloud).

However, wind alone can scarcely account for interference effects causing complex patterns with circular symmetry revolving near the observers, in the air or on the water. [328] Moreover, Occam's razor seems to demand that the trigger for aerial wheels has to be the same as the trigger for the analogous aquatic wheels, not just because they resemble one another but because they occur in the same sea areas and conditions. And yet the coupling between wind and wave in the open ocean is, generally, even more chaotic, with no opportunity for standing waves to develop on such fine scales.

The least implausible natural mechanism so far proposed to explain some complex geometrical displays in water is interference between internal seismic waves from different sources on the seafloor, a theory first proposed in 1960 by oceanographer Kurt Kalle.[329] But according to the most recent study this does not appear to work to explain rotating water wheels except perhaps at the largest scales.[330] And how could interfering seismic waves in the sea – internal waves – be causally connected to similar wheel patterns in an elevated atmospheric layer many meters above the surface of the medium? Kalle himself thought that

substrate we should perhaps be thinking about how dark lanes occur in what would be – left undisturbed – a flat bright field of luminescence. However, it seems very unlikely that the tiny temperature differential could be significant, absent some critical threshold effect for which, as far as we know, there is no evidence.

328 Winds above 3 m/sec (10.8 k/hr; 7kt) can cause regular raster-like bands of turbulent agitation in the sea, due to an interaction between surface gravity waves and a wind-driven shear current known as Langmuir circulation. The resulting parallel 'windrows' are the result of vortices that accumulate foam and other floating materials – including, potentially, *noctiluca* – where their downwelling flows converge. But these bands form along the wind direction and could not travel transversely at speed as the "wheel" spokes do.

329 Kurt Kalle (1898–1975), a pioneer in marine chemistry working for the Deutschen Hydrographischen Institut in Berlin, wrote the often-cited paper 'Die rätselhafte und unheimliche Naturerscheinung des explodierenden und des rotierenden Meeresleuchtenseine Folge lokaler Seebeben' (The mysterious and eerie natural appearance of the exploding and rotating marine lights – An effect of local see quakes), published in *Deutsche Hydrografische Zeitschrift* Vol. 13 (1960), pp. 49-77. Kalle based his study on 70 reports.

330 Stijn Naus, *An analysis of marine light patterns*, Institute of Marine and Atmospheric Research Utrecht, University of Utrecht, 2014.

aerial wheels might be caused by seaquake shockwaves causing little "fountains" of spray, carrying luminous plankton into the air. But, again, it is very hard to understand how this would explain distinct moving patterns meters above the surface, especially when no luminosity is visible on or below the surface.

There is a mode of coupling between ocean waves and atmospheric structures that could be relevant, in principle. Microbaroms are air pressure waves with infrasound frequencies, caused by high-amplitude sea wave groups generated in interference between oppositely directed wave trains, such as when ocean swells are reflected back from a coast. These standing wave groups transmit their energy upwards to the air, which oscillates in sympathy, with effects that can travel to the top of the atmosphere – unless the energy is trapped by acoustic refraction/reflection effects near the surface, when waves can propagate horizontally.[331] These microbaroms cause the anxiety-inducing sub-audible infrasound effects by which their existence was first suspected. Intriguingly, the experience of encountering phosphorescent wheels has been "variously described as 'eerie', 'weird', 'almost frightening' and 'alarming'."[332]

In one wheel case a lookout on the bridge became 'quite scared' and feared he was hallucinating, while in another the quartermaster 'became panic stricken' and left the helm, having to be ordered back three times.[333] The ship *Moffat*, in the Atlantic near the equator on the evening of March 5, 1821, encountered a bright luminous sea. No banding or wheel effects were seen; but as the luminosity grew to "great intensity" all those observing experienced symptoms of "headach [sic], giddiness, pain in the eyeballs, and slight sickness".[334] It is interesting that headache, dizziness and nausea are typical symptoms of infrasound exposure; and "pain in the eyeballs" is suggestive, given that the anxiety-inducing effects of infrasound have been linked specifically to the 18 Hz resonant frequency of the human eyeball.[335] In 170 m of water in the Bay of Bengal on October 12, 1969, the research vessel *Vladimir Vorobyov* saw a glowing white patch 300–400 m in diameter rotating counter-clockwise which broke up into eight rotating curved beams like turbine blades. Samples of water revealed no luminous organisms. When the beams appeared, "sleeping sailors woke up from a sense of fear",[336] whilst during the manifestation members of the crew felt "pressure on the eardrum and, according to the head of the expedition Edward Petrenko, 'were close to panic'."[337] In February 1977, experienced crewmen of the cargo ship *Anton*

331 https://en.wikipedia.org/wiki/Microbarom

332 P. J. Herring & P. Horsman, 'Phosphorescent wheels: fact or fiction?' *Marine Observer*, Vol. 55 (1985), p. 195.

333 *Ibid.*

334 J. Henderson, 'On A Luminous Appearance of the Ocean', *Transactions of the Medical & Physical Society of Calcutta*, Vol. 1 (1825), pp. 107-110; credit: Mikhail Gershtein, Magonia Exchange.

335 https://littlefield.co/the-psychoacoustic-effect-of-infrasonic-sonic-and-ultrasonic-frequencies-within-non-lethal-cf05e1fd8673

336 Col. V. L. Pravdivtsev and Capt. E. P. Litvinov, On the history of the study of anomalous phenomena by reconnaissance of the USSR, p. 15; https://www.rulit.me/books/k-istorii-izucheniya-anomalnyh-yavlenij-razvedkoj-voenno-morskogo-flota-sssr-read-548628-1.html

337 In a conceivably related report from Uzbekistan, witnesses on the shore of a large reservoir near Yusuphona in early July 1975 "woke up from unaccountable fear" to see a cold "fluorescent" light in the shape of a "ball" silently emerging from the water surrounded by "concentric circles of various thicknesses and

Makarenko are reported to have felt "dizzy and sick, as if on a merry-go-round" during a wheel display in the Malacca Strait.[338]

It's most unlikely, of course, that microbaroms with infrasound wavelengths of tens to hundreds of metres (about 1-20 Hz) could themselves be agitating airborne *noctiluca* into patterns of luminescence with a characteristic scale of meters, or less. But perhaps infrasound waves from great distances – travelling possibly hundreds of miles – are revealing the presence of a widespread acoustic duct in the atmospheric boundary layer at times when wheel displays occur, and perhaps this is important. Could it be that the top of a sharply capped duct is registering the effect of reflected and interfering internal atmospheric waves inside the duct, in much the same way as does the shallow coastal ocean below it in Kalle's seismic theory? The presence of such an acoustic trapping duct below an inversion cap could be consistent with frequent reports that the luminous effects appear located co-altitudinally in an elevated layer, and with occasional references to a mist layer. The fact that aerial wheels favour the same sea areas as their watery relatives might be explained if stable oceanic boundary layer inversions of large horizontal extent tend to occur over the same warm, shallow, tropical, continental-shelf waters that suit Kalle's theory and also happen to favour plankton abundance.

But this is only a suggestive analogy. And again, what is the source of the interfering waves in the atmospheric layer? If Kalle's internal seismic shockwaves in the ocean cannot somehow couple to waves propagating on a stable atmospheric layer metres above the sea surface – which seems very difficult – we need to explain why these wheel-like interference products, due to waves of different origins, in these different media with different properties, can appear the same. Not to mention: how does a population of *noctiluca* come to be suspended in an aerial mist layer whilst being often absent from the water below?

An escape from this dilemma seems to bring us back to the one condition common to all reliable sightings – the presence of the ship. Whilst the evidence of emotional infrasound effects (merely suggestive, to be sure) could implicate microbaroms, or indeed seismic P-waves (the type of internal pressure waves able to travel through water),[339] which both have frequencies in the range 1-20 Hz, it happens that the frequency of engine revolution in most ships is also infrasonic at around 1-2 Hz.[340] There are almost no observations made by people not on ships.[341] Herring & Horsman noted in 1985 that there were no reports from small

---

brightnesses", for 6-7 minutes, all the time experiencing "a feeling of animal fear that fettered movement". See: Col. V. L. Pravdivtsev and Capt. E. P. Litvinov, *op. cit.* p. 16; http://nyos.lv/f/uploads/EN-TEXT-Microsoft-Office-Word-Document.pdf

338   It is possible this was merely an optical disorientation effect, although the rotation was "not rapid" (Paul Stonehill, 'Soviet UFO Sightings in International Waters', *Nexus*, June-July 2011). Also reported by Psalomschikov (*NLO*, St. Petersburg, 2006, #18). This is probably the same Malacca Strait case reported by Corliss as happening on Feb. 14, 1977. Psalomschikov's reported date of Feb. 28 appears to be an error, probably coming from the date of the article which is his source (Soviet newspaper *Vechernyaya Odessa*, Feb. 28, 1977, also cited by Stonehill, *op. cit.*). An event date of Feb. 14, 1977, would fit.

339 Possible animal 'prediction' of earthquakes by infrasound has long been an active field of study. See: A. Bedard Jr., & T. Georges, 'Atmospheric infrasound', *Physics Today*, 53(3), March 2000, pp. 32-37.

340   Stijn Naus, *op. cit.*, p. 9.

341   It is possible that some find their way, incognito, into the UFO literature. Besides the Uzbekistan case mentioned in note 337, our only other marginal candidate is a sighting from a beach in Togo, West Africa, on

boats, no local traditions to speak of, and no wheel sightings from aircraft (which, in truth, might be thought a little strange whether the wheels are associated with ships or not).[342] Does this mean that the engine vibrations of a ship inside an atmospheric duct can directly cause similar standing waves both in the sea and in a low-level atmospheric layer laden with *noctiluca*-rich mist droplets? Perhaps. But the problem is not thereby halved, rather it is doubled: how, exactly, does this account for similar patterns of spinning wheels in the water *and* in the air?

So much is speculation. Despite the interest of a few marine scientists, and more than 200 reports logged in good faith by seamen, most of them archived assiduously for 80 years in the pages of *The Marine Observer*, the phosphorescent wheels have remained a fringe topic of Forteana, with almost no active investigation. To some extent they were probably shoved under the carpet as just being too weird to deal with. They are certainly the most spectacular species in a mysterious marine menagerie of related phenomena including "erupting luminescence", glowing boomerangs, rings, coloured rays, and so forth. But there can be little doubt that the phosphorescent wheels are as real as any of them.

Or, at least, they were.

The dearth of reports of wheels since the 1990s is striking. At the time of writing (2020) we have found only a couple of possible cases so far in the 2000s,[343] and none from the decade just past.

In one case, glowing "spiral designs", "concentric rings" and other "geometric shapes" seen on or under the surface of the Strait of Hormuz over two nights on May 18-19, 2007, resemble the patterns created by colonies of often-bioluminescent molluscs. Reports of this type also predate the phosphorescent wheels proper.

---

the Gulf of Guinea. On a dark night in March 1974 a French vacationer and a Togolese girl saw a dark mass with an estimated size of 25 to 30 m, 200 to 300 m out on the sea. From it three beams of blinding light of white-yellowish, rosy, and blue-green colours shone out in their direction. Almost immediately, a big wave flooded the beach threatening to drag the couple into the sea if they hadn't been able to hold onto the trunk of a coconut tree. Powerful waves lashed the shore. Underneath the mass the sea "was hollowed out in the form of a basin", "some five metres or maybe even six metres deep". A published drawing based on a sketch made by the French witness shows illuminated waves in concentric rings emanating from the mass. Impressed by the blue and green colours of the waves, the principle witness also mentioned having felt a paralyzing and terrifying heat coming from the beams. He suffered distress afterwards. (*Phénomènes Spatiaux*, # 47, March 1976, p. 23; *Flying Saucer Review*, Vol. 22, No. 6, pp. 4-5 and back cover.) The colours, the season, duration, and location, not to mention emotional disturbance, are all consistent with a display of bioluminescence., and the Gulf of Guinea hosts "high concentrations" of *noctiluca scintillans* (Richard V. Lynch, *An Assessment and Annotated Bibliography of Marine Bioluminescence Research: 1979-1987*, Ocean Sciences Branch, Oceanography Divison, January 1993, p. 160 [733]). However, other aspects of the story cast doubt on this interpretation.

342 Herring & Horsman record one aircraft sighting only, of an interesting linear wave phenomenon but not of a mature wheel. It may be that the relatively small scale of true wheels and their proximity to lighted ships at night makes them difficult to notice from the air.

343 The two cases, involving expanding rings, spirals, bars, blobs, and crescents, date from May 2007 and April 2009. Neither has all the features of fully mature wheels, but both have some of the component features of classic displays; and each can boast different detailed accounts from multiple witnesses, something rare in old reports. Also, notably, in the April 2009 case two of the three accounts describe the effect as being "just above the surface of the sea" and "hovering and spinning just above the water". See: http://www.cropcircleanswers.com/cca-sightings/marinelightwheels.htm
http://www.cropcircleanswers.com/marinelightwheels_arabiangulf.html

The engraving in Fig. 81 shows a composite of various bioluminescent phenomena witnessed from the schooner *La Découverte* in September 1851, off the coast of Florida. Next to waves "enveloped in white light" we see luminous jellyfish that glowed with "brilliant red light", the spouts of dolphins looking like "jets of fire", and in the foreground a remarkable barred circle of light. The crew hauled up water samples in which were found many small molluscs able to "form colonies of billions of individuals aggregating to form *perfect geometric figures*" (our emphasis). [344] The mollusc in question was identified as *Salpa biforis*, otherwise known as "salp".

Fig. 81. Plate from *La terre et le ciel* (1893) showing luminous phenomena recorded off the coast of Florida in September, 1851. [345]

Today many kinds of related colonial organisms are known. Hundreds – in some cases hundreds of thousands – of tiny luminous animals assemble into long tubes, called pyrosomes, or even longer strings called siphonophores, which rise to feed at night near the surface where they can make rectilinear figures or curl into rings and spirals. These colonies can be many meters long, like a 60-foot (19 m) luminous pyrosome filmed in 2011 off Tasmania, Australia,[346] or the enormous siphonophore, *siphonophore Apolemia*, recently

---

344 From a letter by a Frenchmen, Mr Poussielgue, traveling from Washington on the schooner *La Découverte* with the purpose of exploring 'the oriental part of Florida', in: Amédée Guillemin, *La terre et le ciel*, Librairie Hachette et Cie, Paris, 1893, pp. 159-162.

345 Amédée Guillemin, *La terre et le ciel*, Librairie Hachette et Cie, Paris, 1893, p. 161.

346 http://www.deepseanews.com/2013/08/the-60-foot-long-jet-powered-animal-youve-probably-never-heard-of/

filmed off New Zealand, which was estimated to be as long as 390 ft (124 m) or more, coiled into a spiral "feeding posture" that some headlines likened to an underwater UFO.[347]

All these organisms are far too large to be present in the air above the sea. Their appearance is strange and beautiful, but very different from the hovering mist-like wheels and bands seen in phosphorescent wheel displays.

Our most recent sighting on April 11, 2009, in the Arabian Gulf, boasted something closer to a fully-featured classic display, taking place "above the water", with fast-moving linear waves of light, expanding rings, and alignments of rotating spirals "like something that belonged on a dance floor". But finding only one 21st-century "phosphorescent wheel" in our net is a paltry catch for a species that was once, if not commonplace, at least a regular presence in the record. In these days of instant mass communication, where have they gone?

According to the most recent academic research we have located concerning phosphorescent wheels, "almost all of the reports on the luminous phenomena were originally published in the Marine Observer."[348] We note the closure of *The Marine Observer* in 2003 (after 80 years and a World War, finally a victim of Meteorological Office budget trimming[349]), followed by the demise of the pioneer anomalist and archivist William Corliss in 2011; and we speculate that these factors together may go some way towards explaining the near disappearance of reports in the 21st century, implying that the phenomena may still be out there.

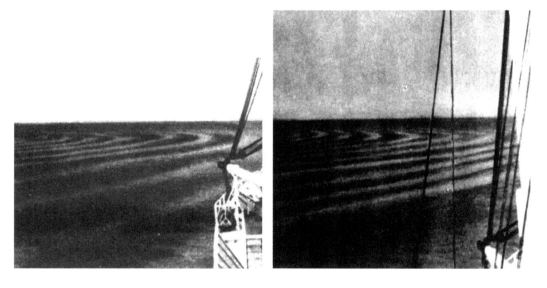

Fig. 82. Not bioluminescence. These unusual light-coloured rings photographed in the Adriatic Sea, near the coast of Yugoslavia, June 14, 1985, are due to a suspension of lime particles caused by fault displacement or collapse of limestone karst formations on the seabed. [350]

---

347 https://www.newsweek.com/otherworldly-150-foot-long-string-like-organism-deep-sea-millions-interconnected-clones-1496512

348 Stijn Naus, *An analysis of marine light patterns*, op. cit.

349 Malcolm Walker, *History of the Meteorological Office*, Cambridge University Press, 2012, p. 442.

350 Left: http://www.radionetplus.ru/teksty/poznavatelnye/61206-tayna-dyavolskoy-karuseli.html
Right: https://coollib.com/b/227044/read

Nevertheless, we still find it curious that no photos or videos of wheels exist, especially given the near-ubiquity of modern phone cameras and the rapid growth of the internet in the last two decades. Other, not dissimilar, phenomena have been seen and filmed. So why not phosphorescent wheels? The pyrosomes, siphonophores and their relatives are cases in point; and Fig. 82 shows rare daylight photos of a strange geometrical pattern of pale rings appearing on the surface of the Adriatic, which was eventually traced to a geological cause. One doubts that huge, blue, phosphorescent wheels rotating on or above the sea surface at night would be any less spectacular. Yet we have found nothing.

How do we explain this? In a few cases an observer reports that he had a camera but didn't think of using it. In the April 2009 case just mentioned, the observer, who himself had the conn and was unable to get to his camera, made the interesting remark that some crew members did take photographs but that none of them captured what could be seen with the eye. A possible implication is that the light's intensity may be poor, or its frequency not optimum for emulsions and sensors, so that over the years disappointing images may have been discarded. There is some evidence that sighting frequency may be inversely correlated with the phase of the moon, which would be consistent with the idea that the luminescence is faint and harder to observe in bright moonlight. [351]

Unlike a CCD or CMOS sensor, or most 20th-century film emulsions, the fully dark-adapted human retina (using rod cells only) is almost exclusively sensitive in a blue-green region centred around 530 nm, which is close to the peak emission wavelength of marine dinoflagellates like *noctiluca scintillans*. The eye also has an extremely good response to patterns of fleeting motion, subjectively enhancing fugitive, fast-moving bands that might be smeared into featureless uniformity by the long exposure times needed for faint light sources at night.

On the other hand, we do find an abundance of internet images of *noctiluca*, in its ordinary manifestation, glowing very photogenically around beaches and boats all over the world (Fig. 83). Why, then, is there not a single one of the classic "wheel"-type patterns? [352] Wheel reports often describe what sound like very vivid displays; but we have no easy way to calibrate subjective impressions. Have they always been, in fact, relatively very faint? Or have they gone – faded from the oceans and from history altogether? If so, what has changed recently?

---

351   Our colleague Manuel Borraz classified 114 cases of marine luminescent displays detailed by W. R. Corliss (GLW1-GLW8 in *Lightning, Auroras, Nocturnal Lights*, Sourcebook Project, 1982) according to the nearest lunar phase, finding about 5 times as many cases near New Moon as near Full Moon (email from Manuel Borraz to Wim van Utrecht, July 20, 2020. New Moon: 39, First Quarter: 26, Full Moon: 7.5, Last Quarter: 41.5. The decimals are adjustments reflecting cases on the mid-point between phases). Borraz points out (email to Martin Shough & Wim van Utrecht, Aug. 27, 2020) that this would also be consistent with the idea that bright light suppresses the bioluminescence, as has been observed in certain dinoflagellates – though not the most common suspect, *noctiluca scintillans* (see: https://academic.oup.com/plankt/article/35/1/177/1520566).

352   We were initially deceived by an impressive 'photo' of a rotating 'wheel' observed in 1967 in the Gulf of Thailand (see: http://www.radionetplus.ru/teksty/poznavatelnye/61206-tayna-dyavolskoy-karuseli.html, and several other Russian sites that deal with UFOs and the paranormal), only to discover that it is not an authentic photograph, merely a realistic 'reconstruction from eyewitness accounts'
(http://tonnel-ufo.narod.ru/tonn_28.html)

Fig. 83. The blue glow of *noctiluca scintillans* – also known as "sea sparkle" – illuminates breaking waves on the shore of Pingtan, Fujian province, China.[353]

If it is possible to explain the initial late-19th century peak by the appearance of powered iron and steel ships, and if ship construction is still basically the same, has something changed in the environment? One thing might be sea surface temperatures. Could there be a climate change angle here? Probably not. It seems *noctiluca* likes it hot, and so on that basis wheel phenomena in warming seas ought to be *increasing*, all things being equal, not decreasing.[354] On the other hand it is possible that increased ocean pollution, particularly perhaps in oil-producing areas, might affect the prevalence or behaviour of surface plankton.

In summary: It has often been said that the deep ocean is less explored than the environment of space. Phosphorescent wheels show that the surface of the ocean, too – not to mention in some cases the atmospheric boundary layer above it – still holds mysteries. It seems almost certain that the source of light is bioluminescence, probably supplied by *noctiluca*; and it is a reasonable suspicion that most if not all wheel phenomena are associated with the presence of powered, iron- and steel-hulled ships. But beyond this, to date, there seems to be no completely convincing explanation.

Dutch researcher Stijn Naus had this to say of the various theories available in 2014:

353   https://twitter.com/ChinaDaily/status/1118405648226619393/photo/1
354   Warming climate has been blamed for expanding blooms of *noctiluca scintillans* in many parts of the world, largely tracking the explosion of plankton populations which are the organism's food (https://www.zmescience.com/ecology/environmental-issues/global-warming-plankton-27052015/). There is also a direct relation between the bioluminescence and water temperature. It has been known since the mid-19th century that warming *noctiluca*-laden water to 35° C causes it to glow more brightly. (Leopold Gmelin, *Handbook of Chemistry: Cohesion, adhesion, affinity, light, heat, and electricity*, Volume 1, Cavendish Society, 1848, p. 184). True, on further heating to 43° C the luminosity was completely destroyed. But it's very unlikely that excessive temperature could explain a disappearance of phosphorescent wheels. NASA measurements of changing SST (https://earthobservatory.nasa.gov/global-maps/MYD28M) show maximum surface temperature in the Persian Gulf increasing in area over the period 2002 to 2020 but topping out at around 35° C, which ought to suit *noctiluca* quite nicely. Much higher sub-surface temperatures have been recorded, up to 56° C in the Red Sea; but not near the surface of the open ocean. Even if SSTs approaching 43° C might conceivably occur in a few rare hotspots it seems very unlikely that this could be disabling *noctiluca* on any significant scale.

[A] closer look shows that they all fall short in explaining some aspects of the observations. This either means that the final theory concerning the phenomena has not yet been found, or that different versions of the phenomena also need different theories. This last option may seem like a stretch, because the different phenomena all seem to take place in the same area and in the same time frame, which would indicate that the different theories that have been discussed should all have the same very specific requirements. However, using the same explanation for all of the different observations is also unsatisfying, because of the great variation between them. [355]

All quite bizarre, and frustrating. We have many apparently reliable eyewitness accounts, most of them clearly relating to the same phenomenon. Yet after more than a century there is still no satisfying explanation. We are reminded of the will-o-the-wisps, so prominent in the records of pre-20th century naturalists. They, too, departed from us, and took their secret with them into history. With virtually no one reporting the wheels anymore (the most recent 2009 case being a lonely outpost in the new millennium) we are afraid that marine scientists will have little attention to spare for them in the future. Are phosphorescent wheels destined to go the way of flying saucers, becoming creatures of myth?

There is something remarkable about the way Charles Fort's submarine "wheel shaped constructions" prefigured the flying saucers of a later era, a resonance not lost on modern writers when Fort was rediscovered after Kenneth Arnold's sighting of mysterious discoidal aircraft. From one point of view, the amplifying effect of this resonance may be considered a negative factor, promoting an unholy alliance. On the other hand, it may have been helpful in furthering the data-conservation project that began with Fort – if not directly in terms of case research and explanations, then indirectly, by encouraging a tradition of chronicling anomalies which, *via* the work of Corliss and others, kept the phosphorescent wheels spinning on the periphery of scientific awareness. They are still there. We can hope to do little more here than perpetuate Fort's role in this.

---

355 Stijn Naus, *An analysis of marine light patterns, op. cit.*

CHAPTER 12 – **Paced by a Fireball off Cape Race**

One night in November 1887 the British ship *Siberian* was steaming near Cape Race, Newfoundland, when according to her Captain "a large ball of fire appeared to rise out of the sea to a height of about fifty feet" then approached the ship and matched its course for a mile and a half before moving away, remaining visible in total about five minutes.

Charles Fort was critical of *Nature*'s "supposition" that it was ball lightning. He points out that the famous astronomical populariser Camille Flammarion had said it was "enormous" (which is true, although the captain's own chosen adjective was "large"), that "the object had moved 'against the wind' before retreating" and that "Captain Moore said that at about the same place he had seen such appearances before."[356]

> 21. GLOBULAR LIGHTNING. — The following report from the Hydrographic Office relates to one of the rarest and most inexplicable forms of lightning. Can any of the readers of *Science* give any information on the subject? A globe of fire floats leisurely along in the air in an erratic sort of a course, sometimes exploding with great force, at other times disappearing without exploding. On land it has been observed to go into the ground and then re-appear at a short distance, and where it entered the soil it left a rugged hole some twenty feet in diameter. Although there is no doubt as to the facts regarding the phenomenon, no satisfactory explanation of the cause has ever been given. It is, of course, entirely different in character from St. Elmo's fires, so often seen on board vessels during thunder-storms : these remain stationary at the yard-arms and mast-heads, and are analogous to the 'brush discharge' of an electric machine. Captain Moore, British steamship 'Siberian,' reports, " Nov. 12, midnight, Cape Race bearing west by north, distant ten miles, wind strong south by east, a large ball of · fire appeared to rise out of the sea to a height of about fifty feet, and come right against the wind close up to the ship. It then altered its course, and ran along with the ship to a distance of about one and one-half miles. In about two minutes it again altered its course, and went away to the south-east against the wind. It lasted, in all, not over five minutes. Have noticed the same phenomenon before off Cape Race, and it seemed to indicate that an easterly or south-easterly gale was coming on."

Fig. 84. *Science*, Vol. 10, No. 256 (December 30, 1887), p. 324.[357]

This is another well-known sighting, re-quoted in numerous sources, usually from Fort. It was widely reported in 1887–1888, but all of the accounts appear to stem from a short "report from the Hydrographic Office" first published in December 1887, in the *New York Times* (December 2, calling it "an electric phenomenon") and in *Science* (Fig. 84) which described it as "globular lightning . . . one of the rarest and most inexplicable forms of lightning."

---

356   Fort, *Damned,* p. 261, citing *Nature,* 37-187, and *L'Astronomie,* 1887(sic)-76 ('La foudre globulaire,' *L'Astronomie,* 7, 1888, p. 76). See also: Camille Flammarion (Trans. Walter Mostyn), *Thunder and Lightning,* Chatto & Windus, London, 1905, p. 68.

357   http://science.sciencemag.org/content/ns-10/256/324.3

Many such cases have been reported as "globular lightning" since the idea became fashionable in the 19th century. Today this would be called "ball lightning", but in truth the notion is no great advance on the kind of hand-waving notions about "meteors" of "electrical fluid" (not rocks from space) that were already old hat by the time Charles Fort raised a sceptical eyebrow at them in *The Book of the Damned*.

First of all, is the story reliable?

Capt. Moore's account, as printed, was preserved on a Hydrographic Office Pilot Chart by the man in charge of the Hydrographic Office in New York, a serious-minded young US Navy Lieutenant named Vincendon Lezare Cottman (1852–1917). Lt Cottman moved on in 1889 to take up shipboard posts, his "energy, tact, and sound judgment" having been responsible for expanding and systematising the work of the Office and leaving it in an "enviable position," according to the *Annual Report of the Secretary of the Navy* (1890). He later rose to the rank of Rear Admiral and retired as Commandant of the US Navy Yard, Puget Sound, Washington.[358]

We identified Capt. Moore as Robert P. Moore, 47 years of age at the time of the incident, and confirmed that he was Captain of the SS *Siberian*.[359] Capt. Moore appears to have come from a family line of ships' Masters.[360]

The *SS Siberian* was a 372-ft single-screw steam passenger/cargo vessel weighing around 3900 tons built on the Clyde at Govan, Glasgow, in 1884. She was British registered, operated by the Allan Line, and regularly carried livestock and migrant passengers (see Fig. 86) across the Atlantic between Scotland and Quebec or, later, New York.[361] On November 19, 1910, she left St John's, Newfoundland, on her final voyage to Glasgow. She was scrapped at Falmouth in 1912.[362]

358   Several useful pieces of information on this case were provided by members of Magonia Exchange email group, 18-27 Feb. 2016; in particular, Richard Spiers, Drew Richardson, and Bob Skinner. Richard Spiers points out that the *NY Times* story was probably the earliest newspaper article. Biographical information on Lt. Cottman: http://freepages.military.rootsweb.ancestry.com/~cacunithistories/RADM_Cottman.html
Hydrographic Office Pilot Charts are archived at:
http://www.archives.gov/research/guide-fed-records/groups/037.html
http://www.archives.gov/research/guide-fed-records/groups/019.html
359   http://archiver.rootsweb.ancestry.com/th/read/TheShipsList/2004-11/1100308619; Robert P., Capt. Moore, born July 19, 1830 in North Carolina, United States, son of Charles Augustus Moore and Lucinda Killian, died Mar 08, 1919. See: http://www.wikitree.com/wiki/Moore-4818;
http://www.wikitree.com/genealogy/Moore-Family-Tree-4818
360   Information attached to a 1903 letter from Robert's son, Judge Charles A. Moore:
http://www.martygrant.com/genealogy/moore/moore-charles-letter-1903.htm
361   In 1891 she rescued the crew of the stricken ship *Little Wader* in an Atlantic storm, for which her Master (then Capt. John Park), 2nd Mate and other crew members were awarded medals for gallantry. See National Archives, P.R.O. BT.261.5; http://www.dnw.co.uk/auction-archive/special-collections/lot.php?specialcollection_id=101&specialcollectionpart_id=28&lot_id=64021
362   N. R. P. Bonsor, *North Atlantic Seaway*, Vol. 1, p. 316;
http://www.theshipslist.com/ships/descriptions/ShipsS.shtml
http://www.clydesite.co.uk/clydebuilt/viewship.asp?id=13257

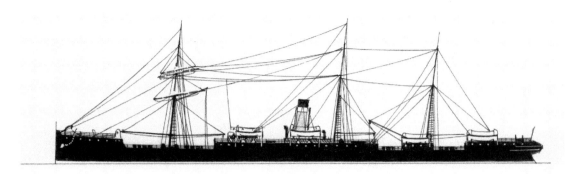

Fig. 85. The Allan Line ship SS *Siberian*.

Fig. 86. A migrant party on the deck of SS *Siberian*, June 13, 1885. [363]

The date of the incident is potentially ambiguous, because "Nov. 12, midnight" might mean either midnight November 11-12 or midnight November 12-13. There is today a popular convention that "Nov. 12, midnight" would refer to the midnight that ends the given calendar day. But this is *only* a convention, not inevitable.[364] The 1884 International Meridian Conference rationalised a variety of civil, astronomical and nautical calendars into a common 24 hour day anchored to the Greenwich meridian – although it took many years for things to change in practice, with a number of nations not adopting the new conventions until well into the 20th century, and merchant fleets were typically slow to implement changes. Officially, the international day was now "to begin for all the world at the moment of mean midnight of

---

363 http://content.iriss.org.uk/goldenbridge/photoalbum/zoom_08022.html (credit: Richard Spiers, Magonia Exchange).

364 Conventions of date and time have evolved laboriously. Indeed, 150 years ago, the civil day, the nautical day, and the astronomical day, were all officially different. The old nautical day started at noon on the day before the civil date, and so had two ambiguous noons. The US was 40 years behind Britain in matching the start of the nautical and the civil day, but from the middle of the 19th century, when the American-born Capt Moore was still a boy, the official US nautical day became the same as the civil day, beginning and ending at midnight – at least officially; it may well be that some sailors' habits were slow to change.

the initial meridian, coinciding with the beginning of the civil day" and the Conference expressed "the hope that as soon as may be practicable the astronomical and nautical days will be arranged everywhere to *begin at midnight*." The Conference did not explicitly resolve the ambiguity of midnight.[365] But if midnight belongs to the beginning of the calendar day, then strictly "Nov. 12, midnight" in a ship's log ought to mean 24 hours before the change to November 13, or 00:00 on the night of November 11-12. As for common usage, an exactly contemporary newspaper account, published November 12, 1887, of the foundering of the steamer *Plover* off Newfoundland at midnight November 11-12, records the accident as occurring at "12 o'clock, a.m., today", implicitly attaching the prior midnight to the current date, November 12. [366] So it isn't quite as obvious as one might first think that the phrase "Nov. 12, midnight", reported by the American Captain of a British-registered ship in 1887, as quoted by a US Navy Lieutenant, should be interpreted to mean the local midnight[367] between November 12 and November 13.

Sidestepping this uncertainty over the date, we are still able to perform a crude check on the weather at the time of the sighting, which was reported by Capt. Moore as "wind strong, south by east." The US War Department Daily Weather Maps for the mornings before and after the sighting (Fig. 87) show that on Friday, November 11, a deepening low-pressure system is moving east out over the shore of New England "with increasing energy", heading towards Nova Scotia.[368] A Maine newspaper reported that a trans-Atlantic vessel had to turn back to shore until the 12th because of "one of the roughest times ever experienced on the bay."[369] By 0700 Washington time on November 13 the low has drifted over the north of Cape Breton. Therefore, during the 24 hours bracketed by the two possible incident times, the centre of the low should have remained somewhere over Nova Scotia, approximately 400-600 miles (640-960 km) WSW of Cape Race. Measurements for the sea area of interest to us are not available; but the cyclonic gradient wind implied by the isobars, and in particular the surface wind rotating a little further anticlockwise in the friction layer, would probably have been blowing from the S or SE towards the Avalon peninsula of Newfoundland during this

---

365   On the 12-hour civil clock, this has persisted into the 21st C, so that legal contracts and the like especially in the US would replace "Nov. 12, midnight" with "11:59" or "00:01" on the 11th, 12th, or 13th for the avoidance of doubt. Generally, midnight is held to be 12 a.m., whilst noon is 12 p.m. And yet there are opportunities for confusion here, too. The US Govt Printing Office style manual defined midnight as 12.00 *p.m.,* and noon as 12.00 *a.m.*, until 2008, presumably because making midnight 12 hours *post meridiem* seemed to respect the popular convention that associated it intuitively to the prior calendar day – even though that same convention had long accepted midnight as 12.00 a.m.!

366   *The Colonist* (St John's, N.F.), Nov. 12, 1887, p. 1.

367   Probably Atlantic Standard Time, approximately. Ship's time may or may not be local time. Usually a merchant vessel would adopt local time at the port of departure, adjusting *en route* to local time for the port of arrival.

368   Central pressure on Nov. 11 is equivalent to a Category 1 hurricane, less than 29.1 inches of mercury (<985.4 mbar). After Nov. 11, as the low moves out over Nova Scotia and the Atlantic where observations are sparse, central pressure is no longer recorded and isobars are few; but the Daily Weather Maps show that this cyclone has been well-defined for only a day or so. The Nov. 11 map tracks the centre moving north from Nantucket over the previous 24 hours. It is evident there on the Nov. 10 map, but not on Nov. 9. Therefore, as the typical lifetime of a mid-latitude cyclone is 3-10 days, it may well still be deepening during Nov. 11-13.

369   *Bangor* (Maine) *Daily Whig and Courier*, Tuesday, Nov. 15, 1887, p. 3 (credit: Richard Spiers, Magonia Exchange).

period. By interpolating roughly between the surface windspeeds shown on the weather maps at a comparable radius from the centre of the low one can infer that winds over the ocean near Cape Race might have been in the region of 20 mph from the SE, a reasonable approximation to the "strong" wind reported by Capt. Moore (a "strong breeze", Beaufort force 6, would today be associated with wind speeds of 25-31mph [22-27 kt; 40-50 kph][370]).

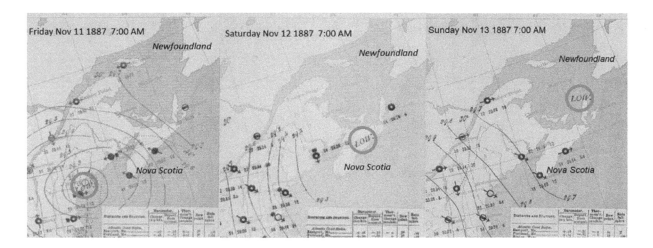

Fig. 87. US War Department Daily Weather Maps for November 11, 12 & 13, 1887, showing progress of the low-pressure centre from Maine across Nova Scotia towards Cape Breton.[371]

We are not told which way SS *Siberian* was sailing during the sighting – either Glasgow to Montreal or Montreal (*via* Boston) to Glasgow. Records of her sailing dates are incomplete,[372] but knowing the journey time and combining known dates with newspaper

---

370 The Beaufort scale conceived by ship commander Francis Beaufort in 1805 (first mentioned in his private log book in January 1806 and developed over several years), was officially adopted by the Admiralty in 1831. It was operational, not quantitative. It characterised Forces 1, 2, 3 & 4 in terms of ship speed increases in knots, but above Force 4 was entirely qualitative, defining Force 6 or "strong breeze" as "that in which a well-conditioned man-of-war could just carry, in chase, full and by: Single-reefed topsails and top-gallant sails", which is not very helpful (https://rmets.onlinelibrary.wiley.com/doi/pdf/10.1002/wea.153). The modern Beaufort scale was not really formalised in terms of wind speeds until the early 20th century and Capt. Moore's characterisation in 1887 would have been based on these very practical understandings. However, they were far from casual, and observations were becoming ever more systematised. Logging wind force and direction at the start of each nautical day (originally noon) then updating the log through the day as conditions changed had been established practice on Royal Navy and many merchant company ships since the 18th century (Dennis Wheeler & Clive Wilkinson, 'The Determination of Logbook Wind Force and Weather Terms: The English Case', *Climatic Change*, 2005, 73: 57-77). The practice was not universal; however in 1853 international conventions on consistent weather recording had been adopted at the Brussels Maritime Conference, where an international network of marine weather data acquisition had been agreed, according to which *all* merchant vessels as well as warships would carry log books in which regular "observations related to the weather should be carefully recorded" (Robert M. Schoner & Patrick M. Brady, 'National Weather Service Marine Data Collection, Past-Present-Future,' Mariners Weather Log, U.S. Department of Commerce, National Oceanic and Atmospheric Administration, Environmental Data and Information Service, 1976, p. 267). Recording of instrument observations, previously limited to East India Company logbooks, became widespread after this date.
371 https://library.noaa.gov/Collections/Digital-Collections/US-Daily-Weather-Maps
372 http://www.norwayheritage.com/p_ship.asp?sh=sibe1

articles placing her in Glasgow on November 3, 1887,[373] and in Boston on November 21 departing for Glasgow,[374] we are able to prove that *Siberian* must have been westbound to Montreal when off Cape Race, as shown (approximately) on Fig. 88.

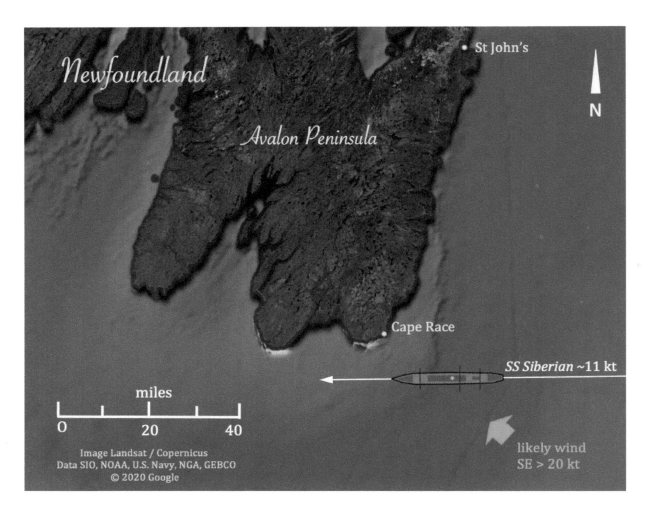

Fig. 88. Approximate position of SS *Siberian* SE of Cape Race (adapted from Google Earth).

These facts help, in turn, to interpret the motion of the object. After approaching close to the ship, moving "right against the wind" – that is, from the NW, to starboard – it then "altered its course and ran along with the ship to a distance of about one and one-half miles." During this close-observation phase of the sighting the object's perceived direction of motion would have been roughly towards the west, so it might have been moving somewhat with the wind at this time, or at least not directly against it. But its apparent change of course was acute, through an angle of about 135°. Then "in about two minutes it again altered its course and went away to the south-east." When it left the ship on the port side, it would have changed course again through about 135° heading away "to the south-east against the wind."

Capt. Moore's times and distances don't quite add up. An object travelling "a distance of about one and one-half miles" in "about two minutes" would be making nearly 40 kt, whereas

373 *Manitoba* (Winnipeg) *Free Press*, Fri., Nov. 4, 1887.
374 *Manitoba Free Press*, Wed., Nov. 23, 1887, p. 1.

the *SS Siberian*'s speed was only 11 kt; [375] so having "come close up to" the ship it could not literally have "run along with" it – i.e., paced it at a constant bearing. Perhaps a number is misreported. Howsoever, the substance of the account is not significantly affected.

What might the object have been? There are many other reports of balls of fire seeming to emerge from the sea and other bodies of water. In a few cases the proximity of subsea volcanic vents is suspicious; but in this case the location was over the geophysically inert seafloor of the continental shelf, the nearest seamounts (the Fogo and Newfoundland chains) being hundreds of miles away. So-called "erupting" bioluminescence might explain some cases. This is an as-yet unexplained type of natural bioluminescence (see Chapter 11) consisting of "balls, or patches of light, shooting up from the depths of the ocean. The balls start out small, but when they come close to the surface they expand and above the surface they explode into large discs of light above the water. These discs disappear in seconds afterwards. In all events the light that appeared was reported to be extremely bright, which would indicate strong bioluminescent triggering." [376] But this phenomenon is a feature of deep tropical waters only, not the shallow North Atlantic continental shelf.[377]

Another phenomenon that can occur in shallow continental-shelf waters is a methane eruption from organic hydrate deposits on the seafloor. There may be some chance of methane bubbles spontaneously igniting (see Chapter 9 for a discussion). But in any case, the ascent into the sky would remain unexplained.

It is a common reflex to pigeon-hole a report of this type as "ball lightning," as did *Science* in 1887 whilst nevertheless admitting bafflement. Interesting experiments have been done in recent years in which artificial lightning balls, so-called 'Gatchina' water plasmoids, have been generated fleetingly by electric discharges in salt water, a partially understood mechanism which might conceivably one day help explain a fireball rising from the sea.[378] There is no mention of atmospheric electricity in Capt. Moore's account; however the correlation between ball lightning and thunderstorms is imperfect, and we have at least established that there was a deep cyclone moving towards Newfoundland, which might have given rise to the vertical atmospheric instability associated with thunderstorms. Five minutes is an exceptional duration for ball lightning, but not unique in the literature.

On the other hand, the apparent emergence from the sea could have been some kind of illusion. And the impression of curiosity suggested by the object pausing in its southeastward

375 Most sources give the *Siberian's* cruising speed as 11kt. *The Railway News & Jointstock Journal* (Vol. 42, 1884, p. 479) records the ship's launch and says she "made her official trip on Saturday last, when an average speed of thirteen knots an hour was attained." Perhaps they were proud to show off a little extra zip from her engine, but in commercial operation, laden with cargo, it would be pegged back. A speed of around 11 kt better fits the typical 10-12 day voyage time from Scotland to Quebec.

376 Stijn Naus, *An analysis of marine light patterns*, Institute of Marine and Atmospheric Research Utrecht, University of Utrecht, 2014, p. 4.

377   R. J. Turner, *Notes on the Nature and Occurrence of Marine Bioluminescent Phenomena*, National Institute of Oceanography (UK), July 1965, p. 7 (https://eprints.soton.ac.uk/392084/1/00473569.pdf).

378 'Ball-lightning in the laboratory', Max Planck Institute for Plasma Physics, Press Release 08.05.2006 (https://www.ipp.mpg.de/ippcms/eng/presse/archiv/05_06_pi); Karl D Stephan, *et al.*, 'Initiation, growth and plasma characteristics of "Gatchina" water plasmoids', *Plasma Sources Sci. Technol.* 22 (2013) (https://drive.google.com/file/d/0B08kTWc1vxHcZE9hTGhfaExMcVk/view); Eric Canan, 'Great Balls of Fire', *New Scientist*, Oct. 24, 2020, pp. 46-49.

course to follow the ship could be an illusion of parallax, much like the moon appearing to follow a moving car. Perhaps multiple light sources were involved. For example, might the witnesses have seen a bright star or planet low on the horizon, then transferred their attention to a coincidental bright meteor arcing over the ship?

However, there was no moon or other celestial body visible that could account for this "ball of fire". At midnight November 11-12 the 14% illuminated moon was well below the horizon (-29°), whilst on November 12-13 it was only 7% illuminated and fully 40° below the horizon. Neither Venus nor any other bright planet was in the sky. Only the magnitude 0.0 star Vega was low in the NNW; but it was at 5° elevation, and descending, so it is difficult to understand what illusion might all of a sudden have fooled Captain Moore into thinking it had risen from the sea.

Fig. 89. The Cape Race iron lighthouse and steam fog whistle in 1895. The original fixed light had been replaced by a flasher in 1866 (photo courtesy Canadian Coast Guard and [379]).

Cape Race is said to be a corruption of Cabo Raso meaning "bare" or "flat" cape in Portuguese. There was nothing there in 1887 except the Cape Race lighthouse, which would have been more-or-less in the direction of the mysterious light when first seen from SS *Siberian*. Could an experienced ship's Captain have confused this treacherous coast's vital navigational beacon with a ball of fire emerging from the sea? It can be argued that Capt. Moore does not explicitly describe seeing both the ball of fire *and* the lighthouse together, although the latter might have provided a point of reference. On the other hand, when he says "midnight, Cape Race bearing west by north, distant ten miles" he is probably referring specifically to the visible lighthouse, not merely to the general geography.[380] Had the light *not*

379 http://www.lighthousefriends.com/light.asp?ID=1308

380 The original seal-oil light installed in 1853 was "visible for 15 miles" (W. H. Davenport Adams, *The Story of our Lighthouses and Lightships,* Thomas Nelson & Sons, 1891, p. 324) even though it was "not particularly

been operating, on this notoriously dangerous headland, that fact surely would have been recorded in Capt. Moore's report to the Hydrographic Office. In any case, the original fixed light had already been replaced in 1866 by a very distinctive flashing light, turned by clockwork (Fig. 89), and this was in operation until 1907.

Fig. 90. A sensationalized impression of the sighting from the November 1947 issue of *Amazing Stories*.

A slow, Earth-grazing, superbolide with a long over-the-horizon trajectory would be more convincing as "a large ball of fire [that] appeared to rise out of the sea to a height of about fifty feet". The approaching fireball might appear to rise only gradually at first, so that it appeared to "run along with the ship" for an appreciable duration, whilst brightening; then its angular rate would accelerate nonlinearly as it gained elevation and soared overhead. (A similar illusion was proposed to explain the 1749 "Ball of blue Fire" in Chapter 9.)

However, 5 minutes would be an impossible duration for a single fireball. There have been famous sky-crossing trains of Earth-grazing meteors lasting several minutes in total (e.g. the "great meteor procession" of February, 1913; see *Redemption of the Damned*, Vol. 1, pp. 383-385); but in even the most sedate cases no individual fireball is in view for more than a

powerful, the ray being only of some 6000 candle power" (Frederick A. Talbot, *Lightships and Lighthouses,* William Heinemann, London, 1913, p. 164). Following complaints from mariners that it was "too feeble" it was replaced in 1866 with the more powerful lamp that would certainly have been visible from SS *Siberian*, weather permitting, at only 10 miles. See also: http://www.lighthousefriends.com/light.asp?ID=1308

159

few tens of seconds. And from the ship's deck, perhaps 20 ft (6.5 m) or more above the water, the northwest horizon would have been filled with the lighthouse-topped cliffs of Cape Race at 10 miles (16 km), so that a bolide should have appeared to ascend from the land, not from the sea.

One other fact tends to indicate a local cause rather than an astronomical one. Capt. Moore had "noticed a similar phenomenon before off Cape Race" in conditions of an impending SE gale. Could this common weather factor be a clue?

Many a British lighthouse[381] had its "rocket house" where signalling pyrotechnics were kept for use in emergencies, or in fog or snow. The rocky reefs off the headland of Cape Race were notoriously dangerous. It is very likely that, as well as its flashing lamp and steam whistle, the lighthouse provided rockets that might be fired in warning.[382] Many rocket houses, especially those shared with associated Coast Guard stations, would also store Dennett rockets[383] or, after 1865, two-stage Boxer rockets,[384] which could carry a lifeline several hundred meters to a ship foundering on the rocks. It would be surprising if Cape Race did not also have such rockets, given its situation and history.[385]

Remembering that Capt. Moore does not, specifically, mention the lighthouse beam in his report, could it be, after all, that the lamp was for some reason not operational that night? If that were the case, the keepers may have resorted to rockets to warn off approaching ships – or may even have been engaged in some kind of rescue operation at the time.

However, whilst this theory might explain a rising fiery light in the NW, it would not explain a fireball crossing the course of the ship 10 miles from shore and heading away SE. Clearly, SS *Siberian* was far beyond the reach of any rocket or flare fired from Cape Race itself. Only a device launched from a nearby vessel could behave like this, perhaps a rocket fired from a passing ship in distress, or a signal from a lightship which would be well-supplied with rockets.

We found no record of shipping accidents off Cape Race around the date of interest, only the previously-mentioned loss of the *Plover*, several hundred kilometers away. But we did find evidence that plans had been laid in 1863 to station a lightship off Cape Race. The Cape Race Electric Telegraph and Lightship Company was incorporated with a capital of £100,000 to provide a light vessel permanently connected to the shore by a submarine cable, the latter to fulfill the needs of Associated Press who since 1859 had kept a boat off Cape Race for the purpose of intercepting messages in waterproof canisters thrown overboard from passing steamers, thus to collect advance news from Europe. It is possible that signal rockets would

---

381 Newfoundland was a British colony at this time. The lighthouse had been built and maintained by Trinity house, the British lighthouse authority, although in 1886 management responsibility was ceded to the Canadian Government's Department of Marine and Fisheries.

382 In the 1880s both light- and sound-emitting rockets were used, the latter being more effective over distance than gunshot (http://www.cyber-heritage.co.uk/rocketrocket/rockets.htm).

383 The Dennett rocket (https://en.wikipedia.org/wiki/Gunville#John_Dennett,_rocket_inventor) made obsolete the less accurate and shorter-range Manby mortar, which explosively launched an iron shot with a line attached (https://en.wikipedia.org/wiki/Manby_mortar).

384 http://www.cyber-heritage.co.uk/rocketrocket/rockets.htm

385 At Christmas 1856, only ten days after the light began operation, the ship *Welsford*, from New Brunswick bound for Liverpool, was smashed on the rocks, the keepers managing to save only 4 of her 26 crew by paying ropes down the sheer cliff; https://www.lighthousefriends.com/light.asp?ID=1308

have been fired to facilitate this operation at night. However, AP's news boat had been rendered obsolete – along with their interest in the abortive lightship project – with the completion of the new transatlantic telegraph in 1866.[386]

That leaves a passing vessel of some type. But would not SS *Siberian*'s crew have recognized signal rockets from a nearby vessel? Furthermore, a duration of several minutes would be far too long for any simple signal rocket available in 1887. For that we need to be looking at military ordnance.

Since the beginning of the 20th century, a luminous object rising from the surface of the sea then floating over the water with a brilliant fiery light would immediately be interpreted by seamen as a parachute flare, fired from a ship in distress. But early parachute-borne lights launched by rockets were heavy munitions designed for battlefield-illumination purposes, advanced descendants of the earlier "ground light balls" – perforated iron balls containing a brightly burning mixture which could be fired into the midst of an enemy to reveal positions and guide artillery, but which were easily extinguished on the ground, or buried. Parachute lights were more efficient, and were beyond reach. These date from about 1819, when Sir William Congreve[387] adapted his 1804 explosive rocket to a parachute version.[388] When the rocket attained the top of its arc it would explode, releasing a canister of slow-burning pyrotechnic mixture which would drift down over the target area on a 5-foot (1.5 m) cotton parachute (Fig. 91).

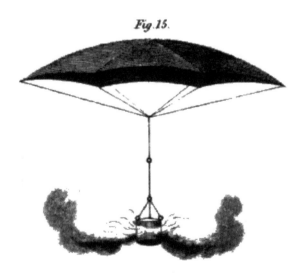

Fig. 91. An engraving of a Congreve parachute light-ball rocket in action.[389]

386 *The Nautical Magazine & Naval Chronicle* for 1863, Cambridge University Press, 2013, pp. 323-325; https://www.lighthousefriends.com/light.asp?ID=1308

387 https://en.wikipedia.org/wiki/Sir_William_Congreve,_2nd_Baronet

388 William Theobald Wolfe Tone, *Essay on the Necessity of Improving Our National Forces*, Kirk & Mercein, New York, 1819, p. 103; Allen H. Mesch, *Preparing for Disunion: West Point Commandants and the Training of Civil War Leaders*, McFarland, 2018, p. 18.

389 Aerospace Engineering blog, *The History of Rocket Science*, March 20, 2016; https://aerospaceengineeringblog.com/history-of-rocket-science/

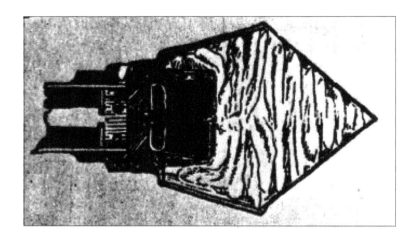

Fig. 92. Austrian rocket head for a Hale rotatory light-ball rocket, date 1887, showing the parachute packed in the nose. [390]

Owing largely to its inaccuracy in flight (only partially corrected by moving its original side-mounted guide stick to an axial position), the Congreve rocket was superseded in 1867 by the spin-stabilised rotatory rocket developed by British inventor William Hale,[391] including a parachute flare version for battlefield illumination (Fig. 92).[392] Hale rockets were used first by the US in Mexico and by the British in several African campaigns,[393] including bombardments of Zululand by 24-pound explosive rockets fired from Naval ships in 1879. [394]

And at about the same time, a different munition was being introduced: the "parachute light-ball" developed by Colonel Boxer, a heavier piece of ordnance which, being launched by a mortar and thus needing no internal propellant, could carry a greater volume of pyrotechnic mixture and might potentially burn longer. The parachute light-ball, "the direct antecedent of the present-day illuminating round",[395] was adopted by the British Army in 1866. The hollow iron sphere of the light-ball was timed to split into two halves when at maximum height, releasing an inner iron hemisphere containing a pyrotechnic chemical

390 Frank H. Winter, 'A History of Austrian Rocketry in the 19th Century', in: *Essays on the History of Rocketry & Astronautics: Proceedings of the Third through the Sixth History Symposia of the International Academy of Astronautics*, Vol. 1, NASA, 1977, p.34;
https://cors.archive.org/details/NASA_NTRS_Archive_19770026086/page/n39/mode/2up?q=flare+balls
391 John Timbs, *The Year Book Of Facts In Science And Art*, London, 1874, p. 61;
https://archive.org/details/in.ernet.dli.2015.222422/page/n63/mode/2up?q=rocket
392 *Proceedings of the Third through the Sixth History Symposia of the International Academy of Astronautics* Vol. 1, 1977, pp. 34-35;
https://cors.archive.org/details/NASA_NTRS_Archive_19770026086/page/n39/mode/2up?q=flare+balls)
393 Ian Knight, *Companion to the Anglo-Zulu War*, Pen and Sword Books, Barnsley, 2008, pp. 169-171.
394 "The rockets, as I expected, proved of little value . . . to my mind, the Zulus displayed the utmost contempt for them. The enormous 24-pr. Hale's war rocket fired from tubes by the Naval Brigade seemed to cause as much anxiety to our own men as to the enemy." Lt W. N. Lloyd, R. H. A., *The Defence of Ekowe*, Royal Artillery Institution Proceedings (1881): 451-465;
http://www.natalia.org.za/Files/5/Natalia%20v05%20article%20p15-28%20C.pdf
395 Philip Jobson, *Royal Artillery: Glossary of Terms and Abbreviations: Historical and Modern*, The History Press, Stroud, 2008.

mixture, attached by chains to a parachute (Fig. 93). According to an 1870 technical encyclopedia[396] the parachute ball "possesses the advantages of being serviceable at sea, or to illuminate an enemy's fleet", suggesting that a "light and handy mortar" for launching might be carried on the deck of a ship. The device was made for use in 5.5-inch, 8-inch, and 10-inch caliber mortars.[397] The 10-inch ball had the longest burn duration of 3 minutes[398] and was the last version to fall into disuse, not being officially declared obsolete until 1920.[399]

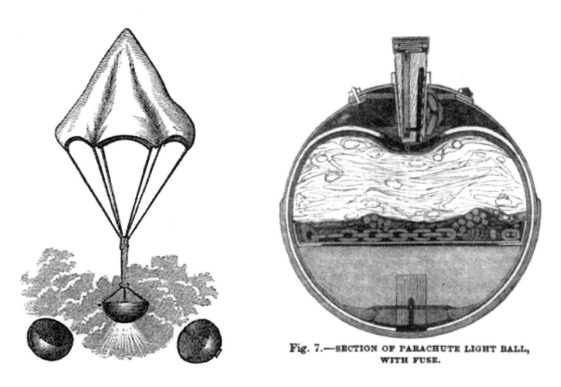

Fig. 7.—SECTION OF PARACHUTE LIGHT BALL, WITH FUSE.

Fig. 93. The parachute light ball, from: *The Technical Educator: An Encyclopædia of Technical Education*, Vol. II, Cassell, 1870.

So, all these devices could be fired from ships, and even – in the case of the Congreve and Hale rockets – from smaller boats (Fig. 94).[400] Also, all these pre-1887 devices were manufactured for military applications. Therefore, it is possible that the captain and crew of a commercial vessel like SS *Siberian* could have been unfamiliar with their appearances and behaviours. The question, then, is whether it is possible and likely for this kind of ordnance to have been deployed from a vessel off Cape Race in 1887.

---

396   *The Technical Educator: An Encyclopædia of Technical Education,* Vol. II, Cassell, 1870, p. 9.

397   https://en.wikipedia.org/wiki/Shell_(projectile)

398   http://www.cyber-heritage.co.uk/rocketrocket/rockets.htm

399   Philip Jobson, *op. cit.*

400   Indeed, the main early user of Congreve rockets was the Royal Navy, which during the Napoleonic Wars (1803–1815) converted HMS *Galgo* and HMS *Erebus* into rocket ships and trained men from the Royal Marine Artillery to become expert rocketeers. They were also deployed on a large scale by the Royal Navy in America during the War of 1812, where the bombardment of Fort McHenry by ship-launched Congreve rockets inspired the fifth line of the United States' National Anthem, *The Star-Spangled Banner*: "and the rockets' red glare, the bombs bursting in air"; https://en.wikipedia.org/wiki/Congreve_rocket

Fig. 94. From "The Use of Rockets on Boats", in: Major-General Sir W. Congreve, *A Treatise on the General principles, Powers, and Facility of Application of the Congreve Rocket System as Compared with Artillery*, London, 1827, p. 81.

Considering first the parachute light-ball: We have no evidence that this was ever used as a civilian marine signal; indeed a primitive mortar in 1887 would be a cumbersome device for emergency use on ship – having to be charged and loaded a bit like a giant musket, heavy work with long re-load times (the game-changing portable Stokes mortar of WW1 still needed several minutes between firings); whereas multiple rockets might be fired in quick succession with relatively little work. The big 3-minute light-balls weighed 30 lb (13.6 kg), not surprising for a 10-inch, riveted, cast iron sphere, ¼-inch thick, packed with more iron and chemicals. [401] This is quite a lump to launch. It certainly was not the type of thing that would be carried by local fishing boats or the like, especially off a remote coast like Cape Race.[402]

Together with the fact that the culprit vessel needs to be the better part of 10 miles (16 km) off shore, within, let us say, a kilometre of SS *Siberian*, in conditions of strong wind and a fairly lively sea,[403] once again an ocean-going vessel of fair size seems implied. Perhaps a passing US or Canadian naval vessel illuminating a target in an exercise? Or a revenue vessel

---

401 *Reports of the United States Commissioners to the Paris Universal Exposition, 1867*, Vol. 5, U.S. Government Printing Office, 1870, pp. 130-131.

402 *Ibid*, p. 79. A contemporary 10-inch military mortar was a cast iron monster weighing over 2000 lbs (getting on for 1000 kg or an imperial ton) mounted on a big iron-banded wooden block and transported by a cart and 2 or 3 horses. Granted there may have been specialized, lighter, static mortars used for light-balls on ships – nevertheless we find it hard to imagine any small boat or merchant ship routinely carrying a mortar capable of firing 30 lbs of iron over hundreds of meters, presumably along with a supply of balls.

403 The sea state associated with a "strong breeze", Beaufort Force 6, is "rough", wave height of 3 m (10 ft), extensive foam crests, and some blown spray.

watching for contraband, trying to identify the *Siberian*? The precursor organisations of the Canadian Coast Guard did have official "patrol vessels" in some places on the Eastern seaboard of the confederation at this time, although we can't confirm the types or locations of any such vessels around Newfoundland.[404] But whilst a little boat might go unseen at night, surely any larger ship, passing so close between SS *Siberian* and a dangerous coast, would not escape the attention of lookouts? (And there is the noise of a mortar in relatively close proximity to be considered – although it's true the wind direction would not favour sound carrying.)

A parachute rocket light-ball was capable of being fired from a much smaller and less conspicuous boat, more quietly, and is much more likely to have been carried by a non-military vessel – even if that would, presumably, be far from usual. And it appears possible that some of these rocket light-balls could burn at least as long as the 10-inch mortar light-ball. It was claimed, according to one 1825 source, that Congreve's parachute-borne "rocket light-ball" would remain "suspended in the air for five minutes at least, so as to afford time and light sufficient to observe the motions of an enemy, either on shore or at sea; where it is particularly useful in chasing, and for giving more distant and extensive night signals." The author adds a caveat: "We have seen no account of any experiments which have been made with it." [405] But, if true,[406] five minutes would nicely fit Capt. Moore's estimate of the duration of his mystery "ball of fire".

Let us suppose that, with the *Siberian* rounding Cape Race on a WSW heading at 11 kt, an unseen vessel, perhaps a half a mile (~1 km) to the NW of her position, launched a parachute rocket light-ball towards her. Initially climbing into a south-easterly surface headwind, the rocket's trail would appear to rise vertically from near the sea. At the top of its climb, say 1000 ft (300 m) above the sea, when the parachute light-ball ignited and separated from the rocket carcass (A – B in Fig. 95), it would grow rapidly brighter, thus seeming to approach the ship. In reality it would have been in the order of hundreds of feet high and thousands of feet away, yet appearing to be tens of feet high and only hundreds of feet away ("a height of about fifty feet" and approaching "close against the ship"). Let us further suppose that somewhat below this altitude the wind direction rotated from SE to NE (we will return to this later); so that, when the parachute opened, and the motion became more subject to the wind, it would have begun to drift SW while slowly descending. We can fine-tune the wind speed and direction (11 kt – the same speed as the *Siberian* – from the NE works well) in such a way that the line of sight from the *Siberian* to the approaching and descending light could have remained roughly constant for a minute or two, in both azimuth and elevation, whilst the inverse-square brightening of the light due to reducing distance could compensate the slight early fading of the pyrotechnic, so that the light appeared to pace the vessel whilst remaining at fairly constant intensity (B – C). Then, as it neared the *Siberian*, it would become apparent that the light was crossing the course of the ship. Once on the port side and moving away

---

404 https://www.ccg-gcc.gc.ca/corporation-information-organisation/history-eng.html.
405 James Cutbush, *A System of Pyrotechny, Comprehending the Theory and Practice, with the Application of Chemistry, Designed for Exhibition and for War*, Philadelphia, 1825, p. 539; http://www.tinyurl.com/yk6zbzhz
406 The parachute flares developed by several nations before WW1 typically burned for about 40 seconds, as do modern distress flares; but some are said to have achieved "several minutes". *Military Explosives*, Technical Manual TM 9-1300-214, HQ Dept. of the Army, Washington D.C., 1984, pp. 2-11.

again from the ship, the pyrotechnic mixture would be starting to burn out, the line of sight beginning now to fall a little astern of the *Siberian*, and the dwindling light descending slowly, then vanishing (C – D). The nett effect, from the point of view of an observer on the moving ship, could be of a rising fireball flaring in the NW and pacing the ship for a time, before overflying it and receding rapidly towards the SE horizon.

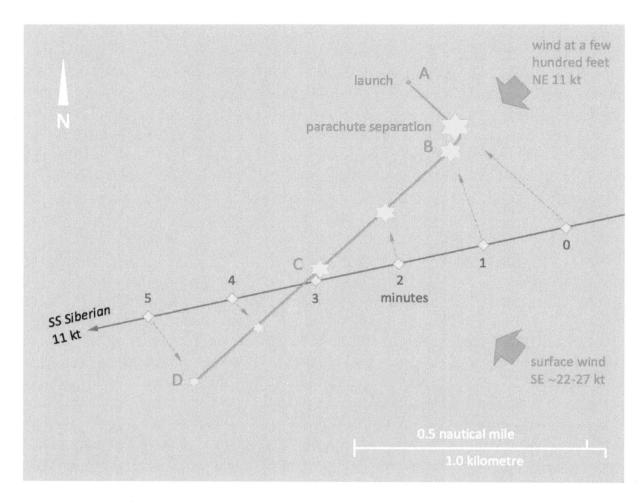

Fig. 95. Diagram illustrating the parachute rocket light-ball theory.

One major advantage of this theory is that it explains a 5-minute duration better than does the fireball meteor theory. A second is that it might explain why Capt. Moore had "noticed a similar phenomenon before off Cape Race", seemingly heralding "an easterly or southeasterly gale". Storms and dangerous currents are common here. In 1913, by which time there had been a beacon on the Cape for more than half a century, Frederick Talbot could write that "over one hundred vessels of all descriptions have been smashed to pieces in the vicinity of Cape Race alone", adding: "More fearful catastrophes have been enacted within hail of the lights at Cape Race and Cape Ray, hard by to the west, and more millions sterling of cargo and ship have been shattered and lost here than upon any other corresponding stretch of coast in the world."[407] An unusual frequency of incidents involving distress rockets would not be surprising. But we have to assume Capt. Moore was well aware of all this. A signal rocket would likely have been the first thing to spring to the mind of a captain familiar with this coast – had the light resembled such a rocket.

We found what may be an account of one of the precursor incidents off Cape Race mentioned by Moore, dated 10 months earlier in January 1887 (Fig. 96). Although no location is given, the phrase "balls of fire" predicts Capt. Moore's later account of the November event. But in other respects, the January phenomenon is rather different. It is unclear what might be meant by "St. Elmo's fire" which, as was well known even at the time, is a corona discharge attached to the masts and spars of a ship, not a free-flying ball of fire. Any atmospheric luminosity was typically assumed in the 19th century to be electrical in nature, so perhaps it was just used as a casual generic term. Yet lights "shooting up from the horizon" so much suggests coloured signal rockets that again one wonders why this was not the natural immediate conclusion of the *Siberian*'s crew. Presumably, in this instance, the number of these lights and their distribution on the horizon "all around the vessel", if not also their behaviour and appearance, precluded such a theory.

> The British steamer *Siberian* reports that on January 17, 1887, a brilliant display of St. Elmo's fire was observed, taking the shape of *balls of fire* shooting up from the horizon all around the vessel and bursting at an altitude of about 5°; one ball showing a green light was mistaken for a vessel's side light.

Fig. 96. *American Meteorological Journal* Vol. VI, No. 10 (February 1890), pp. 442-444

When it comes to the November "ball of fire", we would emphasise again that a parachute rocket light-ball was *not* a familiar signal rocket. It was a military device, its long duration, appearance, and drifting motion, all being possibly unfamiliar to a merchant sailor in 1887.

Of course, the same point cuts both ways: it speaks to the likelihood of this kind of ordnance being deployed by an unobserved small boat off a remote headland on a winter's midnight in peacetime. It is much less likely than a common signal rocket. However, it is certainly possible.

The only other issue of concern is the wind. If Capt. Moore's report of the wind condition at midnight ("strong, south by east") is reliable – and there seems to be no good reason to discount it[408] – then our scenario requires a wind shear, with the strong SE surface wind

---

407 Frederick A. Talbot, *Lightships and Lighthouses*, Heinemann, London, 1913, p. 162.

408 Could Capt. Moore be referring to conditions recorded earlier? The times of SS *Siberian*'s weather observations are unknown; but the last entry in the log might be hours old at midnight. However, the 'south by east' wind direction doesn't seem to be merely appended to the report as though quoted from a logbook; rather it is embedded in Capt. Moore's description of what he actually saw happen: the object 'came right against the wind close up to the ship' at the start, and finally 'altered its course and went away to the south-east against the wind'. Note that he also adds: 'Have noticed the same phenomenon before off Cape Race, and it seemed to

rotating to a weaker NE flow a few hundred feet over the sea. There are two separate but related problems here.

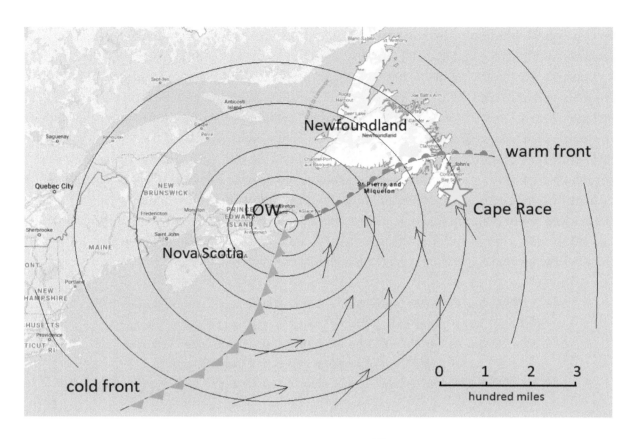

Fig. 97. A mid-latitude cyclone showing typical fronts[409] and isobar-crossing surface winds. Schematic illustration of plausible synoptic-scale weather on sighting date, extrapolated from Fig. 86. (adapted from Google Maps).

The first problem is that the reported SE surface wind south of Newfoundland would be consistent with the typical mid-latitude cyclone indicated in the daily weather maps (Fig. 87), whose low-pressure centre a few hundred miles to the WSW near Nova Scotia would be surrounded by an anticlockwise circulation, as approximated crudely in Fig. 97 . The vertical structure of such a cyclone means that the expected gradient flow at the top of the surface layer, a few hundred feet[410] above the sea, would not be backing towards the NE as required: indeed, it would be veering (clockwise), tending to become opposed, blowing from between

---

indicate that an easterly or southeasterly gale was coming on', which would be consistent with his being aware of the 'strong, south by east' wind blowing at that time. We don't really see how this can be explained by reliance on a redundant weather observation recorded hours previously. However, see also p. 173.

409 No fronts are marked on the US War Department Daily Weather Maps in Fig. 87 because the concept of frontal systems did not exist in 1887. It would be another 30 years before Norwegian meteorologist Jacob Bjerknes and colleagues formalized their post-WW1 theory of "frontiers" or "front lines" between air masses. See: https://dspace.mit.edu/bitstream/handle/1721.1/59075/33053940-MIT.pdf?sequence=2

410 https://en.wikipedia.org/wiki/Planetary_boundary_layer#Cause_of_surface_wind_gradient

SE and S.[411] A second problem is that wind speed almost universally increases with altitude through the friction layer,[412] whilst our scenario requires this gradient to be locally inverted, at the same time as the unexpected directional shear.

It will be apparent from our model in Fig. 95, where a steady NE wind of 11 kt is assumed, that the faster this wind is (and the faster, therefore, the parachute light drifts), the steeper the angle of intersection with the course of SS *Siberian* must become in order to keep the line of sight, from the ship to the vanishing flare, within the SE sector over the course of 5 minutes ("it went away to the south-east against the [surface] wind"). In other words, a stronger wind would tend to mean that the origin of the wind needs to lie even further N,[413] putting added pressure on the already problematic directional shear.[414] So, we would like this wind to be significantly slower than the surface wind, about equal to or less than the speed of the ship. But, given a typical wind speed profile, the wind above SS *Siberian* would be expected to strengthen about 130% from a "strong" surface breeze of 22-27 kt to one in the range 27-34 kt.[415] Exceptions can occur; a reversed gradient is not impossible. But turbine engineers have had to carefully study the incidence of anomalous offshore wind gradients. Thousands of wind profiles were recorded at 10-minute intervals over a year or more at offshore turbine sites in the Baltic and the North Sea. Reversed gradients were detected in only 0.58% of all profiles (1/170); moreover, these short-lived fluctuations were correlated

---

411   The warm sector of a mid-latitude cyclone like this is an air column through which the surface wind direction is generally southerly, rotating clockwise (veering) with increasing height. The surface wind in the friction layer is being slowed and dragged inwards along the pressure gradient towards the low, which diverts it somewhat anticlockwise. The effects over the open sea are usually smaller than over land, depending on the roughness of the sea state; so, the surface wind would be perhaps 70% -80% of the gradient wind speed and rotated 10° -20° anticlockwise. But a few hundred meters up, the friction effect lessens and the airflow would transition from "strong, south by east" towards the isobar-following geostrophic wind, that is, speed increasing and direction rotating clockwise, until by about the 500 mbar level (~5000 m) air is flowing along the direction in which the low-pressure centre is moving – which, due to the zonal winds and Coriolis effect, is always northeastward in the N Atlantic. The recorded motion of the low from November 11-13, 1887 fits this picture (*Mid-Latitude Cyclones: Vertical Structure*, University of Wisconsin, Department of Atmospheric and Oceanic Sciences, Spring 2006;
https://web.archive.org/web/20060903120723/http://www.aos.wisc.edu/~aalopez/aos101/wk14.html.
See also: https://en.wikipedia.org/wiki/Extratropical_cyclone).
412   The fact that winds 100-150 feet above the sea are up to 10 kt stronger than the wind at sea level is the reason a ship's top sails are made smaller in area than those lower on the masts. See: Peter Reaveley, *Navigation and Logbooks in the Age of Sail*, US Naval Academy, 2012;
https://www.usna.edu/Users/oceano/pguth/website/shipwrecks/logbooks_lesson/logbooks_lesson.htm
413   In fact, to reproduce the geometry of apparent motion with an upper wind only equal in strength to the strong surface south-easterly, we would need the upper wind to be blowing from due north.
414   Of course, this assumes a steady wind of constant N-S direction through the lifetime of the flare. Why couldn't there be a clockwise veer with height in the upper flow, as in the lower, bringing the parachute further round towards a SE heading as it descends? Because, by definition, this upper wind is to be decoupled from the veering friction layer. We require this in order to (try to) explain its adverse flow. As a result it is already, *ex hypothesi*, an anomalous *backing* shear; if on top of this we propose a countervailing (and unexplained) *veer* through its depth, bringing the two flows into direct opposition at a thin boundary, this would be even more thoroughly unphysical.
415   https://en.wikipedia.org/wiki/Wind_gradient

strongly with the lowest wind speeds, occurring only below about 3 m/sec (6 kt).[416] Another study was undertaken in Nantucket Sound, an ocean location closer to Newfoundland but in a situation where, aerologically speaking, there is "something special going on". In this area subject to significant low-level turbulence, the normal pattern of vertical speed shear was degraded in unstable conditions, but not overturned.[417] In short, the type of vertical wind shear our theory predicts appears to be unlikely in the reported conditions without some local source of anomalous smooth flow.

Our search for local contemporary evidence led us to the St John's newspaper *The Colonist* which regularly carried brief telegraph reports of weather from Cape Race. At this point the issue of the date comes back into play. Given the uncertainty discussed above, we looked at the reports for November 11 and November 12, 1887 (there was no Sunday 13th edition of *The Colonist*), and, for context, the available reports several days either side, with the result shown in Table 1.

date	07	08	09	10	11	12	13	14	15	16
direction	N	-	NW	NW	W	ENE	-	NW	W	SE
strength	fresh	-	stiff	strong	light	fresh	-	strong	brisk	fresh

Table 1. Winds reported from Cape Race, November, 1887 (*The Colonist*, St. John's).

The wind was somewhat variable through this period, generally favouring the historical average direction for November – the W quadrant.[418] The November 11 wind was "light" from the W, which is not helpful. But the edition of November 12 (Fig. 98) carries the report "Wind E.N.E., fresh", which looks very promising. We should register a note of caution, however.

Firstly, the time of the observations telegraphed to *The Colonist* – evidently an evening paper – would not have been midnight; most likely, it was in late-afternoon on the day of the date given. If, for example, it was 4:00 p.m.,[419] then this would have been 16 hours after the

---

416 Mathias Møller *et al*., 'Comparing abnormalities in onshore and offshore vertical wind profiles', *Wind Energ. Sci.*, Vol. 5 (2020), pp. 391–411; https://wes.copernicus.org/articles/5/391/2020/wes-5-391-2020.pdf

417 The study found that turbine-height winds could be unexpectedly strong in Nantucket Sound, due to turbulence bringing even faster upper winds downwards (holding out the promise of 'extra wind power'); but that the typical profile of vertical shear from the surface to the turbine top tended to become somewhat flattened ('relatively' uniform) when there was turbulent mixing happening. See: Anthony Watts, 'Study: Wind power fiercer than expected', August 11, 2016; https://wattsupwiththat.com/2016/08/11/study-wind-power-fiercer-than-expected/

418 In mid-November, the wind on Cape Race is historically from the W quadrant ~45% of the time, from the E quadrant ~10% of the time, and from N or S each about 20-25% of the time. The mean windspeed is 15 kt, lying between 7-22 kt about 60% of the time. On Nov. 12, Cape Race is 57% cloudy on average, has ~4 hrs sunlight on average, and the hourly averaged night-time temperature range is 32-45°F (0-7°C); https://weatherspark.com/m/147559/11/Average-Weather-in-November-at-Cape-Race-Nfld;-Canada#Sections-Clouds and https://www.windfinder.com/windstatistics/cape_race

419 Checking the times of passage of ships reported in these Cape Race telegraph despatches in *The Colonist* through November 1887 indicates that those recorded as 'today' tend to be, roughly speaking, pre-4:00 p.m.,

midnight between 11th and 12th November, and 8 hours before the midnight between 12th and 13th. Clearly, no time of day would necessarily be representative of conditions at the sighting time. Secondly, this would be the local surface wind measured on land, subject to possible coastal vagaries, and it is not immediately obvious that this need be relevant to SS *Siberian*'s position 10 miles out to sea.

Nonetheless, assuming (for the moment) November 12-13 to be the correct night, it is worth asking if an ENE wind on the headland is evidence of conditions consistent with the required wind shear 10 miles offshore.

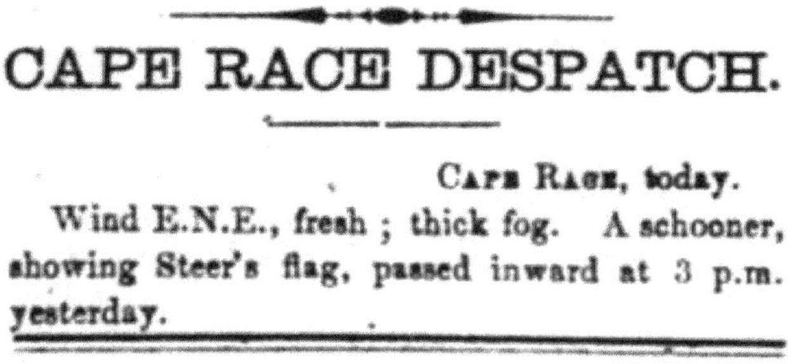

CAPE RACE DESPATCH.

Cape Race, today.

Wind E.N.E., fresh ; thick fog. A schooner, showing Steer's flag, passed inward at 3 p.m. yesterday.

Fig. 98. *The Colonist*, St John's, N. F., November 12, 1887, p. 1.[420]

There are several possible causes of directional wind shear. These include mountain winds, cold and warm frontal temperature inversions,[421] land breezes, and thunderstorm downdrafts. Mountain winds are clearly not relevant to the marine situation; but cliffs and headlands affect wind direction in sometimes similar ways. In particular, Cape Race is notorious for its "cornering" effect, compressing surface wind streamlines into a fast jet where they round the headland. But this is only relevant in a NE flow and cannot account for the shear we need. More relevantly to our case, a SE wind blowing at an angle onto a line of cliffs will be diverted along the line. But not at a distance of 10 miles.

Synoptic-scale cold and warm fronts could be relevant (see e.g. Fig. 97), the former[422] less so than the latter. A warm front could be expected to extend east of the low pressure centre, generally towards Cape Race. Speed and directional shear can occur ahead of the warm front. But again, the shear in wind direction above the surface will always be a veer, clockwise.[423]

---

whilst those recorded as 'yesterday' are post-4:00 p.m. This would be shortly before sunset. (The same despatches appeared on the same dates in the St John's *Evening Telegraph* datelined "this evening"; http://collections.mun.ca/cdm/compoundobject/collection/telegram18/id/32699/rec/1)

420 http://collections.mun.ca/cdm/ref/collection/colonist/id/808

421 Radiative inversions produced by stable stratification in light air would be precluded by boundary layer mixing due to a strong SE surface wind. In any case, there is typically a fast "jet" above the inversion level, the opposite of what we are looking for. Subsidence inversions are associated with high pressure and light winds.

422 Likely trailing in the southwestern wake of the cyclone until possibly catching up and occluding, first at the centre of the low then progressively further eastward, late in its life.

423 K. Haroon, 'Veering and Backing Wind', Airline Pilots Forum, 2011; https://www.theairlinepilots.com/forum/viewtopic.php?f=22&t=267

And the speed gradient would also be unhelpful to our model. Wind shear due to warm fronts typically brings stronger winds aloft. [424]

More promising, on the face it, is the "land breeze" that may blow offshore at night, behaving basically like a weak cold front, independently of the synoptic wind. A land breeze develops because the thermal capacity of the sea is greater than that of the land, and as the land cools more rapidly at night an offshore flow develops. Typically, the land breeze begins flowing perpendicular to the shoreline, but during the course of the night it begins to rotate clockwise, tending to parallel the shore towards dawn.[425] Therefore, a land breeze off Cape Race might well become ENE by midnight, conceivably extending far enough out to sea (as much as 20 km in some well-developed cases[426]) to blow our parachute light-ball across the path of the *Siberian*.

Problems with this theory are several. The offshore wind is a surface-level flow, drawn in *under* rising air over the warmer sea surface – it does not flow above, and contrary to, the mesoscale wind; in fact, it is smothered by it. Even in favourable conditions the land breeze is quite weak, much weaker than its diurnal onshore cousin the sea breeze, typically reaching a maximum of a few knots in the hour before sunrise; and it only develops at all if not overwhelmed by a contrary prevailing wind, as would almost certainly be the case here.

Which perhaps leaves a thunderstorm downdraft as the least unlikely culprit. Thunderstorms may be triggered by the passage of a warm front, locally disrupting the neat synoptic picture suggested illustratively in Fig. 97. According to this idea, the reported strong SE wind might actually have been a gust front expanding rapidly away from a storm downdraft a further 10 or 15 miles out to sea, pushing its cold "nose" in under the relatively warm less-dense air near the sea surface (Fig. 99). In this convergence, the cold air is forced to rise, then curls back at higher level, forming a weaker contrary stream in the "head" of the gust front, typically rising a few thousand feet then curling down again towards the surface, whilst above the head warmer air flows back in towards the base of the storm.

This theory is not without its issues. It may be a difficulty that the depth of the gust front head rotor is thousands of feet, rather than the hundreds we would prefer for our model.[427] And it's a little unsatisfying that the match between the SE direction of the wind and the cyclonic synoptic situation would be reduced to coincidence by this theory. On the other hand, although winds in the gust front are likely to be erratic, as the name suggests, the average speed of propagation of the gust front (16 kt, in the range 7.5-28 kt) is in the right ballpark to fit Capt. Moore's account. Open ocean thunderstorms, although much more likely

424 http://www.tpub.com/weather3/6-15.htm

425 J. Neumann, 'The Coriolis Force in Relation to the Sea and Land Breezes - A Historical Note', *Bulletin of the American Meteorological Society*, Vol. 65, No. 1, Jan. 1984, p. 24; www.tinyurl.com/1osctv3v

426 Rajib Pokhre & Heekwan Lee, 'Estimation of the effective zone of sea/land breeze in a coastal area', *Atmospheric Pollution Research*, Volume 2, #1, Jan. 2011, pp. 106-115;
https://www.sciencedirect.com/science/article/pii/S1309104215305225

427 A Doppler radar study of 115 thunderstorm outflows found that the "head" of the gust front was 1.3 km (4100 ft) deep on average, in the range 0.8–2.3 km (2600–7400 ft). The study also found a "very complex flow pattern" characterised by turbulence, "strong vortices" and "microbursts", rather than a smooth circulation. William P. Mahoney III, 'Gust Front Characteristic and the Kinematics Associated with Interacting Thunderstorm Outflows', *Monthly Weather Review*, Vol. 116 (1988), pp. 1474-1491.

in summer in the far western North Atlantic,[428] do occur in winter, and they do tend to favour nighttime. A few problems may be a price worth paying for a reversed current of air aloft that might carry our parachute across the direction of a strong surface wind.

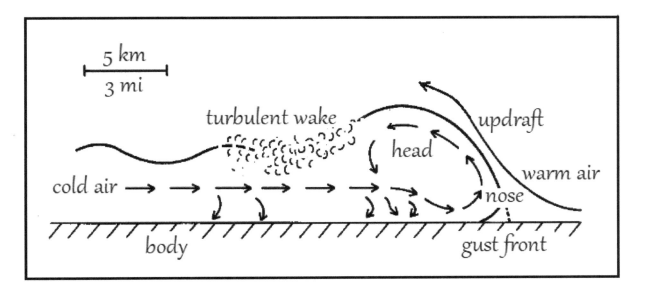

Fig. 99. Schematic diagram of a thunderstorm gust front passing left to right. The vertical scale is exaggerated (adapted from: Droegemeier & Wilhelmson, 1987[429]).

A final question: Can we be certain that the *Siberian* was 10 miles from the cliffs as reported? There is another scenario. On a moonless night, the distance to the lighthouse atop the dark granite cliffs may have been hard to judge. If the *Siberian* was much nearer the coast than her crew believed (as, no doubt, other, less fortunate, crews have believed over the years), she might have been close enough to lie within a zone of diverted wind caused by the cliffs. Perhaps her proximity to the rocks was the very reason someone in a boat fired a rocket in her direction.

The scenario requires Capt. Moore to have been unaware that the wind had swung NE during the sighting, although, as mentioned in note #408, the reported wind direction "south by east" seems to be structurally embedded rather than merely tagged on. And the departure "away to the south-east against the wind" seems coherent with an initial approach "right against the wind" as long as that implies essentially a N-quadrant to S-quadrant trajectory crossing the ship from the land side (which would, of course, fit a signal rocket or distress rocket fired in warning from a boat nearer the rocks – even though what was seen cannot have been a familiar signal or distress rocket). Nevertheless, it is possible that for 5 minutes or more Capt. Moore, preoccupied with the strange object, failed to notice that the ship was

428 Specifically, in our area of interest south of Newfoundland, where US continental influence dominates. Frederick Saunders & John C. Freeman, 'Thunderstorms at Sea' in *Thunderstorms: A Social, Scientific, & Technological Documentary, Vol. 2, Thunderstorm Morphology and Dynamics*, U.S. Department of Commerce, National Oceanic and Atmospheric Administration, Environmental Research Laboratories, 1982, pp. 53-77.
429 K. Droegemeier and R. B. Wilhelmson, 'Numerical Simulation of Thunderstorm Outflow Dynamics', *J. Atmos. Sci.*, 44, 1180-1210.

passing through a coastal zone of ENE wind during the sighting, recalling only that the wind had been SE before and was SE again afterwards.

On the other hand, when it comes to evidence, Capt. Moore's first-hand testimony of a SE wind is what we have to deal with. It ought to be borne in mind that the wind and sea state are rarely insignificant for navigation; and in a situation with strong wind- and wave-pressure on one beam, and dangerous rocky shoals on the other, even a steamship navigator needs to be aware of drift or "leeway" and compensate accordingly.[430] A risk of passing Cape Race too close in such conditions would give the *Siberian*'s captain every incentive to pay attention to the wind.

In summary, a slow, Earth-grazing, fireball meteor is one conceivable explanation. The main problem with this theory is the duration of ~5 minutes. A gross overestimate of duration is not impossible but seems a little strained. Alternatively, a wind-blown parachute light-ball launched by rocket from a nearby vessel can account for the duration. But this theory has its own problems: the question of why said vessel would be carrying and launching an item of military ordnance (not a common distress or signal rocket); the question of why this nearby ship or boat was not itself observed from SS *Siberian*; and the need for a meteorologically problematic wind shear. But although the account of the event and the conditions seems essentially self-consistent and historically plausible, we are unable to prove that the wind was SE, or that SS *Siberian* was really 10 miles offshore, as reported. And in the end, it is impossible to be certain about local air movements over 130 years ago. Therefore, the theory cannot be ruled out, although it would be fair to say that its assumptions incur a certain compound improbability. Some may conclude that a true anomaly would be more improbable still.

---

430 Indeed, a steamship or motorboat, lacking the water resistance offered by a deep keel, may be more subject to leeway than a small sailing boat. See: Malcolm Pearson, *Reeds Skipper's Handbook*, A&C Black, 2013.

Part 5

Plunging Fireballs

CHAPTER 13 – A Falling Mass of Fire
CHAPTER 14 – Black Meteor: Plummeting Fire & Ice

CHAPTER 13 – A Falling Mass of Fire

That, at midnight, Feb. 24, 1885, Lat. 37 N., and Long. 170 E., or somewhere between Yokohama and Victoria, the captain of the bark *Innerwich* was aroused by his mate, who had seen something unusual in the sky. This must have taken appreciable time. The captain went on deck and saw the sky turning fiery red. "All at once, a large mass of fire appeared over the vessel, completely blinding the spectators." The fiery mass fell into the sea. Its size may be judged by the volume of water cast up by it, said to have rushed toward the vessel with a noise that was "deafening." The bark was struck flat aback, and "a roaring white sea passed ahead." "The master, an old, experienced mariner, declared that the awfulness of the sight was beyond description." [431]

Thus, Charles Fort paraphrases a report in the journal *Science*, received *via* the US Hydrographic Office in early March 1885. A startling story, copied in dozens of UFO and fortean books. But there are several errors here. Two of them are down to *Science*, and one is down to Fort.

First, the name of the ship was not *Innerwich*, but *Innerwick*. Second, according to the earliest source we have found[432] – a dispatch datelined "Victoria, B.C., March 2", mere hours after Capt. Waters[433] brought the *Innerwick* into that port on the night of 1-2 March[434] – the

---

431 Fort, *Damned*, p. 260, citing *Science*, 5-242 (March 20, 1885).

432 Thanks to Chris Aubeck for assistance with research and text-editing for an unpublished early draft of a part of this chapter, prepared during co-writing of *Return to Magonia*, Anomalist Books, 2015.

433 According to a Waters family genealogy (Marjory McGillivray Waters, *Waters in depth, 1648–1978: a genealogy of the Waters family of Caithness, Scotland, and the Livermore family of Devonshire, England, 1736–1978, in Canada and U.S.A.*, Waters, 1978) *Innerwick* was captained by John Waters (born 1830), an experienced sea captain from Caithness, Scotland, since her maiden voyage. *Innerwick* was a 1,200 net-ton wooden barque built at the James Kitchin shipyard on the River John, Pictou, Nova Scotia, in 1882. At the time of the sighting she was recorded in various papers as British-owned (see Note #207). She was re-registered in 1898 at Pictou, Nova Scotia, according to the Canadian government Registration Index (# NS 83187, *Library & Archives of Canada*; and see, for example, *New York Evening Telegram*, Jan. 14, 1897, p. 1); however various sources still record her as British from 1889 into the 20thC (e.g. *New York Herald*, Feb. 15, 1889; *Boston Globe*, Dec. 23, 1894 & April 24, 1900). She operated out of Liverpool according to the Hong Kong Maritime Museum (http://m.hkmaritimemuseum.org/). From 1905, the ship sailed under an Italian flag as the *Scillin*, later *Elvo*, until being wrecked in 1913 (F. W. Wallace, *Record of Canadian Shipping*, Musson, Toronto, 1929). The *Innerwick* left many traces in contemporary newspapers, including an amusing notice in the *Melbourne Argus* (Sept. 5, 1885, p. 6) stating: "BARQUE INNERWICK - Capt. JOHN WATERS will not be responsible for debts contracted by his crew in this port. D. Blair, Agent."

434 "British bark Innerwick, 30 days from Yokohama, arrived Sunday night" (*Daily British Colonist*, Victoria B.C., March 3, 1885, p. 3). Later reports confirm the ship in port in British Columbia that March prior to sailing for Australia: "MOODYVILLE, BC, March 23 - In port, barks [...] Innerwick (Br), Walters [sic], for Melbourne" (*New York Herald*, April 5, 1885, p. 18); "MELBOURNE - Arrived Aug 24, [...]; Br bark Innerwick, Burrard Inlet" (*Daily Alta California*, Oct. 6, 1885, p. 8). Credit: Roberto Labanti, Magonia Exchange email group, March 31, 2013.

fiery mass did not appear at midnight, but at 5:00 a.m.[435] Finally, the longitude given in *Science*, 170° 15' E (Fig. 100), is copied incompletely by Fort.

— The following account of unusual phenomena was received March 10, at the Hydrographic office, Washington, from the branch office in San Francisco. The bark Innerwich, Capt. Waters, has just arrived at Victoria from Yokohama. At midnight of Feb. 24, in latitude 37° north, longitude 170° 15' east, the captain was aroused by the mate, and went on deck to find the sky changing to a fiery red. All at once a large mass of fire appeared over the vessel, completely blinding the spectators; and, as it fell into the sea some fifty yards to leeward, it caused a hissing sound, which was heard above the blast, and made the vessel quiver from stem to stern. Hardly had this disappeared, when a lowering mass of white foam was seen rapidly approaching the vessel. The noise from the advancing volume of water is described as deafening. The bark was struck flat aback; but, before there was time to touch a brace, the sails had filled again, and the roaring white sea had passed ahead. To increase the horror of the situation, another 'vast sheet of flame' ran down the mizzen-mast, and 'poured in myriads of sparks' from the rigging. The strange redness of the sky remained for twenty minutes. The master, an old and experienced mariner, declares that the awfulness of the sight was beyond description, and considers that the ship had a narrow escape from destruction.

Fig. 100. The story as inaccurately reported in the AAAS magazine *Science*.[436]

Another version appeared in the *Richmond Dispatch* (Fig. 102) giving a few more details in what purports to be a first-person account by Capt. Waters. Alone among the sources available, this account disambiguates the phrase "midnight on February 24"[437] by specifying that the sighting began "at 5:00 AM on February 25." And whereas other accounts merely say that the fireball fell "all at once" when Capt. Waters reached the deck, here the captain is quoted as saying that 5 minutes elapsed between his first sight of the red sky and the fireball.

Such details could indicate a genuine source, although newspapers have never been above making up quotes, and we note this version mis-spells "Waters" as "Walters" and "Innerwick" as "Innewick". But *if* this is a verbatim quotation then it is important that the longitude is given as "170 degrees 15 *west*". instead of "east", giving a position about 1000 miles nearer Victoria B.C. than the position earlier reported in *Science* and, before that, in an original dispatch from Victoria B.C. dated March 2, probably first published in the *San*

---

435 The dispatch begins "At midnight" but this introduces a weather and position report, not the sighting. A misreading of this dispatch by the Hydrographic Office or by *Science* possibly also corrupted the phrase "towering mass of white foam" to "lowering mass."

436 *Science*, 5:242, March 20, 1885; also see: http://adsabs.harvard.edu/full/2001M%26PSA..36..175R

437 In common usage the phrase "midnight on February 24" may mean either the night of Feb. 23-24, implying a sighting time of 0500 on Feb. 24, or the night of Feb. 24-25. We find both forms in contemporary accounts, and this issue will become significant later.

Francisco Call and from there picked up by various newspapers around the world, e.g. the New Zealand *Bruce Herald* (Fig. 103) and the *United States Miller* (Fig. 104).

Fig. 101. Painting of the barque *Innerwick*. [438]

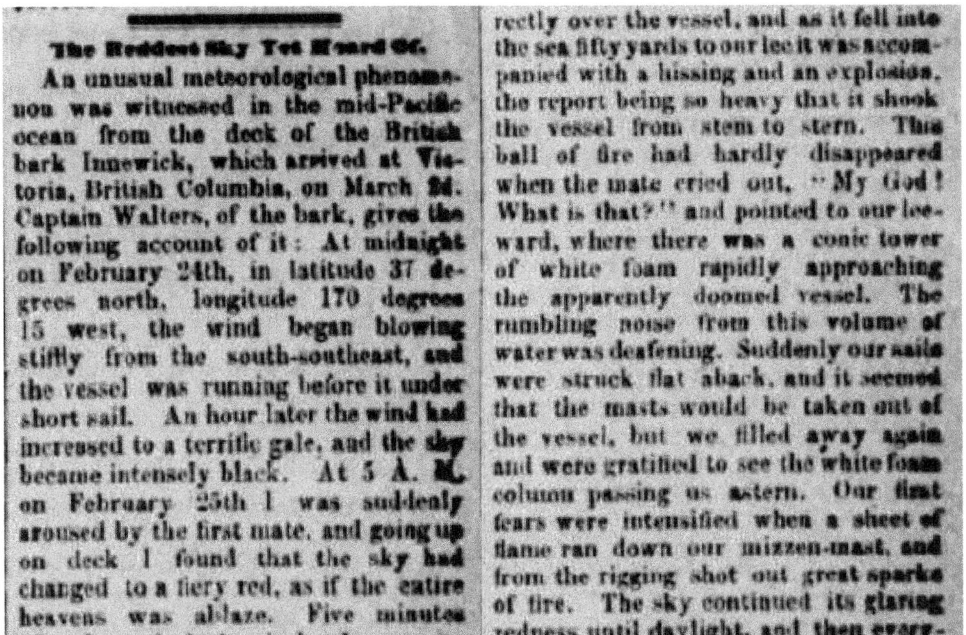

The Reddest Sky Yet Heard Of.

An unusual meteorological phenomenon was witnessed in the mid-Pacific ocean from the deck of the British bark Innerwick, which arrived at Victoria, British Columbia, on March 2d. Captain Walters, of the bark, gives the following account of it: At midnight on February 24th, in latitude 37 degrees north, longitude 170 degrees 15 west, the wind began blowing stiffly from the south-southeast, and the vessel was running before it under short sail. An hour later the wind had increased to a terrific gale, and the sky became intensely black. At 5 A. M. on February 25th I was suddenly aroused by the first mate, and going up on deck I found that the sky had changed to a fiery red, as if the entire heavens was ablaze. Five minutes after I reached the deck a large mass of fire shot out from the heavens directly over the vessel, and as it fell into the sea fifty yards to our lee it was accompanied with a hissing and an explosion, the report being so heavy that it shook the vessel from stem to stern. This ball of fire had hardly disappeared when the mate cried out, "My God! What is that?" and pointed to our leeward, where there was a conic tower of white foam rapidly approaching the apparently doomed vessel. The rumbling noise from this volume of water was deafening. Suddenly our sails were struck flat aback, and it seemed that the masts would be taken out of the vessel, but we filled away again and were gratified to see the white foam column passing us astern. Our first fears were intensified when a sheet of flame ran down our mizzen-mast, and from the rigging shot out great sparks of fire. The sky continued its glaring redness until daylight, and then everything resumed its normal condition.

Fig. 102. Capt. Waters' account, as reported by the *Richmond Dispatch,* April 2, 1885.

438 Documentary Art Collection, Nova Scotia Archives accession no. 1979-147 322; https://novascotia.ca/archives/brigsbarqs/archives.asp?ID=73

STRANGE ATMOSPHERIC DISTURBANCE.

Victoria B. C., March 2.—The bark Innerwick, Capt. Waters, thirty-one days from Yokohama, has just arrived and the master reports a very stormy passsage. At midnight on February 24th in latitude 37deg. north, longitude 170deg. 15min east, the wind was blowing heavy from the south-south-east, with the ship running before it under short sail. At 1 in the morning it increased to a living gale with the sky of a pitchy darkness. At 5 o'clock the Captain who was aroused by the mate, went on deck and found the sky, changing to a fiery red, as if the entire heavens were in conflagration. All at once a large mass of fire appeared all over the vessel, completely blinding the spectators, at the time and as it fell into the sea some fifty yards to the leeward it created a hissing sound, heard even above the blast, causing the vessel to quiver from stem to stern. Hardly had this disappeared when the mate, clutching the Captain's arm, cried: " My God what's that ?" pointing to a towering mass of white foam rapidly approaching the apparently doomed vessel. The noise from the advance of the volume of water is described as deafening. As the bark was struck flat aback, and before there was time to touch a brace, the sails filled again and the roaring white sea could be seen passing away ahead. To increase the horror of the situation another vast sheet of flame ran down the mizzenmast, from whose rigging poured myriads of sparks, and for twenty minutes the strange red of the sky remained. The master, who is an old and experienced mariner, declares that the awfulness of the sight was beyond description. He considers that the ship had a narrow escape from destruction.

Fig. 103. *Bruce Herald* (New Zealand), July 3, 1885, p. 5.

AN AWFUL NIGHT AT SEA.

The *Morning Call*, San Francisco, received the following report of a terrible storm at sea:

"The bark Innerwick, Captain Waters, thirty-one days from Yokohama, has just arrived, and the master reports a very stormy passage. At midnight, on February 24th, in latitude 37° north, longitude 170° 15' east, the wind blowing heavy from the south-southeast with the ship running before it under short sail. At one o'clock in the morning it increased to a living gale with a sky of pitchy blackness. At five o'clock the captain, who was aroused by the mate, went on deck and found the sky changing to a fiery red as if the entire heavens were in conflagration. All at once a large mass of fire appeared over the vessel, completely blinding the spectators, at the time, and as it fell into the sea some fifty yards to the leeward it caused a hissing sound, heard even above the blast, causing the vessel to quiver from stem to stern. Hardly had this disappeared when the mate, clutching the captain's arm, cried: 'My God! what's that?' pointing to a towering mass of foam rapidly approaching the apparently doomed vessel. The noise from the advance of the volume of water is described as deafening. As the bark was struck flat aback, and before there was time to touch a brace, the sails filled, and the roaring white sea could be seen passing away ahead. To increase the horror of the situation another vast sheet of flame ran down the mizzen mast, from whose rigging poured myriads of sparks, and for twenty minutes the strange red of the sky remained. The master, who is an experienced mariner, declares that the awfulness of the sight was beyond description. He considers that the ship had a narow escape from destruction."

Fig. 104. *The United States Miller,* Vol. 18, No. 6 (April 1885), p. 89.

Another factor which throws a spanner in the navigational works is that *Innerwick* arrived on the night of March 1-2 after 31 days at sea, or 30 days according to one local source.[439] This 30/31 day ambiguity may simply reflect the fact that, during passage from Yokohama, *Innerwick* has crossed the International Date Line, W to E, at which point her clock is turned back one day, or rather one day is double-counted in the log. This means that she spends 30 real days, or 720 hours, at sea, but she arrives 31 *calendrical* days after leaving Yokohama. Therefore she must have departed Yokohama on or about January 29, meaning that the sighting happened about 27 days out from Yokohama, only 4 or 5 days from landfall in Victoria, B.C.; which in turn means that she should not have been more than about 800 miles from Victoria B.C. at the time of the sighting. Yet the two sea positions mentioned are 2500 and 3300 miles from Victoria B.C. by the shortest Great Circle. How could *Innerwick* possibly have been anywhere near either position on February 24-25, yet still have arrived in Victoria B.C. by March 1-2? What is wrong here?

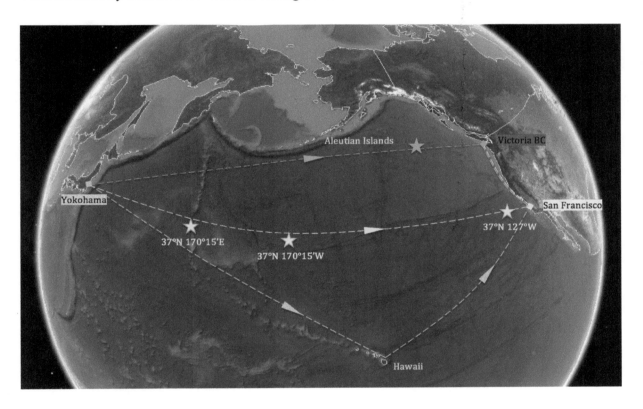

Fig. 105. Schematic of three possible routes taken by the *Innerwick*: top, shortest practical route; centre, *via* reported latitude 37°N; bottom, *via* Hawaii. Yellow stars indicate: left, longitude given in most newspaper accounts; centre, longitude attributed to Capt. Waters in the *Richmond Dispatch* (Fig. 102); right, "probable" longitude offered by the *New York Maritime Register* (Fig. 107). Orange star: possible location 7-800 miles west of Victoria, B.C.

The most direct route from Yokohama would be the near-Great Circle route past the Aleutians to Victoria B.C. (orange route in Fig. 105), whence *Innerwick* could afterwards head south with the strong California Current before picking up the Trade winds and west-

---

439 *Daily British Colonist* (Victoria, B.C.), March 3, 1885, p. 3.

flowing North Equatorial Current for return to the Southeast Pacific.[440] However, the Aleutian route would not automatically be the most natural and economical; a sailing vessel might be hampered by the easterly prevailing winds and opposing Alaska current flowing close to the Aleutians, not to mention the risk of severe weather and icing in February at this high latitude.[441] Which reminds us that all sources consistently report a latitude of 37° N.

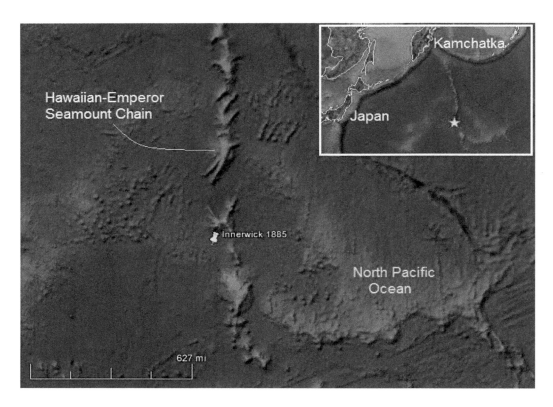

Fig. 106. Showing the *Innerwick's* reported midnight position at 37°N,170°15'E in relation to the Emperor Seamount chain.

Such a route further south, picking up the favourable North Pacific Current and prevailing sou'westerlies at around 40° N, outside the region of heavy winter icing (yellow route, Fig. 105), might fit either of the two reported longitudes, "170°15' east," or "170°15' west", bringing *Innerwick* to the point of divergence of the Alaska Current and California Current and their associated winds,[442, 443] offering unopposed sailing on to Victoria, or a stop at San Francisco.

Howsoever, the fact remains that none of these reported coordinates makes any sense if the incident happened on February 24/25, with only 4 or 5 days of her 30-day voyage left.

440   *Innerwick* left Moodyville B.C. (Burrard Inlet, Vancouver) on March 23 for Australia. See note #434.
441   *Forecaster's Handbook for the Arctic*, US Navy, 1988. Ch. 10. 'Icing', Fig. 10-1, p. 10-2; https://www.nrlmry.navy.mil/forecaster_handbooks/Arctic/Forecasters%20Handbook%20for%20the%20Arctic.10.pdf
442   http://oceanmotion.org/html/background/wind-driven-surface.htm
443   http://studyofplace.terc.edu/ActivityContent/M2_A3_S02b.html

Another source, the *Monthly Weather Review* (Fig. 107), itself citing the *New York Maritime Register,* March 18, 1885, ought to be authoritative, but gives the mysterious coordinates "N. 37°, E. 70° 50', ? (probably W. 127°)".[444] The first reference is in the middle of the Hindu Kush mountains of Afghanistan. The "probable" alternative longitude does put the ship in the Pacific, about 800 miles from Victoria, B.C. – but off the coast of California at San Francisco. Where this longitude comes from, we can't be sure. One possibility is that the *Maritime Register* spotted the anomaly and, knowing the range of a ship like *Innerwick* in the 4 or 5 days available, did their sums. If a radius of 800 miles is dropped from Victoria B.C., it does intersect the 37th parallel of latitude near the "probable" longitude, off San Francisco.

But it is hard to conceive of any reason for *Innerwick* to have charted a course for the Pacific hub port of San Francisco without putting in. She didn't.[445] And if their first landfall after the incident *had* been San Francisco, one would expect the story to have been datelined San Francisco, not Victoria B.C. Anyway, a first call at the Bay would only be logical if the ship had travelled *via* Hawaii (the southernmost white route in Fig. 105); but this is not very likely either, and there is no trace of the *Innerwick* having arrived at or departed from Honolulu during that period.[446]

The following is from the "New York Maritime Register" of March 18, 1885:

The bark "Innerwick" (Br.) from Yokohama, at Victoria, B. C., March 2, reported that at midnight of February 24, in N. 37°, E. 70° 50',? (probably W. 127°) the wind was blowing heavily from sse.; at 5 a. m. the sky changed to a fiery red, and all at once a large mass of fire appeared over the vessel and fell into the sea some fifty yards to leeward, with a hissing sound, causing the bark to quiver from stem to stern. A towering mass of white foam was then seen rapidly approaching the vessel. The bark was struck flat aback, and before there was time to touch a brace the sails filled again, and the roaring white sea could be seen passing away ahead. Another sheet of flame then ran down the mizzenmast, from the rigging of which poured myriads of sparks, and for twenty minutes the strange redness of the sky remained.

Fig. 107. *Monthly Weather Review*, February 1885.[447]

---

444 It is a reasonable suspicion that the *New York Maritime Register* blindly lifted this questionable longitude from a story which had appeared in the local *New York World* newspaper just 5 days before, on March 13, 1885 (requoted in the *Harbor Grace Standard,* April 11, 1885, see Fig. 109.). The value "E. 70° 50'" appears in no other known source.

445 For completeness we checked all ship arrivals for San Francisco in the *Daily Alta California* from mid-February to March 1, 1885. There's no mention of the *Innerwick*.

446 We checked all issues of *The Pacific Commercial Advertiser* (Honolulu, Hawaii) from Feb. 10 to Feb. 28, 1885 (https://chroniclingamerica.loc.gov/lccn/sn85047084/issues/1885/). Many trans-Pacific sail voyages in the 1880s would have been made *via* a lay-over in Hawaii – known as "the crossroads of the Pacific" – for re-provisioning and to put off and pick up passengers and cargo. But the fact that *Innerwick*'s next destination was Australia (departed Vancouver March 23, arrived Melbourne Aug. 24; see note # 434), inevitably passing Hawaii *en route*, makes a prior visit to Hawaii on the eastward trip less likely. Also, given the time needed for landfalls, a trip time of 30 days from Yokohama is uncomfortably short even assuming consistently good headway in favourable weather; and in conditions described as "a very stormy passage" (dramatised by the fact that a few hours before the strange incident the *Innerwick* was "running before" a strong SSE wind under short sail – i.e., forced to head NNW in the wrong direction) it seems very improbable.

447 'Meteors', *Monthly Weather Review* (Feb. 1885) 13(2), pp. 51-52.

So, in the end we cannot be sure of the position of the ship. But given: a) that the date and the number of days at sea are arguably the least ambiguous data; b) that the incoherence of the coordinates makes the reliability of the reported latitude of 37°N suspect; and c) the circumstantial unlikelihood of a route bypassing San Francisco; then the most likely position is near latitude 48°N, longitude 140°W, around 800 miles west of Victoria, B.C. (orange star in Fig. 105).

Why does the location matter anyway? An example of why it might matter is that 170°15'E would put the ship close to a major chain of Pacific submarine volcanoes, the Emperor seamount chain, which is the northern part of the mighty Hawaiian-Emperor chain tracing the 80-million-year movement of the magma hotspot presently responsible for the active Hawaiian volcanoes (Fig. 106).

A glowing mass or ball of fire; hissing and roaring; a foaming sea; electrical discharges – these are features quite suggestive of an active volcanic seamount (electrical discharges due to friction-charging of ash particles in volcanic plumes are far from unknown). So, the coincidence is worth noting, and this is not the only such report where we notice a similar coincidence. One of the best is the sighting from the brig *Victoria* in the Sea of Sicily in 1845. But in that case there is historical evidence of active venting in the immediate area, and the depths are shallow (see Chapter 10, *Victoria's Secret*). Unfortunately, we find no evidence that any of the deep ocean volcanoes in the Emperor chain have been active in historical times.

Of course, a red sky near dawn is hardly unusual, so we are bound to ask why this fiery appearance was thought so significant. According to one account published in several papers:

> There was not a speck of white or blue or black in the sky. All was fiery red. When it faded the atmosphere took on a yellow tinge, then it changed to a blue, and finally faded away in a mist. Suddenly the sun came up and for an hour was dancing on the waters . . . .[448]

This display reportedly started at 5:00 a.m. and lasted "for 20 minutes."[449] Unlike some commentators, we should resist as long as possible the temptation to explain one remarkable phenomenon with another.[450] A plausible *prima facie* possibility is a widespread thin stratus

---

448 *Oswego Palladium*, March 14, report datelined New York, March 13,1885, also: *Eau Claire (Wisconsin) News*, Dec. 19, 1885, p. 2, from *New York World*.

449 Elsewhere it is said that this red sky persisted "until daylight", or until "suddenly the sun came up" – in which case it should probably have lasted more like 80 minutes, given that dawn on Feb. 25, 1885, at 48°N, would be about 6:40 a.m. local solar time (or about 6:25 a.m. at 37°N). But see note # 460.

450 A story that appeared in several newspapers (e.g. *The Indiana Democrat*, July 2, 1885, citing *The New York World*) quoted an "old sea captain" who likened the *Innerwick*'s encounter to his own experience near Norway "some years ago". His ship was becalmed in the middle of a large patch of bioluminescence, or "phosphorus on the water", a mile across, "looking exactly like a sea of fire. Then the fire worked its way up our anchor chain to the bow of the boat, thence to the bowsprit, up the rigging to the foremast in a straight column to the sky. It was a sublime sight. The sky was red for half an hour. I think the experience of those on the *Innerwick* was the same as mine." However, apart from the red sky no other feature of this extraordinary account resembles the *Innerwick* encounter, and it fails to dovetail with other reports of marine bioluminescence (see Chapter 11). A sketchy anecdote, years old at the time of telling, probably ought not to be relied upon.

or fog forming at the top of a marine layer, a shallow temperature inversion over colder water brought down from Alaska by the California Current. Such a layer is typically most marked around dawn when, in the right conditions, the fog might be luridly underlit for some minutes by reddened light from the rising sun. But such an effect ought not to be so very unfamiliar to experienced seamen, surely? One could of course argue that it would not have been memorable were it not for a chance association with the subsequent fireball and electrical effects. Yet it does seem to have been thought extraordinary at the time – the First Mate would not ordinarily drag the Captain out of bed just to see a sunrise.

Another plausible cause of an extraordinarily red dawn at an unusually early hour would be volcanic dust injected into the stratosphere from a major eruption somewhere distant, an effect similar to the global fiery twilights that had occurred for several months after the eruption of Krakatoa in 1883 (reportedly[451] prompting fire-fighters to mobilise on the streets of New York and elsewhere). We looked at eruptions around the world close to the sighting date but found no very plausible culprits (see Table 2). Neither have we found other records of amazing sunsets/sunrises around the Pacific (or indeed anywhere else) in February 1885, which would be expected if the lurid sky were caused by stratospheric ash. [452]

Merapi	Indonesia	1885 Feb 24 ± 4 days	1887	1
Shikotsu	Japan	1885 Jan 4	1885 Mar	2
Tungurahua	Ecuador	1885 Jan (?)	1885 Oct 16	2?
Suwanose-jima	Japan	1885 Jan	1885 May	2?
Tongariro	New Zealand	1885 ± 1 year	1887	1
Karkar	Papua New Guinea	1885	Unknown	2?
Gamkonora	Indonesia	1885 ± 5 years	Unknown	2
Isluga	Chile	1885	Unknown	1?
Irazú	Costa Rica	1885	Unknown	2?
Izalco	El Salvador	1885	Unknown	2
Semeru	Indonesia	1884 Dec 10 (?)	1885 Sep	2
Concepción	Nicaragua	1884	1886	2
Etna	Italy	1884	1886 Apr	1
Bogoslof	United States	1883 Sep 27 (or before)	1895 ± 2 years	3
Láscar	Chile	1883	1885	2
Kita-Iwo-jima	Japan	1880	1889	0
Vesuvius	Italy	1875 Dec 18	1906 Apr 22	4?
Kaba	Indonesia	1873	1892 Nov 1 ± 30 days	2
Stromboli	Italy	1857	1889 Jun 26	3
Kilauea	United States	1823 Aug (on or before)	1894 Dec 6	0
Yasur	Vanuatu	1774 (in or before)	2011 (in or after)	3
Sangay	Ecuador	1728 Sep 30 ± 30 days	1916 (in or before)	3

Table 2. Worldwide list of volcanoes in an active phase on February 24, 1885, showing start and end dates and maximum Volcanic Explosivity Index (scale from 1 to 8). [453]

---

451 Numerous sources, e.g. https://science.nasa.gov/science-news/science-at-nasa/2004/07jul_bluemoon, attribute this claim to University of Hawaii volcanologist Scott Rowland.

452 For more about red skies associated with the Krakatoa eruption, see *Redemption of the Damned – Vol. 1*, Ch.15, pp. 211-220.

453 http://www.volcano.si.edu/world/find_eruptions.cfm

The least unconvincing prospect is the island of Bogoslof in the Aleutians, the summit cone of a submarine volcano that had been in an active state since September 1883 with eruptions reaching a VEI (Volcanic Explosivity Index) of 3. Bogoslof is 1500 miles from 170°15'E, or 1200 miles from the orange star in Fig. 105. But we ought to be suspicious of this as an explanation for an isolated report made from only one place in the entire North Pacific region. And even if an eruption >1200 miles away could explain a lurid pre-dawn sky, it does nothing to explain the blindingly-bright "large mass of fire" that "seemed to be forty feet long and twenty feet wide"[454] and fell hissing and roaring into the sea not fifty yards away. Do we have to invoke a coincidental meteor?

The impact reportedly shook the ship physically. But a true near-miss by a large meteorite is highly unlikely in itself; and occurring at the same time as a rare volcanic sunrise it must be improbable in the extreme. Of course, near misses by meteors are not rare in sea stories because bright fireballs reported from ships at sea are often perceived to fall nearby although they are probably far beyond the horizon in most cases.[455] But such a common illusion could not explain the impact shock causing the ship to "quiver from stem to stern." Another coincidence? A chance gust of wind?

There is nothing for February 1885 in the fireball database of the American Meteor Society.[456] One interesting story, though, was sitting under our very noses. In the same issue of *Monthly Weather Review* that reported the *Innerwick's* sighting there is the report of an "enormous meteor" resembling "a mass of molten iron" which passed, remarkably enough, over the town of Victoria B.C. – the destination port of the *Innerwick* – just one or two mornings previously, at 9:00 a.m. on February 23 (Fig. 108).

The following is from the "Washington Post" of February 24, 1885:

VICTORIA, B. C., *February 23.*—A meteor passed over this city this morning about 9 o'clock. It was of enormous size and appeared like a mass of molten iron. The noise caused by its passage was like that of escaping steam. Smoke and flames were thrown off by the meteor. It was seen to descend into the sea, a cloud of spray and steam marking the spot.

Fig. 108. From the *Monthly Weather Review*, 13(2), February, 1885.[457]

---

454 *Oswego Palladium*, March 14, report datelined New York, March 13, 1885; *Eau Claire (Wisconsin) News*, Saturday, Dec. 19, 1885, p. 2, from *New York World*.

455 But the *Innerwick* story is far from alone in claiming physical effects from nearby impacts of strange bolides at sea. Chapter 14 in this book is case in point. A few similar cases are mentioned here: http://olkhov.narod.ru/gr1997.htm#5e. For example, a book cowritten by Bulgarian yachtswoman Yuliya Papazova and her husband Doncho Papazov, describing their round-the-world voyage in 1979–1980, reports an incident in the Pacific Ocean on Nov. 28, 1979, when a luminous body fell in the sea about 100 meters from them, causing a "pillar" of water and waves that rocked the yacht. The light of the object could still be seen underwater for 1-2 seconds after the fall, disappearing in the depths.

456 http://amsmeteors.org/members/fireball/

457 *Monthly Weather Review*, 13(2), Feb. 1885, pp. 51-52.

What should we make of this? Given the great distance between the ship and the coast of British Columbia, at first sight it appears to be no more than another odd coincidence. However, when we calculate the time difference, we find that time on board a ship at 170° 15' E at the moment of the Victoria "meteor" (9:00 a.m. on the 23rd) would have been 19.5 hours ahead, or 4:30 a.m. on the 24th. This time is quite close to the pre-dawn time of the *Innerwick* sighting. It is on the "wrong" date – February 24, not February 23. But dates during an eastbound Pacific voyage are vulnerable to exactly this potential confusion due to crossing the International Date Line.[458]

During a lonely Pacific crossing in 1885 the changeover of ship time from Japanese to Canadian time is at the sole discretion of the captain; and whilst clock time might be altered regularly during the voyage to match changing local solar time (one hour advance per 15° longitude), retarding the date, by entering an extra blank day, has no practical urgency until approaching the port of arrival. Thus the event date may be correctly calculated from the day of departure, Yokohama time, and entered in the log as February 24, even if by this time *Innerwick* has already crossed the International Date Line at longitude 180° and has notionally gained (repeated) a calendar day.[459] In this case an event date of February 24 Yokohama time recorded in the log would be February 23, Victoria time.

We have already mentioned that "midnight, February 24" is, in any case, a potentially ambiguous phrase meaning either 23/24 or 24/25. The ambiguity was earlier resolved tentatively in favour of 24/25 and a sighting time of 5:00 a.m., February 25, by a newspaper story quoting Capt. Waters, although we noted problems with this source. If the time logged was really 5:00 a.m. on February 24, however, an issue with the Date Line could make the *Innerwick* and Victoria fireballs nearly simultaneous. And, in fact, some news sources did explicitly give the date as February 24 (see Figs. 109 & 110).

But, of course, now that we have raised significant doubt about the reliability of the reported 170° longitude, this argument needs to be revisited. The potential date error remains, but we need to recalculate the time of day. If the *Innerwick* was near the most reasonable inferred position indicated by the orange star in Fig. 105, roughly 48° N, 140° W, 800 miles west of Victoria B.C., then a superbolide seen to fall at 9:00 a.m. PST from Victoria would be seen at 7:40 a.m. local solar time on the *Innerwick*.[460] The problem here is that this would have been one hour after sunrise at the vessel's likely position (which was at 6:40 a.m. solar time), whereas according to Capt. Waters the strange phenomena *terminated* at sunrise. This discrepancy does tend to undermine the theory of a single huge fireball or superbolide.

---

458   As already mentioned, the IDL was globally formalised at the International Meridian Conference of 1883; https://www.livescience.com/44292-international-date-line-explained.html

459   http://maritimesa.org/grade-10/international-date-line/; https://www.livescience.com/44292-international-date-line-explained.html

460   Solar time at the event point was about 17° of longitude or 68 minutes of time behind Victoria B.C. (123° W). Subtracting 68 mins from the meteor time of 9:00 a.m. we would get 7:52 a.m. for the meteor time as it might have been measured from the *Innerwick*. But since 1883 mean time zones had been introduced across Canada. The Pacific Standard Time zone was based on solar noon a bit further east of Victoria, at 120° W, so the difference between Victoria B.C. clock time in 1887 and local solar time at *Innerwick*'s position would have been about 80 minutes.

However, given the inevitable uncertainties of time and position,[461] perhaps a single superbolide is not impossible.

An Extraordinary Electrical Phenomenon at Sea.

The bark Innerwick, which recently arrived at Victoria, B. C., from Yokohama, reports an extraordinary phenomenon in the North Pacific. On the morning of the 24th ult., with a southeasterly gale blowing out of the trade wind belt, a fiery mass appeared over the vessel and fell into the sea with a hissing noise, the sky having previously assumed a strange redness. Though no explanation of the phenomenon is offered by the master of the Innerwick, we may possibly infer that the fiery meteor was globular lightning. Some physicists have denied the possibility of its existence, but since Arago reported instances of the kind many years ago able observers have confirmed his records of ball lightning. Dr. Tripe, an English meteorologist, observed, on July 11, 1874, a large ball of lightning, which at first had a very slow motion, and two years latter Mr. Fitzgerald, an Irish observer, noticed, in the Clendowan Mountains, a distinct "globe of fire floating leisurely along, and after passing the crown or the ridge it gradually descended into the valley, where it drifted along the earth for some minutes, finally burying itself in a peat bank and exploding with terrific force." The latter meteor, it was reported, travelled leisurely over a mile after its first appearance, consuming about twenty minutes. In one case, cited by Arago, the fiery mass appeared like the moon enlarged, and when its envelope burst with a terrible explosion there darted from it ten or twelve zigzag lightnings. The sheet of flame which, after the descent of the fireball, ran down the Innerwick's mizzenmast, illuminating the rigging, was, no doubt, a "corposant," or St. Elmo's fire—an electrical display distinct from lightning and quite harmless. If the explanation which we suggest of the phenomenon observed on board the Innerwick proves to be correct the record now published by her captain will be highly prized by students of atmospheric electricity.—*N. Y. Herald.*

Fig. 109. *Democratic Northwest*, March 19, 1885.

---

461 Might the reported 9:00 a.m. time of the Victoria meteor be wrong? Yes. The source appears to be a single recopied news dispatch. A reporting or converting error is possible, even a typo. (One newspaper, the *Indianapolis Journal* of February 24, 1885, uniquely claims the incident occurred at 'about 3 o'clock', which is almost certainly a typo.) William F. Allen's 5-zone time system (Intercolonial, Eastern, Central, Mountain, and Pacific) had been introduced by the railways in 1883, rapidly adopted everywhere in practice, and ratified globally at the International Meridian Conference; but it was not given legal status for many years, during which time the potential for confusion did still exist (http://www.thetimenow.com/pst/pacific_standard_time). Another solution would be to put *Innerwick* another 15° further away, at about 155° W, thus pushing the equivalent time back one hour to local dawn. This position is about 1440 miles from Victoria B.C. Given at most six days to get there (144 hours; 1887 was not a leap year) *Innerwick* would need to have made an average 8.7 kt (10 mph). This seems plausible. Most 19th-century sailing ships averaged 5-8kt, depending on vessel size. The fastest 19th-century Atlantic crossing under sail, by the big clipper *Red Jacket* in 1854, averaged 10.5 kt. Analysis of logbook records of speed and weather shows that, by 1830, East India Company ships were generally making about 1/3 of the surface wind speed, i.e. ~8 kt in a 25 kt fresh breeze (https://voxeu.org/article/speed-under-sail-during-early-industrial-revolution). Half a century later one might expect better. 8.7 kt would be well within *Innerwick*'s limiting hull speed. (A ship's hull speed is calculated as a ratio $r = v/\sqrt{w}$, where v = speed in knots, w = length of waterline in feet, and a typical maximum value of r = 1.3. *Innerwick*'s total length was 194.7 ft., probably excluding bowsprit; therefore, a waterline length of ~175 ft allows a theoretical maximum hull speed of ~17 kt. Average speed would be much lower. See, e.g.: http://www.oldsaltblog.com/2012/09/are-modern-ships-slower-than-sailing-ships-probably-not/; https://voxeu.org/article/speed-under-sail-during-early-industrial-revolution) Nothing in the reports justifies a longitude of 155° W, it is true – but then nothing directly justifies 140° W or 48° N either!

In 2012 a fireball was visible for 40 seconds as it travelled at least 1100 km (700 mi) from the Baltic to the west of Ireland.[462] This is not so unusual. A bolide might easily travel 1700 miles if entering at a low angle, perhaps passing through the upper atmosphere on an Earth-grazing trajectory. During the remarkable 1913 fireball-procession investigated by Clarence Chant (see *Redemption of the Damned, Vol. 1: Aerial Phenomena*, Case #79) the individual fireballs survived, conservatively, in the order of one minute, the entire train taking some 5 minutes to traverse each observer's sky, and the procession was observed from Canada to the South Atlantic over an estimated ground track of 7000 miles.[463] So a single exceptional fireball, entering over the North Pacific and heading down towards Victoria B.C., might have been seen from *Innerwick* as a fiery mass burning out on the ship's eastern horizon, yet appearing to fall nearby.[464]

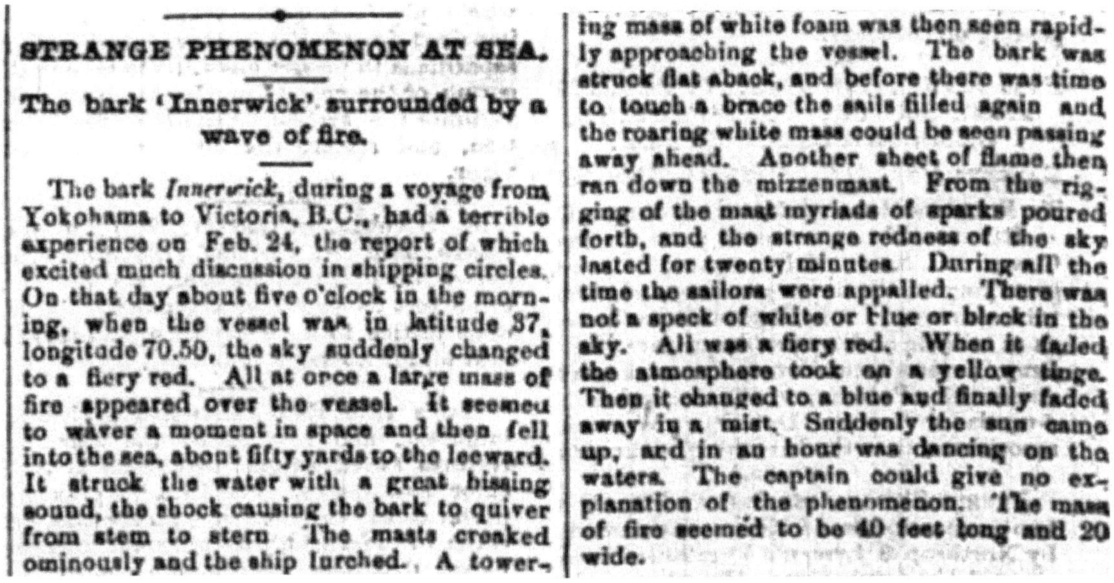

STRANGE PHENOMENON AT SEA.

The bark 'Innerwick' surrounded by a wave of fire.

The bark *Innerwick*, during a voyage from Yokohama to Victoria, B.C., had a terrible experience on Feb. 24, the report of which excited much discussion in shipping circles. On that day about five o'clock in the morning, when the vessel was in latitude 37, longitude 70.50, the sky suddenly changed to a fiery red. All at once a large mass of fire appeared over the vessel. It seemed to waver a moment in space and then fell into the sea, about fifty yards to the leeward. It struck the water with a great hissing sound, the shock causing the bark to quiver from stem to stern. The masts creaked ominously and the ship lurched. A tower-ing mass of white foam was then seen rapidly approaching the vessel. The bark was struck flat aback, and before there was time to touch a brace the sails filled again and the roaring white mass could be seen passing away ahead. Another sheet of flame then ran down the mizzenmast. From the rigging of the mast myriads of sparks poured forth, and the strange redness of the sky lasted for twenty minutes. During all the time the sailors were appalled. There was not a speck of white or blue or black in the sky. All was a fiery red. When it faded the atmosphere took on a yellow tinge. Then it changed to a blue and finally faded away in a mist. Suddenly the sun came up, and in an hour was dancing on the waters. The captain could give no explanation of the phenomenon. The mass of fire seemed to be 40 feet long and 20 wide.

Fig. 110. The *Harbor Grace Standard*, April 11, 1885, quoting *New York World*, March 13, 1885.

Both reports refer to a similar sound – in one case a "hissing" as the object plunged into the sea near the *Innerwick*; in the other a sound "like escaping steam" as the meteor passed through the air over Victoria. There is some doubt that these sounds could be acoustic, particularly in the latter case where the sound was associated with the passage of the meteor across the city, presumably at some height (unlike the *Innerwick* story where the "hiss" was associated with the object apparently plunging into the sea). Not only do high-frequency sounds travel especially poorly over large distances, the speed of sound in air means that

---

462 A rare collision between Earth and an Aten asteroid:
http://sattrackcam.blogspot.nl/2012/09/more-on-21-september-2012-fireball-why.html

463 http://en.wikipedia.org/wiki/1913_Great_Meteor_Procession

464 The position "to our lee" or "to leeward" means in the compass quarter opposite to the eye of the wind. Unfortunately, we have no information regarding wind direction or sailing direction at the sighting time (only at midnight); but we would expect the prevailing wind direction on *Innerwick's* chosen route (see above) to be westerly or sou'westerly; therefore, if we had to guess, "to leeward" would most likely be in the eastern quadrant.

witnesses would typically hear meteor sounds some minutes after the visual sighting, not simultaneously with it. This could be interpreted as evidence that the meteor (if such it was) passed very low over Victoria. But not necessarily. This type of sibilant hiss is suggestive of the "electrophonic" sound which has been reported by meteor observers for centuries[465] in these very words – "hissing", "fizzing", "like steam hissing out of a railway engine", "swishing", "crackling" and the like.[466]

What, then, of the "sparks" and "sheet of flame" that seemed to run down the *Innerwick*'s rigging? This suggests St Elmo's fire. Corona discharge occurs on masts and spars; and can also cause a hissing sound. But given the hissing Victoria fireball this would seem an unlikely coincidence – unless we invoke a very speculative idea due to Stephen Hughes, a physicist at Queensland University of Technology, who has theorised that frictionally-charged meteoroids, even though many kilometres high, could discharge into ionisation tracks formed between them and the ground, causing ball lightning near the surface. [467] Hughes argues that this effect has been observed. It may be imprudent to rule it out, however unlikely.

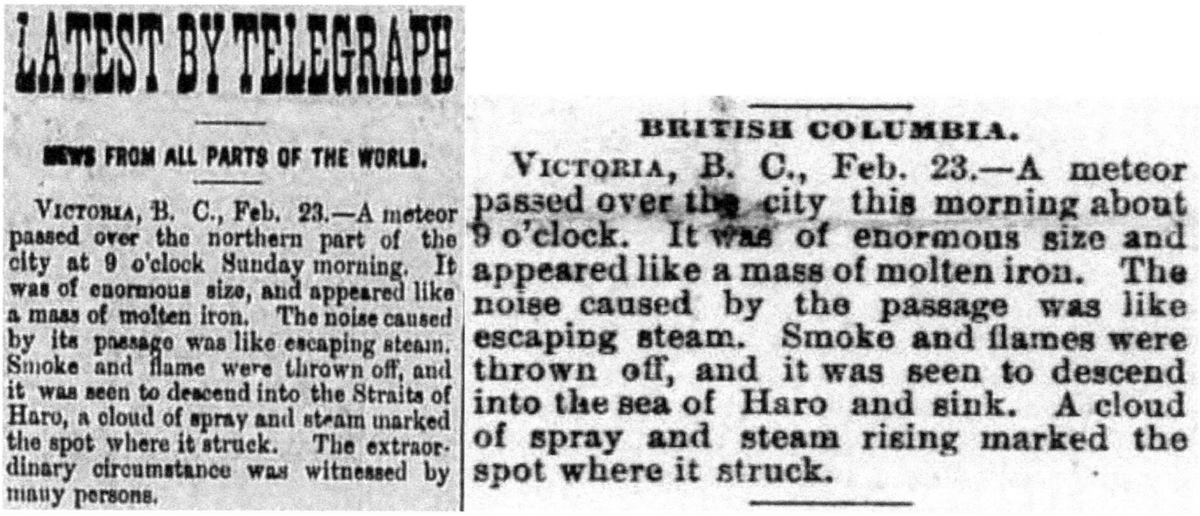

LATEST BY TELEGRAPH

NEWS FROM ALL PARTS OF THE WORLD.

VICTORIA, B. C., Feb. 23.—A meteor passed over the northern part of the city at 9 o'clock Sunday morning. It was of enormous size, and appeared like a mass of molten iron. The noise caused by its passage was like escaping steam. Smoke and flame were thrown off, and it was seen to descend into the Straits of Haro, a cloud of spray and steam marked the spot where it struck. The extraordinary circumstance was witnessed by many persons.

BRITISH COLUMBIA.

VICTORIA, B. C., Feb. 23.—A meteor passed over the city this morning about 9 o'clock. It was of enormous size and appeared like a mass of molten iron. The noise caused by the passage was like escaping steam. Smoke and flames were thrown off, and it was seen to descend into the sea of Haro and sink. A cloud of spray and steam rising marked the spot where it struck.

Fig. 111. Left: The *British Columbian*, March 4, 1885. Right: The *Daily Ohio State Journal*, February 24, 1885.

---

465   This is unexplained, but is believed to be direct transduction of electromagnetic waves emitted by the bolide and picked up either by nearby conductive objects acting as resonant antennae or by structures in the inner ear itself. According to Carl Koppeschaar, writing in the Dutch popular science journal *Kijk* ('Sissende vuurbol', *Kijk*, Aug. 1992, p. 54), people with luxuriant curly hair have a better chance of 'hearing' fireball sounds. And the American Meteor Society FAQ states: 'those with a large amount of hair seem to have a better chance of hearing these sounds.' (https://www.amsmeteors.org/fireballs/faqf/#6). We note, for what it may be worth, that this is the type of hair one would expect from sailors having been at sea for 27 days.
466   J. A. Finnegan, *Electrophonic Meteors*, Armagh Observatory; https://ethw.org/Electrophonic_Meteors
467   S. Hughes, 'Green fireballs and ball lightning', *Proceedings of the Royal Society A: Mathematical, Physical and Engineering Sciences,* Vol. 467 (2010), Issue 2129, pp. 1427-1448; https://royalsocietypublishing.org/doi/full/10.1098/rspa.2010.0409 (See also Ch. 9.)

Accounts of the Victoria B.C. meteor appeared in many newspapers. Almost all of them specify that the object was seen to fall into the Haro Strait (Fig. 112), between Vancouver Island and San Juan, no more than a few miles to the east of the city, with a visible plume of "spray and steam" marking "the spot where it struck" (Fig. 111). This could have been an illusion similar to that perhaps experienced simultaneously by the crew of *Innerwick* hundreds of miles to the west. A high-altitude superbolide descending over the horizon might have appeared to land in the Strait, leaving a dusty trail visible for some minutes by scattered sunlight, apparently rising from the sea and possibly resembling a plume of spray or steam.

One serious problem with this theory is that it implies a track continuing east over Canada with potentially wide visibility. Yet we have found no record of a major fireball – or indeed any burning airship or similar meteor-like spectacle – being observed from anywhere else (excepting Capt. Waters' story, of course). We searched many sources for corroborating reports from other parts of Canada, the U.S, or even the rest of the world; but despite reports on the 2nd, 8th, 12th, 14th, 16th, 18th, 19th, 20th, 22nd, and 27th of February,[468] we found nothing corresponding to the Victoria meteor. We can't prove that reports didn't exist; but the dispatch from Victoria does seem to have been picked up very widely. Why would others not be? Especially given that newspapers in Seattle and Vancouver did carry the meteor story from Victoria.

Fig. 112. Location of the Haro Strait east of Victoria B.C.

Perhaps if most of its path had been over the open Pacific, far to the west where the only potential witnesses were those lookouts on ships like the *Innerwick* who were awake just before dawn; and if its final trajectory over land passed low over or near Victoria B.C. and terminated there, this might help to explain why it was not observed more widely in western Canada. An impacting meteoroid, or fragment thereof, might conceivably make a real splash

---

468   The same February 1885 issue of *Monthly Weather Review* containing the *Innerwick* and Victoria reports contains 15 other North American meteor reports for the month of February.

with visible spray; but would never arrive hot enough to cause "steam" as reported.[469] Still, meteorites have popularly been assumed to arrive burning hot for centuries, so it is perhaps not difficult to understand how such an idea might arise and be perpetuated, fostered by the impression of "escaping steam" conveyed by the sound of its passage.

Yet, how low over Victoria could a meteoroid be and still look like a smoking mass of molten iron? Most fireballs burn out and enter dark flight at an altitude of tens of miles. And is it plausible that the crew of the *Innerwick* – or at any rate her Captain – could have been fooled by the illusion that a fireball descending far beyond the horizon was "a mass of fire 40 feet long and 20 feet wide" falling into the sea just 50 yards away (implying a visual angular area about 15 full moons wide and 30 long)? Moreover, this theory offers no easy interpretation of the fiery red sky which first alerted the crew of *Innerwick* before the appearance of the fireball.[470] And, if no impact occurred near *Innerwick*, what explains the "towering" or "conical" mass of foam that swept past the ship?

---

469 "Never" may be too strong. Most meteoroids are slowed to terminal velocity many thousands of feet up and, once they enter "dark flight", the deep-space cold of the body's interior rapidly cools the thin, molten, exterior layer to a fusion crust as they fall. Thus, heat is averaged through the body, which arrives at the surface merely warm. But another factor, possibly relevant to some cases of reported heat, is fragmentation: If a part of the incandescent molten layer is detached from the main body of the meteoroid near the beginning of dark flight, then, separated from the cooling heat-sink of the parent mass, it may survive to the ground still hot. Poorly conductive stony meteoroids will tend to have thinner hot crusts; iron meteoroids are fused to a greater depth, and so hot fragments will tend to be largest in the case of iron meteoroids. This may explain some well-reported cases of hot meteorites. The Muzzaffarpur iron ataxite fragment that fell in India in April 1964 was said to be "hot enough to burn the fingers" when recovered from its small impact pit within a minute of falling. Its parent was a "luminous white red-hot ball" trailing "thick dark black smoke" that apparently broke up with thunderous sounds, following which a fragment fell in a field with – interestingly – "a hissing sound" (https://www.lpi.usra.edu/meteor/metbull.php?code=16885). Another case recorded by the Smithsonian is the Mazapil, Mexico, meteorite of November 1885, "a hot stone, which we could barely handle, and which on the next day looked like a piece of iron". It buried itself in the ground of a corral with a "loud thud" preceded by – again, interestingly – "a loud sizzling noise exactly as though something red-hot was being plunged into cold water" (G. P. Merrill, & W. F. Foshag, *Minerals from Earth and Sky*, Smithsonian Science Series, Vol. 3, New York: Smithsonian, 1938, pp. 21-22; http://digital.library.wisc.edu/1711.dl/HistSciTech.MinMerrill).
470 Although Russian meteor researcher Dr Andrei Ol'khovatov notes that there were reports of a "red sky" at the time of the Tunguska event (http://olkhov.narod.ru/gr1997.htm#5e). And our colleague Manuel Borraz alerted us to one other story, a rediscovered 1930 event in Brazil, in which a red sky is associated with a claimed meteorite fall, and which has been compared to the *Innerwick* incident by meteoriticist M. C. L. Rocca-Mendoza who described both as "puzzling superbolides" (M. C. L. Rocca-Mendoza, 'Two Puzzling Superbolides', 64th Annual Meteoritical Society Meeting, 2001; https://www.lpi.usra.edu/meetings/metsoc2001/pdf/5002.pdf). The Brazilian case was first described in 1931 by a Catholic missionary, Father Fedele d'Alviano, who is said to have talked to hundreds of eyewitnesses in the remote rainforest of the Curuçá River (*L'Osservatore Romano*, March 1, 1931). The story he assembled was that on the morning on Aug. 13, 1930 (the peak date of the annual Perseid meteor shower) "the sun became blood-red and darkness spread over everything" due to a "reddish dust in the atmosphere, giving the impression of an immense fire that would reduce to ashes all the elements of nature." As fine ash fell over forest and river, "a multiple hissing noise" came from the sky, "sounding like the whistles of artillery shells", and as the hissing seemed to come closer to the ground "large balls of fire" fell out of the sky into the forest "with a triple shock similar to the rumble of thunder." There were "three distinct explosions" causing "earth tremors like earthquakes." According to an uncorroborated London newspaper story of March 6, 1931, the impacts set forest fires that burned for months. Later researchers located possible impact sites on satellite photographs; and found matching impact-like seismic traces recorded by a Bolivian seismic observatory, fixing the time as just after dawn local solar time at the site. But there is no clear explanation of

WATER-SPOUTS.

The " New York Maritime Register " of March 11, 1885, contains the following:

Captain Simmons, of the British brig "Charley," at Point à Pitre, February 17th, reports that on the 6th, in latitude N. 37° 30′, and longitude W. 72° and 71°, passed near a water-spout, the water flying hundreds of feet into the air and going around at a fearful rate; the water-spout covered a space of five hundred or more square feet.

Sandy Hook, New Jersey: at 9.45 a. m. on the 10th a water-spout was observed in the direction of the Scotland light-ship, about four miles distant; it was clearly defined and lasted about one minute.

The s. s. "British Princess," F. H. Freeth, commanding, reports that on February 21st, in latitude N. 39°, longitude W. 62°, several well-defined, and many imperfectly formed water-spouts were observed between noon and 8 p. m., Greenwich mean time.

The British bark "Artizan," J. Dwyer, master, reports having observed on February 22d, two large water-spouts in latitude N. 39° 10′, longitude W. 60° 10′.

Fig. 113. Reports of waterspouts in *Monthly Weather Review*, February 1885, p. 52.

The latter resembles nothing quite so much as a waterspout funnel, but surely an experienced crew knows a waterspout when it sees one. Ships' reports of waterspouts were logged routinely in journals such as *Monthly Weather Review*. In fact, the same issue reporting *Innerwick's* encounter contains reports (Fig. 113) from four different ships of spouts observed in the Atlantic; they are hardly rare. Yet what is the probability of a waterspout almost engulfing a ship at the same time as a spectacular meteor causes rare electrical effects? Although there do exist uncommon reports of tornado funnel clouds emitting glows, fireballs, and lightnings of various kinds, [471] that would not account for everything either. The Victoria B.C. meteor would now be just a coincidence, as would that persistent lurid sky. Moreover, 5:00 a.m. is a quite unusual time for a violent waterspout. Relatively benign "fair weather" waterspouts do tend to form in the morning hours, although not usually at dawn; tornadic waterspouts usually form in the afternoon, associated with thunderstorms. [472]

---

how the red dust or ash, which "continued to fall for a few hours", could have preceded the arrival of the bolides; and the report of forest fires serves only to raise questions about the direction of causation. The same issue arises in the *Innerwick* case: the red sky preceded the fall of the fiery mass. Presumably, there may be no causal connection between the livid dawn and the supposed superbolide in either case. References: Mark. E. Bailey *et al.*, 'The 1930 August 13 "Brazilian Tunguska" Event', *The Observatory*, 115 (1995), No 1128, pp. 250-253; http://adsabs.harvard.edu/full/1995Obs...115..250B. Almost everything published after that focuses only on the possible correlation with seismic data and impact craters, for example: A. J. Vega, 'Possible Evidencia Sismica del Evento "Tunguska" del 13 de Agosto de 1930, Ocurrido en Brasil', *Revista Geofísica Instituto Panamericano de Geografía e Historia*, 44, (Jan.-June 1996), pp. 201-211. The most complete overall discussion known to us is by Patrick Huyghe, 'Anecdotal Evidence: Incident at Curuçá', *The Sciences*, March/April 1996, pp. 14-17.

471 Martin Shough & Wim van Utrecht, *Was the Saint-Prouant "Cloud-Cigar" of September 14, 1954 a Funnel Cloud?* (http://www.caelestia.be/saintprouant.html)

472 https://earthsky.org/earth/all-about-waterspouts

Perhaps we should give up the attempt to connect the Victoria meteor with Capt. Waters' "mass of fire". According to the *British Columbian*, March 4, 1885, the meteor passed over "the northern part of the city", which might suggest something in local airspace. True, only one source has this detail, and the phrase does not necessarily mean its *ground track* crossed the north of the city; it may only mean that it was seen at a relatively low elevation in the northern sky from some other part or parts of the city. But if the "meteor" was really a local phenomenon, what might it have been?

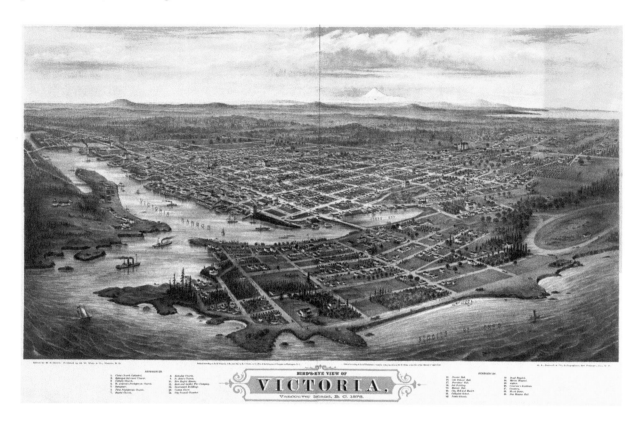

Fig. 114. View of the City of Victoria B.C. from the southwest in 1879.

Another prosaic explanation of a fiery object that makes a hissing sound and falls into a body of water with a cloud of steam would be a rocket. On the other hand, all sources say it passed "over the city" before falling in the Haro Strait (Fig. 111). The old city of Victoria was centred on what are now the downtown and dock areas in the SW of the modern city, several miles from the Haro Strait. The suburban area today spreading towards Oak Bay in the east was undeveloped rural farmland in 1885. [473] If a rocket was seen, from the city, to "pass over the city" it would need to have been launched from west of the city. A ship carrying military rockets (see Chapter 12) might have been in the harbour here (Fig. 114). But this is a long way from the Strait. The larger Hale rockets of the time had average ranges of 1200 yards (1100 m) and in exceptional cases were said to achieve 4000 yards (3770 m), or about 2¼ miles.[474] Even if launched from land inside the city, the best such effort would

473 http://oakbaychronicles.ca/?page_id=1180

474 Elmo Phillips, *The Hale Rocket and Rocket Launcher-The American Connection*, American Society of Arms Collectors Bulletin 82:7-15;

not even reach the coast. We searched the press carefully for mentions of any special event such as a military rocket experiment or a firework display in or near Victoria B.C., finding nothing. But unreported official or private ventures using larger ordnance or pyrotechnics cannot of course be ruled out.

If we accept Capt. Waters' lurid description – fiery sky, falling projectile, erupting sea, and all – what else might explain something that sounds like a scene from an epic naval battle? A mighty "shock" causing the *Innerwick* to "lurch" and "quiver from stem to stern" sounds like a hard impact – could she have been rammed by an unmanned torpedo boat fitted with explosive spar torpedoes?[475] But to what purpose, and how would that have been accomplished in the middle of the ocean? The 19th-century torpedo boats were small steam-powered craft (Fig. 115), and because of their limited fuel load their deployment was restricted to coastal areas. No battles were fought anywhere near the Aleutian Islands, western Canada, Hawaii, or the US West Coast in 1885.

Fig. 115. Etching depicting two self-propelled torpedo boats attacking the Chilean ship *Almirante Cochrane* during the 1891 Chilean Civil War.

https://americansocietyofarmscollectors.org/wp-content/uploads/2019/06/2000-B82-The-Hale-Rocket-and-Rocket-Launcher-The-.pdf (See also https://airandspace.si.edu/collection-objects/rocket-solid-fuel-hale-3-pounder/nasm_A19790731000 and http://weebau.com/history/hale_rock.htm)
475 The explosive charges, usually mounted on nose spars at the waterline, often failed or went off prematurely; https://en.wikipedia.org/wiki/Torpedo_boat

Perhaps *Innerwick* got in the middle of a peacetime naval gunnery exercise, or (less likely) encountered a naval ship firing experimental pyrotechnics, perhaps some combination of explosive Hale rockets[476] (see Chapter 12) and smoke bombs designed for close naval engagements. Smoke bombs containing red phosphorous might help explain the fiery red sky. No detonations were heard; but still, rockets might explain the hissing sound, and an exploding rocket could have rocked the ship and perhaps created "myriads of sparks". During the 20 minutes it took for the fiery sky to clear, smoke might have helped cloak the retreat of the culprit vessel – though not beyond the horizon.[477]

How might a rocket – or other fiery projectile – falling into the sea generate a "towering mass of white foam" surging towards the ship? Well, the Pacific is the habitat of a large number of different types of whales. If the object fell amid, say, a passing pod of humpbacks, in the resulting panic an animal may have lunged towards the ship and breached the water in a great plume of spray, ramming the hull, either accidentally or deliberately.[478] When the smoke and confusion had cleared, there would be no sign of the submerged animals. Of course, the coincidental proximity of whales, unrecognised by experienced seamen, would add a further order of unlikelihood to our scenario.

Other unlikely theories are that *Innerwick* fell victim to a bungled interdiction on suspicion of contraband (again, improbable out in the open ocean so far from Coast Guard jurisdictions), or of piracy – or was herself attacked by pirates. But all such theories fail to convince. Again, no gunfire or explosions were heard, there was no hailing, or attempt to board.

Perhaps a ship on fire, with exploding powder kegs on deck, could have resulted in a similar display of columns of spume and burning projectiles? But again, no detonations were heard, and we checked various sources, finding no record of a maritime disaster having occurred during the final week of February 1885.[479] If the burning vessel had been merely

---

476 https://en.wikipedia.org/wiki/William_Hale_(British_inventor)#Rocketry

477 Only if it was a steam ship, and only if the duration of the smokescreen was longer than the reported "20 minutes" of red sky before full sunrise. Two sailing ships' rate of separation, subject to the same wind, cannot be more than a fraction of either ship's typical speed, or only a few knots; meaning that a sailing vessel should have been easily spotted when the sky cleared. From a vantage on deck, say 20 ft above the water, the horizon distance would be 5.5 miles, and the masts and superstructure of a ship would be visible at ranges far beyond this; from the crow's nest the horizon distance would be in excess of 15 miles. In fact, another ship would have needed to make an impossible 40 kt to have travelled this far, about twice the plausible speed of a ship in 1885 even under steam (the record speed would only exceed about 30 kt by the turn of the century). Even if "20 minutes" is a gross underestimate, the fastest vessel should not have been more than a few miles away and still easily visible to any lookout.

478 Breaching, or lunging, is a type of behaviour thought sometimes to be used to warn off rival males and might happen if a ship's hull was mistaken for another whale. Deliberate attacks on ships are rare but have been recorded. See:
https://en.wikipedia.org/wiki/Cetacean_surfacing_behaviour#Breaching_and_lunging;
https://www.wildaboutwhales.com.au/whale-facts/about-whales/whale-behaviour;
https://www.canadiangeographic.ca/article/how-often-do-whales-attack-ships;
https://www.independent.co.uk/environment/killer-whales-orcas-ramming-attacking-sailing-boats-spain-portugal-b434745.html

479 https://bel-memorial.org/books/Dictionary_of_Disasters_at_Sea_during_the_Age_of_Steam.pdf;

damaged, rather than destroyed and sunk, she may not have made it into the historical record; however, this would increase the strangeness of the fact that this ship and its crew were nowhere to be seen, or heard, when, after some minutes, the fiery dawn faded and the sun was "dancing on the waters". And aside from the improbability of such a dawn encounter hundreds of miles out in the Pacific, the theory doesn't then convincingly explain the towering sea, or, truthfully, the corona discharge-like sparking effects.

To escape from some of these problems we may have only two options, both somewhat radical. The first would be to accept that several unusual, not to say unexplained, local phenomena happened concurrently around the *Innerwick*; and that the fall of a spectacular meteor was a further coincidence. The second option would be to doubt the veracity of Capt. Waters' account almost entire; and replace coincidence with deliberate confabulation.

The idea would be that when *Innerwick* docked at Victoria her crew visited the town's bars, pockets full and ready to impress with exotic tales of the Far East, only to be greeted with the news that they'd just missed an amazing fireball over Victoria. (For the purposes of this theory it wouldn't matter if it was really a fireball meteor, or a rocket, save only that it was hot gossip.) Crestfallen, they may have made up an elaborate tale of their own to trump the story, inventing a fireball that not only fell nearby but almost destroyed their ship, complete with burning sky, monstrous waves, and lightning, no less.

Either way, we still have a story of coincidences. The alert reader may have noticed the weird synchronicity between, on one hand, this case of 1885, in which a fireball plunging into the sea is seen by a captain from Caithness whilst *en route* to Victoria, and, on the other hand, the fireballs seen bursting from the sea near the ship *Victoria* by Captain Caithness in 1845 (Chapter 10), both sightings in conjunction with meteors seen hundreds of miles away. And we raise our eyebrows a little further when we discover yet another sighting (of unknown date) of a "great meteor", this one splashing audibly into the sea off the bow of SS *Deccan*, causing "gigantic bubbles" of gurgling hot air under the ship (Fig. 116). It was published, in London, on March 7, 1885, just a few days after Capt. Waters brought the *Innerwick* into Victoria harbour and *3 days before* Capt. Waters' story reached the Hydrographic Office in Washington D.C. What should we make of these coincidences? Probably nothing, as – absent magic – no causal connection seems feasible in either case.[480]

---

https://en.wikipedia.org/wiki/List_of_shipwrecks_in_1885#February;
https://en.wikipedia.org/wiki/List_of_accidents_and_disasters_by_death_toll

480   The time window is too tight for local knowledge of the article to predate Capt. Waters' story. The date of the first newspaper report of the latter is not known with certainty; but according to *Science* the Hydrographic Office report was received in Washington D.C. from San Francisco on March 10. *Chambers's Journal* was a weekly, printed in London. A copy of the March 7 issue would have taken at least 8 days or so to cross the Atlantic, then another 4 or 5 days minimum to get by steam train from the east to the Canadian Pacific coast. So, even if the magazine was printed and dispatched more than a week ahead of its nominal cover date (most unlikely for a weekly) it still could not reach Vancouver Island in time to influence Capt. Waters to invent, write and disseminate a story which was then picked up by the San Francisco Hydrographic Office branch and retransmitted to Washington some time before March 10. A quote from *Chambers's Journal* could in theory have been sent immediately by telegraph to someone in Victoria; but where would Capt. Waters have encountered it? (The earliest published trace we have found of the story across the Atlantic is in the *New York Times*, March 22, 1885, p. 11.) Moreover, the report sent on from the San Francisco office was probably taken from the same news dispatch datelined "Victoria – March 2" beginning "The bark *Innerwick* has just arrived…"

Howsoever, assuming a hoax, or a tall tale got out of hand, can we imagine *Innerwick*'s captain having gone along with this imposture, to the extent of manufacturing a story, complete with details of date, times, and weather, and reporting it to the newspapers? Perhaps, yes, if backed into a corner by a public *fait accompli*.

Yet, if it is merely a tall tale, unrelated to the February 23 meteor story except as it was intended to trump that event for drama, why choose to date it one day after, on February 24? If, on the other hand, the motive is to exploit the meteor story as corroboration for a fake marvel, it would seem odd to mis-date it by (almost exactly) one day, without explanation, leaving it to 21st-century anomalists to figure out that the fake discrepancy is designed to simulate a plausible laxity in the logbook routine of a ship crossing the International Date Line.

160 CHAMBERS'S JOURNAL. [March 7, 1885.

With these introductory remarks, let me offer my short story. We had left Aden, and were steaming rapidly Bombay-wards, over a placid sea, under a magnificent star-lit sky; I was occupying my favourite resort, the platform of the gangway ladder, of the good ship *Deccan*, and Colonel P—— shared it with me. Our conversation turned on the magnificence of our surroundings. Above us was the heavenly host, each unit shining with the splendour peculiar to tropical skies; beneath us, great masses of phosphorescence rolling in the depths, seemed to emulate the stars above; and behind us, Venus cast a long brilliant reflection on the deep. While watching her effulgence, Colonel P—— suddenly drew my attention with : 'By Jove, H——, she is coming at us !' And true enough it seemed so for a moment; but immediately we both recognised the fact that a great meteor was approaching; and no sooner was this fact apparent, than it had passed ahead and disappeared under the following astonishing circumstances. At first, of a dazzling white, it rivalled Venus in brilliancy, and seemed to emerge from her; then the white rapidly passed into red, then dull red, almost black, and in this condition it flew over our heads, passing over the *Deccan*, and falling into the sea with a splash, apparently a mile ahead of her, and slightly on her starboard bow. Involuntarily, we both rushed forward to *see* the fall, but were too late; but every one on deck heard it; and we all saw and heard the outsplashed water falling back into the sea. As the steamer sped on, we passed over, at an interval, I should say, of five hundred yards, three gigantic bubbles of hot air gurgling up from the depths, and marking the slanting course of the meteor to the bottom of the sea.

This adventure formed a topic of conversation during the remainder of our voyage to Bombay.

Fig. 116. 'A Remarkable Meteor', *Chambers's Journal of Literature, Science and Art*, March 7, 1885, p. 160. [481]

In summary, we can suggest some part-explanations, some of which might be made to seem persuasive if one is not too scrupulous. But it must remain up to the reader to weigh the likelihoods, pending any future research that may clarify some of the issues raised here. There could be significant errors or inventions in the report, of course, and ambiguities in the

which seems to have first appeared in the *San Francisco Call*, as quoted e.g. in the *US Miller* (the Hydrographic Office text quoted in *Science* is essentially the same). A dispatch sent March 2 clearly could not in any way be influenced by a magazine published March 7 – albeit that we can't guarantee the March 2 date as we only have it second-hand.

481 The SS *Deccan* did exist. She was a passenger vessel launched in 1868 and did sail to and from Aden and Bombay at various times. The story mentions a "Colonel P ---" on board, suggesting a military transport roll. This could fit periods of her service history between Aug. and Nov. 1882, or between Sept. 1884 and May 1886, at which times she was taken up for troop transport in the Egyptian campaigns (according to http://www.poheritage.com/Upload/Mimsy/Media/factsheet/93039DECCAN-1868pdf.pdf). Therefore, it *could* have been a very recent story when published – but not so recent as to be contemporaneous with *Innerwick*'s sighting, of course (SS *Deccan* was in the Mediterranean at that time, not the Arabian Sea).

ship's position and time could be taken as evidence of a basic unreliability. Indeed, we cannot prove any of it really happened. On the other hand, if the account is taken to be broadly accurate it is quite difficult to explain neatly.

And, as we have mentioned, this is not an isolated case. In fact, barely two years later another ship's captain reported a similar plunging fireball causing a "sea of fire" and "tremendous breakers" that swept over his vessel. The details of that report are at the core of our next story.

CHAPTER 14 – **Black Meteor: Plummeting Fire and Ice**

This 1887 report of aerial "balls" nearly sinking the Dutch vessel *J.P.A.* in a "sea of fire" is well known, being one of the most striking accounts collected by Charles Fort in *The Book of the Damned*. Fort is especially delighted to note that "solid lumps of ice fell on deck" after the object plunged into the sea. "It is our acceptance," he writes, "that these things had entered this earth's atmosphere, having first crashed through a field of ice."[482]

RARE ELECTRICAL PHENOMENON AT SEA.

Capt. C. D. Swart, of the Dutch bark "J. P. A.," makes the following report of a remarkable phenomenon observed by him at 5 p. m. March 19, 1887, in N. 37° 39′, W. 57° 00′:

During a severe storm saw a meteor in the shape of two balls, one of them very black and the other illuminated. The illuminated ball was oblong, and appeared as if ready to drop on deck amidships. In a moment it became as dark as night above, but below, on board and surrounding the vessel, everything appeared like a sea of fire. The ball fell into the water very close alongside the vessel with a roar, and caused the sea to make tremendous breakers which swept over the vessel. A suffocating atmosphere prevailed, and the perspiration ran down every person's face on board and caused everyone to gasp for fresh air. Immediately after this solid lumps of ice fell on deck, and everything on deck and in the rigging became iced, notwithstanding that the thermometer registered 19° Centigrade. The barometer during this time oscillated so as to make it impossible to obtain a correct reading. Upon an examination of the vessel and rigging no damage was noticed, but on that side of the vessel where the meteor fell into the water the ship's side appeared black and the copper plating was found to be blistered. After this phenomenon the wind increased to hurricane force.

Fig. 117. Fort's source, *Monthly Weather Review*, Vol. 15 (March 1887), p. 84.

Research for the book *Return to Magonia*, co-authored by Martin Shough and Chris Aubeck, showed that Cornelis Dirks Swart[483] – appropriately named for a witness to a "black meteor" – was indeed a ship's captain, born on October 9, 1853, in Kinnum on the West Friesian island of Terschelling, the Netherlands. He was buried nearby in May 1909. He is registered as commander of the 179-foot (55m), 1,173-ton, copper-clad wooden barque *J.P.A.*. She was originally built in 1867 in Quebec by Dunn & Samson as the naval frigate *Pladda*, sold re-rigged one year later as the Dutch barque *Maasnymph*, then in 1885 re-sold in Rotterdam for 15,000 Dutch guilders to G. Mauritz of Dordrecht and renamed *J.P.A.* (giving rise to the nickname "Jan pak an," a colloquial Dutch expression translating literally as "John catch it" and meaning something like "a go-getter!"). She was wrecked in a storm on January

---

482 Fort, *Damned*, pp. 271-272, citing *Monthly Weather Review*, March 1887.
483 "Swart" is given correctly in several contemporary newspapers but others have "Captain Swan." Many modern versions have "Captain Sweet" copied from an error in print editions of *The Book of the Damned* (Boni & Liveright, 1919, p. 271; Sphere/Abacus, 1973, p. 292) and the *Complete Books* (Dover, 1974, p. 284).

6, 1893, on the coast of Brazil at Barra de Santo Antônio.[484]

The reported coordinates place *J.P.A.* in the North Atlantic on March 19, 1887, 700 miles south of Newfoundland and 600 miles northeast of Bermuda. This fits her known movements. She left Rotterdam for New York on February 2, arrived in New York on April 14, stayed there for about one month, then departed for Québec where she arrived on June 3.[485]

What could the ship have encountered in the middle of the ocean?

Stories of ships being narrowly missed or even struck by huge meteorites are commonplace in old sources – too common. Most cases are probably lightning strikes, illusions caused by fireball meteors descending far beyond the horizon, (signal) rockets, or else "fishermen's tales." The probability of a near-miss by even a moderately-sized meteorite is tiny. As in the *Innerwick* case discussed in Chapter 13, a super-rare giant bolide can't be completely ruled out; but it would not explain everything in that case, and the same is true here.

Perhaps there are other explanations.

The crew perspired and gasped for air whilst "everything appeared like a sea of fire." A thermometer reading of 19°C (66.2°F) is certainly unusual for a March afternoon in the North Atlantic; but does not suggest scorching radiance. Nor does the "blistered" and blackened copper plate, because heat sufficient to blister copper with a melting point over 1,080°C (1,976°F) would probably cause timber fittings to burst into flame[486] as well as seriously burn the crew.

On the other hand, even moderate heating of the copper might speed up chemical patination caused by exposure to sulphurous gas (a trick known to "antique" restorers).[487] Copper blackening might point to the effect of hydrogen sulphide fumes,[488] and hydrogen

---

484 https://www.genealogieonline.nl/en/klein-eyckenstein/I3464.php; *Geboren of overleden aan boord van 1800 tot heden*, http://www.zeemansleed.nl/?p=5363; F. W. Wallace, *Record of Canadian Shipping 1786–1920*, Musson, Toronto, p. 216; https://archive.org/stream/recordofcanadian00wall/recordofcanadian00wall_djvu.txt; 'Ships Shattered at Sea,' *NY Times*, Feb. 23, 1893; *Times Picayune*, New Orleans, Jan. 13, 1893; http://www.maritimephoto.info/downloads/archief-zeebrieven/send/4-archief-zeebrieven/67-zeebrief50-oranje-2-anthony-veder.html; https://www.marhisdata.nl/schip&id=16421

485 See: *De Maasbode*, Feb. 4, 1887; *Nieuwe Rotterdamsche Courant*, June 5, 1887; *The Boston Globe*, May 8, 1887; *New York Times*, April 15, 1887.

486 Flaming autoignition of wood occurs at a few hundred degrees C, and for large samples heated by radiant heat on a timescale of minutes (rather than hours): Babrauskas, V., 'Ignition of Wood: A Review of the State of the Art,' in *Interflam 2001*, Interscience Communications Ltd., London (2001), pp. 71-88; https://doctorfire.com/pages/wood_ign.pdf

487 "For a black copper patina, this involves the application of heat to your copper [with a blowtorch] followed by a mixture of sulphurated potash. The heat activates the material, resulting in an aged look to the copper that would normally require decades of exposure" (http://www.ehow.co.uk/how_8496366_make-black-copper-patina.html). Conceivably copper sheeting might be heated by induction if exposed to a rapidly alternating magnetic field associated with an electrical phenomenon, but this is sheer speculation.

488 According to Wikipedia (http://en.wikipedia.org/wiki/Hydrogen_sulfide): "a diagnostic clue to extreme poisoning by H2S is the discoloration of coins in the pockets of the victim." Blackening and pitting of copper pipes has been associated with small quantities of sulphur in well water or even in so-called Chinese drywall (plasterboard), etc. See: http://www.finishing.com/258/66.shtml.
See also: http://www.inspectionnews.net/home_inspection/plumbing-system-home-inspection-commercial-inspection/30458-copper-pipes-turning-black-new-home.html

sulphide is a principal constituent of hot gases emitted from active volcanic vents. H_2S or "sewer gas" may form an explosive mixture with air. It reacts violently with copper oxide and causes potentially severe symptoms if inhaled.[489] So it may be significant that most sources say "the air was full of sulphur" on the deck of the *J.P.A.* (see Fig. 118), or that the crew suffered "greatly oppressed breathing from the great amount of sulphur in the air".[490] But it seems unlikely that volcanic H_2S could have achieved sufficient concentration for a sufficient time, in the open air in a "severe storm", to cause significant chemical deterioration of the hull copper. Moreover, the position given was in very deep water. The nearest group of seamounts – the New England Seamount Chain – is over 100 miles away, and anyway there is no record of eruptions or hydrothermal venting there in historical times.

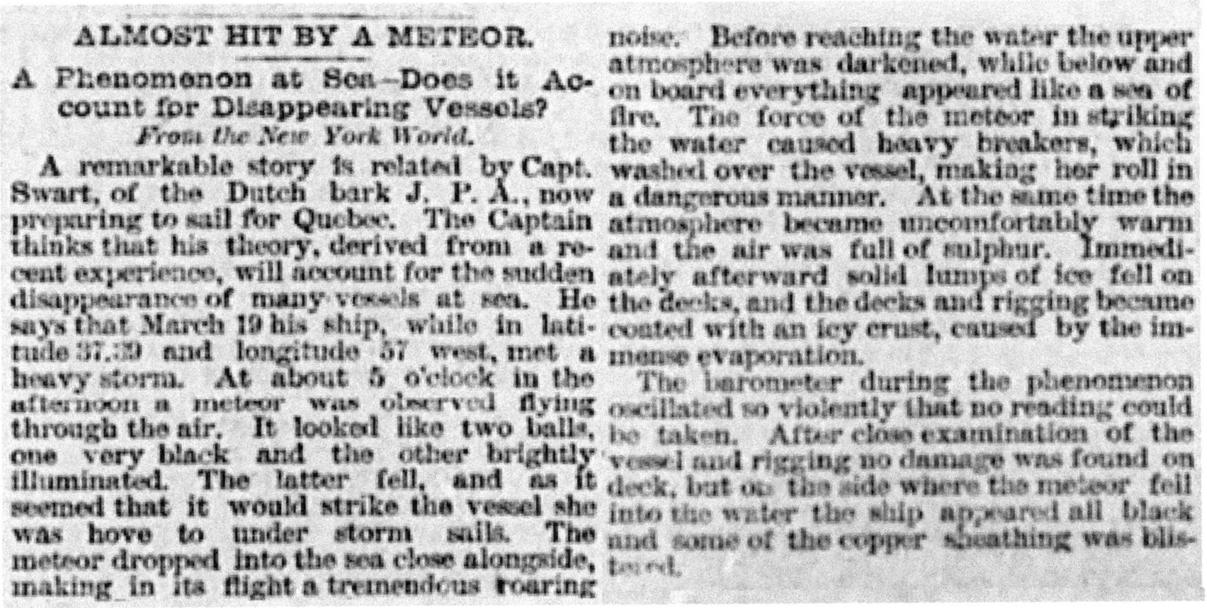

ALMOST HIT BY A METEOR.

A Phenomenon at Sea—Does it Account for Disappearing Vessels?

From the New York World.

A remarkable story is related by Capt. Swart, of the Dutch bark J. P. A., now preparing to sail for Quebec. The Captain thinks that his theory, derived from a recent experience, will account for the sudden disappearance of many vessels at sea. He says that March 19 his ship, while in latitude 37.39 and longitude 57 west, met a heavy storm. At about 5 o'clock in the afternoon a meteor was observed flying through the air. It looked like two balls, one very black and the other brightly illuminated. The latter fell, and as it seemed that it would strike the vessel she was hove to under storm sails. The meteor dropped into the sea close alongside, making in its flight a tremendous roaring noise. Before reaching the water the upper atmosphere was darkened, while below and on board everything appeared like a sea of fire. The force of the meteor in striking the water caused heavy breakers, which washed over the vessel, making her roll in a dangerous manner. At the same time the atmosphere became uncomfortably warm and the air was full of sulphur. Immediately afterward solid lumps of ice fell on the decks, and the decks and rigging became coated with an icy crust, caused by the immense evaporation.

The barometer during the phenomenon oscillated so violently that no reading could be taken. After close examination of the vessel and rigging no damage was found on deck, but on the side where the meteor fell into the water the ship appeared all black and some of the copper sheathing was blistered.

Fig. 118. *Morning News* (Savannah, Ga.), May 15, 1887. [491]

If the heat and copper damage are hard to explain, what about the ice? These were not just flecks of frost, but "solid lumps," and Swart says that "everything on deck and in the rigging *became* iced, notwithstanding that the thermometer registered 19° Centigrade" [emphasis added]. This implies that the icing happened during the event, rapidly. But could the rigging have become iced by weather during the storm, unnoticed by captain or crew, so that when the anomalous heat overwhelmed the ship this ice melted and fell to the deck? There was "a severe storm", so the *J.P.A.* was no doubt subject to heavy driving spray. In such conditions icing on superstructure and rigging can occur anywhere if the sea surface temperature is below about 42-44°F (6°-7°C) and if the air temperature is close to the freezing point of

---

489 Acute exposure causes respiratory paralysis, eye irritation, dizziness, and unconsciousness, and can be fatal in a few minutes. See: Health Protection Agency, Chemical Hazards; www.hpa.org.uk/webc/HPAwebFile/HPAweb_C/1246260029655

490 E.g., *Democrat and Chronicle* (Rochester, NY), May 8, 1887; *Morning News* (Savannah, Ga., citing *New York World*), May 15, 1887.

491 https://gahistoricnewspapers.galileo.usg.edu/lccn/sn86063034/1887-05-15/ed-1/seq-12/

seawater. But these conditions are unlikely. The *J.P.A.* was well south of the Arctic area of heavy icing. On this date, the environmental air temperature and the sea surface temperature would both have been well above the threshold for spray icing.[492] It "became dark as night" at the moment of the event, but at 5:00 p.m. (ship's time) it was broad daylight. Large ice build-ups occur over many hours or days and surely would not have escaped notice until chunks began falling to the deck. And when it did it would be recognised: icing can be very serious.

Unusual warmth, fluctuating pressure, and rapid icing make little meteorological sense together in any normal storm conditions. Capt. Swart reports "hurricane force" winds. There may have been no true hurricane[493] but we wondered about a tornadic waterspout: "Tornadic waterspouts . . . are associated with severe thunderstorms, and are often accompanied by high winds and seas, large hail, and frequent dangerous lightning."[494]

Baseball-sized hailstones are not uncommon, and they have been recorded up to 8 inches (20 cm) in diameter, like the record-breaking 2 lb conglomerate that fell in Vivian, South Dakota, in a violent thunderstorm in July 2010.[495] Giant hail is a possible cause of "solid lumps of ice [that] fell to the deck," but would not explain the statement that at the same time "everything on the deck and in the rigging became iced."

"The barometer during this time oscillated," states Capt. Swart, "so as to make it impossible to obtain a correct reading." Rapid and intense pressure and temperature fluctuations might occur across the wall of a powerful tornadic funnel. Understandably there is limited testimony about conditions inside tornado funnels, but transient pressure drops approaching 200 mbar (20% of sea-level atmospheric pressure) have been recorded,[496] and although instrumental temperature data are all-but non-existent the air ought to cool significantly. However, it would not suddenly freeze seawater on the deck and rigging, and certainly not while the crew are experiencing a suffocating warmth confirmed by the ship's thermometer.

The appearance of the object allegedly causing these effects is no less curious:

---

492   Typical environmental norms of 10°-15°C are recorded nearby by the NOAA National Data Buoy Center. See http://www.ndbc.noaa.gov/. See also *Forecaster's Handbook for the Arctic*, Section 10.1.1. 'Precipitation Types,' Figure 10-1; *Canadian Coast Guard, Ice and Weather Environment*, '3.1.6 Freezing Spray and Superstructure Icing Conditions' (http://www.tinyurl.com/3kgeau89)

493   No Atlantic hurricane is recorded for that month. However, the 1887 Atlantic hurricane season was one of the most active on record. It was also one of only four Atlantic seasons to have experienced hurricanes outside the "official" season. In 1887 "there were four storms that occurred outside the season, the most in a single year". See: http://en.wikipedia.org/wiki/1887_Atlantic_hurricane_season; http://en.wikipedia.org/wiki/Atlantic_hurricane#cite_ref-NOAA_Book_82_26-0   ; http://www.wunderground.com/hurricane/at1887.asp

494   http://oceanservice.noaa.gov/facts/waterspout.html

495   https://www.ncdc.noaa.gov/monitoring-content/extremes/ncec/reports/vivian-hailstone-final.pdf; http://commons.wikimedia.org/wiki/File:Record_hailstone_Vivian,_SD.jpg

496   A 100 mbar drop was recorded in South Dakota in 2003 (http://www.spc.noaa.gov/faq/tornado/), and in 2007 a funnel in Tulia, Texas, induced an astonishing drop of 194 mbar. A drop of 192 mbar was claimed for a tornado in Minneapolis, Minnesota, in 1904 (S. F. Blair, D. R. Deroche, and A. E. Pietrycha, 'In situ observations of the 21 April 2007 Tulia, Texas tornado,' *Electronic J. Severe Storms Meteor*, 3(3), 2008; http://www.ejssm.org/ojs/index.php/ejssm/article/view/39/40

... a meteor in the shape of two balls, one of them very black and the other illuminated.[497] The illuminated ball was oblong, and appeared as if ready to drop on the deck amidships. In a moment it became as dark as night above, but below, on board and surrounding the vessel, everything appeared like a sea of fire. The ball fell into the water very close alongside the vessel with a roar, and caused the sea to make tremendous breakers which swept over the vessel.

We should bear in mind that English was not Cornelis Swart's first language; but the notion of an "oblong ball" suggests that the word "ball" has a loose meaning here, perhaps closer to "blob", and an "oblong" blob might be something quite elongated. Occasionally witnesses who have been in a position to look up into the funnel of a tornado as it passes overhead have described intense and frequent lightning, even a continuous electrical illumination, inside the funnel. Controversial reports also exist of an external glow being seen around a funnel, although usually at night.[498] Could a waterspout really "transform everything into a sea of fire" even on a gloomy afternoon? And what could the "very black" ball have been? The shadowed interior of a second, unilluminated, funnel? Multivortex tornados and waterspouts do occur that contain two or more intense subvortices orbiting or twisting around a common center inside the main vortex.[499] However this theory feels extremely strained, not least because waterspouts would have been familiar to experienced seamen.[500]

Apart from a brief mention in the beginning of the narrative, nothing more is said about the unusual black body. Did everybody see it? How big was it? How did it behave? And what happened to it when the luminous object fell into the water? Was it lost from sight when the sky turned dark? A curious enough object, to be sure, but also very ill-defined – arguably too elusive for us to be sure it was real. It is perhaps worth considering the possibility that the black ball was merely an afterimage caused by staring at the "brightly illuminated" ball.

The only other explanation we can think of for this black ball is a vagrant balloon caught up in the storm. Admittedly it seems unlikely that a stray balloon could be blown hundreds of miles out over the Atlantic and chance to come down right on top of the *J.P.A.*; yet readers of the first volume of *Redemption of the Damned* may recall that just such a derelict balloon puzzled witnesses on the island of Bermuda in August 1885, having probably been swept hundreds of miles from the US East coast by Tropical Cyclone #2 of that year's Atlantic hurricane season (see Vol. 1, Case #51, pp. 227-231). There was no hurricane in March 1887,[501] but it was an unusually stormy month over the western Atlantic, especially from the

---

497 Some 1887 newspapers described "two balls of fire," but as these contain less detail and more errors they are presumably not reliable. See e.g.: http://trove.nla.gov.au/newspaper/article/65600570/6385125#; http://trove.nla.gov.au/newspaper/article/9136616#

498 B. Vonnegut & J. R. Weyer, 'Luminous Phenomena in Nocturnal Tornadoes', *Science*, Vol. 153 (Sept. 9, 1966), pp. 1213-1220. See also: Martin Shough & Wim van Utrecht, *Was the Saint-Prouant "Cloud-Cigar" of September 14, 1954 a Funnel Cloud?* http://www.caelestia.be/saintprouant.html

499 http://www.spc.noaa.gov/faq/tornado/index.html#multivortex1

500 Reports of waterspouts taken from ships' logs were published routinely in, for example, the *Monthly Weather Review* and maritime journals of the period.

501 See Note #493.

1st to the 20th, with many continental low pressure systems following their typical northeastward tracks off the US East Coast.[502] One of these might easily be responsible.

Stretching this idea a bit further: we know that balloons dispensing fireworks for public display were around in those days and were involved in some spectacular accidents (see: *Redemption of the Damned*, Volume 1, Case #35, pp. 146-150; Case 74, pp. 363-364); also that military balloons designed to drop explosives had been used since at least July 12, 1849, when a manned bomb-balloon was launched over Venice from the Austrian vessel SMS *Vulcano* (without success due to adverse wind). The *Vulcano* also participated on August 22, when her crew, and land forces, flew a total of 200 pilotless 23-foot (7.3 m) hot-air bomb-balloons over Venice, equipped with fuses timed to drop 33-pound explosive charges into the city, with limited success. US patents for more sophisticated "dynamite balloons" were granted in the 1860s.[503]

So, there is a possibility that an unmanned firework-balloon or bomb-balloon broke loose in an East Coast storm and drifted far out to sea. Rainwater collected by the balloon gondola might freeze as it was lofted to great height in a storm updraft, until the weight of water ice and failing gas buoyancy brought it down to sea level, where lightning chanced to set fire to its payload over the *J.P.A.*. The blazing gondola full of pyrotechnics could have burned free from the stricken balloon (the "black ball", which was destroyed) and fallen like a ball of fire, crashing into the water nearby and damaging the copper hull plating (typical "black powder" pyrotechnic mixtures can burn at 1,200°-1,400°C, hotter than the 1,080°C melting point of copper[504]). The burning powder and clouds of smoke might have resembled "a sea of fire" and darkened the sky, causing a "roaring" noise and a "great amount of sulphur in the air".[505]

Possible. But not very plausible. Could pyrotechnics survive dry and viable through many stormy hours or days aloft? Would freezing rain stay frozen during a balloon's descent from somewhere above the freezing level (typically about 9800 ft, or 3000 m, over the Northwest Atlantic[506]) to near sea level? Possibly – yet how could the fall of lumps of ice have occurred after the basket had already plunged into the sea? Perhaps some ice also accreted on top of the balloon envelope. Then again, what could explain the simultaneous icing of the ship's

---

502   "Eleven depressions are traced . . . During the first two decades of the month the more important Storms which appeared were confined to the western half of the [Atlantic] Ocean, where deep barometric depressions, accompanied by storms of great violence, followed one another in rapid succession . . . As compared with the corresponding month of previous years, the weather over the North Atlantic during March, 1887, was unusually severe west of the thirty-fifth meridian, this being due rather to the frequency of storms than to their exceptional individual strength." ('North Atlantic Storms During March, 1887', *Monthly Weather Review*, March 1887, p. 71; https://www.ncei.noaa.gov/sites/default/files/march-1887-monthly-weather-review-final.pdf)

503   http://www.ctie.monash.edu.au/hargrave/rpav_home.html; https://en.wikipedia.org/wiki/Incendiary_balloon; https://longstreet.typepad.com/thesciencebookstore/2018/10/mad_balloon.html

504   M. E. Brown and R. A. Rugunana, 'A Temperature-Profile Study of the Combustion of Black Powder and its Constituent Binary Mixtures', *Propellants, Explosives, Pyrotechnics* 14, 69-75 (1989), 69; http://tinyurl.com/53ak37nv

505   The latter two details were left out by Fort's source, the *Monthly Weather Review* (Fig. 117), but were widely reported elsewhere.

506   Gettys N. Harris, Jr., *et al.*, 'Comparison of Freezing-Level Altitudes from the NCEP Reanalysis with TRMM Precipitation Radar Brightband Data', *Journal of Climate*, 13(23), 2000, pp. 4137-4148; https://journals.ametsoc.org/jcli/article/13/23/4137/29256/Comparison-of-Freezing-Level-Altitudes-from-the

rigging? And "tremendous breakers that swept over the vessel" could hardly be caused by a plummeting balloon gondola.

At this point it is time to admit failure. If we are to preserve the phenomena as reported, without resorting to exotic hypotheses, we are reduced to ever more far-fetched speculations.

We will close this chapter with another coincidence, one which picks up echoes from Chapters 10 and 13. In the former we described the sighting by Capt. Caithness, of the brig *Victoria*, and a near-coincident fireball meteor seen hundreds of miles away. In the latter we considered sightings by citizens of Victoria, British Columbia, and by Caithness-born Capt. Waters, on the barque *Innerwick*, of what may have been the same "hissing" superbolide. The pattern is becoming something of a theme: This time, we find that Captain Swart encountered his plunging "meteor" not long after a remarkable superbolide exploded over far-off Australia – alarming the populace of the State of . . . Victoria! [507]

This fireball soared 400 miles across Australia's most southeastern state on Thursday, March 17, 1887, at about 4:15 p.m., with rumbling explosions like artillery and a hiss "like escaping steam", causing "earth tremors", "shaking houses severely", and scaring livestock and wildlife. Around 5:00 p.m. the sky was "obscured by a kind of vapour at a great height" – not "dark as night", as reported by Capt. Swart, but a lead-grey mist "such that all objects looked green or greenish in the strange light". Reports from various districts appeared in the Australian press on the following days, [508] and an article was published in *Nature* (Fig. 119).

This event occurred at about the same local time of day as the *J.P.A.* episode, but two days earlier. In this case there seems no prospect of reconciling the dates. Nevertheless, it remains odd that our two cases of plunging "meteorites" were both preceded – calendrically, at least – by a superbolide that entered the atmosphere in a different part of the world, each time in a place called Victoria. Daylight meteors producing sonic booms, shaking houses, and leaving a trail of white cloud in the sky, don't occur every year, nor even every ten years. In fact, the description of the Australian bolide is nearly identical to that of the daylight fireball seen, heard, and felt at Chelyabinsk in February 2013, the most spectacular close encounter Earth has had with a bolide during modern times.

So, where does all this leave us? The *Monthly Weather Review* reported Capt. Swart's observation as a "rare electrical phenomenon at sea", no doubt having in mind stories of ball lightning. But anything luminous has too often been labelled ball lightning, especially in the late-19th century. Still, today, scientists' ignorance of the nature and properties of so-called ball lightning make this a not-very-profitable conclusion, especially in a case which strains the theory in multiple directions. Even if we combine rare lightning phenomena with a violent waterspout funnel, we can only reproduce some of the effects. We have seen that other theories have their problems too. If these things occurred as stated, then Capt. Swart's double "meteor" deserves its status as a famous fortean mystery.

---

507   Cornelis Swart was from the Dutch province of North Holland. Australia was still officially known as "New Holland" even into the 1830s. Dutch explorers were the first to circumnavigate, map, and name the country; and in the 21st century Victoria still had "the largest number of Netherlands-born people of any state in Australia". See: 'Immigration History from Netherlands to Victoria';
https://origins.museumsvictoria.com.au/countries/netherlands;
https://en.wikipedia.org/wiki/New_Holland_(Australia)
508   Melbourne *Argus*, March 18, 1887, p. 5; *Argus*, March 19, p. 12.

ON March 17 last, about 4.15 p.m., the track of a brilliant meteor in the southern heavens, at an altitude of 30°, was observed by Mr. R. Brough Smyth, of Sandhurst, Victoria, Australia. Writing to us on March 19, Mr. Smyth says :—
" The line was silver-white and of considerable breadth. The sun was shining in a clear sky. Owing to the view being intercepted by large gum-trees growing in the grounds around my house, I could see only a portion of the arc described. Subsequently, a little after 5 o'clock p.m., the sky was obscured by a kind of mist or vapour at a great height—in colour between steel-grey and lead-grey, and with tints similar to those of the metal bismuth over the whole. All objects looked green or green-ish in the strange light. The meteor was observed at Salisbury in South Australia, at Coleraine in the extreme west of Victoria, and at various places eastward—say over a distance of 400 miles. It travelled apparently from east to west, and as far as known was visible in the southern part of Australia only. In some places it presented the appearance of a blood-red ball, and at Beaufort the ball is said to have exploded with a loud report, sending up a streak of fire, accompanied with the hissing of escaping steam, as from an engine. It left a cloud of greyish smoke. This smoke-like cloud was observed in other places. At Warrnambool on the west coast, and at Terang, twenty-five miles north-eastward, shocks of what were supposed to be earthquakes were felt at the time of the disappearance of the meteor. Cattle and horses galloped about in alarm, houses were shaken, windows rattled, and the wild fowl in the lakes were disturbed, and took wing. I inclose cuttings from the *Argus* containing accounts of this phenomenon."

The " cuttings " inclosed by Mr. Smyth are a series of tele-grams, describing the phenomenon as seen in various parts of Australia. At Coleraine, " a brilliant ball of fire shot from the zenith in a clear sky to 30° above the horizon, and then disap-peared as it exploded, leaving a large cloud of white smoke, which was visible for half an hour. Exactly six minutes subsequently, two distinct shocks like cannon reports were heard, with a percept-ible tremor of the atmosphere. The phenomenon was witnessed by 500 persons." At Merino, " a most unusual phenomenon appeared in the eastern sky. A streak like smoke from a vol-cano appeared. Immediately after the appearance, a report like distant thunder was heard from the same direction. It was thought that an aërolite of immense size had fallen between Merino and Hamilton." At Stawell the " meteor appeared to burst just beyond the town in a cloud of smoke, which was immediately followed by a loud crash like thunder." From Terang it is reported that at Lake Keilambete " the black swans were noticed to rise suddenly off the lake. A rumbling noise appeared to pass under, causing the cattle grazing on the banks of the lake to scamper away, and on gaining some distance they were seen to look back. The noise was heard in other places, and seemed to pass to the south-west." At Port-land, " three distinct reverberations like the booming of artil-lery were heard about 4 p.m." The people at Warrnambool, hearing, shortly after 4 o'clock, loud detonations like a volley of musketry, with subsequent dropping shots, rushed out of their houses ; and " the cattle were paralyzed with fear at the sounds." The disappearance of the meteor over Beaufort, where it is said to have exploded, " was followed by earth tremors and a rumbling sound as of the firing of heavy artillery. The vibrations lasted for ten seconds. Several houses were shaken severely. No substance appears to have fallen to the earth."

Fig. 119. 'A Remarkable Meteor', *Nature*, May 26, 1887, p. 93. [509]

And yet, when all is said and done, and despite our reassuringly positive "background check" on the captain, his ship, and its movements, we are free to doubt the veracity of a story which rests on the word of a single witness. It may not be a coincidence that in 1873 English translations of Jules Verne's book *Around the Moon* were published. That novel – sequel to Verne's influential 1865 science fiction novel *From the Earth to the Moon* – has a story that sounds all too familiar, illustrated in Fig. 120. The scene is the deck of the U.S. corvette *Susquehanna* which is taking soundings in the Pacific Ocean:

> . . . At that moment (it was seventeen minutes past one in the morning) Lieutenant Bronsfield was preparing to leave the watch and return to his cabin, when his attention was attracted by a distant hissing noise. His comrades and himself first thought that this hissing was caused by the letting off of steam; but lifting their heads, they found that the noise was produced in the highest regions of the air. They had not time to question each other before the hissing became frightfully intense, and suddenly there appeared to their dazzled eyes an enormous meteor, ignited by the rapidity of its course and its friction through the atmospheric strata.

> This fiery mass grew larger to their eyes, and fell, with the noise of thunder, upon the bowsprit, which it smashed close to the stem, and buried itself in the waves with a deafening roar!

> A few feet nearer, and the Susquehanna would have foundered with all on board!

---

509 https://www.nature.com/articles/036093a0.pdf

Fig. 120. Jules Verne's fictional moon-shot projectile falls from space to impact the US Navy vessel *Susquehanna,* from the 1870 illustrated edition of *Around the Moon*.[510]
Credit: Mary Evans Picture Library.

510 https://www.maryevans.com

Around the Moon was first printed in 1870.[511] Since most of Verne's work was about adventures at sea, it is safe to assume that by 1885–1887 a great number of ship captains in the Western world would have read one or more of his books.

It is true that other, much earlier, sources of influence could have been encountered by Capt. Swart, in newspapers, books and scientific journals, reporting hissing and whistling meteors, some falling in the sea near ships, dating back hundreds of years. Verne is said to have been noted for his assiduous research for ideas in scientific journals, and his own fictional 1870 description of a hissing re-entry may itself have been influenced by earlier meteor stories he had read.[512] Nevertheless, the similarity of language is undeniably striking. Could a work of popular fiction explain why stories of fiery, steam-producing objects splashing down near ships were around in those days – and are not around anymore?

511 https://en.wikipedia.org/wiki/Around_the_Moon
512 For example, these from Greg's well-known 1861 catalogue:
1676, March 31 (21st Old Style), a fireball twice the size of the moon fell into the sea near Corsica with a hissing sound and detonated; **1749**, Nov. 4, Atlantic Ocean, a fireball shattered a ship's mast, leaving a strong sulphurous smell (see Chapter 9); **1810**, Nov. 28, a fireball "evidently aerolitic" fell into the sea between Cape Matapan and the Island of Cerigo, Greece; **1821**, Sept. 18, seen from a ship at sea, a fireball the size of the moon fell obliquely from the zenith, burst and fell into the water; **1848**, 29 Oct., near Bombay, a large, "dazzling" meteor leaving a streak travelled horizontally, then fell down into sea; **1852**, Dec. 17, Dover, a fireball half the diameter of the moon in the centre of a black cloud fell into sea the with a hissing noise and a cloud of spray (see: Aubeck & Shough, *Return to Magonia*, Anomalist Books, 2015, pp. 153-166); **1856**, Sept. 17, Rome, Italy, a large bolide exploded and fell vertically into the sea with spray and a hissing sound, close to a vessel.
See: R. P. Greg, F.G.S, 'A Catalogue of Meteorites and Fireballs, from A.D. 2 to A.D. 1860,' *Report of the Thirtieth Meeting of the British Association for the Advancement of Science*, held at Oxford in June and July 1860. published by John Murray, Albemarle Street, London, 1861;
http://www.meteoritehistory.info/GREG/GREG.HTM#cat

CONCLUSION

Charles Fort urged independent thinkers to rescue his "damned data" from the abyss to which he believed scientific intolerance had cynically abolished them, promising that we should discover wonders. He was persuasive. We have accepted his challenge and redeemed from damnation a wide spectrum of remarkable stories. What have we found?

As we discovered in Vol. 1 of this work, some of the anomalous observations recorded by Fort in *The Book of the Damned* dissolve away on inspection. But some remain mystifying. Is this simply for lack of the information that would allow them to be explained in a conventional way? In many cases that seems very likely to be true. Can we argue – as some sceptical critics will – that it must be true in all cases? Appealing to long experience, and playing the percentages, it is possible to justify this conclusion as the most economical.

Of course, in terms of investigatory effort it would have been even more economical to dismiss the strangest reports out of hand as too fantastic to justify the effort of analysis in the first place. Some would have advocated doing so; but that would have been the lazy obverse of credulity, rather than rigorous scepticism. Throwing out difficult claims as fantasy does not qualify as a solution, just as in a game of chess overturning the board will never be a winning move, and could never be honourable between self-respecting players who have thought it worthwhile to set up the pieces in the first place.

In the same spirit, when a claim so strange that one half-expects it to evaporate immediately into fantasy survives detailed checking of witnesses and circumstances, and acquires every appearance of being a sincere account of an anomalous physical event, one has a responsibility to respect the possibility that it might be so. This means giving respect to a conscientious process of eliminating even very unlikely fusions of rare conventional events, to the point where it is no longer possible to proceed "as if" the report is broadly true without invoking novel, exotic phenomena.

To those who are impatient with this process we would reiterate that it isn't only proponents of exotic theories who need first to have journeyed down this road: only by having given this much respect to a report do we earn the right to defend the suggestion – should we so wish – that it may, after all, be fiction.

As in Vol. 1, there are different grades and flavours of strangeness across the spectrum of fortean anomalies examined in Vol. 2. Broadly speaking, on the one hand we have phantom moons and planets (Chapters 1 & 2), lights and other phenomena on the Moon (Chapter 6) and on Mars (Chapter 8), or luminous wheels in Earth's oceans (Chapter 11) – each intriguing and with incompletely explained aspects, but not implying fundamentally novel phenomena. On the other hand, we have a number of observations like the "super-Zeppelin" seen against the sun from two different locations (Chapter 3), and assorted balls of fire, sometimes destructive, crashing into or bursting out from the sea, reported by ships' captains (Chapters 12, 13 & 14).

Among these latter observations there is a residue of cases that not only fail to dissolve under the light of inquiry but even seem to harden. In some cases this may be because a rare but genuine conventional phenomenon, or more than one, can be identified as a plausible cause; but in a few cases we have to accept that this process ends in an impasse. One or two of these obdurate reports are simultaneously so remarkable and so circumstantial that, despite our best explanatory ingenuity, we cannot rule out the possibility of an exotic event.

But it is fair to say that we have found no single case where an exotic explanation is inescapable. In all cases there remain uncertainties, omissions, contradictions, and unresolved issues of various kinds that create room for doubt. And, frustratingly, this remainder concerns phenomena that are no longer reported in recent decades, despite sophisticated detection tools being almost ubiquitous.

Vast luminous wheels near the surface of oriental waters, bright fireballs terrorizing ships at sea, and dark objects appearing in front of the sun, the moon or neighbouring planets . . . . In the new millennium, these things should not escape the attention of smartphone and security cameras, of military radars that monitor the skies constantly, of Google Earth satellite cameras, and of all-sky camera networks that exist around the world and register hundreds of fireball meteors every year, none of which ever display the uncanny behaviour mentioned by our witnesses from previous centuries. Were these historical observations flawed or simply invented? Or are we missing something? As lifelong investigators of the unknown we have given it our best shot, but the answer remains unclear.

Extraordinary claims famously require extraordinary evidence, and although the evidence in *The Book of the Damned* – as rationalised and expanded in our books – is, at its best, provocative, it is not good enough to conclude with certainty that there is something going on in our atmosphere, our oceans and our solar system that transcends our general understanding of physics.

Martin Shough & Wim van Utrecht, January 2021

INDEX to VOLUME 1

Abbe, Prof. Cleveland ... 84, 292, 293, 297, 301

Aberystwyth Observer 143

Académie des Sciences, Paris 17, 132, 148, 172, 306, 308, 309, 311

Acharius, Erik .... 18-23 *passim*, 28, 29

achromatic objective (optics) 15, 16, 197

actinic light 204

Adrianople (Edirne) 231, 232, 402

afterimages, retinal 22, 23, 399

Agé, M 238

Air Intelligence Digest (USAF) 354

airglow 98, 99

airships 1, 230, 300, 301, 342, 344, 359-361, 384, 391

Airy disc (optical resolution) 17, 60

Airy, Sir George Bidell 17, 46, 60

Aisne, France 121

albedo 160, 163, 164

Alexander, William H. 356

Alexandria (Virginia) *Gazette* 284

Algol 156, 160

Alkaid 307

Allingham, Cedric 18

Alpha Centauri 242

Alpha Gemini 157

Alpha Pavonis 390

Altair (Alpha Aquilae) 369, 373

altocumulus lenticularis, *see* lenticular cloud

America (airship) 230

American Car & Foundry Company 394

American Ephemeris and Nautical Almanac 83

American Journal of Science and Arts 39

American Meteorological Journal 221

American white pelican 351

Andes Lights (Andes Glow) 210, 211

Angels of Mons 347

Anglo-French Conference on Time-keeping at Sea (1917) 332

Annalen der Physik und Chemie 36, 38

Annales des Sciences Naturelles 172

Anthropological Institute of Great Britain & Ireland 317

antisolar corona 297

antisolar point 317, 318

Antwerp, Belgium 114, 325, 397

Aquarius (constellation) 117-119

Aquila (constellation) 364, 365, 368, 369, 373

Arago, François (1786-1853) 7, 232, 240, 361, 362, 364

Archives des découvertes (1839) 44

Argentinian Navy 349

Argo Navis (obsolete constellation) 242

Ariake Sea, Kyushu, Japan 270

Aristotle, bird hibernation theory of 11

Armagh Observatory 247

Arnold, Kenneth 1

Ashland, Kentucky 395, 396

asteroid 160, 163-165

Astronomical & Physical Society of Toronto 156

astronomical day, *v.* civil day and astronomical day 331, 332, 377

Astronomical Society of the Pacific 284, 377, 390

Astronomische Nachrichten 311, 312, 373

atmospheric waves 64

Atoyac river, Mexico 138

Aubeck, Chris 21, 29, 73, 105, 112, 143, 269, 300

Auber, Prof 41

aureole (atmospheric optics) 214, 215, 304, 327, 328

Aurora Australis 96

Aurora Borealis 38, 40, 39, 67, 69, 96, 121, 151, 183, 235, 247, 259, 365, 369, 392
   aurora, interaction with noctilucent cloud 95
   auroral arch 97, 151, 166, 184, 186, 242, 247, 249, 369, 370
   beam 95, 99, 181, 182, 249
   conjugacy 96
   oval...167
   patch... 97, 166, 167, 182, 185, 235, 399
   streamer 235, 242
   zone 97, 98, 243
Aylesbury, Buckinghamshire 63, 66, 67

Baden Powell, Rev. Prof......44, 45, 53, 61, 64, 65, 67, 76, 195
Bahamas 137
Balearic Islands 75
ball lightning 2, 5, 48, 54, 129, 132, 149, 171-173, 231, 232, 238-240, 292, 296, 297, 301, 310, 353, 356, 359, 361, 362, 364, 370, 372, 400
   horses stunned by 354
   internal structure of 371
Ballester Olmos, Vicente-Juan 136, 244
balloons............ 23, 27, 46, 76, 77, 92, 148-150, 165, 227-230, 249, 295, 300, 306, 308-310, 312, 313, 319-322, 349, 359-364, 371, 374, 379, 381, 383, 388, 395, 400
ballooning spiders 14, 24, 57
Ballot, John 220
Ballyarthur, County Wicklow, Eire ...322-328 *passim*, 402
Baltimore & Ohio Railroad...................300
Banbury Guardian 124, 126
Banbury, Oxfordshire .. 124, 125, 127-129, 401
Bancroft, Joseph FRS.............................64
Bangalore, India........................84, 86, 401
Banner, Capt. Frederick William.... 89-111 *passim*

'Barbazon, Mr', *see* Lord Brabazon
bar-headed goose (*Anser indicus*) 175
Barlow lens 194, 195
Bassett, Adelina D. 227
bat colonies 245
bat migration 245
Bat's Cave, East London, S. Africa......245
Bath, England. 377, 378
Bath, Maine..366
Bay of Bengal 51
Beaufort weather system..........22, 57, 160, 272, 295, 303, 313, 334, 351
Becker, Johannes.........................34, 25, 38
Beesley, Thomas 126
Bell, Dr Alexander Graham........ 247, 249
Bellerophon, HMS 255
Béraud, Mr 74
Berlin, Germany............. ..111-116 *passim*, 313, 401
Berlin Observatory...............................116
Bermuda.................227-230, 273, 384, 402
Berson, Arthur 313
Beta Carinae...242
Beta Ursa Majoris.................................156
Biddeford Daily Journal 365, 366
bioluminescense
   of insects.........................70, 244, 310
   of marine animals...........................263
   of plant material 310
   of unicellular organisms.................263
Biot, Jean-Baptiste 20, 398
birds, as possible explanation...........42, 84, 121, 132, 144, 173-175, 189, 192, 207, 244, 249, 251, 252, 310, 375
   migration of......11, 12, 133, 134, 143, 174, 176, 198, 200-202, 305
Birmingham Morning/Evening News ... 124
Birt, William Radcliffe FRAS.......... 64-68
Biskopsberga, Sweden..........18, 20-23, 27, 29, 55
Blanchard, Sophie.......................149, 363
Blanche, HMS 255

blast furnace, light pillar caused by......392, 394-397

Blomme, Dr Ronny.......136, 199, 200, 204

blue jets (atmospheric phenomena).......370

blur-circle (optics).......15, 60, 62, 87, 124, 196

Boggs, Edward M..........296-298

Bon Matsuri (Festival of Lanterns)......266, 268, 269

Bonilla, José Árbol y.............132, 189-207 *passim*, 213

Boötes (constellation) 368

Borraz Aymerich, Manuel.....199, 200, 390

Borsig steel foundry, Berlin..................115

Boscovich, Roger Joseph 10-17

Bosphorus Strait....................................232

Boston Herald 364

Brænne, Ole Jonny......................234, 236

Brecon Beacons, South Wales 382

Brendel, Dr Martin.................................311

British Association for the Advancement of Science 42, 45, 53, 56, 61, 64, 76, 144, 145, 285

British Museum...............................55, 255

British Rainfall (Symons)................66, 127

Brock's Fireworks, London 72

Brooks, W. R..............................304-306

Brorsen's Comet 155, 156

Broughty Ferry, Dundee 186

Brown Mountain, South Carolina 143

Bruguière, H...189

Brunswick Record 364-366

Brunswick, Maine 364

Buchner, Christian Ludwig Otto.............42

Buckminster Fuller, Richard 2

Bucks County Gazette 169

Bucyrus Foundry and Manufacturing Company 225

Bucyrus, Ohio 225, 226

Bulletin of the Society for Geographical Studies, Mexico 136

Bunsen, Prof. Robert W. E.....................116

Burlington Free Press...................359, 371

Burlington, Iowa....................................298

Burlington, Vermont ... 173, 354, 357, 359-361, 364, 366, 370, 371, 400, 402

Buys-Ballot, Mr 41

Caelestia website 108

Callendreau, Prof. Octave 306-308, 311

Calman of Dundee (shipbuilder).............90

Cambrian News 142

Cambridge, Mass 121

Canadian Weather Review....................319

candle balloons, *see* fire balloons

Canterbury Times 236

Cape Breton, Nova Scotia.....................249

Cape Verde 101, 102, 105, 106

Capella 278

Capocci, Ernesto 74, 195, 219, 251

Capodimonte Observatory 74

Capricorn (constellation).......117, 118, 178

Capron, John Rand 95, 182-184, 186

carbon-arc lamps............................116, 232

carbon-arc searchlights..........116, 346, 350

Cardigan Bay, West Wales 151

Carlsbad (Karlovy Vary), Czech Republic 103

Carmelite Order of Dijon.....................132

Caroline, HMS ....253-279 *passim*

Carrington event (geomagnetic storm, 1859)..99

Cartwright, T. L. M.......125, 127, 130, 131

Cassiopeia (constellation) 286, 288

Castle, Capt..257

Catalogue of Meteors and Fireballs (Greg, 1860)..42

Catalogue of Observations of Luminous Meteors (1849), see Baden Powell

Cave, Charles J. P 103, 379, 381, 382

celestial sphere 157

Chamberlain, B. H. 266

Chant, Prof. Clarence A........144, 170, 384

Charles Scribner and Sons....................121

Cheju-do, *see* Jejudo

Chelyabinsk superbolide..............239, 342

Cherbourg, France................... 41-44, 401

Chicago & Rock Island Railroad 296
Chicago Tribune...........................96, 259
China Sea 255, 256, 258, 262, 264
China, early pyrotechnics in...................73
Chinese lanterns............................256, 271
Chisbury, England...............379-381, 383
Chisholm, Sarah 261
Chladni, Ernst 18, 21, 31-33, 35-38
Cilfton, Sir Gervase..............................153
Clifton, Leonard Worsley.....................153
Cincinnati Enquirer 286
circle of confusion (optics)............193, 194
City of Boston (ship)......................108, 109
Claimant, The (Satan) 130
Clarke, Dr David 79
Clemens, Dr A 38
Clifton, Leonard Worsley.....................153
'Clifton, S. W.', *see* Clifton, Leonard
clouds
    cirrus........70, 71, 93, 94, 102, 103, 105,
    113, 215, 217, 218, 224, 320, 321, 387
    cumulus 93, 99, 100, 102, 104,
    105, 234, 320, 354, 371, 381, 382, 387
    lenticularis 100, 101, 105, 321, 381-
    382
    optical transparency of.............341, 343
    shadow cast by...... 379, 382, 383, 386,
    387
    stratus.................... 304, 321, 327, 333,
    335-337, 341, 343, 345, 347, 351, 382
    see also, funnel, hole-punch, nacreous,
    noctilucent, vortex
Coffin, Prof. John H. C 81-84
Coggia, Jérôme Eugène.........117, 118, 121
cold core funnel cloud..........................136
Coleman, Peter.....................................131
collotype process.................................204
comet....... 66, 67, 102, 104, 112, 113, 155,
    156, 158, 164, 165, 168, 206, 213, 220,
    221- 224, 241, 242, 389-391
Comet 2P/Encke...................................236
cometary dust grains, optical scattering by
    206

Comptes-Rendus 117-119, 147, 148,
    171, 172, 209, 210, 212, 309, 311
condensation level 336
Condon Report....................................107
condor..174, 175
Congreve, Col. William...........................73
controlled burning of vegetation...........262
Copeland, Prof. Ralph..........................247
Cordoba Observatory...........................389
Cordoba, Argentina..............................390
Corliss, William R 5, 27, 29, 145, 210
corona (atmospheric optics)..................327
Coronal Mass Ejection (CME)...............95
Cosford Incident 378
Cosmos 2238......................................379
Coutances, France...............................42-44
Cowley, Les 226
cranes (birds)........173, 174, 175, 176, 189,
    201, 202
Croghan Kinsella (Cruachán Uí
    Chinnsealaigh)..................322, 325, 326
Crotsenburg, C. N....... .291-293, 295, 296,
    297, 301, 304
Crow Agency, Montana................291, 292
Crow Indian Reservation, Montana 292
cubic ice 219
Curlew, HMS......................................255

Daily Journal-Gazette, Mattoon, IL.......27
Daily Record, Long Branch, NJ............360
Dann, Kevin...361
dark meteors 76, 77, 249-252, 304
David Dunlap Observatory...................385
Dawes, William Rutter 61
daylight fireball..............................31, 154
de Lan-Lusignan, Mr 75
De Natuur 250
'Death Ray Matthews', *see* Grindell-
    Matthews, Harry
De Cuppis, Mr......................................41
Defiance, HMS 255
Denning, W. F.........86, 288-290, 377, 378,
    384, 385

Devoe, J. Spencer.........156, 157, 159, 161, 163-165, 168, 177

Dharamsala (Dhurmsalla), India......69-71, 399, 401

diamond dust (ice crystals).........55, 70, 71

diffraction

optical phenomena created by....24, 27, 328, 340

with telescopic lenses............16, 17, 24

diffraction corona, non-circular (atmospheric optics) 327

Dijon, France...................17, 132, 134, 401

Dimanche des Brandons (Sunday of the Firebrands)..149

dispersion (optics) 197

Dollond, Peter......................16, 58, 61, 63

Doubt (magazine).....................................2

dragonflies, swarm of 244

Drayton, N. S 176-178

Dreiser, Theodore 2

Dreyer, J. L. E.......................................249

Du Celliée Muller, A. M..............249-251

duct, atmospheric-optical 259

dunlin, migration of 244

Durham, England 69, 77, 79, 401

dust devils, electric field in 129

dust satellites...................................67, 165

dust, atmospheric, fall of 211, 213

dusty plasmas 217, 285, 287, 371

optical transparency of....................206

Eager, Walter H. 392

Earle, John W...287

earth(quake)lights.....................2, 143, 232

earthquake 2, 69, 211, 222, 263, 364

East Twickenham, England 240

echelon formation 342

eclipse,

lunar...241

eclipse, solar 41, 82-84, 194, 306

ecliptic plane 54, 68, 95, 206, 214, 366, 368, 369

Eddie, Major L. A. FRAS............. 241-249 *passim*

Edgar, HMS..255

Edirne (Adrianople) 232

Eiswerder Island, Berlin................115, 116

electrical apparatus, geomagnetic disruption of 183

electrojet (ionospheric current)..............96

electrical effects

associated with auroras 183

with insects 244

with meteors...................47-49

with thunderstorms...359, 398

with tornadoes...................129

electrostatic interactions of airborne particles 219

Elementary Cosmography (Bonilla, 1877) 191

Ellery, Robert L. J...............................154

elves (atmospheric phenomena)............370

Emmert, Emil 23

Emmert's Law..23

emulsions, photo, colour bias of 197

EPB, *see* equatorial plasma bubble

Epsilon Lyrae 113

EQL *see* earth(quake)lights

equatorial plasma bubble (EPB) 97-99, 217

Esparza Sánchez, Cuauhtémoc 191

Espert, Mme........................362-364, 371

European gypsy moth 121

Evans, Rev. J 142

Evelyn, John FRS 141

eye, motion tracking of.........................197

eyepiece projection (telescopic)...176, 189, 196, 200

faculae, solar 194, 204

Fairfield, Connecticut 359

fall-streaks (virga)..... 71, 93, 100, 102-104

'falling leaf' motion 122

'false lights' of Durham....................77, 79

Fata Morgana, *see* mirage

Fatima, 'Miracle of the Sun' 399

fermentation heat...................................108

Festival of Lanterns, *see* Bon Matsuri, FuTzuki

The Field...141

field of view (telescopic) *see* FOV

fire balloons......23, 54, 69, 70, 71, 73, 119, 172, 178, 179, 239, 300, 307, 308, 310

fire tornados 130

fireball meteors..........33, 38, 44, 107, 112, 217, 232-236, 239, 285, 287, 289, 377
  booms and vibrations caused by 385
  Earth-grazing...........119, 144, 170, 333, 338-343, 384, 385, 400
    size and brightness of...................... 341
    trail of...284

fireflies 70, 244, 310

fire-lures, in night fishing.........52, 71, 264, 270, 271, 275, 278

firework balloons........148-150, 361, 363, 364, 371

fireworks ....…...71-73, 147-150, 267, 310, 361, 363, 364, 371

Flammarion, Camile.....171, 172, 175, 232, 238, 240

flare up lights (nautical)...........................271

Floor, Kees..103

Flora, HMS..255

Flying Saucer From Mars (1954) 18

flying saucers.....1, 3, 4, 7, 27, 28, 265, 284

folklore 73, 143, 269, 318

forest fires 130, 262, 275, 340

Fort Belvoir smoke ring (1957).............107

Fortean Studies............................359, 364

Fortean Times 2, 79, 347

forward gloss..................84, 132, 143, 198

Fourth of July 178, 293, 295, 300, 361

FOV (field of view)........59-62, 111, 113, 165, 251

Franco-Prussian war...............................116

Fremantle, Australia..............153, 154, 401

Fuller, Paul....................................130, 131

funnel cloud......37, 38, 129, 136, 138, 172, 320

furnace, of foundry, light from.............114

FuTzuki, Japanese festival....................268

Gais, Switzerland 55-58, 401

Gamma Pegasi (star)...................65, 67, 68

Garvey, Acting Boatswain Frank........331-335, 342-345, 348, 350

Gaussian thin lens equation 195

geological faulting 143

geomagnetic activity 151

geomagnetic pole 167, 184

Georget, M. le Commandant..........306-310

Georgian Military Highway 238

Gershtein, Mikhail 104

Gervais, Mr..75

Gibbs Hill lighthouse, Bermuda 229

Glaisher, James 46, 47, 49, 144, 145

Glancy, A. Estelle 389-391

Glorieux, Jean-Baptiste.........................310

Gloucester, England.....................287, 288, 377, 378

Gosling, W. H...............................227, 228

Gouka, Mr...251

Gouzon, France................................74, 75

Grace, Mr 64-66

Grahamstown, South Africa.......241-245, 247, 402

gravure process 204

'great meteor procession', *see* Chant, Prof. Clarence A.

Green, Charles...............................149, 363

Greenwood, Barry..........332, 333, 337-340

Greg, R. P 42, 43, 76

Greifswald, Germany.....................311, 402

Grímsfjall, Iceland (volcano)................134

Grímsvötn volcano complex, Iceland. 134

Grindell-Matthews, Harry.....................347

Guam, Western Pacific 329

Guillemin, Mr 117, 119

hail................................13, 17, 91, 146, 249

Hallasan (mount.), Jejudo 257

Hallet, Marc 204

halo........... 55, 93, 102, 104, 215-217, 219, 372, 393

Hamar Stiftstidende 236

Hamar, Norway 233

Handbook For Travellers in Japan (1898) 265

Handlingar Svenska Vetenskap Akademein 19

Harding, Charles 227

Hare, A. T......................................240

Harries, Henry...................................91

Harris, Dr Frank B 374

Harrison, Henry .... 155-168 *passim*, 177

Harvard College Observatory 121, 159, 391

Haute-Marne, France..............................232

Havana 41

Hawke's Bay Herald............................236

Hawke's Bay Philosophical Institute 236

Heidelberg-Königstuhl State Observatory 373

Heis, Prof. Eduard 76, 77

Henningsen, Ole.................................108

Henry, Paul 191

Henry, Prosper 191

Herrick, Mr....................................41

Herschel, Lieutenant.........................84-87

Herschel, Prof. Alexander Stuart............85

Herschel, Sir John 64, 66

Hertzsprung, Ejnar 392

Hertzsprung-Russell diagram.................392

Himachal Pradesh, India........................73

Himalayas....................................70, 175

Himes, Prof....................................83

Hiroshima Higher Technical School.....270

Hobart College, New York 304

hole-punch cloud 102-104

Holmes, Edwin Alfred.........................252

Hopman, Frits 250-252

Hraschina, Croatia 285

Hughes, Dr Stephen.............................48

Hughes, R. F 391

Humacao, Puerto Rico 222, 402

Huntington, West Virginia 82, 391-395, 402

Hutcheon, Steve.................................385

Hwawangsan (mount.), S. Korea..........262

hyperfocal plane.......11, 12, 14, 15, 60, 87, 193-195, 251, 374

ice crystals, formation of 102, 103

optical diffraction by.......................327

reflection by 114, 215, 217, 219, 224, 226

ignis fatuus................................. 73, 79, 265

illusory motion.............................301, 303, 321, 339

Iloilo, Philippines.............................233

Inglis, Sir Robert 55-58, 82

insect pillar 244

insects.....2, 57, 86, 87, 121, 122, 143, 192, 262

electrostatic luminosity of................244

migration of, and lunar phase 244

International Date Line 331

International Meridian Conference (1884) 331

International Meteor Conference (1996) 76

interstellar dust, particle size of 206

Inverness, Scotland........................ 53, 401

ionosphere 48, 67, 97, 98, 168, 217, 218, 370, 399

iridescent film 25

Ironton, Ohio...............................395, 396

Isaribi, *see* fire-lures

Isis (journal)...108

Janssen, Pierre Jules César 191

Jeju Weekly.....................................265, 267

Jejudo Island 257, 259, 262, 263, 269, 271-275, 277, 278

'jellyfish' cloud 102

Jersey City, NJ 153, 155, 159, 165, 176, 177, 399, 401, 402

Jessup, Morris K 161, 163, 164
Jinta Hirayama's Fireworks, Japan 72
Journal of Mathematical Sciences 108
*Journal of the British Astronomical
    Association* 241, 250, 251
Journal of the Franklin Institute 83
*Journal of the Geological Society of
    Dublin* 69
*Journal of the International Meteor
    Organisation* 76
junk (boat) 264, 274, 275, 279, 280
    rig, efficiency of 273
    speed of 271
Jupiter (planet) 46, 47, 54, 60, 63, 145,
    252, 286, 302

Kamchatka Peninsula 105
Karman line (start of space) 206
Kasanka National Park, Zambia 245
Kattenau, Germany 169, 170, 401
Kelley, Mike C 98
Kennebec Journal 366
Kennebunkport, Maine 366
Keswick, Cumbria 316
Keyhoe, Maj. Donald E 111
Khao no-Khao Kaeo, Thailand 246
Khao Yai National Park, Thailand 245
Kiel, Germany 317, 318, 402
Kincardine, Lake huron 261
King, Bob 182, 185, 370
King's Sutton, Oxfordshire 124
Kittery, Maine 364
Knipovich (seamount) 105
Knowledge 176, 186, 187
Kobé, Japan 257, 265
Kodak 203
Koellner, Rev. Father 34-36
Kolosimo, Peter 265
Komun-do, S. Korea ... 258, 260, 269, 272-
    274, 277
Königliches Stutamt Trakehnen 169
Korea Forest Research Institute 262

Korea Strait 253, 258-260, 263, 269,
    270, 272, 274, 399, 402
Krakatoa 127, 206, 209, 211, 213, 215,
    217-222, 224, 226, 243, 399
Krakatoa Committee... 127, 213, 215, 218-
    220
Kuhnian "normal" science 398
Kurushio Current 260
Kyauk Phyu (Kyook Phyoo) 51

L'Aigle, meteorite fall 20
Lake Champlain Tercentenary
    Independence celebrations 360, 361
L'Année Scientifique et Industrielle 41,
    74, 75, 121-123, 132, 133, 146, 237-239
La Nature 143, 306, 307
lanterns, on boats 264, 268, 269, 271
Lady Elizabeth (ship) 154
Lady of the Lake (ship) 89-91, 94, 95,
    97-102, 105, 106, 108, 109, 217, 399
Lagrange point 67, 165
Laki, Iceland (volcano) 134
Lamey, M. l'abbé Charles 132-134
The Lancet 81
LaPaz, Dr Lincoln 384
Laplace's extinction theorem 277
L'Astronomie 42, 174, 175, 182, 189-
    192, 194-196, 203, 204, 206, 231, 283
lava tubes 257
Lawrence, Sir Alexander 71
Leander, HMS 253, 257
Lefroy, General Sir John Henry FRS ....
    227-229
Leipzig Museum of Ethnography 209
Leonid meteor shower 38-40, 121, 236
Lewiston, Maine 364-366, 369
Lichtenberg, Georg 18
Liège, Belgium 309
lieue (unit of distance) 146
light pillar 71, 113-116, 224-226, 391,
    393-395, 397
lighthouse 79, 229

lightning in volcanic ash plumes 213
ligne, unit of length 15
Lineville, Iowa ....291-303 *passim*
Lister, Martin FRS 14
Litchfield Observatory, New York 156
Little Bedwyn, Wiltshire 379
Llanberis, Wales 286, 288, 402
Lloyd's Register 90, 91
locusts 57, 85, 86, 244
Lord Brabazon, Reginald 111-113, 115, 116
Louisville, Kentucky 96
low pressure system 127
Lowe, Edward Joseph FRAS 53, 195
Lowell, Mrs. L 227
Lowery, George H. 11

Maccabee, Dr Bruce 332, 333, 342, 345
MacGowan, Dr Daniel J 267, 269
Magazine of Natural History 43
Magin, Ulrich 33, 38
magnetic declination (variation) 101, 260, 276
Magonia Exchange 19, 27, 33, 38, 104, 183
Magrogordato, M 232
Makela, Prof. Jonathan 98, 99
Malaysian Airlines MH370 108
Manchester Evening News 142
Manhattanville, New York 156, 157, 161
Mannheim, Germany 148
Manterola, Hector 206
Marfa, Texas 143
marine bioluminescence 263, 270
marine chronometer 101
marine layer 102, 336, 337
Mars (planet) 18, 54, 60, 302, 307
Marseille, France 41, 117, 118, 160, 189, 401, 402
Marseille Observatory 117
Martin, Howard H 387
Martyn, Arthur J. K 316
Mary Celeste 109, 127

Mason, W. B 266
Massingill, Kay 24, 27, 111, 149, 158, 166, 183, 320
Master Clock 116
Maunder, Edward Walter 95, 97, 166, 181-183, 249, 252
Mauritius 220
McLeod Ganj, Dharamsala 70, 71
Mebane, Alexander D 384
megacryometeors 5, 13
Meiji era, Japan 268
Melbourne Observatory 153, 154
Meldrum, Dr C 220
Mémoires de l'Académie Royale (Mem. Acad.), Paris 7-9
Menzel, Dr Donald H. 344, 345
Mercer, Missouri 295, 297-299
Mercury (planet) 59, 60
Merksem, Belgium 225
mesopause 218
mesosphere 67, 95, 217-219, 243
Messier, Charles ..... 7, 9-18 *passim*, 41, 82, 86, 87, 132, 134, 249
'meteor smoke' 218
meteorite 20, 154
meteoroid, shock wave from 32, 239
Meteorological Journal, The 224
Meteorological Service of Canada 319
meteors 38-40, 44, 46-48, 58, 61, 64, 76, 77, 83, 84, 86, 132, 134, 144, 145, 151, 174, 232, 236, 249-251, 287, 330, 331, 333, 336, 337, 339-341, 344, 346, 351, 384
    aero-braking of 338, 339
    durations of 343
    procession of 144, 145, 170, 343, 383-385
    trails of 39, 40, 48, 112, 232, 233, 239, 242, 285, 289, 389
    visual colours of 340
methane 143
Meudon Observatory, Paris ... 121, 122, 191
Mexico City 138, 192, 198

Miaplacidus (obsolete star name, *see* Beta Carinae)

Michaud, Bishop John S 173, 354-359, 371

Michel, Aimé...111

microburst..37, 38

mirage 52, 53, 114, 143, 256, 258, 259, 261-264, 268, 270, 271, 275-281, 399

    Fata Morgana...................................280

    inferior..280

    Novaya Zemlya........................259, 280

    superior...280

Miyanishi Machika, Prof 270

Mizar (star)..307

Modern Mechanix 347

Mongolfier balloon 149, 308-310

Mongolfier brothers 308

Monstrator..166

Monthly Meteorological Magazine
    (Symons)........... ....127, 372

Monthly Notices of the Royal Astronomical Society 58, 59, 61, 63, 64, 67, 84-87, 241, 340, 378

Monthly Weather Review 200, 293, 295-297, 301, 319, 320, 329, 330, 353-356, 359, 371, 386

'Moon illusion' 23

Moon, as possible explanation 214, 302, 322

    reddened appearance of 304

Moore, Sir Patrick 18

Morning News, Birmingham, UK.........124

'mother of pearl' cloud, *see* nacreous

motion blur.....................196, 197, 203, 205

Mount Auckland, *see* Hallasan

Mount Rainier 382

mountains, shadow cast by 379, 382

mountain-top electricity 210

Mt Etna, Sicily..............................105, 106

Mulu National Park, Borneo 245

Muntz metal 90

murmuration of starlings 12

'mystery airship' sightings 301

nacreous cloud 94, 95, 243

Nagasaki, Japan 255

NASA 371

Nassr, Anthony.............................359-361

National Maritime Museum, Greenwich
    331

National Museum of Natural History,
    France 172

National Oceanic and Atmospheric
    Administration (NOAA) 37, 137, 335, 336

Nature..........73, 74, 124, 125, 143, 153, 154, 169, 182, 218, 227-229, 233-242, 247-249, 253, 255, 256, 264, 278, 285-290, 306, 307, 315, 317, 319-323, 325, 373, 374, 379-381, 383, 391

nautical compass, points of...................277

nautical day, *v.* civil day and astronomical
    day..331, 332

nautical twilight 93, 94, 243, 335

Naval Advisory Staff (US) 329

Naval Observatory, Washington...157, 158

naval searchlight drills 349

Neff, Robert 265

Nelson Evening Mail (NZ) 96

New Haven, Connecticut........................96

New York Herald..................................305

New York Times 3, 96, 151, 177, 244, 267

New York Tribune 156-160, 166

New Zealand Mail................................236

New Zealand Times..............................236

Newbottle, Oxfordshire......125, 127, 128, 130-132

Newcomb, Simon...................................331

Newfane, Vermont................................359

Newman, Robert J 11

Niagara Falls..38

Ningbo, China..267

Nininger, Harvey Harlow 145

nitrogen dioxide....................................130

Nobuyuki Marume 268

noctiluca scintilans................................270

noctilucent cloud 94, 95, 217-219, 243, 399

Nogaro, France...75

Noguez, Luis Ruiz................190, 191, 196

Norcock, Capt. Charles J...253-281 *passim*

Nordenskjold, A. E............... 209-213, 218

North American Review 19, 21, 22, 28

North Declination...............................157

northern lights, *see* Aurora Borealis

Notes and Queries 141, 156

Nottingham Evening Post 183

Nusseerabad, Rajasthan, India................86

Oaxaca, Mexico.............135, 136, 138, 401

Observatoire de Cluny, Paris....... 10, 16, 17

Observatoire de Meudon, Paris............121, 122, 191, 194

Observatory of Palermo 173

Observatory of Zurich 73, 74

Observatory, The.... 17, 63, 67, 74, 86, 116, 156, 181, 194, 377, 378

Office of Naval Operations (US) 329

Olson, Donald W 385

Ommanney, Admiral Sir Erasmus.......285-289

Ophiucus (constellation) 117

Oplandenes Avis....................................234

Oregon..49

Orionid meteor shower 236

orographic forcing, *see* lenticular cloud

Oswestry Advertiser 151

Oswestry, Shropshire 141

Otago Daily Times 126

Owl nebula 165

Oxford, England 53, 401

Oxford University 55

ozone 130

Palagaud, M 220

Palermo Zoological Museum................174

Pall Mall Gazette 130

Pampa (Texas) *Daily News* 144

parachute flares 71

parachute light-balls 72, 73

parallax.....64, 66, 102, 164, 198, 221, 224, 225, 259, 278, 288

Parc Randon, Saint-Ismier, France 149

Paris, France......7, 10-13, 16, 17, 44, 112, 116, 119, 121, 122, 129, 148, 149, 150, 172, 173, 191, 228, 238, 271, 306, 361-363, 371, 401

Parkhurst, Henry M...............................159

Parry arc (ice halo feature)............216, 217

passenger pigeon.................................... 12

Payne, F. F 319-321

Peace River, Florida.............................. 137

Pedgley, David E 103

Peenemunde, Germany 311

pelicans, *see* American white pelican

Perrine, C. D. 390

Perseid meteor shower...........................83

Perseus (constellation) 82, 83, 286

perspective, illusion of.......10, 23, 44, 337, 339

    foreshortening........ 232, 320, 342, 344, 382

Peters, Prof. C. H. F 156

Pettitt, G..44, 45

Pezza, Rubén J 191

Philadelphia Inquirer............................. 28

Philadelphia, Pennsylvania 220

Philippi, Dr Rodolfo 209

Philosophical Magazine, The 182

Philosophical Transactions of the Royal Society 102, 141, 142

Phnom Sampeu, Cambodia...................246

Phoebe, HMS.......................................255

'Phoenix lights' 71

photocollography 204

Picton-Jones, Mr 142

Pinus densiflora....................................262

Pisces (constellation).............. 67, 118, 377

plasma rings, from fireball meteors 107

plasma tubes...................................67, 97

plasma, optical transparency of 205

plasmasphere 97

Pleiades 156, 160

Poland, Ohio 38

polar mesospheric cloud, *see* noctilucent

Polaris...177

pollen grains, optical diffraction by 327

Pons, Jean-Louis.................................304

Pony Express 298

poplar seeds...57

Popular Astronomy 114, 159, 241, 374, 384, 385

Popular Electricity.........................211, 348

Popular Science Monthly 84

Port Hamilton, *see* Komun-do, S. Korea

Porter, T. C................................382, 383

Portland, Maine 365

Powell, Rev. Prof. Baden.....44, 45, 53, 64, 65, 195

prime focus (optics)..............................194

Princeton, Missouri.......291, 293, 295, 296, 298, 301, 302, 402

printing plate, retouching of.................204

Proceedings of the Royal Society....51, 236

Puebla Observatory, Mexico 198

Puebla, Mexico.....................................192

Pwllheli, North Wales 141-143, 401

pyrotechnics.....................71-73, 149, 364

Quarterly Journal of the Royal Institution
.... 31

Quarterly Journal of the Royal Meteorological Society..................92, 99

Queensland, Australia 48, 90, 143

Queensland Technical University 48

Quetzalcoatl 138

radioactivity, discovery of....................210

radiosonde balloon readings..................395

RAF Cosford, Shropshire......................378

Railway Post Office car 295

rainbow 25, 104, 236, 340, 364

red 315-318

Rajkote, Gujarat, India...........................86

Raleigh, N. Carolina.............................284

Rastpfuhl, Germany 34-36

Rayleigh criterion (optical resolution) 17

Read, Rev. William. 58-63, 73, 87

Reade, Rev. Joseph Bancroft FRS.....63-66

Reading, Berkshire 128

Reaumur temperature scale....................56

Redemption of the Damned, Vol. 2, Sea and Space Phenomena 5, 84, 263

Report of the British Association 42, 45, 53, 56, 61, 64, 76, 144, 145

Report of the Krakatoa Committee (1888)
....215, 219

retinal persistence.................................197

Return to Magonia (2015)...... 73, 143, 269

Revue Scientifique 307

Ricco, Signor 173-176

Rice, Jacob................................221-224, 226

Richard Coeur de Lion 192

Rickard, Bob...2

Right Ascension....157, 160-162, 168, 199, 377

Rio de Janeiro Observatory...................143

'road mirage', *see* mirage, inferior

Rochester, Indiana (meteorite impact site).....................................145

Rosenberg, G. V. 335

Royal Astronomical Society 55, 58, 59, 61, 63, 84, 87, 156, 241, 285, 340, 378, 384, 385

Royal Astronomical Society of Canada
....156, 384

Royal Circus of the Netherlands........... 149

Royal Gazette, Bermuda.......................227

Royal Geographical Society 285

Royal Meteorological Society (R.M.S.)........................89, 90, 127, 227

Royal Navy (UK)............22, 253-255, 271, 285, 331

Royal Observatory of Belgium 136, 192, 199, 204

Royal Observatory, Edinburgh.............249

Royal Observatory, Greenwich.............181

Royal Society of Canada's Phenology
Survey.................................319
Royal Swedish Academy of Sciences 18,
20
Rüppell's vulture (*Gyps rueppellii*) 175
Ruppelt, Capt. Edward J 354
Russell, Albert Rollo...........................219
Russell, Bertrand 219
Russell, Prof. Henry Norris 392
'Ryook Phyoo', *see* Kyauk Phyu

Saarbrucken, Germany 31-34, 38, 401
Sabine, Col. Edward 55
Sagittarius (constellation) 117
Saint Benedict, Order of 132
Saint-Prouant, France...................127, 131
Sakuhei Fujiwhara, Dr 270
Salyut 6 95
San Fernando, Chile 209, 222, 399
sandhill crane (*grus canadensis*)...........201
Santinez, Dr Pedro 210
Saturn 66, 68, 117, 118, 302
scattering (atmospheric optics).........26, 58,
205, 215, 243, 250, 277, 316, 335, 339-
342
Schofield, Lieut. Frank H.............. 329-350
passim
Schofield, USS 329
Schooling, William 252
Science...................................... 304, 305
Science Gossip 304
Scientific American 135, 136, 138, 155,
156, 158-160, 176, 210, 221-224, 249,
250, 346, 362, 389, 392
Scott, Robert Henry FRS 90
Scutari, Constantinople (Istanbul).........232
'sea fireworks', *see* shiranu-hi
Sea of Japan...........258, 264, 270, 274, 275
seamounts...105
searchlight spots on cloud, as possible
explanation 344-351, 400
Secretan telescope..............................194
Sedbergh, Cumbria.......................315, 402

seeds, airborne..........11, 14, 57, 61, 62, 74,
84, 86, 121, 123, 124, 169
Selenographical Society..........................64
Serpens (constellation) 117, 118
Sewell, William Elbridge......................329
Shaoyang, China 107
Shimbara Gulf.....................................265
Shiokawa, Prof. Kazuo 98
shiranu-hi............................... 265, 267-270
Shōwa era, Japan.................................270
Sicily 105, 106, 175, 176, 257, 402
Sidereal Messenger...................... 156, 224
Sidmouth, Dorset 183
Siege of Paris 116
signal-flares, *see also* parachute
flares/light-balls 147, 271
Skänninge, Sweden 18, 21, 398, 401
Smith Observatory, N.Y. 304, 306
smoke ring...................................107, 108
Snell's Law (optics) 279
soap bubbles..............24, 26, 147, 149, 372
soap, manufacture of...............................27
Société Astronomique de France 307
Solar Cycles...... 40, 67, 96, 242, 249, 259,
369
solar granulation, *see* faculae................204
'soleil d'artifice' (pyrotechnic)...............363
Souter Point lighthouse 79
South Mimms, Hertfordshire............58, 73
Southern Taurids, meteor shower 47
Spandau Citadel, Berlin 115, 116
spectral dispersion...............................316
spectroscopic emission lines...........183
spider webs 24
Spiers, Richard................................27, 28
sprites (atmospheric phenomena)...........48,
370
squid fishing..... 52, 53, 263-265, 267, 268,
270, 274-278
St David's Point lighthouse 229
St Elmo's Fire.......................211, 244, 257
St Petersburg, Russia 237, 238
standing waves...................100, 102, 321
steam rings 106, 108

Steele, Prof. J. D 84

STEVE (Strong Thermal Emission
Velocity Enhancement) 166, 167,
186, 249, 369, 370, 400

stipple engraving 192, 204

Stolp, Carlos (Karl) 209-215, 217-220

Stone, Buckinghamshire 63

Stony Lake, Ontario 320, 321, 402

Stralsund, Germany...............................311

Strong Thermal Emission Velocity
Enhancement, *see* STEVE

Sub-Auroral Ion Drift (SAID)...............166

subsidence inversion 336

subsun...215

sulfur dioxide 219

Sulphur Springs, Ohio.............. 223-226,
402

sulphur, smell of................35, 44, 125, 130

sun pillar............ 51, 215-218, 224, 325,
391, 397, 399

sun, reddening & dimming of 26

sundogs..104

sunspots............10, 11, 14, 69, 74, 96, 122,
123, 151, 183, 193, 196, 200, 201, 204

supercooled water vapour.... 102-104, 218,
219

supersun *see* sun pillar

Supply USS.....….……329-354 *passim*, 400

Svahn, Clas..22

Svalbard, Spitzbergen 225

Swedish Acadamy of Sciences..............209

Swift, Lewis A 84

Swiss National Observatory.....................74

Sydney Morning Herald..................86, 254

Symons, George James 66, 127, 129,
215, 372

The Tablet...96

Talbot, William Henry Fox......................63

tangent arc (ice halo feature).........216, 217

Taranaki, New Zealand 96

Tarazed (Gamma Aquilae)....................373

Taurid meteor shower........47-49, 235, 236

Taylor, Mr.. 236

Tebbutt, John FRAS 220

telegraph, effects of aurora on 96

temperature inversion.....66, 259, 263, 270,
344

Thayer, Tiffany 2

Theory of Natural Philosophy (Boskovich,
R., 1758)..10

thermosphere...218

The Times (London)... 54, 77-79, 111, 149,
151, 182, 227, 241

The Times of India 86

Thomas, Northcote Whitridge 317

'thousand lanterns', *see* shiranu-hi........265,
267, 269

Tilden Smith, Charles 379-381

*Timb's Year-Book of Facts in Science and
Art* (1845)..46

Tinguirica Canyon, Chile......................212

Tlatelolco, Mexico 138

Todarodes Pacificus......................264, 274

toise, unit of length 11, 146

Toledo, Ohio..131

Topley, William FRS.......................... 129

tornados 35-37, 124, 127-129, 131,136,
138, 139

Tornado and Storm Research Organization
(TORRO)..131

trade cumulus 93, 99, 100, 102-105

Trainor, Joseph.......................359, 364-366

Trakehnen (Yasnaya Polyana),
Kaliningrad Oblast 169

Trécul, Auguste A. L 171-173

Tremadog Bay, North Wales.................141

Trinity House 78

tromba marina (waterspout)...................138

tropical cyclone 230

Trouvelot, Etienne 121-124, 132

Trowbridge, C. C 391

TRUE Magazine....................................301

Tsushima warm current.........................260

tumbler pigeon 252

Twin Lakes, Missouri............292, 293, 302

typewriters, early US ownership of.......324

UAP (Unexplained Aerial Phenomena)..... 79
UFOs..........4, 28, 29, 51, 75, 81, 107, 136, 142, 143, 149, 154, 161, 164, 168, 204, 205, 232, 234, 244, 265, 270, 301, 324, 332, 333, 359, 366, 379, 381, 384, 398-400
Uintah Basin, Utah..............244
Universidad Nacional Autónoma de México......206
University of Heidelberg......373
University of Münster......76
University of Zacatecas......190, 196
'Unknown Light of Japan'......265, 278
Ursa Major......287, 307
Ursa Minor......177
US Army Signals Corps......160, 161, 178
US Bureau of Statistics......296
US Department of Agriculture......366
US Highway 65......298
US National Weather Service......292
US Nautical Almanac Office......331
US Naval Academy......82
US Naval Observatory......83, 121
US Navy......267, 329, 334, 348
US Navy Atlantic Battle Fleet......349
US Navy Bureau of Ordnance......329
US Weather Bureau......292-294
Üsküdar, Istanbul......232
Utrecht, the Netherlands......149

Vallée, Jacques F......74, 112
Vallot, Jacques-Nicolas......17
Vannes, Brittany, France......306-309, 402
vapour droplets, reflectivity of......173
Vega......113, 115, 116, 278
Vence, France......146, 147, 149, 153, 363, 401

Venus..........54, 59, 60, 84, 118, 145, 186, 187, 195, 215, 224, 242, 301, 302, 323, 326-328, 393
Vermont, New England......166, 173, 354, 357, 361, 366, 400, 402
Vernon, HMS......255
Vevay, Indiana......83
Viborg, Denmark......107, 108
Villafañe, Lucas......136
virga, see fall-streaks......93, 102
visual magnitude......163
Vladicaucase, see Vladikavkaz......238
Vladikavkaz, Russia......237-239, 402
volcanic ash......213
volcanic dust......104, 132, 213, 217, 218, 222, 224, 226, 399
volcanic eruption......67, 134
volcanic glass......213, 214, 217, 219, 224, 243, 399
vortex cloud, from volcano......105
vortex flow, 19thC physicists and......108

Waipawa Mail......236
Waldner, Henry......73, 74
Walthamstow, Greater London......66
warbler, migration of......244
Warmley, England......377, 379, 402
waterspout......5, 127, 138, 139
Weather (journal)......132
Weatherwise......95, 103
West, Mick......103
Western Australian Times......154
Western Union Telegraph Company......298
Westphalia, Germany......76, 77, 401
Wettermark, Knut Gustaf......20, 21, 24
Whanganui, NZ......96
whirlwind..........34-36, 38, 124, 125, 127, 129, 131, 132, 138, 139
whooping crane (grus americana)......201
wild fires......262
Williams, Capt......51
will o' the wisp......79, 142
wind shear......60, 136

Windhoek Cave, S. Africa 245
Winlock, Joseph 121
Woburn Square, London........................81
Wolf, Dr Max..373
Wolf, Prof. Rudolph..................................74
Wonders in the Sky................................112
World Heritage Site, Jejudo.................257
Wylie, Charles Clayton.........................384

Yloilo, Philippines, *see* Iloilo
Yokohama, Japan 72, 257

Zacatecas Observatory, Mexico... 189-191,
    193, 198, 199, 201, 206, 402
Zentmayer, Mr 83
Zeppelin 181
zodiacal light......67, 68, 76, 165, 209, 214,
    222, 224, 364-370
    conditions for viewing 368
Zomergem, Belgium 324
Zurich, Switzerland 55, 73, 74

INDEX to VOLUME 2

2002VE68 (quasi-satellite)............. 9, 10

2006 RH120 (asteroid) 20

2020 CD3 (asteroid) 20

Académie Royale des Sciences, Paris.... 6, 34, 35, 37, 43, 45

Adalia (Antalya), Turkey 115–117

Adanson, Michel 134, 135

Adriatic Sea...................................146

Ainab, Mount Lebanon 116

Alasehir (Philadelphia), Turkey 116

Alaska current 182

Aldebaran.......................................73–75

Aleutian Islands............................182, 195

Allan Line, shipping company 152, 153

Amazing Stories....................................159

American Journal of Science 17, 23

American Meteor Society.............186, 190

American Meteorological Journal 167

Annual Register...........................33, 34, 75

Annual Report of the Secretary of the Navy (1890) 152

Antarctica...................................87, 129

Anton Makarenko (ship)......................143

Antoniadi, Eugène Michel 48

Arabian Gulf 146

Arago, François 20

Aristarchus (lunar crater).......... 53, 65, 67, 69, 77, 79, 81–83, 86

Arnold, Kenneth...................................149

Around the Moon (Jules Verne)............208

asteroid.......10, 11, 20, 39, 40, 41, 42, 44, 53, 189

Astronomical Unit..................................44

Astronomische Nachrichten 18, 19

Atalanta, HMS 129

Athenæum, The.............105, 106, 115, 116

atmospheric duct 144

Aubeck, Chris.....15, 33, 84, 106, 116, 177, 201, 210

aurora borealis 80, 83–85, 87, 91, 100

Avalon, Newfoundland.........................154

Avern, Capt. J. 132

ball lightning........109, 114, 151, 152, 157, 190, 207

balloon............ 13, 20, 21, 36, 58, 81, 205-207

Banks, Joseph PRS 75

Baratta, Mario 125

Barber, John T. 85

Barlow, William Henry 83

Barr, Edward M. 83

Basel, Switzerland 6, 33, 34, 36

Bay of Bengal.....................................142

Beaufort scale...............................155, 164

Bermuda.......................129, 135, 202, 205

Bintang SS 134

bioluminescence (*see also* noctiluca)...130, 134, 138, 140, 144, 146, 147, 148, 157, 184

Blue Mountains, New South Wales......47, 48

Bogoslof, Aleutian Islands....................186

bolide ...112, 114, 160, 189, 190, 202, 207, 210

Bombay.......................................198, 210

Boxer rocket.......................................160

British Alliance, mv (ship)....................137

British Arctic Expedition.......................129

British Association for the Advancement of Science..............48, 80, 105, 115, 210

British Columbian..........................190, 194

British India Company...........................132

British Meteorological Office...............139

Bruce Herald (NZ) 178, 180

Bruges...87-89

Bulldog, HMS..............127–136 *passim*

Caithness, Capt. George Henry....118, 119, 123, 197, 207

California Current 181, 182, 185

Campi Flegrei Mar Sicilia (volcanic seamount zone).........................120, 124

Canadian Coast Guard 158, 165, 204

Cape Race, Newfoundland....103, 151–174 passim

Cape Matapan.. 210

Cape Town, South Africa.................78, 79

Cassini, Giovanni Domenico 7, 9

Cerigo, Island of...................................210

Chalmers, Mr................107–114 passim

Chambers, Capt./Adm.............89, 107, 197

Chambers's Journal of Literature, Science and Art......................................198

Chant, Prof. Clarence............................189

Chelyabinsk superbolide.......................207

Chevalier, Rev. Prof..............................81

China Sea 130, 134

Chladni, Ernst...................34, 44, 112

Ciel et Terre....................................7

Climatic Research Unit, University of East Anglia..107

Clyst St. Lawrence, Devon 87

Colonist, The, St. Johns (NF)......154, 170, 171

cold front...172

comet...............................15–17, 37, 42–44

Congreve, Sir William.. ....161–165 passim

Conrad, Joseph....................................132

Copernicus (lunar crater) 53

copper, blistering of 203

Corliss, William ...130, 137, 139, 143, 146, 147, 149

corona discharge 109, 190

coronal mass ejection 100

Corsica.................................107, 111, 210

Coste, Mr.............33, 36, 38, 40, 41, 44, 45

Cottman, Lt Vincendon Lezare.............152

Coumbary, Aristide................................23

Curuçá River...192

cyclone 154, 157, 168, 169, 171, 205

Daily Ohio State Journal 190

Danjon scale.................................89–91

Danjon, André-Louis 89

Davy, Sir Humphrey, PRS.....................75

d'Alviano, Father Fedele.......................192

De Blauwe Wimpel (journal)................ 139

De Hullu, P...139

De Rostan, Mr.....................33–45 passim

De Vaucouleurs, Gérard Henri 90, 91

De Vico, Father Francesco 20

Deccan SS....................................197, 198

Delta SS 132

Democratic Northwest 188

Dennett rocket.....................................160

Denning, William Frederick 24

Denver, Colorado...........................24, 25

diffraction..75

digit (angular measure) 38

Douglass, Andrew Ellicott..........93, 94, 98

Dover..210

dynamite balloons................................206

eardrum, pressure on............................142

earthshine 69, 77, 79, 81, 86

eclipse
    missing..87
    of the Moon............. 47, 67, 68, 80, 81, 87-91
    of the Sun................. 13, 24, 25, 38, 69

Eddington, Sir Arthur 13

Einstein, Albert 13, 28

Electric Telegraph and Lightship Company, Cape Race........................160

electrophonic meteor sound 113, 190

Emperor seamount chain 184

Encyclopædia Britannica...............110, 111

engine vibrations, of ships 135, 144

Erebus, HMS.......................................164

eyeball, resonant frequency of................142

eyepiece projection (telescopic) 36, 45

Fallows, Rev. Fearon 69, 77, 79

fear, sense of...............................142, 143

Ferdinandea, Isola 120–122, 125
Flammarion, Camille 22, 25, 49, 82, 151
Fogo seamount chain 157
Fontana, Francesco...............................5, 8
Forster, Dr Thomas 87–89, 91

Gabe, Capt...134
Galgo, HMS..164
Gatchina plasmoids 157
General Relativity, Theory of 13, 28
geostat 38
Glasgow Daily Herald 122, 123
Govan, Glasgow......................................152
Graham Island, *see* Ferdinandea
Greenacre, James Clarke.........................83
Greenwich meridian................................153
Greg, R. P. FGS......................................210
ground light ball 161
Gruithuisen, Franz von............15, 16, 82
Gulf of Aden 138
Gulf of Carpentaria 140
Gulf of Oman...................................139, 140
Gulf of Thailand..........130, 137, 139, 147
gust front.......................................172, 173

hailstones, size of 204
Haiti......................................128, 129, 135
Hale rocket 162, 163, 194, 196
Hale, William, *see* Hale rocket
Harbor Grace Standard 183, 189
Hardwicke's Science Gossip (1886)..........7
Haro Strait, B.C., Canada..............191, 194
Harris, Commander R. E.......................131
Harris, Sir William Snow FRS.......82, 105,
    106, 108
Harrison, John 108
Herring, Dr Peter...130, 135, 137, 142–144
Herschel, Frederick William FRS....11, 63,
    64–68, 77, 81, 83, 88, 91
Hicks, Col. William (Hicks Pasha) 26
Hind, J. R...22
Hirst, George Denton.............................48
Histoire de l'Académie Royale de Sciences
   35

History and Present State of Electricity
    (1775), *see* Priestley, Joseph
Horrebow, Christian 7, 8
Horsman, Paul...............130, 135, 142–144
Houzeau de Lehaie, Jean-Charles ... 5, 7–
    10, 28
Hubble space telescope 95, 100
Huggate, Yorkshire................................81
Hughes, Dr Stephen......................114, 190
Humboldt, Alexander von 84
hurricane 154, 204, 205
Huyghe, Patrick 139, 140, 193
hydrogen sulphide, volcanic gas........111,
    120, 202
Hydrographic Office, US.....151, 152, 159,
    177, 178, 197, 198

icing (of ship at sea)......182, 203, 204, 207
Indian Ocean.................................130, 134
infrasound exposure, symptoms of 142
Innerwick (ship) .....177–198 *passim*, 202,
    207
Institute of Marine and Atmospheric
    Research Utrecht................138, 141, 157
interference (of waves).........134, 137, 138,
    141-143
International Date Line.........181, 187, 198
International Meridian Conference (1884)
    ....153, 187, 188
Itinda, SS 132
Itola, SS 132

J.P.A. (ship) ....201–207 *passim*
Jessup, Morris Ketchum 52, 53
Johnson, Rev. S. J...................................91
Journal of the Society of Telegraph
    Engineers 83
Jurende's Vaterländischen Pilger 18

Kalle, Kurt 141, 143
Kater, Capt. Henry FRS..............75–77, 82
Kepler (lunar crater) 53
Kepler, Johannes.....................................44

Kingsmill, Mr L..........................51

Klinkenberg (1762 comet) 41, 42

Kopal, Zdeněk.................83, 86, 90, 91

Koppeschaar, Carl..........................190

Krakatoa.............................27, 185

La Découverte (ship)............................145

Lagrangian point 10, 39

land breeze 172

Langmuir circulation............................141

L'Année Scientifique 22, 24

Lausanne, Switzerland ....33–45 passim

Le Verrier, Urbain.....13, 14, 20, 22–24, 28

Lebanon, Connecticut 55

Lescarbault, Edmond 15, 22

lighthouse, at Cape Race...............158-160,
    166, 167, 173

Litvinov, Capt. E. P......................130, 143

Livingstone, Dr David...........................130

Lizard Point, Cornwall..................107, 108

Lloyd's Register 118, 119

Lockyer, Sir Norman.............................24

Loomis, Elias 69

Lowe, E. J..22

Lowell Observatory...............83, 93, 95, 98

Lowell, Prof. Percival..................93, 95, 98

lunar phase, re "phosphorescent wheels"....
    147

Lunar Reconnaissance Orbiter................83

Macaluso, Domenico 125

Madrepore Bank, volcanic seamount...
    121–124, 126

magnetic perturbations............................84

Mahsuri, mv (ship)..............................139

Malacca Strait 132, 143

Malta 115, 116, 118, 120, 121, 124

Malta Mail Times 116

Mare Procellarum............................50, 53

Marine Observer 130, 135, 137–139,
    142, 144, 146

Maritime Register, New York........181, 183

Mars Express, Mars orbiter.............99, 100

Mars, aurora on 100
    unusual clouds on 95

marsh gas 111

Martin, Martha 6

Maskelyne, Rev. Dr Nevil 72, 73

MAVEN, Mars orbiter..........................100

Max Planck Institute for Plasma Physics....
    157

Mazapil (meteorite)..............................192

Mercalli, Giuseppe.................................125

Mercury (planet)......13, 14, 15, 17, 18, 20,
    23, 29

Messier, Charles 37, 39, 41, 42, 43

meteor 44, 53, 81, 86, 91, 111–117, 158,
    159, 166, 174, 186–189, 191, 192–194,
    197, 198, 201, 205, 207, 208, 210

meteorite........82, 112, 114, 186, 192, 202,
    207, 210

methane hydrate....................................111

microbaroms 142, 143

minimoons 20

mirage..........................27, 36, 58, 59, 140

Moffat (ship) 142

Montague, HMS ....107–112 passim

Montaigne, Jacques Laibats- 6, 9

Monthly Notices of the RAS ...9, 14, 15, 25,
    49, 81, 87, 88, 91

Monthly Review 44

Monthly Weather Review 172, 183, 186,
    191, 193, 201, 205– 207

Moon
    eclipse brightness and aurora.............91
    red colour during eclipse 87, 89
    surface brightness anomaly................90
    volcano observed on......64, 65, 67–69,
    75, 77, 81-83, 91

Moore, Capt. Robert P......151–174 passim

Moore, Sir Patrick..................................89

Morgan, John H. 85

Morning Glory, cloud phenomenon 140,
    141

Morskoi sbornik (journal)....................130

Moss, Cdr Edward Lawton, R.N.......127–
    130, 135

Muzzaffarpur (meteoroid).....................192

Nantucket Sound...................................170
NASA......29, 39, 67, 82, 83, 90, 99, 148, 162
National Institute of Oceanography 130, 139, 140, 157
Nature......22–24, 83, 106, 127–131, 136, 138–140, 151, 157, 207, 208
Naus, Stijn....138, 141, 143, 146, 148, 149, 157
nautical day, *v.* astron./civil day............153
Neith, phantom planet...........5, 7, 9, 10, 28
Nerita Bank, volcanic seamount vent ...122
New Zealand.................146, 178, 180, 185
New Philadelphia, Ohio Democrat.........56
Newfoundland seamount chain.............157
Newton, Sir Isaac.....................................13
Newton, CO Peter 139
Niesten, Leopold 7
NOAA... 28,204
noctiluca scintillans 134, 140, 141, 143, 144, 147, 148
North Pacific Current............................182
Nova Scotia...........154, 155, 168, 177, 179

Observatory, The...........8, 10, 48–50, 68, 91, 193
ocular glare...75
occultation, of stars….......73-75, 78, 86, 90
Olbers, Heinrich Wilhelm...........15–17, 82
Optical illusion 5, 58, 140, 143
Orford Ness (light house) 72
Oumuamua, interstellar asteroid.....29, 39, 40

Papazova, Yuliya..................................186
parachute flare...............................161, 162
parachute light-ball 161, 162, 164, 165, 172, 174
parallax............ 13, 33, 36-38, 41, 43, 44
Paris, France......20, 22, 33–35, 37, 39, 42, 43, 145, 164
Pastorff, J. W...............................16, 18–20

Patna, SS 131, 132, 137
Persian Gulf.......130, 131, 132, 134, 137, 148
Petrenko, Edward.................................142
Philosophical Transactions of the Royal Society ...42, 64, 67, 68, 71, 75–77, 105–107
phosphorescent wheels (*see also* bioluminescence, *noctiluca scintillans*)......130, 132, 135, 137, 140, 142, 144, 146–149
photographs, absence of........................147
Pic-du-Midi Observatory 83, 90
Pickering, William Henry 82, 93, 98
Pingtan, China.....................................148
Plover SS 154, 170
Pravdivtsev, Col. V. L. 130, 143
Priestley, Joseph, FRS 110–112
Pringle, Commander J. Elliot......129–131
Proctor, Richard A. 48, 49, 51–53
Puget Sound, Washington....................152
pyrosomes 135, 145, 147
pyrotechnics.........161, 162, 165, 166, 195, 206

quasi-satellite, *see* Venus
Queensland University...........................114

Rackham, Thomas 83
Rankin, Rev. Thomas 80, 81
Rawlins, Wyoming...........................24, 25
red sky.................177, 178, 184, 185, 192, 193, 195, 196
Redemption of the Damned Vol.1, Aerial Phenomena...........................1, 112, 206
refraction
    atmospheric optical..................... 27, 59
    acoustic..142
retina, sensitivity of 147
Return to Magonia.......84, 106, 116, 122, 177, 201, 210
Ricciardi, Leonardo 124, 125
Richmond Dispatch...............178, 179, 181
Robinson, J. W.....................................132

Rocca-Mendoza, M. C. L. 192
rockets, *see* Congreve, Sir William; Boxer
    rocket; Dennett rocket; Hale rocket
rocket house 160
Roedkiær, Peder...................................8, 11
Rome...210
Rotterdam.............................139, 201, 202
Royal Academy of Sciences, Paris, *see*
    Académie Royale
Royal Astronomical Society......9, 14, 15,
    21, 25, 48, 49, 88, 91
Royal Observatory of Belgium.................7
Royal Rotterdam Lloyd (ship)...............139
Royal Society
    of Edinburgh...........................27
    of London....42, 47, 64, 68, 69, 71, 75,
        76, 77, 105–107, 111, 114, 190
    of New South Wales 48
Russell, Henry Chamberlain 47

Salpa biforis (mollusc)..........................145
San Francisco Call........................178, 198
Santa Maria dell'Itria 125
Santhia SS 132
sea sparkle...148
Schröter, Johann....................65–67, 82, 83
Sciacca, Sicily 125, 126
Science (journal) 151, 157, 178
Scientific American 55, 56, 83, 133, 134
Scott, Benjamin.......................................21
Scott, Capt. Robert Falcon......................87
seismic waves, in the sea................141, 142
Senegal, West Africa...............................134
Serviss, Garrett P....................27, 28, 65, 66
Shahjehan (ship) 131
shock wave, as possible explanation.....137
Siberian, SS.......................151–174 *passim*
siphonophores 135, 145, 147
Slipher, Dr. Vesto Melvin........................95
Sole, Switzerland 33, 34, 36
Soleure, *see* Sole
Solothurn, *see* Sole
specific orbital energy 44
St John's, Newfoundland........................152

Strait of Hormuz...........................137, 144
Stroobant, Paul...11
Stuart, Dr Leon H. 82
Stuyvaert, Charles-Emile 6, 7, 8, 82
sulphur, smell of.........106, 109, 111, 113,
    116, 120, 121, 124, 202, 203, 206, 210
Sun, green colour of..........................26-28
sunspots......15, 16, 18, 19, 22, 23, 27, 28,
    37, 45, 50, 53, 83, 91, 93
superbolide.........113, 116, 159, 187, 191,
    193, 207
Susquehanna (ship)......................208, 209
Swart, Capt. Cornelis Dirks 201–210
    passim
Swift, Lewis A..24
Sydney Observatory..........................47, 51

Talbot, Frederick...................159, 166, 167
Tasmania 145
temperature inversions 171
Terschelling, Netherlands.....................201
Thunder Storms, *see* Harris, Sir William
    Snow
thunderstorm downdraft........................172
Times of Malta 115
Titius, Johann Daniel 10
Togo, West Africa.........................143, 144
tornado...................................193, 204, 205
torpedo boat 195
Transient Lunar Phenomena (TLP)......53,
    63, 67, 81–84, 86, 90, 91
tribocharging 114
Tunguska event............................192, 193
Turner, R. J. 139, 140, 157

United States Miller 178, 180
US Government Printing Office.........154
US War Department Daily Weather Maps
    ....154, 155, 168

Valentijn (ship) 134, 139
Vallée, Jacques 15, 33
Vallis Schröteri, lunar valley 83

Vatican Observatory.............................. 20
Vega, as possible explanation................158
Venus
    as possible explanation....................78
    quasi-satellite of.................................9
    phantom satellites of 5
    transit of...6
    Trojan asteroid co-orbital with..........10
Veracruz.......................................127-129
Vera Cruz, *see* Veracruz
Verne, Jules..........................121, 208, 210
Vestnik (ship)......................................130
Victoria (ship) 116, 184, 207
Victoria B.C., Canada...................177, 191
Victoria, Australia 207
videos, absence of 147
Vladimir Vorobyov (ship) 142
volcano
    ash and dust...............27, 64, 111, 124,
      184-186
    gases from 111, 120, 202
    lunar, *see* Moon
    submarine......................111, 120, 125,
      184
Vulcan, phantom planet. ...3, 8, 13–15, 20–
    29 *passim*, 50, 121
Vulcano, SMS 206

Vulture, HMS...............129–135 *passim*

Walkey, Rev. C. E. 87, 91
warm front 171, 172
Waters, Capt. John....177–197 *passim,* 207
waterspout....................193, 204, 205, 207
Watson, Prof. James Craig.....................24
wavelengths, scattering....................26, 89
Ways of the Planets, The (1912), s*ee*
    Martin, Martha
Webb, Thomas W. 16, 66-68, 75
Welsford (ship)....................................160
whales 196
Wiener Zeitschrift 123
Wilkins, William....................................72
Wilkinson, Dr Clive 107
Willimantic Chronicle, The..............57, 58
will-o-the-wisp.....................................149
Wilson, Latimer J.................................100
Wiltshire, mv (ship) 138
wind shear.............140, 167, 169–171, 174

Yokohama, Japan..........177, 181, 183, 187
Young, Thomas, FRS 75
Yusuphona, Uzbekistan........................142

Printed in the USA
CPSIA information can be obtained
at www.ICGtesting.com
CBHW061605180624
10294CB00024B/1082